LIFE IN THE RANK AND FILE

Pergamon Titles of Related Interest

Art, Davis & Huntington REORGANIZING AMERICA'S DEFENSE:
LEADERSHIP IN WAR AND PEACE

Bowman, Little & Sicilia THE ALL-VOLUNTEER FORCE
AFTER A DECADE

Goodpaster & Elliott TOWARD A CONSENSUS ON
MILITARY SERVICE

Hunt & Blair LEADERSHIP ON THE FUTURE BATTLEFIELD

Record REVISING U.S. MILITARY STRATEGY

RUSI/BRASSEY'S DEFENCE YEARBOOK 1983

RUSI/BRASSEY'S DEFENCE YEARBOOK 1984

Sarkesian BEYOND THE BATTLEFIELD

Taylor et al. DEFENSE MANPOWER PLANNING

Related Journals*

DEFENSE ANALYSIS

*Free specimen copies available upon request

LIFE IN THE RANK AND FILE

Enlisted Men and Women in the Armed Forces of the United States, Australia, Canada, and the United Kingdom

Edited by
David R. Segal
University of Maryland

H. Wallace Sinaiko
Smithsonian Institution

PERGAMON-BRASSEY'S
International Defense Publishers

Washington New York Oxford London Toronto Sydney Frankfurt

Pergamon Press Offices:

U.S.A. Pergamon-Brassey's International Defense Publishers,
1340 Old Chain Bridge Road, McLean, Virginia, 22101, U.S.A.

Pergamon Press Inc., Maxwell House, Fairview Park,
Elmsford, New York 10523, U.S.A.

U.K. Pergamon Press Ltd., Headington Hill Hall,
Oxford OX3 0BW, England

CANADA Pergamon Press Canada Ltd., Suite 104, 150 Consumers Road,
Willowdale, Ontario M2J 1P9, Canada

AUSTRALIA Pergamon Press (Aust.) Pty. Ltd., P.O. Box 544,
Potts Point, NSW 2011, Australia

FEDERAL REPUBLIC Pergamon Press GmbH, Hammerweg 6,
OF GERMANY D-6242 Kronberg-Taunus, Federal Republic of Germany

BRAZIL Pergamon Editora Ltda., Rua Eça de Queiros, 346,
CEP 04011, São Paulo, Brazil

JAPAN Pergamon Press Ltd., 8th Floor, Matsuoka Central Building,
1-7-1 Nishishinjuku, Shinjuku, Tokyo 160, Japan

PEOPLE'S REPUBLIC Pergamon Press, Qianmen Hotel, Beijing,
OF CHINA People's Republic of China

**Copyright © 1986 Pergamon-Brassey's International
Defense Publishers**

Library of Congress Cataloging in Publication Data
Main entry under title:

Life in the rank and file.

1. Soldiers--Addresses, essays, lectures.
2. Sociology, Military--Addresses, essays, lectures.
I. Segal, David R. II. Sinaiko, H. Wallace.
U21.5.L53   1985   355.12′0917′521   85-12080
ISBN 0-08-032387-1
ISBN 0-08-032386-3 (pbk.)

Printed in the United States of America

CONTENTS

Acknowledgments

Any book of this kind requires effort and support of individuals and organizations other than the editors and authors. This volume is no exception. Sam C. Sarkesian, chairman of the Inter-University Seminar on Armed Forces and Society, pointed out that an important void in the literature needed to be filled and suggested the volume to us. We are grateful to the organizations for which we work—the Department of Sociology at the University of Maryland, the Office of Naval Research, and the Smithsonian Institution—for providing both a supportive infrastructure and a work climate conducive to such an endeavor. We appreciate the efforts of Franklin D. Margiotta, director of publishing for Pergamon-Brassey's, whose personal interest in this project encouraged us and expedited its completion. Finally, there is no way we can adequately thank Becky Graham, Smithsonian Institution, who spent countless hours with the manuscripts (and sometimes with the authors) improving prose that had been written, criticized, revised, and edited.

David R. Segal
H. Wallace Sinaiko

1

Soldiers, Sailors, and Airmen

David R. Segal and H. Wallace Sinaiko

They are known as soldiers and sailors and airmen and, in the aggregate, "enlisteds." They make up 85% of the active duty forces in the U.S. military, and this is a book about these men and women. It is also about their counterpart "other ranks" in the Australian, British, and Canadian armed forces.

The volume came about for several reasons. First, although recent years have seen considerable criticism and debate about America's armed forces, as far as we know there is no comprehensive treatment of enlisted personnel in a single source—a curious gap, since roughly seven out of eight military people are enlisted. Indeed, other than the classic "American Soldier" studies published by Samuel A. Stouffer and his colleagues after World War II and Charles C. Moskos' book, *The American Enlisted Man*, published two decades later, there is very little literature on enlisted personnel.[1]

Second, there has been an explosive growth of public and academic interest in military manpower; the communications media regularly publish and broadcast analyses, criticisms, and defenses of American military manpower policies and programs. The principal international scholarly body in the field, the Inter-University Seminar on Armed Forces and Society, which sponsored this volume and which came into being in the early 1960s with a dozen members, now numbers over 1,000 fellows.

Third, the way in which the United States mans a large standing peacetime military force, with a total reliance on volunteers since 1973, has been one of the most profound changes in national policy and one of the largest-scale social experiments ever attempted. Not only is this nation completely dependent on individuals' coming forward and volunteering to serve, but at the same time its military has been deeply affected by changes in society that have influenced the character of the force. Two of these—changes in gender role definitions and increasing dependence on technical competence in modern high-technology society—have had particular importance for the military, as the chapters to follow demonstrate. Women were moving into roles in American society that they had not occupied previously at precisely the time that the armed forces, deprived of conscription, had to find new non-traditional

1

sources of "manpower."[2] And increasing dependence on technical ability and expertise have required military forces to reward and promote personnel on bases other than leadership and abilities at traditional military skills.

Perhaps for these reasons, more than for any other, we and our colleagues felt that by the mid-eighties it was high time to bring the subject of enlisted forces into a single volume. In commissioning the separate chapters, we set out to include each major component of the active-duty U.S. force and three allied forces that share a common language and cultural heritage. We also sought to acknowledge the entire range of enlisted personnel, from the most junior recruits to the most senior noncommissioned officers. While this range is not emphasized in any single chapter, we hope that the book as a whole reflects the diversity of experiences and responsibilities of enlisted personnel. At the same time we decided to come at the subject from more than one professional perspective; thus, the authors are sociologists, historians, psychologists, anthropologists, and social workers. One is an engineer. Several of them are also professional military officers, and some have served as enlisted personnel.

Sue E. Berryman, whose degree is in social relations, provides an important politico-historical context in which to view contemporary enlisted forces. One of the major issues in the current debate on America's all-volunteer force is how representative it is of American society in general. Berryman notes that the social composition of the American military, how it resembled (and differed from) the larger society, and how the image of the social composition of the force differed from the reality, have been issues since the birth of the Republic. She addresses the question of whether the all-volunteer force in America has become an extension of the welfare state and finds that recruits, on the average, do not come from the most marginal strata of society, but rather are of somewhat higher status than those who enter the civilian labor force after high school. Nonetheless, these recruits are likely to have been users of social welfare programs. By contrast, volunteers who served in the American military in earlier periods were more socially marginal, although military service compared more favorably to civilian employment than many analysts have recognized. To many early volunteers, the military was a good job—or a way of achieving geographical mobility in search of a good job. Berryman suggests parallels in the motivations of volunteer soldiers throughout American history. She also points out that, historically, draftees have been less of a cross-section of society than the concept of an equitable draft implies. She also defines some of the dilemmas, other than issues of representativeness, presently facing the nation vis-à-vis military manpower: social policy, deterrence, and conflict with civilian values, inter alia. And she points to the political constraints that affect the resolution of these dilemmas.

As a reflection of the dramatic increase in utilization of female military personnel, the U.S. armed forces are treated in separate chapters defined by gender as well as by service. Charles C. Moskos, a sociologist, writes about enlisted males in the Army; and Martha A. Marsden, a social worker, deals with Army women. Continuing the discussion of representativeness of the armed forces, Moskos emphasizes changing demographic characteristics—for example, recent significant increases in the proportion of Army recruits who are high school graduates, the rise in the number of blacks, and a doubling in the proportion of married men—and he points up some consequences of the policy shift from the draft to an all-volunteer force. He also describes life in the Army, from basic training through overseas tours, and the current enlisted culture. Notable features of the latter are less unit cohesion, high turnover rates, more men living off-post, and a new form of post-enlistment disillusionment. Moskos also reports on attitudes toward involvement in combat—intentions which appear to be highly specific to particular scenarios. He elaborates on two major problems of the current Army: race relations and attitudes toward women soldiers. Moskos' chapter concludes with an observation about an important organizational trend: the shift from an institutional to an occupational model of military service (a conceptualization somewhat at variance with Berryman's analysis) that has influenced the thinking of policy makers and military analysts for more than a decade.

Martha E. Marsden's chapter on Army enlisted women treats attitudes toward women soldiers, stressing particularly the issues of the drafting of women and the involvement of women in combat. She emphasizes a typology that has shaped much of the contemporary discourse on military service: the belief systems of male soldiers and the public that have made the expansion and integration of the female cohort difficult. The nation has traditionally been uneasy in the way it views the roles of its women soldiers, and a certain ambivalence continues. On the one hand the Army has expanded women's opportunities, but its policies vis-à-vis their involvement in combat tend toward exclusion. Marsden complements Berryman's historical overview by presenting an historical picture of Army women which goes back to the American Revolution, tracing the development of Army policies regulating women's participation.

The Navy is covered in chapters by James F. Downs, a cultural anthropologist, and Patricia J. Thomas, a psychologist. In writing about naval enlisted men, Downs focuses on noncommissioned officers (NCOs), who outnumber junior enlisted personnel in the Navy. He draws heavily on historical material to explain the occupational structure of the enlisted force and some of the problems it faces as the Navy becomes an increasingly technical organization. Downs explains the role of the Navy petty officer and how the structure of enlisted authority works. He pays particular attention to the shifting balance between military leadership requirements and demands for technical competence and expertise in the petty officer ranks.

Patricia J. Thomas, in portraying navy enlisted women, points out that the Navy was the first service to have women serving as part of the force rather than as an auxiliary. She puts special emphasis on the experiences of women in recent years, as they have assumed other than traditionally female roles, have in some cases gone to sea, and in some cases have proven to be more cost effective than men. She writes about the special environmental problems faced by Navy women operating in a predominantly male world, and she suggests that, in the future, American women will be in the same short supply as men—a demographic fact that has to be recognized. She presents interesting survey data, collected from civilian women as well as from women in the Navy. For example, most women in the Navy feel that women should be allowed to serve aboard ship or be assigned to any job they can handle. Among the first women serving at sea, there was a polarization of opinion regarding that experience: about one-third viewed it positively versus nearly half whose evaluations were negative. (Males, who were also surveyed, were less positive [about one-fourth] and less negative [about one-third].)

Air Force personnel are treated from unusual perspectives. Jacob Neufeld and James C. Hasdorff, both historians, present an oral history of an exclusive group: the six men, now retired, who have served as chief master sergeants of the Air Force since this post (which is the highest enlisted grade in the service) was created. These very senior NCOs reflect on such historically significant events as the desegregation of what had been the Army Air Corps, extending the discussion of race relations that appeared in earlier chapters. Their views of enlisted promotion policies, the employment of Air Force women, problems of drug and alcohol use, and their own roles as the top enlisteds are also described. In this latter context, a theme raised by Moskos regarding the Army, and by Downs regarding the Navy, appears in the Air Force as well: the ambiguous role of the NCO in a military system in which the traditional meaning of discipline is changing and technical expertise, including expertise in human resource management, is coming to the fore.

Military women have increased in absolute number and relative numbers throughout the U.S. military since the all-volunteer force (AVF) came into being. Concurrently, in both the military and civilian sectors of American society, women's roles have expanded in terms of both their occupations and the locations in which they serve. These changes are not without problems, some of which reflect the number of American military personnel stationed overseas. Constance S. Ojile, an anthropologist, deals with these overseas assignments as they affect the lives and work of Air Force women. Ojile's report of interviews and discussions with women stationed overseas reflects the problems that young adults away from home, frequently for the first time, may experience. While not all the problems are unique to women, some are. Many are not unique to overseas tours, although some, such as feelings of cultural isolation, tend to be. The same respondents noted positive aspects of military life as well, although given a chance to talk about their problems, they did. These insights, almost clinical in nature, point to persisting personnel problems that must be addressed. Ojile makes recommendations for policy changes that would, she believes, make overseas assignments much more rewarding for women.

Marine enlisted men and women are the subject of the jointly authored chapter by Michael and Renee Patrow, both of whom are career officers in the Marine Corps. The Patrows explain the mission of the Marine Corps and review demographic trends in its enlisted force which, unlike the other services, is concentrated in the lower ranks. In the context of their service's mission, they point out the unique two-occupation role of enlisted marines, who are both technical specialists and fighters, and who all assume leadership responsibilities as they proceed through their careers. The corps thus has its own solution to maintaining a balance between traditional military and modern technical skills. The Patrows describe in considerable detail the boot camp experience, the crucible in which new marines are shaped and which is also the corps' greatest vulnerability. In discussing NCOs, the Patrows emphasize the particular stresses placed upon the cadre responsible for training the new recruits: the drill instructors. Paralleling the chapters by Marsden and Thomas, much of the Patrows' essay is devoted to enlisted marine women: their early utilization in 1917-20, the part they played in World War II, and the controversies that surrounded them between the 1940s and the 1960s, when decisions about their appropriate roles were dictated by internal requirements. In the current era, they note, policies are being influenced by factors external to the corps, leading to the utilization of women in a wider range of occupational roles and to role combinations that allow the same person to be a wife, a mother, and a marine.

Enlisted Army families are the subject of Mady Wechsler Segal's paper. The military family is an area of new and growing concern in the U.S. (and other) armed forces. As noted above, enlisted personnel are increasingly likely to be married; and the armed services have recognized that the long-term retention of career personnel will be determined, in part, by family circumstances and the success with which military families cope with the special stresses they face. Segal, a sociologist, reports on her recent research among Army families in a housing area for middle enlisted grades at a major southern post. She portrays the structure of the community and the day-to-day life of those who live there. She presents the residents' satisfactions with marriage, children, the community, the Army, and life in general. She also presents their dissatisfactions, noting that some (but not all) of these are unique to military life. Segal describes how the community provides social support through both formal and informal arrangements and points out the importance of recognizing that in times of military emergency, when the needs of family members for social support may be extreme, some of these mechanisms will not be available because they use personnel from operational units.

The last three chapters are about enlisted people in the forces of Australia, Canada, and the United Kingdom. We include chapters on Allied forces because, like the U.S. military, they are manned by volunteers; and because, as hardly needs emphasis, they share a common political, economic, military, and ideological heritage with one another and with us. This heritage includes development from primarily agricultural to increasingly urbanized and industrialized societies, and a common militia tradition perhaps better suited to the former agricultural society in which military occupations required relatively low skill levels, military service was regarded as a duty of citizenship, and conscription was rarely used to raise armed forces.

Malcom van Gelder, a civil engineer and economist, and Michael Eley, a psychologist and an army officer, write about some historical perspectives and, in their words, the "Australian fighting character." Reflecting patterns of and concerns about social representativeness found in the other Anglo-American nations, they describe the present social composition of the enlisted force which, like the U.S. armed forces, has undergone a transition from a mixed force of conscripts and volunteers to an all-volunteer force in the post-Vietnam War years. They note the increased utilization of women and increased dependence on technology in the Australian forces and compare the three component forces—Army, Navy, and Air Force—in terms of conditions of service, turnover, rank structure, and other factors. Van Gelder and Eley discuss attitudes of the Australian populace toward its defense force, and they comment on some inevitable effects on the Australian force which will come out of changing social norms. In many ways these changes parallel trends identified by Moskos in his analysis of the army in a modern industrial society (where formal legal systems, secularism, and commercialism have replaced informal customs and traditions as mechanisms of social organization), by Marsden and Thomas in their analyses of military women, and by Segal in her analysis of U.S. military families and communities.

Charles A. Cotton and Franklin C. Pinch, both of whom are sociologists, deal with the Canadian enlisted force. Both are lieutenant colonels in the Canadian Forces, the former retired and the latter still on active duty. Their chapter treats the structure of enlisted service, entry and socialization, and the pressures—social, political, and economic—for change in a force that has some members who speak both French and English (while most speak only one or the other), and in which the land, sea, and air elements have been integrated. Cotton and Pinch also go into some depth about specific issues facing Canadian manpower planners: early attrition, which is particularly problematic in a force that has moved away from the concept of citizen-soldiers and seeks long-service enlisted personnel (which the authors suggest may be unrealistic); attitudes of enlisteds toward service; the combat soldier's status in a force in which three-quarters of enlisted personnel are in technical and administrative support jobs and can be moved between land, sea, and air assignments; integration of military women, driven by both social change and manpower needs; and "dual" service marriages that result in part from the increased presence of women in the force. They discuss the role of regimental affiliation in maintaining the identity and cohesion of combat troops. The contrasting roles of warrior and technician are no less problematic in Canada than in the other nations discussed in this volume, and Cotton and Pinch use Moskos' institutional and occupational models as the basis for developing a typology of enlisted personnel: soldiers, employees, and ambivalents. A unique aspect of the Canadian military is the formal recognition of re-entry into civilian life as one phase of the serviceman's career pattern, a transition that the military feels a moral and pragmatic obligation to ease. Cotton and Pinch make some suggestions about future strategies which will enable the Canadian force to continue to meet its obligations and, at the same time, accommodate changes as the nation moves into the twenty-first century.

The final chapter, on the enlisted force in the United Kingdom, is by Gwyn Harries-Jenkins, a sociologist. It is appropriate that this chapter deal with Great Britain, for it was the British militia tradition that served as the foundation for the military manpower systems of all of the nations considered in this volume, and the British regimental system which served as the model for the traditional organization of the Canadian land forces and the recent regimental renaissance in the U.S. Army. Noting the impacts of technology and changing military organization which have been raised repeatedly in this book, Harries-Jenkins suggests that there are three different images of the "other ranks" in the British forces: warriors, workers, and technicians. He notes that these types (which differ somewhat from those proposed by Cotton and Pinch) reflect different motivations to join the forces and are associated with differing and more long-term orientations toward military service: those of the traditionalist, the opportunist, and the careerist. This typology of three enlisted subcultures is an alternative elaboration of the institutional and occupational models introduced by Moskos and is used by Harries-Jenkins to address the issues of technological impact, utilization of women, and social representativeness. Harries-Jenkins notes that despite differences between enlisted subcultures, enlisted personnel as a group differ from officers, reflecting the class structure of British society while at the same time differing in important ways from the civilian working class as well.

The analysis in this book in some ways comes full circle: from Berryman's demonstration that from the time of the American Revolution, military service was a job and a mobility opportunity to many, particularly poor immigrants; through Moskos' conceptualization that postulates a *recent* trend toward military service as a job; to demonstrations that in recent decades the military has been a mobility channel and a source of employment for people disadvantaged in the civilian labor force (such as women, members of minority groups, and the poor); and ultimately to conceptualizations such as that of Harries-Jenkins, postulating that traditional military and contemporary occupational types may co-exist in a modern all-volunteer force, and that a mixture of the two may be the most common form. At the same time, the book documents other important changes that have taken place in enlisted service: from short-term to more career-oriented and professionalized manning; toward higher skill levels needed in more technologically sophisticated forces; toward rank structures affected by technical ability as well as leadership ability; toward greater utilization of women reflecting both broader social trends and internal personnel requirements of the services; and toward new adaptations between the military and the family as social institutions. These changes demonstrate that we have not truly come full circle. Rather, change has been dialectical and, as in most institutions, a synthesis has been achieved between the structures and traditions of the past and the technical and social innovations of the present. What is certain is that a true end state will probably never be achieved. Society, its military organization, and its enlisted force will all continue to change. We feel that adaptation to that change will be eased by a fuller understanding of how we have arrived at our present state. We hope that this volume will make a contribution to that process.

NOTES

1. Samuel A. Stouffer et al., *The American Soldier*, vols. I and II (Princeton: Princeton Univ. Press, 1949); Charles C. Moskos, Jr., *The American Enlisted Man* (New York: Russell Sage Foundation, 1970).
2. Mady Wechsler Segal and David R. Segal, "Social Change and the Participation of Women in the American Military, pp. 235–258 in Louis Kriesberg, ed., *Research in Social Movements, Conflicts and Change*, vol. 5 (Greenwich, CT: JAI Press, 1983).

2

Images and Realities: The Social Composition of Nineteenth and Twentieth Century Enlisted Forces*

Sue E. Berryman

Americans use information about the social composition of our enlisted forces to judge the quality of their military performance, their political reliability, the fairness of the combat burden, and the access of minority groups to the opportunities associated with service. This paper assesses the congruence between the actual social composition of American enlisted forces in the nineteenth and twentieth centuries and public and defense policymakers' images of that composition.

"Social composition" refers to the background characteristics of the enlisted forces. Some of these characteristics such as race, ethnicity, recency of immigration, citizenship, age, sex, family socioeconomic status, or geographic origin, locate enlistees in the nation's social, political, and economic structure. Other characteristics locate them in the nation's talent distribution, for example, their educational attainment, verbal and mathematical abilities, and aptitudes such as mechanical skills.

Questions of composition are not of academic interest only. As Eitelberg notes, these issues have surfaced in most contemporary discussions of military manpower programs and policies.[1] They appear in congressional hearings, congressional reports, government commissions, scholarly articles, the popular media, government-sponsored research reports, and congressionally mandated annual Department of Defense reports on the composition of new recruits and the active duty forces.

---

*Author's Note: This chapter is based on a larger study of the American enlisted force, financed by The Ford Foundation and entitled *The Social Composition of American Enlisted Forces: 19th and 20th Century Images and Realities, Political Dynamics, and Questionable Assumptions.*

Potential *discrepancies* between compositional images and realities are also consequential. Since 1973 the Congress has proposed several measures to alter the composition of the all-volunteer force (AVF) based on *assumptions* about that composition and its implications to members of the Congress. Some of these proposals have been vaguely formulated and casually entertained; others, more carefully framed and seriously debated. They have included bills to increase pay, to reintroduce the G.I. Bill (educational benefits), and, the most drastic, to return to the draft.

All proposals have implied economic and political costs. All have been predicated on the assumption that the AVF is not attracting and retaining the "right" kinds—or enough of the right kinds—of youth. Different policymakers have different definitions of "right," but the definitions have usually involved background characteristics such as race, ethnicity, gender, recency of citizenship, socioeconomic class, educational attainment, and mental ability.

Today the defense policy community is less concerned with composition than it was at the end of the 1970s, partly because the recession of the early 1980s converted the recruiting market from a seller's to a buyer's market. However, the historical materials that we examined showed that, since the founding of the Republic, compositional issues have persistently arisen and affected defense manpower policy choices. This historical continuity suggests that we can expect compositional issues: (1) to re-emerge in policy debates about the AVF; (2) to differ little in substance from issues raised several times in American history; and (3) to affect the military manpower policies considered and chosen.

THE AVF: EXTENSION OF THE WELFARE STATE?

Since the AVF's inception in 1973, policymakers have monitored and criticized its numeric strength, quality, and social composition, the discussions becoming somewhat ferocious in the late 1970s and early 1980s. One of the implicit assumptions in these debates was that the AVF had become an extension of domestic youth and welfare policy—an "employer of last resort," an employment and training activity for youth who can't succeed "on the outside." Also implicitly assumed was that this extension jeopardized the effectiveness, efficiency, and fairness of our national defense.

We assessed the accuracy of this image through comparison with data from the 1979 *National Longitudinal Survey of Labor Force Behavior, Youth Survey* (1979 NLS). This survey, sponsored by the Department of Labor, samples 17 to 22-year-olds in the civilian and military sectors, thus allowing comparisons of active duty enlistees with their age mates who are not in the military.

We classified the 17 to 22-year-old male respondents by their primary activity at the time of the *1979 NLS* interview. Here we only discuss the results for the five major in-school and out-of-school activities: active duty military, full-time civilian labor force, unemployed, two-year college, and four-year college.

The data showed incontestably that 17 to 22-year-old enlistees in 1979 did *not* come from the more marginal groups on *any* of three dimensions: family socioeconomic status, achievements (basic skills and education), and motivations. We used four indicators of the family's socioeconomic status (SES): father's education, mother's education, the Duncan socioeconomic score[2] of father's occupation, and an index of reading in the home. The five major groups have this rank order of parental SES: (1) four-year college, (2) two-year college, (3) military, (4) full-time civilian labor force, and (5) unemployed. Thus, on average, the military is drawing from families with a higher average socioeconomic status than full-time civilian employers.

When we look at the parental socioeconomic status of the different activity groups by race and ethnicity, we find that whites have the same parental SES rank order as that for all males, i.e., (1) four-year college, (2) two-year college, (3) military, (4) full-time civilian labor force, and (5) unemployed. However, for blacks and Hispanics, the military moves up in the parental SES rank order: blacks and Hispanics in the military and those in two-year colleges come from families with the same SES. In other words, for black and Hispanic youth the military *and* two-year colleges are drawing from socioeconomically similar families.

We find about the same results for measures of educational attainment and abilities. Of the out-of-school groups, enlistees have about the same average educational attainment as their counterparts in the full-time civilian labor force and higher average attainment than the other out-of-school groups. Black and Hispanic enlistees have higher average educational attainment than their racial and ethnic counterparts in all other out-of-school groups. The active duty military group has a substantially lower percentage of high school dropouts than all of the other out-of-school groups with the rate, even for males, in the full-time civilian labor force being about double. This military group also has a smaller percentage of those with at least one year of college than several of the other out-of-school groups, although the picture is more mixed for black and Hispanic enlistees.

In the absence of direct basic skill measures,[3] we used knowledge-of-work scores as an ability measure.[4] The analyses show that enlistees have higher knowledge-of-work scores than the other out-of-school groups, but, except for black enlistees, lower than the college groups.

The Department of Defense compared the Armed Forces Qualifying Test (AFQT), i.e., basic skill, scores of 18 to 23 year old FY81 accessions and the population of *1980 NLS* youth. For males, the analyses showed that white enlistees and the white youth population had the same median AFQT scores. Black and Hispanic enlistees had median scores almost double those of the black and Hispanic youth populations.[5]

We assessed the motivations of different subgroups with measures of educational aspirations, occupational aspirations, work orientation, and willingness to ask the federal government for financial help. The *1979 NLS* data strongly indicate that enlistees are educationally and occupationally ambitious and work-oriented. Although their educational and occupational expectations are lower than those of the college groups, they are substantially higher than those of members of the other out-of-school tracks. Those in the military were less likely than any other track to say that they would stop working if they suddenly acquired plenty of money. The military group also had one of the smallest percentages who said they would turn to the government for welfare or food stamps if they were in financial difficulties.

Perhaps a final test of whether the military represents an extension of the welfare state is to determine whether youth who participate in federal youth programs move disproportionately into the military. The *1979 NLS* asked respondents whether they had participated in any of a wide range of federally-sponsored training and job programs, e.g., the CETA Summer Program, In-School Work Experience Program, Job Opportunities in the Business Sector (JOBS), Public Service Employment, CETA training, Job Corps, SER-Jobs for Progress.

Of the five major groups, the military track had a participation rate second only to that of the unemployed group. If we look at participation for the different racial and ethnic groups, blacks in the military group had a higher participation rate than blacks in any of the other four groups.

At first blush these data imply that the military *has* become an extension of the welfare state. However, when we looked at participation by the four indicators of family SES, we found that participation in federal job and training programs has penetrated the higher family SES levels far more than is popularly assumed, especially in the black and Hispanic communities. Thus, participation in federal job and training programs does *not* indicate a family at the bottom—or even at the lower levels—of the nation's SES distribution. What the higher participation rate among those in the military means is, therefore, much less clear. In conjunction with the other data about AVF youth, it suggests making use of opportunities—the classic behavior of up-wardly mobile individuals. For example, our analyses showed that black participation in these programs increased as the amount of reading in their homes increased. More reading in the home is one indicator of parents' higher achievement drives for themselves and their children.

In conclusion, even in 1979 the younger members of the enlisted force by no means came from the most marginal families or from youth with the most marginal attainments, aspirations, or work attitudes. The military profile is that of a classic upwardly mobile group. Its members come disproportionately from the racially, ethnically, or socioeconomically less-enfranchised sub-groups in the population. Its minority members tend to come from the middle classes of their subgroups; its white members, from the lower middle classes. Whites in the military come from families with higher levels of reading in the home than their parents' education and fathers' occupations would lead us to expect, suggesting upwardly mobile families. Whites in the military attained more education than we would expect, given their parents' educational attainment and the status of their fathers' occupations, but their levels were commensurate with levels of reading in their homes. The average basic skill levels of those in the military, in general and for all racial and ethnic groups, are higher than the averages for their counterparts in the youth population. Their aspirations and attitudes toward work and economic independence are solidly middle class.

THE SOCIAL COMPOSITION OF VOLUNTEER FORCES

Analyses of the nineteenth and earlier-twentieth-century enlisted force are consistent with those of the AVF in that they indicate that historically we have rarely had accurate images of our enlisted forces. The American military has been more selective under volunteer conditions and less representative under draft conditions than our public images would suggest. This section describes and assesses these images for our volunteer (usually peacetime) enlisted forces prior to World War II. The following section describes our draft (usually wartime) enlisted forces in the Civil War and World War I and from 1940 to 1973.

Images

Before and after the Civil War, the officer corps commanded social esteem, but the enlisted forces had negative social images. Prucha states that the pre-Civil War army

> comprised a rather sorry lot, recruited from the dregs of American society and the newly arrived immigrants from Great Britain and Continental Europe . . . . Almost every traveler from overseas who came in contact with the army was struck with the fact that the American army was scarcely American at all, but Irish, English, and German, and that those native Americans who did enlist seemed to be the "scum of the population of the older states."[6]

In his examination of the political and social institutions of the United States almost a century and a half ago, de Tocqueville commented that in "times of peace, the Army is always inferior to the country itself." A countryman of de Tocqueville, Guillaume Tell Poussin, concluded as Prucha reports

> The recruits are generally men, who, as laborers and mechanics [would] receive much higher compensation than in the military service. They must, therefore, be infected with some moral infirmity, which renders them unfit for a useful and laborious life.[7]

The image of the post Civil War regular army was not much better. As Rickey reports, many civilians felt that the regulars who remained in service after the Civil War were shiftless men, either too lazy or unable to succeed in the competition of civilian life.[8]

Several social facts raise questions about the validity of the social images of the nineteenth century enlisted forces. First, since the founding of the

Republic, Americans have distrusted the centralized power inherent in a regular standing army. For example, in the late eighteenth and nineteenth centuries they preferred militias under the control of the states.[9] As Huntington observes:

> Military forces, particularly professional military forces, and military institutions have been viewed with suspicion and hostility. The ideals of liberty, democracy, equality, and peace have contrasted with the military's concern with authority, hierarchy, obedience, force, and war.[10]

Distrust of an institution tends to generalize to its members, although this fact does not explain why the enlisted force, *but not the officer corps*, had such a negative image.

Second, *peacetime* American militaries have always suffered an image problem, the public esteem of the military varying directly with the geographical or temporal proximity of hostilities. Rickey provides a nice example of this phenomenon:

> Until the Sioux and Northern Cheyennes were confined to reservations, the merchants, saloonkeepers and other inhabitants of the town [Miles City, Montana] were almost totally dependent on the soldiers stationed across the Tongue River at Fort Keogh. When Miles City became a booming cow town in the eighties, soldiers fell rapidly in public estimation. Later, when the Ghost Dance craze swept the northern plains tribes in 1889 and 1890, and wholesale outbreak seemed imminent, the regulars quickly became very much appreciated.[11]

Third, those who recorded impressions of our nineteenth century enlisted forces were necessarily literate, a fact which placed them in the middle to upper classes of their countries of origin. American militaries have always reproduced the class structure of the larger society, the officer corps representing the professional and managerial classes and the enlisted force representing the low-level white collar, blue collar, and laboring classes. The differential regard accorded the officer corps and enlisted forces may say less about the quality of the enlisted force than it does about the greater status compatibility between observers of American militaries and the officer corps.

Realities

Since these factors give us reason to suspect a distortion in nineteenth century public views of the enlisted force, it seems useful to ask how much nineteenth century peacetime enlisted forces *in fact* differed from the rank and file of the total nation. It must be remembered that peacetime enlisted forces in the nineteenth century were small, ranging from about 14,000 in 1820 to about 40,000 in 1897.[12] Thus, small changes in the absolute numbers of enlistees with particular characteristics considerably affected the social composition of the total enlisted force.

The statistics support the image of the peacetime enlisted forces as disproportionately foreign-born. In 1850, the country's male population was about
10% foreign-born; from 1860-1900, about 15%.[13] However, from the 1820s to
the 1880s, 25 to 70% of the Army was foreign-born, averaging at least 50%
during the peacetime periods between 1840 and the mid-1870s. For example,
of the 5,000 recruits who entered the service in 1850-51, 70% were born in
Europe; of this group, about 60% came from Ireland, 20% from Germany,
and 12% from England and Scotland.[14] In terms of country of birth, the 1850
distribution of foreign-born enlistees was roughly comparable to that of immigrants to the United States in 1850. In that year 83% came from Europe.
Of the European-born, 53% were from Ireland, 26% from Germany, and
17% from Great Britain.[15]

Blacks, representing a declining percentage of the population across the
century (18% in 1820 and 12% by 1900),[16] were substantially under-represented in the military. At any point in the century, their representation reflected a compromise between (1) blacks' attempts to gain their freedom and
full enfranchisement through military service; (2) white policymakers' attempts to frustrate the achievement of these objectives or to control the rate at
which they were achieved; and (3) military manpower requirements. In general, they were more under-represented under peacetime volunteer conditions
than during wartime.[17]

Thus, during the nineteenth century, military service clearly attracted those
trying to enter the mainstream more than those already in it. In judging the
quality of those in the military, however, characteristics of the civilian, native-
born, white population should be kept in mind.

We assessed the quality of the nineteenth century enlisted force by comparing their probable educational attainments with those of the larger society,
their occupational skills relative to those of the civilian labor force, and their
wages relative to the wages of the civilian labor force.

We can assume that members of the enlisted force were more apt to come
from the lower than from the higher end of the nation's distribution of
educational attainment. As now, the nineteenth century military was a two-
class system, but, much more than today, enlisted military jobs were primarily
laborer and blue collar jobs. Under any reasonably efficient allocation of
human capital among the nation's jobs, we would not expect the more educated classes to staff the enlisted forces.

We can probably also assume that the educational levels of the nineteenth
century enlisted forces were somewhat below those of the rank and file white,
native-born population. The large percentage of foreign-born suggests higher
rates of illiteracy in the English language and in any language. Comparative
data for 1850 indicate that Germany and the United States had about the
same ratio of students to the total population. However, other countries that
supplied large numbers of recruits to the U.S. military, especially Ireland,[18]

had lower rates. If foreign-born recruits spent their school years in their countries of birth, those from certain countries had smaller chances of attaining the educational levels of their social class counterparts in the United States.

If the nineteenth century enlisted forces had limited education, however, so did the nineteenth century American population. Although no sound analytical methods can provide reliable estimates of the population's educational attainment for specific dates before 1910,[19] fragmentary data give us some sense of the level of the population's education and of the incidence of illiteracy.

In 1870 the U.S. Office of Education estimated that 2% of all 17-year-olds were high school graduates.[20] The Census determined illiteracy in different ways, and the data points are therefore not strictly comparable. However, the first estimate in 1840 found that 20% of the white native and foreign-born population was illiterate. This percentage declined to 11.5% in 1870 and to 6.2% in 1900.[21]

In sum, for much of the nineteenth century large percentages of the civilian population had limited schooling. Noticeable percentages of even the white native-born population were illiterate. Although the immigrant contingent in the enlisted forces probably had less average education than their white, native-born, blue collar civilian counterparts, it is not clear that the educational differences between the two groups were that great.

Although nineteenth century recruits were usually described as "unskilled," the *civilian* labor force itself was not particularly skilled. Farmers and farm laborers dominated the labor force for much of the century, representing 72% of the civilian male workers in 1820, 64% in 1850, 49% in 1880, and 38% in 1900.[22] As late as 1900 only 18% of the civilian labor force had high or low level white collar occupations, most being concentrated in the manual worker/laborer occupations (45%) and farmer/farm laborer occupations (38%).[23]

Several nineteenth century observers used the military's low pay as a basis for inferring that anyone who enlisted at such rates must be of low quality—unemployable, dissolute, or worse. However: (1) at least after the Civil War, it is not clear that military pay was worse than civilian pay in some of the large blue collar and farm-laborer occupational categories; (2) even if military pay was lower, observers did not consider the availability and stability of those civilian jobs that paid higher wages; and (3) observers did not consider the implications of high percentages of immigrants in the armed forces for the relationships between wages and manpower quality.

The first issue is the relationship between military and civilian wages. We have no statistics that let us compare pre-Civil War military wages and allowances with the average annual earnings of different civilian occupations. Foreign observers commented on the discrepancy between an enlisted man's $5 per month and a civilian laborer's $1 per day.[24] However, these observers did not consider military allowances or compare the annual earnings of enlistees and civilian laborers. Civilian wage earners often did not have steady work, and their wage rates reflected the expected duration of their employment. Thus, from 1832 to 1860 civilian laborers employed by the day earned from 35-55% more per day than laborers employed on a monthly basis.[25] At the same time, if before the Civil War military pay was in fact about $5 per month (excluding allowances), military annual pay was less than that of the largest category of wage earners, farm laborers. In 1830, state-specific data indicate that farm laborers made from $7 to $10 per month plus board, annual pay for those steadily employed being about $80 to $100.[26]

Although we do not have post-Civil War wage data for exactly the same years for the enlisted force, farm laborers, and nonfarm employees, it is probable that enlistees' annual pay was higher than that of farm laborers for the 1865 and 1898 periods.[27] When we recall that in 1870 30% of the total male civilian labor force was in the farm laborer category, military service may have been more attractive economically than observers would have us believe.

Data on the 1898 annual wages for selected industries and occupations show that enlistees received higher annual pay (including allowances) than workers in manufacturing, bituminous coal miners, farm laborers, and public school teachers.[28] Even if we exclude all craft occupations from the manufacturing category, these first three civilian occupations comprised 36% of the male civilian labor force in 1900.[29]

In sum, although the wage data are fragmentary, they suggest that enlistees, while not highly paid, were paid as well as, if not better than, a substantial percentage of the civilian labor force.

The second issue is the availability and stability of nineteenth century civilian jobs. When nineteenth century observers talked about higher civilian wages, they did not consider the availability of civilian work or its steadiness in relation to military service. Nineteenth century military desertion rates were very high[30] and were often interpreted as evidence of enlistees' inferior moral character.[31] However, analyses show that these rates tell us more about problems in the civilian economy and men's use of military service to adjust to these problems than they do about the moral character of those in the military.[32]

Unemployment levels were generally higher in the nineteenth century than in the twentieth, as the result of uneven geographic distributions of labor, substantial seasonal unemployment, and periodic recessions and depressions.[33] The society lacked minimum wage laws, collective bargaining, and unemployment insurance. Certainly the need for patching together jobs across the year was greater.

The uneven geographical distribution of new immigrants, lack of information about jobs in other places, and the high cost of transport combined to create serious unemployment in some areas (especially the eastern coastal cities) and labor scarcities in others (especially the frontier states).

The nature of the economy exposed large numbers of workers to four or five months of seasonal unemployment. Agriculture, the major employer for much of the century, was notoriously affected by the weather. Farming could provide only seven or eight months of steady work, even to employees considered regular workers. Prior to 1860 the largest employer of adult men, second to agriculture, was the merchant marine. Ocean trips, however, varied in length: one or two months along the coast, five months from New England to the West Indies, and six to eight months to Liverpool. Between trips sailors were subject to unemployment.

Non-farm industry was also more subject to the weather in the nineteenth century, with outdoor operatives losing four or five months a year. The country grist and oil mills were the largest nineteenth century manufacturing industry. In the North and West, millers hired only for the autumn or "so long as the mill can run before freezing up." The ironworks commonly shut down for several months during the winter. Weather affected those in transportation occupations who depended on roads and internal waterways. The roads between towns were usually ruts that became impassable in winter, and the waterways closed for an average of four months every winter. As today, outside construction ceased during the winter months in much of the country.

Finally, workers were subject to cyclical unemployment during the recessions and depressions of 1818 to 1820, 1837 through the early 1840s, 1857 to 1861, 1873 to 1879, 1885, and 1893 through the late 1890s. These economic crises affected different industries and different parts of the country. The 1818 to 1820 crisis, for example, primarily affected manufacturing. Manufacturing employment fell by an estimated two-thirds, but only about 5% of the labor force was employed in manufacturing at this time. Some of the crises, however, were severe and general, the 1890s depression being among the worst prior to the 1930s, with unemployment reaching 18.4% in 1894.[34]

In sum, although men enlisted and deserted for many reasons, such as escaping financial or social embarrassment in their home towns,[35] the two major reasons for both enlistment and desertion were economic: (1) free transportation from the eastern states to the western frontier where most army units were stationed—and where there were shortages of civilian workers; and (2) patching together a year-round income. As General O.O. Howard observed in 1885:

> Excellent young men every day solicit the privilege of enlisting, but they do it in a strait for work. A workman in Omaha has had from $1 to $1.50 wages, but in winter he is often discharged and not able to get work again until spring, so when a young man finds himself without means and without bread he enlists. Good offers in spring and summer tempt him to desert.[36]

Thus, even if military wages were lower than those for civilian jobs, military service was a job that paid money in places and at times of the year when civilian jobs were scarce. The very fact that men moved so freely between military service and civilian jobs indicates that the quality of servicemen and civilian workers could not have been that different.

The final issue is the relationship between immigrant members of the enlisted force, pay, and quality. Nineteenth century observers assumed that if military pay was low relative to civilian pay, enlistees must be of low quality. However, they did not take into account what economists call the "reservation wage" of the large percentage of immigrants in the Army and Navy. This concept refers to the wage below which the individual declines to supply his labor. Nineteenth century American wages for laborers were higher than European wages for the same occupation. For example, in 1850 wages of Dutch and German laborers were about $0.50 per week, whereas the average American wage was $0.87 per day.[37] Thus, military pay may have been lower than civilian pay, especially before the Civil War. It could, nonetheless, be attractive to recent European immigrants, however, and their acceptance of these wages cannot be interpreted to imply low quality. When we recall the high percentage of immigrants in the armed services, the possible difference between immigrant and native American wage expectations is an important issue.

In sum, the pay issue, and what it implies for enlistee quality, needs to be interpreted in the context of the nineteenth century economy. If a pay discrepancy existed between civilian and military employment before the Civil War, the discrepancy was less than that reported. Observers compared military monthly wage rates with civilian daily wage rates. However, in compensation for short-term employment, labor employed by the day earned more per day than labor employed by the month or year. It is by no means clear that post-Civil War annual military pay was lower than the annual earnings of major civilian occupations. In contrast to several major civilian industries that could employ workers for only about two-thirds of the year, military employment was nonseasonal, a benefit that we would expect to be reflected in wages somewhat lower than those paid in less secure civilian industries. Finally, evidence suggests that relative to wages in their home countries, immigrants might have found military pay rates quite attractive.

Like the AVF, the nineteenth century peacetime enlisted forces had a negative social image, even when they were compared to civilian laborers. Again as for the AVF, this image does not seem consistent with the facts. Whatever else they imply, the military's high desertion rates indicate high permeability between the civilian and military labor forces. The workers in each could not have been that different from each other. Lebergott's classic analysis of the American nineteenth century economy indicates that much of the male labor force had to string jobs together across the year. Military service was less sensitive to seasonal and cyclical employment fluctuations than many civilian occupations, and analyses of desertion rates indicate that male workers—

probably younger and unmarried ones, especially—used military service as one employment option in this patching process.

The discrepancy between image and reality, shared by the nineteenth century and today's enlisted volunteer forces, begs explanation. As noted earlier, Americans distrust centralized power, their regard for the military varies with the proximity of danger, and in peacetime the status of the military declines. However, these facts do not explain why, even in peacetime, the officers corps traditionally enjoys public esteem and the enlisted force, public distaste or contempt.

The typical social composition of American enlisted forces under volunteer conditions is a key to the discrepancy between image and reality. Like the AVF, the nineteenth century enlisted force attracted those who wanted to enter the mainstream more than those already in it—the working class, immigrants, and blacks. Class bias, racial and ethnic bias, and nativist bias seem to maintain the chronic discrepancy between the image and reality of volunteer enlisted forces in this country. We explore this issue in greater detail later in this chapter.

THE SOCIAL COMPOSITION OF DRAFTED ENLISTED FORCES

While our peacetime enlisted forces have been more select than public images would have them, our draft enlisted forces appear to have been less representative than public images would indicate.

Civil War

We have had federal conscription during the Civil War, World War I, 1940 through 1947, and 1948 through 1973.[38] The inequities of the Civil War draft were legendary and partly responsible for the bloody draft riots of 1863. A man could buy an exemption for $300 or procure a substitute for an agreed-upon amount. Inevitably the burden of the draft fell disproportionately on the working classes, although we cannot estimate how unrepresentative the Union forces were. What we know about pre-Civil War annual earnings suggests that $300 would have represented a large sum for many, not just poor, families. Certainly both Confederate and Union soldiers complained that they were caught in "a rich man's war and a poor man's fight."[39]

World War I

In response to the abuses of the Civil War draft, the 1917 Congress tried to design an equitable draft law, in part by decentralizing draft decisions to the level of local selective service boards. In fact, a major National Academy of Sciences (NAS) study indicates that the social composition of the World War I draft was not representative.[40] The study reported that prior to September 1918, 21 to 31-year-old males were registered and more than seven-tenths of these registrants were placed in deferred classes. Of the 6,973,270 deferments and exemptions, 6.8% were deferred for occupational and industrial reasons; 0.5% for religious reasons; 51.1% for various conditions of dependency; 8.9% for current enlistment in the Army or Navy; 7.8% for lack of physical, mental, or moral fitness to be a soldier; and 13.2% for reasons of alien allegiance.

The nature of the selective service deferment rules supports the NAS's conclusion that those who received occupational deferments were "undoubtedly above the average of men in the same occupation."[41] However, a slightly larger percentage of individuals were deferred or excluded from service because they did not meet physical, intellectual, or moral enlistment standards. The major source of deferments was dependency, and the relationships between dependency and representativeness criteria are not known for this time period.

The NAS study provides substantial information about the representativeness of those actually drafted.[42] These data suggest that foreign-born white male immigrants were somewhat over-represented among white male draftees. Black registrants were apparently inducted at higher rates than white registrants, and blacks were over-represented in the military relative to their percentage of the total population. Foner reports an induction rate of 34% for black registrants but only 24% for white registrants.[43] In 1920, black 20 to 29 year-old males represented 10.1% of the 20 to 29-year-old population. However, they provided 13% of all those drafted in World War I.[44]

For all males 25 to 34 years of age in 1920, the age cohort for most of the World War I draftees, the census reports an illiteracy rate of 5.6%[45] The NAS data indicate that World War I draftees had much higher illiteracy rates than the 1920 census shows for the general population. Although military literacy standards were often higher than census standards,[46] the illiteracy rate was still 22.4% for all draftees in army camps that used literacy standards most similar to those of the census (ability to read and write). Even under conservative assumptions, the white illiteracy rate was still 19.2%. Camp Jackson, which used a "read and write" criterion only, found that 7.9% of white northern recruits, 36.5% of white southern recruits, 58.3% of foreign-born recruits, and 83% of black recruits were illiterate.

In general, World War I draftees had lower educational attainments than the average attainments for their age cohort. Relative to the 25 to 29-year-old white population in 1920, the draft of native born whites had a higher percentage of those with less than five years of school and a much lower percentage of those with twelve or more years of school. Relative to the 25 to 29-year-old nonwhite population in 1920, the total black draft had a slightly smaller percentage of those with less than five years of school, but only half the percentage of those with twelve or more years of school.

Unfortunately, we lack both the civilian and the military data that let us compare the skill levels of draftees with their same-age civilian cohort. We can conclude, however, that the average World War I draftee was in his early twenties and unmarried. One in eight was black and one in six an immigrant. Relative to the average for his same-age cohort, the average draftee was more likely to be illiterate, more likely (except for blacks) to have less than five years of school, and less likely to have completed high school or have any post-secondary education.

World War II, Korean War, Korea-Vietnam Interim, and Vietnam War

Except for a 15-month hiatus in 1947-48, the United States had some form of military draft from 1940 to 1973. We have data on the social representativeness of the military for three episodes of war (World War II, the Korean War, and the Vietnam War) and one period of semi-peace (the Korea–Vietnam Interim). The data come from two linked surveys, both conducted by the U.S. Bureau of the Census: the March 1973 Current Population Survey (CPS) and the August–November 1973 Occupational Changes in a Generation Survey (OCG). The OCG sample consisted of 20 to 65-year-old males in the CPS sample. The CPS tallied age, race and ethnicity, veteran status, and, for veterans, period of military service (Vietnam War, Korean War, World War II, other service). The OCG inventoried characteristics of the respondent's family when the respondent was 16 years of age: family income, father's occupation, father's education, and mother's education. It also recorded the respondent's education.

The populations described from World War II to Vietnam are not the same as the one described for World War I. The World War I data pertained to *enlisted draftees*. The CPS and OCG data pertain to *veterans*, both officers and enlisted men, who entered the military as volunteers, draft-induced volunteers, or draftees.[47] Since officers have more education and come from families with higher socioeconomic status than enlistees, these data represent upwardly biased estimates of the characteristics of enlisted forces from World War II to 1973.

For each military period we defined the age cohort most vulnerable to military service. To define a cohort, we used the draft laws on ages of liability that operated in the period and the age distribution of those who actually served in that period. For each age cohort thus defined, we weighted the non-veteran sample to reproduce the age distribution of the veteran sample. The total sample is weighted to represent the population from which it is drawn.

Tables 2.1 through 2.4 tell the basic story for the officer and enlisted veterans from World War II to 1973.

Table 2.1. Socioeconomic and Educational Profile of Veterans and Non-Veterans by Military Period

Characteristic	Military Status	Military Period							
		World War II		Korean War		Korea-Vietnam Interim		Vietnam War	
		Mean	Standard Deviation	Mean	Standard Deviation	Mean	Standard Deviation	Mean	Standard Deviation
Annual income of parental family (dollars)	Veteran	3359	3283	4996	3746	6569	4504	8423	4857
	Non-veteran	2796	3274	4119	3871	5624	4503	8215	5400
Father's occupation (Duncan SEI scores)	Veteran	29	21	30	21	33	22	35	23
	Non-veteran	23	19	26	21	29	22	36	24
Father's education (years completed)	Veteran	7.6	3.9	8.3	3.7	9.3	3.7	10.2	3.5
	Non-veteran	6.5	4.0	7.3	4.3	8.3	4.2	10.0	4.1
Mother's education (years completed)	Veteran	8.2	3.7	9.1	3.5	10.0	3.1	10.8	2.9
	Non-veteran	6.9	4.0	8.1	4.0	9.0	3.8	10.4	3.5
Respondent's education (years completed)	Veteran	11.5	3.4	12.5	3.1	12.7	2.9	12.6	2.4
	Non-veteran	9.5	4.2	10.4	4.1	11.6	3.8	12.6	3.5
Race (percent black)	Veteran	6.9		7.2		5.0		8.5	
	Non-veteran	13.5		14.6		12.6		11.3	

As Table 2.1 shows, before Vietnam, veterans came from families with higher socioeconomic status than non-veterans. Their families had higher annual incomes; their fathers, more prestigious occupations; their parents, more education. The veterans had higher educational attainments.

The means for both veterans and non-veterans steadily increased between World War II and Vietnam. These advances reflect several social trends: increasing constant dollar family incomes, higher levels of educational attainment, and increasing proportions of the male labor force in more prestigious occupations.

The differences between means of veterans and non-veterans declined from World War II to Vietnam. As Table 2.2 shows, by the Vietnam War the means for veterans and non-veterans were virtually indistinguishable from each other.

Blacks were underrepresented among veterans for all military eras, but decreasingly so from World War II to Vietnam.

We see in Table 2.3 that from World War II to Vietnam the veteran and the non-veteran populations each became increasingly homogeneous in family background and educational attainment. The coefficients of variation in Table 2.3 simply represent the ratio of the standard deviation to the mean and give us a standardized measure of variation. As Table 2.1 shows, the means increased for both groups for all variables across time. Thus, the decreasing coefficients of variation in Table 2.3 indicate that the standard deviations for each group either decreased across time or did not increase in proportion to the increase in means.

Table 2.2.   Ratio of Non-Veteran to Veteran Means for Selected Characteristics and Military Periods*

Characteristic	Military Period			
	World War II	Korean War	Korea-Vietnam Interim	Vietnam War
Annual income of parental family	0.83	0.83	0.86	0.98
Father's occupation	0.79	0.87	0.88	1.03
Father's education	0.86	0.88	0.89	0.98
Mother's education	0.84	0.89	0.90	0.96
Respondent's education	0.83	0.83	0.91	1.00
Percent black	1.96	2.03	2.52	1.33

*Source: Table 2.1.

Table 2.3. Coefficients of Variation for Veterans and Non-Veterans by Military Period*†

Characteristic	Military Status	Military Period			
		World War II	Korean War	Korea-Vietnam Interim	Vietnam War
Annual income of parental family	Veteran	0.98	0.75	0.69	0.58
	Non-veteran	1.17	0.94	0.80	0.66
Father's occupation	Veteran	0.72	0.70	0.67	0.66
	Non-veteran	0.83	0.81	0.76	0.67
Father's education	Veteran	0.51	0.45	0.40	0.34
	Non-veteran	0.62	0.59	0.51	0.41
Mother's education	Veteran	0.45	0.39	0.31	0.27
	Non-veteran	0.58	0.49	0.42	0.34
Respondent's education	Veteran	0.30	0.25	0.23	0.19
	Non-veteran	0.44	0.39	0.33	0.28

*The coefficient of variation for a characteristic is defined as its standard deviation divided by its mean.
†Source: Table 2.1.

Veterans were socioeconomically and educationally *more homogeneous* than non-veterans in all military eras, even during the Vietnam War when the means for the two groups were virtually the same.

From World War II to 1973, the ratios of non-veteran to veteran means increasingly approached parity (1.00). Across this same period, however, the ratios of non-veteran to veteran standard deviations increasingly departed from parity, the variance in the non-veteran group, as Table 2.4 shows, becoming greater than that in the veteran group. Together these tables imply that, before the Vietnam War, those from the lower part of the country's SES distribution were less likely to serve. During the Vietnam War, those from the lower *and* upper extremes of the distribution were less likely to serve.

In sum, under different forms of the draft the military has been less representative than the concept of draft implies. The nature of the nonrepresentativeness has varied. Although we lack hard data, Civil War draftees almost certainly came disproportionately from poorer families. World War I draftees were disproportionately black and immigrant. Relative to their same-age cohort, they were more likely to be illiterate, and smaller percentages had achieved high school degrees or had any postsecondary education.

From World War II to 1973, we have data on veterans but not on the enlisted force alone or enlisted draftees alone. In World War II the military was upwardly biased socially; i.e., blacks and the lower end of the educational and socioeconomic distributions were under-represented. By the Vietnam War the means for veterans and non-eterans were virtually indistinguishable from each other. However, the lower *and* upper extremes of the educational and socioeconomic distributions were under-represented.

Table 2.4.   Ratio of Non-Veteran to Veteran Standard Deviations
for Selected Characteristics and Military Periods

Characteristic	Military Period			
	World War II	Korean War	Korea-Vietnam Interim	Vietnam War
Annual income of parental family	1.00	1.03	1.00	1.11
Father's occupation	0.91	1.00	1.00	1.04
Father's education	1.03	1.16	1.14	1.17
Mother's education	1.08	1.14	1.23	1.21
Respondent's education	0.83	1.32	1.31	1.46

Source: Table 2.1.

THE POLITICS OF ENLISTED MANPOWER COMPOSITION

At the most superficial level, discrepancies between images and realities seem easily explained, at least for this century. The fact that different discrepancies emerge under draft as compared to volunteer conditions represents an important clue. Military manpower policies intervene between a given enlistment mechanism and actual enlistment. Under these policies a volunteer mechanism never produces "free flow" entry and drafts never produce random selection.

A volunteer mechanism means that the military is subject to the same labor allocation processes that operate in the general economy. Since enlisted jobs consist primarily of blue collar and lower level white collar jobs, we can expect military applicants to come from the lower and middle parts of the nation's talent and SES distributions. Fluctuations in the civilian economy shift the distribution of applicant talent and SES characteristics up and down, but within a fairly narrow range. However, observers apparently ignore the effects of military enlistment standards such as medical and basic skill standards. These shift the talent and SES composition of enlistees above that expected under entirely free flow volunteer conditions.

Quality standards have the same effect under draft as under volunteer conditions. They eliminate the less educated and less physically fit and therefore raise the SES distribution of draftees. However, as we saw in World War I and increasingly from World War II through the Vietnam War, occupational, educational, and dependency deferments shift the talent and SES composition of draftees down. The combined effect of quality standards and deferments is to create a draft more representative of the lower middle and middle parts of the country's talent and SES distributions than would be expected under a truly random draft.

In sum, military manpower policies create much greater compositional continuity across volunteer and draft conditions and across war and peace than would be expected in their absence. However, this explanation of image/reality discrepancies simply pushes the puzzle to the next level. Why do groups interested in and knowledgeable about military manpower policies omit the implications of these policies from their assessments of the enlisted forces?

The answer seems to lie in the fact that military manpower policies reflect normal political processes. We like to think that military manpower policies, the resources devoted to them, and their compositional consequences reflect the "objective" requirements of national defense. In fact, of course, they represent the results of the usual political trades between multiple groups, or *stakeholders*, that have different objectives for the enlisted force and therefore different compositional preferences. This idea is hardly new. As Huntington noted:

> The most distinctive, the most fascinating, and the most troublesome aspect of military policy is its Janus-like quality. Indeed, military policy not only faces in

two directions, it exists in two worlds. One is international politics, the world of the balance of power, wars and alliances, the subtle and the brutal uses of force and diplomacy to influence the behavior of other states. The principal currency of this world is actual or potential military strength: battalions, weapons, and warships. The other world is domestic politics, the world of interest groups, political parties, social classes, with their conflicting interests and goals. The currency here is the resources of society: men, money, material. Any major decision in military policy influences and is influenced by both worlds.[48]

Images of the composition of the enlisted force, then, reflect differences between the actual composition and the composition that stakeholders want. To the extent that a difference between actual and preferred compositions exists, compositional images and realities will differ.

Some of the most important objectives for our enlisted force seem to be the following. Each objective calls for a particular social composition for the enlisted force.

Loyalty to civilian values. This objective predates the founding of the Republic, appearing first in Western Europe with the gradual transfer of power from kings to subjects. It reflects a fear that centralized military power will subvert democratic liberties either in the form of a military coup or of coalitions of military and civilian leaders. It manifests as a preference for militias under state, not federal, control, and for "citizen armies," i.e., armies manned not by professional soldiers but by civilians who turn soldier "for the duration." The objective calls for a small standing army, limited-time drafts, and a composition that mirrors that of the society on some set of characteristics, for instance, a socially representative enlisted force.

Loyalty to government policies. Even in a society where all men are created equal, some men and groups are "more equal than others." As Machiavelli advises the prince, to stay in power one must control one's military. This objective calls for soldiers whose origins are believed to signal conformity to the values of their military and civilian leaders. It would seem to imply a white enlisted force, drawn from less recent immigrant groups, from less urban communities, and from upwardly mobile groups concerned to demonstrate their acceptability to ruling groups. In terms of socioeconomic classes, these include the upper lower and lower middle classes.

Deterrent and combat effectiveness. The purpose of a standing army is to prevent wars and to win those that have to be fought. The image of effectiveness is crucial for deterrence; actual effectiveness, crucial for battlefield victories. Effectiveness, whether image or reality, seems to require reliability and competence. Discussion of the last two objectives indicates that stakeholders vary in what characteristics they associate with reliability. However, they seem to concur in the characteristics associated with competence. Stakeholders seem to assume that current technically complicated weapons systems require commensurate skills. This vague upward pressure on desired abilities pushes toward an enlisted force drawn from the higher status groups, e.g., whites, higher SES families, and the better educated.

Defense efficiency. Relative to an alternative, the composition of a given force is more efficient if it provides higher quality manpower for the same cost or the same quality for lower cost. This objective is the primary concern of those with managerial responsibilities for the enlisted force, and its compositional implications seem to be established more empirically than normatively. For example, the services have educational enlistment standards that reflect a recognized relationship between high school graduation and retention. However, no optimal composition has been identified relative to a fuller set of costs (e.g., recruiting, training, retention). The compositional implication of this objective is, therefore, not clear.

Equally distributed sacrifice. This objective has its roots in the democratization of society. Social equality is exchanged for equal sacrifice in time of war, a contract that implies a socially representative military. The perceived violation of this contract generated several American draft riots, for example, the New York City riots during the Civil War. In our most recent winter of discontent, Vietnam, the issue arose again, the belief being that the war was being fought disproportionately by blacks and the poor.

The equal distribution of sacrifice issue becomes particularly important in war; however, it also lies behind ideas of national service, the concept being that those entering citizenship (the young) should earn that right through military or non-military service to the nation.

Access to military benefits and entitlements. Today's military offers benefits such as food, shelter, clothing, medical care, income, and pensions. In addition, service carries entitlements in the form of full enfranchisement. As Theodore Roosevelt noted, "Universal service and universal suffrage go hand in hand."[49] Since the founding of the Republic, and especially during war, the United States government has offered citizenship to aliens in exchange for honorable military service.[50] The congressional decision to lower the voting age to 18 years at the end of the Vietnam War occurred in the context of this implicit contract that military service earns suffrage. A democratic society is under constant pressure to extend the franchise. Efforts by the less enfranchised to secure access to the military represent one instance of this pressure. This objective calls for a military composition biased toward the less enfranchised.

Table 2.5 summarizes the compositional implications of these several objectives. It clearly reveals a major source of political conflict in military manpower policy: conflicting compositional objectives. *There is no one composition that satisfies all objectives.* It also hints at reasons for the bobs and weaves that we observe in military manpower policy. External events such as changes in stakeholders' power relationships, changes in domestic priori-

Table 2.5.   Objectives for Enlisted Force and Their Compositional Implications

Objective	Compositional Implication
Loyalty to civilian values	Socially representative force
Loyalty to government policies	Bias toward lower middle and middle class whites from less recent immigrant groups and from less urban areas
Deterrent and combat effectiveness	Bias toward better educated white males
Force efficiency	Compositional implications not clear
Equally distributed sacrifice	Socially representative force
Extension of political and economic franchise	Bias toward less enfranchised groups (minorities, lower socioeconomic status groups, women)

ties, and external or internal security threats that perturb the basis for previous compromises by altering the relative saliency of the objectives that bear on compositional policy. Changes in saliency can then provoke shifts in the policies themselves. Given the basic functions of a military institution, we can expect considerations of military effectiveness to limit the extent to which military manpower policy can respond to objectives whose compositional implications conflict with effectiveness considerations.

Even if the military manpower policy process is political in nature and will always involve multiple and conflicting objectives, it can have "market failures" similar to those observed for economies. Failures consist of not arriving at that composition most consistent with stakeholder interests and power relationships. They often occur because the debate is muddled or rests on empirically untested or unsupported assumptions about the implications of a given social composition for stakeholder objectives, for example, assumptions about the loyalty implications of membership in a particular ethnic group.

An empirical literature is gradually accumulating about the implications of individual or group characteristics for the attainment of different stakeholder objectives. However, this literature focuses on efficiency issues and, to a lesser extent, on performance issues. It rarely, and then usually only speculatively or anecdotally, addresses questions about what the social composition of our troops implies for deterrence, reliability, and the potential conflict between two objectives—access to the opportunities associated with military service and equal sacrifice in combat.

Does the social composition of our troops affect how foreign governments perceive our combat capabilities? If so, do governments vary in the conclusions that they draw? What is the history of the reliability of the racial and ethnic subgroups that made up our polyglot military? What military conditions produce loyalty conflicts and for whom? How do defense policymakers, the American public, and interest groups prefer to resolve the potential conflict between access during peacetime and equality during war? Answers to questions such as these may affect how we judge our ability to deter wars; how we deploy our troops during war; and what public support we can expect for any wars that might be waged.

NOTES

1. Mark J. Eitelberg, "American Youth and Military Representation," *Youth and Society* 10 (1978):5–32.
2. The Duncan Socio-Economic Index (SEI) for occupations reflects the relative social standing or status of occupations in the economy, for example, of receptionists, metal molders, electric power linemen and cablemen. A weighted combination of the education and income of the average incumbent of the occupation determines the Duncan SEI score for that occupation. These scores can vary from 1 to 100. For example, a judge has a Duncan SEI score of 93; an optometrist, a score of 79; a draftsman, a score of 65; a construction inspector, a score of 58; an auctioneer, a score of 40; a plasterer, a score of 25; and a paperhanger, a score of 14.
3. In the first followup (1980) to the *1979 NLS*, all respondents took the Armed Services Vocational Aptitude Battery (ASVAB). Scores on subsections of the ASVAB are combined into a basic skill measure known as the Armed Forces Qualifying Test (AFQT). When my analyses were conducted, the AFQT data had not yet been released. However, a staff member at the Center for Human Resource Research at Ohio State University, the group responsible for cleaning, documenting, and disseminating the *1979 NLS* data, ran a correlation of respondents' AFQT and knowledge-of-work scores for us. The Pearson's R was 0.61, indicating that knowledge-of-work scores predict AFQT scores reasonably well. Another staff member substituted knowledge-of-work scores for AFQT scores in a multivariate analysis and found little difference between the coefficients for the alternative ability measures.
4. A respondent's knowledge-of-work score is the sum of correct answers to questions about what workers in ten occupations do. The occupations include department store buyer, dietician, keypunch operator, assembler, and machinist.
5. U.S. Department of Defense, *Profile of American Youth*, 1982, p. 24.
6. Francis P. Prucha, *Broadax and Bayonet: The Role of the United States Army in the Development of the Northwest, 1815–1860* (State Historical Society of Wisconsin, 1953), p. 36.
7. Francis P. Prucha, *The Sword of the Republic* (Bloomington, IN: Indiana Univ. Press, 1977), p. 323.
8. Donald Rickey, Jr., *Forty Miles a Day on Beans and Hay* (Norman, OK: Univ. of Oklahoma Press, 1977).
9. Prucha, *The Sword of the Republic*.
10. Samuel P. Huntington, "The Soldier and the State in the 1970s," in F.D. Margiotta, ed., *The Changing World of the American Military* (Boulder, CO: Westview Press, 1978) p. 17.
11. Rickey, *Forty Miles a Day on Beans and Hay*, p. 27.

12. Series Y904–916, *Historical Statistics of the United States, Colonial Times to 1970*, Part 2, 1975, pp. 1141–1143.
13. Series A119–134, *Historical Statistics of the United States, Colonial Times to 1970*, Part 1, 1975, pp. 15–18.
14. Prucha, *Broadax and Bayonet*.
15. Series C89–119, *Historical Statistics of the United States, Colonial Times to 1970*, Part 1, 1975, p. 106.
16. Series A6–8 and A119–134, *Historical Statistics of the United States, Colonial Times to 1970*, Part 1, 1975, pp. 8, 15–18.
17. Philip Foner, *The Great Labor Uprising of 1877* (New York: Monad Press, 1977).
18. Lawrence A. Cremin, *American Education: The National Experience, 1783–1876* (New York: Harper and Row, 1980), p. 488.
19. John K. Folger and Charles B. Nam, *Education of the American Population* (U.S. Department of Commerce, Bureau of the Census, Washington, DC: Government Printing Office, 1967).
20. Series H598–601, *Historical Statistics of the United States, Colonial Times to 1970*, Part 1, 1975, p. 379.
21. Folger and Nam, *Education of the American Population*.
22. Series D75–84, *Historical Statistics of the United States, Colonial Times to 1970*, Part 1, 1975.
23. Series D182–232, *Historical Statistics of the United States, Colonial Times to 1970*, Part 1, 1975.
24. Prucha, *Broadax and Bayonet* and *The Sword of the Republic*.
25. Stanley Lebergott, *Manpower in Economic Growth: The American Record Since 1800* (New York: McGraw Hill, 1964), p. 244.
26. Lebergott, *Manpower in Economic Growth*, p. 258ff.
27. Series Y856–903, D705–714, and D735–738, *Historical Statistics of the United States, Colonial Times to 1970*, Parts 1 and 2, 1975.
28. Series Y856–903 and D779–793, *Historical Statistics of the United States, Colonial Times to 1970*, Parts 1 and 2, 1975.
29. Alba M. Edwards, *Comparative Occupation Statistics for the United States, 1870 to 1940*, Sixteenth Census of the United States: 1940 Population (Washington, DC: U.S. Government Printing Office, 1943).
30. In 1823, 25% of the enlistments that year deserted; in 1826, 50%; in 1830, 25% (Prucha, *Broadax and Bayonet*); in 1866, 26%; and in 1871, almost a third (J.D. Foner, *The United States Soldier Between Two Wars—Army Life and Reforms, 1865–1898*, New York: Humanities Press, 1970).
31. Prucha, *Broadax and Bayonet*.
32. Rickey, *Forty Miles a Day on Beans and Hay*; Foner, *The United States Soldier Between Two Wars*.
33. Lebergott, *Manpower in Economic Growth*.
34. Series D85–86, *Historical Statistics of the United States, Colonial Times to 1970*, Part 1, 1975, p. 135.
35. Rickey, *Forty Miles a Day on Beans and Hay*.
36. Foner, *The United States Soldier Between Two Wars*, p. 9.
37. Lebergott, *Manpower in Economic Growth*.
38. During the Revolutionary War the states of Massachusetts and Virginia resorted to conscription. The Continental Congress was considering universal conscription when the French intervention eliminated the need. The Congress again considered conscription toward the end of the War of 1812, but the conclusion of hostilities eliminated the need. See Harry A. Marmion, "Historical Background of Selective Service in the United States," in Roger W. Little, ed., *Selective Service and American Society* (New York: Russell Sage Foundation, 1969).

39. Fred D. Baldwin, *The American Enlisted Man in World War I*, (Ph.D. diss, Princeton Univ., 1964).

40. Robert M. Yerkes, ed., *Psychological Examining in the U.S. Army*, Memoirs of the National Academy of Sciences, Vol. 15 (Washington, DC: U.S. Government Printing Office, 1921).

41. The criteria for occupational deferments were: (1) necessary skilled farm or industrial laborers in essential agricultural or industrial enterprises; (2) highly trained firemen or policemen in service of municipality; (3) necessary assistant, associate, or hired manager of essential agricultural enterprise; (4) necessary highly specialized technical or mechanical expert of essential industrial enterprise; (5) necessary assistant or associate or sole manager of essential industrial enterprise; (6) all legislative, executive, or judicial officers of the United States, or of state, territory, or District of Columbia; (7) ministers or students of religion, and all necessary employees in the service of the United States, necessary customhouse clerks, necessary employees in the transmission of mails, mariners, and licensed pilots. See Yerkes, *Psychological Examining in the U.S. Army*.

42. The study reported characteristics for five statistically drawn samples of draftees. These five samples were labeled Groups I, II, III, IV, and V. Group I represented the white draft for the United States. The sample was prorated by state, one recruit being selected per thousand of the white male population of each state. The 1910 census population figures were used to determine state populations. The group II sample consisted of the Group I sample augmented by additional samples for the small states to bring the number of cases for each state to a minimum of 1,000. The group III sample consisted of the group II sample augmented by additions drawn by camp so that the group approximated 2,500 cases per camp. Group IV represented the black draft for the United States. Like Group I, the sample was prorated by state, one recruit being selected per 250 black males in each state. Group V was comparable to Group II for the black draft. See Yerkes, *Psychological Examining in the U.S. Army*, pp. 555-560.

43. Jack D. Foner, *Blacks and the Military in American History* (New York: Praeger, 1974).

44. Foner, *Blacks and the Military in American History*.

45. Folger and Nam, *Education of the American Population*, p. 121.

46. The usual military standard for literacy was the "ability to read and understand newspapers and write letters home." See Yerkes, *Psychological Examining in the U.S. Army*, p. 743. However, 46% of the camps used the standard of 3 to 7 (usually 4, 5, or 6) years of schooling, either as an additional or as the sole literacy criterion. From 1870-1930 the Bureau of the Census asked respondents two separate questions: could they read, and could they write. Illiteracy was defined as the inability to write "regardless of the ability to read," although the data showed that most persons who could write could also read. See *Historical Statistics of the United States, Colonial Times to 1970*, Part 1, 1945, p. 365.

47. The officer content of the active duty military increased from 10% in World War II to 12% in the Korean War to 14% at the end of the Vietnam War. See Series Y904-916, *Historical Statistics of the United States, Colonial Times to 1970*, Part 2, 1975, p. 1141; Table 614, *Statistical Abstracts of the United States: 1980*, 1980, p. 376.

48. Samuel P. Huntington, *The Common Defense* (New York: Columbia Univ. Press, 1961), p.1.

49. N. Sales de Bohigos, "Some Opinions on Exemption from Military Service in Nineteenth Century Europe," *Comparative Studies in History and Society* 10 (1967-1968):261-289. This contract is not unique to the United States, nor did it emerge here. As M.D. Feld notes in "Military Professionalism and the Mass

Army," *Armed Forces and Society* 1 (February 1975):195, the European nation state and mass army invariably and not accidentally appeared together. "Military service and political rights were closely equated. According to the new political outlook the ballot was the minimal political right and military service the basic civic obligation. The former was widely considered to be justified by the latter. That is, military service represented a claim to full citizenship and was a conventional means whereby the disenfranchised gained civic rights."

50. J.B. Jacobs and L.A. Hayes, "Aliens in the U.S. Armed Forces: A Historico–Legal Analysis," *Armed Forces and Society* 7 (Winter 1981):187–208.

3

The American Enlisted Man in the All-Volunteer Army

Charles C. Moskos

THE AMERICAN ENLISTED MAN

Enlisted service was *the* modal experience for young American men from the eve of World War II until the end of the draft following the Vietnam War.[1] With the advent of the all-volunteer force (AVF) in 1973, this ceased to be the case. Whereas about three out of four eligible men who came of age in the 1940s, 1950s and 1960s had military experience, the corresponding figure in the 1970s and 1980s has been about one in four.

Even in the mid-1980s, however, there are about 600,000 Army enlisted men (EM) on active duty and a slightly higher number in the Army Reserves and National Guard. Despite the reduction in military manpower since the end of the draft, the armed forces have been recruiting on the average between 300,000 and 350,000 enlisted persons a year. Between 100,000 and 150,000 of these have been male Army recruits. The sheer numbers in the Army enlisted ranks are still impressive.

The plan of this essay is straightforward. First, trend data are given on the demographics of the contemporary Army enlisted force. Second, the salient features of enlisted life are described. Third, patterns of enlisted culture are examined. Finally, emerging patterns in military social organization are appraised with a concluding statement on the future of Army enlisted men.[2]

DEMOGRAPHIC TRENDS

Educational Levels

The educational levels of Army male recruits have fluctuated widely over the course of the all-volunteer era. As shown in Table 3.1, during the 1970s entrants with a high school diploma accounted for slightly over half of all recruits. A significant turn around began in 1980, however by 1983, high

Table 3.1. Educational Levels of Army Male Entrants (non-prior-service): Selected Years

Educational Level	Draftees 1964	Enlistees 1964	1975	1977	1979	1981	1983
College—some (%)	17.2	13.9	5.7	5.1	2.2	4.0	6.7
High school graduate	54.1	46.2	48.6	51.1	56.3	73.7	78.8
Non-High school graduate	28.7	39.9	45.7	43.8	41.5	22.3	14.5
Total (%)	100.0	100.0	100.0	100.0	100.0	100.0	100.0
(Number in thousands)	(151)	(108)	(165)	(153)	(109)	(97)	(112)

school dropouts accounted for less than 15% of entrants. The improved educational levels among Army recruits in the 1980s can be attributed to the high youth employment rate, improved recruit pay, new programs of post-service educational benefits, and a significantly improved recruiting command. The long-term appeal of the AVF to draw anything approaching a cross-section of American youth in times of economic prosperity, however, continues to be in doubt.

The data given in Table 3.1 also reveal a sharp decline in the proportion of Army entrants with some college between the pre- and post-Vietnam periods. Where 17.2% of the draftees and 13.9% of the enlistees in 1964 (the last peacetime year before the war in Vietnam) had some college, the corresponding figure has been around 5% in the all-volunteer Army. Not only did the draft directly bring a sizeable college element into the enlisted ranks, it also served as an impetus for well educated draft-motivated volunteers to join either active or reserve components of the Army. The 1964 accession data, if anything, understate the infusion of college enlisted men into the ranks of the pre-Vietnam Army. During the small cohort years of the 1950s to the early 1960s—the time when Depression babies had reached military age—college graduates were more likely to be drafted than in any period since World War II. (Survey data based on Army entrants show one quarter of all draftees had some college in 1960.)

Racial Composition

The rising proportion of black entrants in the Army has generated more discussion about the social composition of the AVF than any other topic.[3] In 1964, as shown in Table 3.2, blacks accounted for about 12% of Army enlisted men, a figure corresponding to the black share of the 18 to 24 year age group in the total population. Blacks were disproportionately underrepresented, however, in the officer and senior NCO grades. The changing racial composition of the Army since the end of the draft is also given in Table 3.2. Blacks made up 17.4% of enlisted personnel in 1972 and 32.2% in 1983. The proportion of black noncommissioned officers (NCOs) has increased markedly over the same time period. The numbers of black NCOs can be expected to increase further, owing to the fact that blacks are about one and a half times as likely to reenlist as whites. Although the rise among black officers has not been as sharp, the increased black representation in the Army officer corps is also impressive. It should be noted, however, that bad economic times decrease the proportion of black Army entrants. It is not that fewer blacks try to get into the Army, but that many more whites (who, on the average, are more likely to score higher on entry tests) are drawn to the recruiter.

That the educational levels of blacks in America have trailed behind those of whites is well known (although the trend is toward a narrowing of the gap).

Table 3.2. Percentage of Black Participation in the Army by Pay Grade:
Selected Years

	1964	1972	1979	1983
Officers:				
0-7 and above (general)	—	1.8	5.2	6.3
0-6 (colonel)	.2	1.5	4.3	4.8
0-5 (lieutenant colonel)	1.1	5.3	5.3	4.9
0-4 (major)	3.5	5.0	4.5	4.8
0-3 (captain)	5.1	3.9	6.9	10.0
0-2 (1st lieutenant)	3.6	3.4	9.7	14.7
0-1 (2nd lieutenant)	2.6	2.2	9.4	11.9
Warrant	2.8	4.5	5.9	6.2
Total Officers	3.3	3.9	6.8	8.8
Enlisted				
E-9 (sergeant major)	3.3	8.6	19.0	24.7
E-8 (master sergeant)	5.8	14.4	23.9	28.6
E-7 (sergeant first class)	7.9	19.9	25.2	23.9
E-6 (staff sergeant)	12.2	23.9	22.8	29.1
E-5 (sergeant)	14.8	16.9	28.6	38.8
E-4 (specialist 4)	12.5	14.1	33.7	38.1
E-3 (private first class)	11.9	16.7	37.8	29.3
E-2 (private)	11.6	18.5	37.9	26.4
E-1 (private)	6.4	18.4	37.3	24.4
Total Enlisted	11.8	17.4	32.2	32.2

Contrary to national patterns, however, the intersection of race and education is quite different among male entrants in the all-volunteer Army. Since the end of the draft, the proportion of black high school graduates entering the Army has consistently exceeded that of whites. In point of fact, today the Army enlisted ranks are the only major social arena in American society where black educational levels surpass that of whites.

Mental Aptitude Levels

All recruits are classified into mental aptitude levels according to their scores on entrance tests. The tested population is categorized into five groups (percentile score given in parentheses): I, much above average (93–100); II, above average (65–92); III, average (31–64); IV, below average (10–30); and V, much below average (9 and below). The Army, in competition with the other services, seeks to recruit from the average-and-above portions of the mental aptitude spectrum. Category V individuals are not eligible to join the services.

Table 3.3 shows the distribution of Army male entrants by mental group level over time. It is interesting to note that, even in the best year of the all-volunteer Army (1983), the proportion of recruits in Category I is substantially lower than during any draft year. In terms of actual numbers, the contrast is even sharper. In 1964, for example, 12,000 male entrants were in Category I compared with 4,000 in 1983 (2,000 in 1979). The proportion of Army entrants in Category IV reached unprecedented numbers in the late 1970s, owing in part to a "mis-norming" of the military's entrance test (i.e., individuals who were presumed to be Category III were actually Category IV). During 1979 about half of all Army male entrants were really category IVs.

Because blacks tend to score lower than whites on aptitude tests, the usefulness of mental scores to evaluate soldierly potential is intertwined with controversy over the inappropriate characterization of racial groups by their differential performance on intelligence tests.[4] Research on prediction of soldierly performance based on social background variables, such as race, education, and mental test scores, is not definitive; but the research consensus, if there is one, seems to be the following: completion of high school is a much more powerful predictor of enlistment completion than mental group level.[5] High school graduates, independent of mental group level, are twice as likely to complete an enlistment as are high school dropouts. High school completion, that is, reflects a certain amount of persistence that helps predict completion of an Army tour. Mental ability shows a positive correlation with soldierly performance in a variety of skills, combat as well as technical.[6] With regard to promotion rates, blacks scoring at the lower mental levels tend to do much better than their white counterparts, while blacks scoring at the higher mental levels tend to do somewhat worse than their white counterparts.[7]

Table 3.3. Percentage Distribution of Army Male Entrants
(non-prior-service) by Mental Group Level: Selected Years

Year	I	II	III	IV	Total
1960	8.2	24.1	50.7	17.0	100.0
1964	5.7	28.0	46.4	19.9	100.0
1969	6.1	28.3	38.1	27.5	100.0
1973	3.4	27.5	51.8	17.3	100.0
1975	4.5	30.3	55.1	10.0	100.0
1977	2.3	17.9	36.4	43.4	100.0
1979	1.7	14.4	35.2	48.7	100.0
1981	2.2	21.4	45.5	30.9	100.0
1983	3.5	33.0	51.5	12.0	100.0

Marital Status

Though usually uncommented upon by observers of all-volunteer trends, a most dramatic change has been in the marital composition of the Army. Since the end of the draft, the proportion of married Army enlisted men has increased from about one-fourth to about one-half. The figures are all the more remarkable because they reflect entirely a change in the marital composition of the junior enlisted grades. As shown in Table 3.4, over four in ten E-4s, the modal lower enlisted pay grade, were married in 1983.

The changes in the marital composition of the enlisted ranks run directly counter to national trends, where the median age at first marriage has *risen* over the past decade. This anomaly suggests that the all-volunteer Army has been recruiting disportionately from a subpopulation with a propensity to marry young—a reflection, I would argue, of marginality in terms of class and culture in American society.

Personnel Turnover

One of the major consequences of the shift to an all-volunteer format was an increase in the average length of enlistment terms. As given in Table 3.5, we see that 58% of entrants in 1964 signed on for two years (mainly as draftees, but some as enlistees), with most of the remainder joining for three years. During the height of the Vietnam War in 1968, as the number of draftees increased, about two-thirds of Army entrants had two-year terms. During the AVF period, a quite different pattern has emerged: few Army entrants are two-year volunteers, the largest number are three-year volunteers, and a growing number are four-year enlistments. Put in another way, the average length

Table 3.4.   Marital Status of Army Enlisted Males by Pay Grade, 1983

Grade	Single	Married Civilian Spouse	Married Military Spouse	Divorced/ Separated*	Total (N)**	
E-9	1.0	93.7	1.2	4.1	100.0	(4,009)
E-8	1.9	91.1	1.3	5.7	100.0	(14,907)
E-7	2.7	88.7	2.3	6.3	100.0	(47,920)
E-6	7.0	83.9	3.6	5.5	100.0	(77,721)
E-5	25.0	66.6	3.7	4.7	100.0	(106,045)
E-4	54.2	40.6	3.0	2.2	100.0	(153,631)
E-3	74.3	23.2	1.0	1.5	100.0	(98,447)
E-2	81.4	17.4	.8	.4	100.0	(45,763)
E-1	83.2	15.4	1.2	.2	100.0	(44,205)
Total	44.6	49.8	2.5	3.1	100.0	(591,648)

*includes annulled and widowed
**excludes 2,989 unreported

Table 3.5. Army Enlistment (Induction) Terms of NPS Accessions

Term of Enlistment (years)	1964	1968	1978	1980	1982
2	58%	67%	—	1%	5%
3	40	31	70%	69	57
4	2	2	30	30	38
5	—	—	—	—	—
6	—	—	—	—	—
Total	100%	100%	100%	100%	100%
(N in thousands)	(264)	(529)	(409)	(158)	(120)
Average length of enlistment (months)	29	28	40	41	40

of initial enlistment from the time of the draft to the volunteer era has increased from twenty-nine months to forty months.

With the increasing length of enlistments, the expectation was that personnel turnover rates would be reduced. Types of enlisted separation and turnover rates are given in Table 3.6. Except for the most recent years (reflecting the higher completion rates of enlistments accompanying the increasing proportion of high school graduate entrants), turnover rates in the all-volunteer period have been about the same as those during the peacetime draft period. In point of fact, turnover rates are certainly *higher* in the AVF period if a "total force" perspective (i.e., inclusion of reserve as well as active force components) is taken. Whereas virtually all two-year draftees upon their expiration of term of service (ETS) were obligated for two years of additional service in reserve units, the best estimates for the all-volunteer Army are that only about one-third of ETS separations enter reserve units.

What has changed significantly, however, is the *kind* of turnover. During the peacetime draft era (1960–64), almost all separations were due to ETS. During the Vietnam War (1965–1973) attrition and desertion rates increased, but ETS still characterized the large majority of separations. Under the AVF, Army personnel losses due to attrition and desertion matched or even exceeded ETS separations.

ENLISTED LIFE

Basic Training

A soldier begins his Army life with basic training. All basic training (excepting Fort Dix, New Jersey) is conducted on posts located in southern or border states: Fort Benning, Georgia; Fort Bliss, Texas; Fort Jackson, South Caro-

Table 3.6.   Army Personnel Losses as Percentage of Total Enlisted Strength: 1960-1983*

Year	Desertion	Attrition	Retirement	Death	ETS**	Total	Enlisted Strength
1960	1.1	4.6	.4	.1	23.4	29.6	770,000
1961	1.2	4.9	.8	.2	25.6	32.7	757,000
1962	1.3	6.2	.8	.2	20.8	29.3	949,000
1963	1.6	5.2	1.5	.2	20.4	28.9	866,000
1964	1.5	6.5	1.6	.2	32.1	41.9	860,000
1965	1.6	5.3	1.4	.2	23.9	32.3	855,000
1966	1.4	4.9	1.2	.2	22.6	30.3	1,080,000
1967	2.1	5.4	1.0	.4	16.7	25.6	1,297,000
1968	2.3	5.4	.8	.6	26.7	35.8	1,402,000
1969	3.7	8.0	1.1	.7	30.5	44.0	1,337,000
1970	5.3	13.8	1.0	.6	37.0	57.7	1,153,000
1971	8.0	18.0	1.3	.5	34.5	62.3	972,000
1972	7.0	25.5	1.8	.2	45.3	79.8	687,000
1973	5.2	25.7	1.9	.2	45.6	78.6	682,000
1974	3.9	16.0	1.2	.2	16.9	38.2	674,000
1975	2.5	14.8	1.5	.2	15.4	34.4	678,000
1976	1.9	16.3	1.6	.2	13.7	33.7	680,000
1977	1.9	14.9	1.0	.1	12.7	30.6	680,000
1978	1.7	10.3	1.1	.1	11.7	24.9	669,000
1979	2.0	10.0	1.3	.1	13.6	27.0	657,000
1980	2.1	12.0	1.2	.1	12.5	27.9	673,000
1981	1.7	11.1	1.1	.1	9.4	23.4	675,000
1982	1.2	12.0	1.1	.1	8.3	22.7	673,000
1983	1.3	9.7	1.1	.1	10.9	23.1	674,000

*Table prepared by Charles Moskos
**Expiration of Term of Service

lina; Fort Knox, Kentucky; Fort McClellan, Alabama; Fort Sill, Oklahoma; and Fort Leonard Wood, Missouri. Even after basic training, there is a strong probability that a soldier will be assigned to one of the large Southern posts: Fort Bliss, Texas; Fort Bragg, North Carolina; Fort Campbell, Kentucky; Fort Gordon, Georgia; Fort Hood, Texas; Fort Lee, Virginia; Fort Polk, Louisiana; or Fort Stewart, Georgia.[8] Thus, to a degree perhaps not appreciated by the uninitiated, Army life in the United States has a distinctively southern cast.

Since the mid-1950s, basic training has been eight weeks long, give or take a few days. Following the basic course, essentially infantry training, the recruit is sent to advanced individual training (AIT) where he receives training in a particular military occupational specialty (MOS). In recent years, an increasing number of recruits are given one-station unit training which combines basic training and AIT into a single continuous course. AIT courses vary from several weeks for so-called "soft skills" (e.g., drivers, clerks, food service), to several months (e.g., most combat MOSs, military police), to a year (e.g., electronics, cryptography, foreign language training). Aptitude scores and recruit preferences combined with Army needs usually determine the soldier's AIT, which in turn largely decides the soldier's eventual MOS and assignment.

Upon completion of AIT, the enlisted man is sent to a permanent duty station where, in most cases, he can expect to complete his initial enlistment. Though some MOS skills can be acquired through on-the-job training (OJT), it is relatively difficult to change one's primary MOS without initiating steps to go to a specialized Army school. Most MOS changes (usually to move from a combat MOS to a support MOS) come at the time of first reenlistment.

During the first enlistment, the soldier can routinely expect to achieve the rank of Specialist Four or Corporal (E-4) within three years, or, in some cases, Sergeant (E-5) within four years. Advancement to senior NCO grades are much more selective. From Staff Sergeant (E-6) upwards, promotions become increasingly difficult and are based not only on available openings but also on a complex formula bringing together test scores, evaluations by superiors, service record, formal education, and interviews with a promotion board. Within twenty years of service, a soldier will almost surely attain the rank of Staff Sergeant, will most likely make Sergeant First Class (E-7), and has an outside chance to reach Master Sergeant (E-8). The Army's most senior enlisted rank, Sergeant Major (E-9), is attained only by exceptional individuals, almost all of whom are making the Army a thirty-year career.

As a rule of the thumb in peacetime, about one-third of all Army entrants leave the service before their ETS, about another third leave the Army at the time of their ETS, and the remaining third reenlist. Among those who reenlist the first time, about half will do so for a second reenlistment. Once into the third enlistment, usually ten to twelve years after service entry, "career" reenlistment rates average over 80% until twenty years is reached—the point at which the soldier becomes eligible for retirement benefits equaling half of his base pay (three-fourths at thirty years).

Overseas

About one in three first-term Army EM will be stationed overseas. A career serviceman can expect to expect to spend about one-third of his Army life in a foreign country before retirement. Thus, foreign duty is a primary feature of Army life. In the 1980s the largest numbers of Army personnel were stationed in West Germany (210,000) and in South Korea (28,000).

For close to four decades, the American GI has been a prominent part of the southern German scene. There are now American soldiers in Germany whose grandfathers entered the country as members of a conquering Army in

World War II. During the 1940s and 1950s assignment to Germany was considered an exceptionally good tour. Since the *Wirtschaftswunder* or German "economic miracle" of the 1950s, however, the buying power of American troops has steadily lost ground on the local economy (with a slight reversal in the 1980s). This has been accompanied by an increasing isolation of the GI from German society—and German women. At one time the American enlisted man was relatively prosperous in Germany, much more so than if he were stationed at home. Today, that same GI is much more likely to be regarded by the middle-class German as someone of lower social status. It is my observation that American GIs' command of the German language (never very impressive) has declined noticeably since the 1960s and that volunteer soldiers are more prone to homesickness than their drafted counterparts of an earlier era.[9]

In South Korea, even taking into account that country's economic development since the 1970s, the GI tends to operate in a social situation long considered typical of overseas American servicemen—relatively affluent GIs located in a country with a material standard of living markedly below that of the United States. This was the situation not only in postwar Germany and Japan, but in Southeast Asia during the Vietnam War. (Apropos reactions to American troops overseas, there was the aphorism in wartime England: "Overfed, oversexed, and over here.") Korea is still a place where the dollar goes a long way. The "ville" outside every post's main gate has a kind of garish charm and offers the soldier inexpensive Korean-made products and the indulgence of tailor-made clothes. Needless to add, "business women" in the bars of the ville fawn over GI customers.

From the viewpoint of the overseas soldier, it frequently seems that much of the local population is directly involved with American military personnel. Yet virtually all GI interaction with the local population occurs within a "boom-town" community catering to GI hedonism. Thus a buffer community exists between United States military personnel and the bulk of the population of the host country. This is not to say that agitation against American servicemen is absent. But such agitation is much more likely to be caused by opposition to American strategic policies than by the occasionally unruly behavior of overseas GIs.

Race Relations

Following President Truman's 1948 order to desegregate the military, there was great resistance to racial integration within the armed services. Nevertheless, starting with the Korean War in 1950, integration proceeded rapidly: first in training bases in the United States, then in combat units in Korea, and finally in garrison units worldwide. In a relatively short period of time, the

Army—in one of the most impressive accomplishments in directed social change—was quickly transformed from a racially segregated institution into the nation's most racially integrated organization.[10] Relatively harmonious racial relations characterized the period between the wars in Korea and Vietnam. But as the years of the Vietnam War rolled on, the military establishment was plagued by the new challenges of black consciousness as well as the persistence of white racism. There was no denying that by the end of the war in Vietnam, the Army was undergoing a racial crisis of major proportions.

The crisis subsided, partly due to the military's establishment of a wide-ranging program of race relations instruction and close monitoring of racial discrimination, probably more due to the calming of racial tensions in civilian life. The all-volunteer Army has experienced a noticeable reduction—though by no means absence—of interracial tension among the troops. One good unobtrusive measure of the relaxation in race relations is the much greater frequency of mixed groups eating together in dining facilities (as the old "mess hall" has been renamed). Informal groupings by race, however, are still the rule off duty, though they are not nearly so rigid as a decade ago. Musical preference continues to be the great symbolic divider of the races in off-duty settings. Conversations with black soldiers will reveal that many still perceive certain "racist" features in military life. Many white soldiers, for their part, perceive "reverse prejudice" in the military. Among some whites there has been the emergence of a "cowboy culture" in opposition to black groups. Occupying somewhat of a midposition are Hispanic soldiers, who often see themselves as the most dutiful and the least complaining.

Three general observations can be made on the interracial climate in the armed forces. One is that the more military the setting, the more favorable are race relations. Racial harmony is more evident in the field than in garrison, on duty than off duty, and on-post than off-post. The second is that the irrelevance of race is most pronounced at the small unit level but gives way to more interracial distance in larger and less intimate groupings. Both black and white soldiers contrast the relaxed and cross-racial camaraderie typical of the squad and platoon with the racial separatism that occurs when the same men move into different settings. Finally, the truly important point is that the degree of racial integration in the Army stands in sharp and favorable contrast to what one will find anywhere else in American society.

Attitudes Toward Women Soldiers

The proportion of female soldiers has increased from slightly over 1% in the 1960s to about 10% in the mid-1980s. As race relations became a less contentious issue over the past decade, it seemed that the utilization of female soldiers moved to center stage among Army personnel issues. The attitudes of

Army men toward female soldiers are in a state of flux, but the following generalizations seem warranted.

Among all ranks, but among certain NCOs especially, there are those who simply believe (and will cite numerous examples as proof) that women cannot do the required work and are a disturbing influence to boot. There are also those noncoms who display a kind of courtly sexism, who make special accommodations to ease the work requirements of women. And there are, of course, those who view women mainly as objects of sexual exploitation. But the largest number of men at all ranks seems to be those who adopt a "show-me" attitude. For this group, a woman will be accorded acceptance, but only after she proves her ability to carry her share of the workload. No amassing of statistics on comparable female/male lost time will convince male soldiers that pregnant women do not "get over" (i.e., avoid work) in traditionally male jobs. Unlike newly arrived male soldiers in heavy labor assignments, women soldiers are not given the initial benefit of the doubt by the men of the unit. In administrative, medical, and technical positions, on the other hand, acceptance of women is generally high; indeed, women soldiers in such capacities are often seen as better performers than men.

Relations Between the Ranks

Enlisted/sergeant/officer relations have undergone important shifts in modern Army history. During World War II, the overriding organizational cleavage was between enlisted men (including sergeants) and officers. This was attested to by sources as varied as James Jones's classic novel *From Here to Eternity*, the war cartoons of Bill Mauldin, the monumental surveys reported in the volumes of *The American Soldier*, and the personal experiences of countless soldiers as well.

During the peacetime years between the wars in Korea and Vietnam, another cleavage appeared, one *within* the lower enlisted ranks. The "US" versus "RA" distinction arose; US was the prefix of the service number of the drafted soldier while RA signified a regular Army volunteer. The US versus RA distinction frequently overlaid differences between more highly educated draftees and volunteers with less education. Thus class variables overlapped degrees of military commitment. The term RA was used by draftees as a negative adjective to describe eager compliance with Army rituals or to denigrate men viewed as unable to hold a decent job in civilian life.

During the Vietnam War, the sergeant became the prime object of enlisted animus. In the Vietnam era, moreover, EM/sergeant strain could typically override that between enlisted men and officers. Whereas the pejorative in World War II was "the brass," connoting an officer, the equivalent expression in the Vietnam period was "lifer," almost always a senior sergeant. Another difference between World War II and the war in Vietnam was that in the earlier conflict men served for the duration regardless of how they entered the service, so that sergeants had often been draftees themselves. In the Vietnam War, on the other hand, virtually all sergeants were regulars.

In the first phase of the all-volunteer Army (1974–1979), yet another pattern emerged. The prevailing antagonism of lower ranking soldiers toward NCOs was reduced. At the same time, EM/officer friction became more pronounced, with more than occasional insolence on the part of soldiers toward company grade officers. During this period the educational gap between officers (virtually all of whom were college graduates) and enlisted men (many of whom were high school dropouts) was at its widest in modern times.

In the second phase of the all-volunteer Army (1980–1985), the relations between the ranks began to resemble, somewhat, those of the peacetime draft period. The strain between NCOs and junior-ranking EMs again seemed to be the main source of friction in the ranks. Indeed, in the middle 1980s the high reenlistment rate of many NCOs who had scored low in entry aptitude tests became a personnel issue within the Army hierarchy.

Broadly speaking, sergeants have the following complaints in the all-volunteer Army: a sense that rank no longer has its privileges, a view that the greater privacy accorded junior enlisted men undermines social control, a belief that there was too much diversion from military training toward civilian education and personnel problems, a feeling that there was too much direction by officers in the work setting and not enough in the barracks, and a widespread belief that the military justice system worked to the disadvantage of the enforcer of discipline rather than that of the offender. Most important, there was an endemic concern with perceived erosion of benefits throughout the career force.

There was a widespread feeling among NCOs in the first phase of the AVF—and only some of it could be put down to normal grousing—that too much time was spent handling recalcitrant enlisted men. The days when many enlisted men might be better educated than their sergeants and smarter than their officers were seemingly gone until the turnaround in recruiting in the 1980s. One is struck by the fond reminiscences which older sergeants have of the college-educated draftees who worked under them and formed a virtual "shadow staff"—as communication operators and clerks in administration, supply, and operations—and made things run smoothly at company and battalion levels.

Another major outcome of the all-volunteer force has been a dramatic compression of pay scales within the enlisted force. The "front-loading" of compensation to attract more recruits after the end of the draft, along with changes to make junior enlisted life more attractive (notably, fewer details and social controls, such as the "permanent pass" policy in stateside units, the abolition of reveille, and the end of kitchen police in garrison), have contributed to a perceptible disenchantment within the NCO corps. Once upon a time sergeants measured their incomes and perquisites against those of the soldiers they led, and felt rewarded; now they see a relative decline of status within the service and compare themselves to civilians and feel deprived.

ENLISTED CULTURE

What follows is an appraisal of enlisted attitudes and culture based on my stays in military units around the world and on in-depth interviews with numerous soldiers over the course of the all-volunteer Army era. Individually, one will always meet soldiers who are motivated, appealing, and intelligent. Until the improved recruitment picture of the early 1980s, however, enlisted men as a group were coming from outside the mainstream of American life. I was most struck by what I did not often find in line units: urban and suburban soldiers of middle-class background.

In the barracks, the edge of violence which characterized many line units in the 1970s had largely receded by the 1980s. Barracks crime continued to be a problem, however, and it exceeded the level of the draft era, though some of this was because there was more to steal from today's better-paid soldier. A level of raucousness, if not rowdiness, existed which exceeded the decibel count and temper of the pre-Vietnam Army. Not that the conscripted peace-time Army was a sanctuary of decorum, but the tone of barracks life was no longer modulated by conventional middle-class standards as it was during the draft. Unit cohesion had been undermined by consolidated dining facilities, centralized personnel systems, and higher personnel turnover (probably averaging over 5% a *month* in most units). Rooms in the new barracks (or partitioned quarters in the older buildings) encouraged a sense of personal space which fostered attitudes and behavior of individual or subgroup privacy contrary to traditional military norms.

Along with the growing number of enlisted marrieds, an increasing number of single enlisted members stationed in the United States were living off post. This was made possible by the fact that the real disposable income of junior enlisted members in the AVF was three times what it had been during the peacetime draft. (By 1985, a private first class made the equivalent of over $15,000 a year.) A visitor to a military base in the 1980s could see clear signs of the young single GI's buying power by observing the automobiles in the parking lots. Overseas, the typical young soldier would purchase an expensive stereo system and save up to fly commercially to the United States to take his 30-day leave back home. It is hard to avoid the judgment that the soldier's new discretionary income in the AVF has undermined the quality of barracks life and unit cohesion.

There can be no serious dispute that improved unit cohesiveness and a stronger attachment to the importance of the military mission aids military effectiveness.[11] The most salient factor in low cohesion is the personnel turbulence caused by the high rates of attrition. Less obvious, but perhaps as important, are contextual factors; that is, one of the important though un-quantifiable contributions of better-educated, more mature junior enlisted personnel is to facilitate the formation of effective peer networks which provide the cohesiveness of military units. The barracks world described by observers of the all-volunteer Army of the late 1970s—of fragmented, competitive, and frequently hostile interpersonal relations—reflects the relative scarcity of such persons.[12] The improved enlistment picture of the early 1980s brought positive change at the unit level by bringing into the Army a recruit with many of the social background attributes and enlisted behaviors associated with the draft era.

There is a source of enlisted discontent in the AVF, however, that has no real counterpart in the peacetime draft era. This is post-entry disillusionment resulting from unrealistic expectations as to what the military would offer. The peacetime draftee never held high expectations of what he would encounter and, therefore, was not unpleasantly surprised; indeed he would often, at least in retrospect, find the Army favorable on its own terms. In all-volunteer recruitment, however, a consistent theme has been the self-serving aspects of military life—that is, pay and what the service can do for the recruit in the way of training in skills transferable to civilian jobs. One unintended result of AVF recruitment is to minimize the distinctions between military life and civilian occupations.[13] Post-entry disillusionment speaks directly to the excessive attrition and desertion rates under the AVF. The irreconcilable dilemma is that many military assignments, by no means exclusively in the combat arms, do not have transferability to civilian jobs.

Among all-volunteer recruits in the 1980s, there were two basic types.[14] By far the larger number were soldiers who joined the Army for job security or the chance to learn a marketable skill, many of whom were ready to give serious consideration to making the Army a career. A smaller but still significant number joined the Army as a hiatus between school and work or school and college; many of these were attracted by a generous post-service educational and short-enlistment package which the Army was able to offer in the 1980s. Neither one of these groups should be considered more or less patriotic than the other.[15]

Throughout the lower enlisted ranks, a kind of diffuse patriotism existed among a large majority of the soldiers, along with an inclination to evaluate the American way of life mainly in materialistic terms. Small numbers of vocal patriots in the lower ranks could be found, but they tended to be defined as marginal to the prevailing enlisted ethos. In the 1970s there had been a pronounced tendency for enlisted men to regard themselves and their comrades as removed from the mainstream of American youth. This negative self-characterization on the part of Army enlisted men was somewhat alleviated by the more representative force recruited during the 1980s. Still, the fact remains that under the AVF concept there is little of a publicly convenient rationale for entering the Army as was available during the draft. It is important to note, however, that although there has always been a strong norm to "bad-mouth" the Army when soldiers are in groups, somewhat more favorable attitudes are likely to be expressed by individuals in private.

The political culture of the enlisted man is fairly meager. As would be expected, factual knowledge of the American governmental system, history, and foreign policy is extremely low. Left to themselves, soldiers will rarely discuss any strategic issues, much less political concerns. What little political awareness exists seems to focus on the office and person of the president. There is receptivity, however, to learning about the role of the military as an instrument of America's foreign policy, especially if the soldier's unit can be related to the broader picture. Although such discussion must rely as much as possible on plain language, soldiers will not necessarily be put off by a modicum of abstract talk. Most importantly, any focusing on the commonality of the military experience cuts across and helps override clique differences emanating from racial lines or divergent lifestyles. In a manner of speaking, the only shared experience for most soldiers as part of any larger enterprise is their present Army service. This may explain the truism that unit morale is highest during basic training and extended maneuvers, times when pre-military social differences among soldiers are minimized.

Although soldiers' behavior in combat is beyond the scope of this essay, a crucial question concerns how Army enlisted men feel about being committed to combat.[16] Over the course of the AVF and before, I have raised this issue in numerous conversations and more systematic interviews with soldiers in the combat arms.[17] Although attitudinal responses in a peacetime situation cannot be construed as predictors of the behavior of soldiers in actual combat, such responses are, nevertheless, indicative of some of the salient factors in the belief systems of soldiers.

When posed with hypothetical combat situations, soldiers' initial reactions are with the operability of equipment and the level of training of their unit; in many cases, the responses are negative. With probing for more normative variables, three general findings consistently appear. First, defense of the American homeland (or rescue of endangered American civilians) is nearly universally supported. Second, all plausible scenarios of an overseas war— defense of Germany or Korea, intervention in the Middle East—are grouped in the same category of much lower commitment. Third, soldiers are much more likely to indicate a willingness to volunteer for an overseas war if that war is seen as widely supported at home than if it were a war to which there was domestic opposition. Soldiers' understanding of the utility of force is firmly anchored in the viewpoint that military commitment should be clearly related to America's defense and requires the support of the citizenry at large. In his own artless manner, the GI may be showing more sophistication about the use of force than some of the nation's political leaders.

ORGANIZATIONAL TRENDS

The Army can be understood as an organization which maintains levels of autonomy while refracting broader societal trends. Indeed, it is the interaction between internal and external variables that characterizes military organization. It is from this standpoint that two models—institution and occupation—are presented to describe alternate conceptions of the military.[18] The contrast between institution and occupation can, of course, be overdrawn. Both elements have been and always will be present in the military system. Our concern here, however, is to describe significant trends within the military and society which bear upon central issues of military manpower, in particular the Army enlisted ranks.

An *institution* is legitimated in terms of values and norms, i.e., as having a purpose transcending individual self-interest in favor of a presumed higher good. Members of an institution are often seen as following a calling. To the degree that one's institutional membership is congruent with notions of self-sacrifice and primary identification with one's institutional role, one usually enjoys esteem from the larger society.

Military service has traditionally had many institutional features. Values are captured in words such as "duty," "honor," and "country." There are the extended tours abroad, the fixed term of enlistment, liability for twenty-four hour service, subjection to military discipline and law, and the inability to resign, strike, or negotiate working conditions. All this is above and beyond the dangers inherent in military maneuvers and actual combat operations. It is also significant that a paternalistic remuneration system evolved in the military corresponding to the institutional model: much of compensation received in non-cash form (e.g., food, housing, uniforms, medical care), subsidized consumer facilities on the base, and a large portion of compensation received as deferred pay in the form of early retirement benefits. Moreover, unlike most civilians—for whom compensation is heavily determined by individual expertise—military members are compensated essentially according to rank, seniority, and need.

An *occupation* is legitimated in terms of the marketplace, i.e., by prevailing monetary rewards for equivalent competencies. Supply and demand rather than normative considerations are paramount. In a modern industrial society, employees usually enjoy some voice in the determination of appropriate salary and work conditions. Such rights are counterbalanced by responsibilities to meet contractual obligations. The cash/work nexus emphasizes a negotiation between individual and organizational needs. The occupational model frequently implies priority of self-interest rather than that of the employing organization.

The occupational philosophy clearly underpinned the rationale of the 1970 *Report of the President's Commission on an All-Volunteer Force*, better known as the "Gates Commission Report."[19] The Gates Commission was strongly influenced by laissez-faire economic thought and argued that primary reliance in recruiting an armed force should be on monetary inducements guided by marketplace standards. This dovetailed with the thought of the systems analysts who had become ascendant in the Department of Defense under both Democratic and Republican administrations. Whether under the rubric of econometrics or of systems analysis, such a redefinition of military service is based on a set of core assumptions. First, there is no analytical distinction between military systems and other systems, especially no difference between cost-effectiveness analysis of civilian enterprises and military services. Second, military compensation should as much as possible be linked to skill differences of individual service members, thereby allowing for a more efficient operation of the marketplace. Finally, social cohesion and goal commitment are essentially unmeasurable and are thereby inappropriate objects of analysis. Such a mindset has contributed to moving the American military toward an occupational format.

The policy corollaries for military manpower of the above assumptions are as follows: (1) recruit pay must be substantially higher than during the draft (in practice, this means compression of enlisted salaries across ranks); (2) more of compensation should be up front and in salary—i.e., "visible"— rather than in kind or deferred; (3) the career force (i.e., second termers and beyond) should become a larger proportion of the enlisted force (on the presumption this will reduce turnover); and (4) the active force becomes a larger fraction of the total force. The outcome of these trends is to replace the concept of the citizen soldier with that of economic man.

Other indicators of the trend toward the occupational format include: (1) the rise in attrition, a movement in all but name toward a system of indeterminate enlistments; (2) the increasing proportion of military members living off post, a separation of work and residence locales; (3) the growing number of enlisted men holding second jobs outside the military, an undermining of the soldier's total role commitment to the Army; and (4) an increasing reliance on contract labor to perform tasks previously carried out by soldiers.

Although antecedents predate the appearance of the AVF, the end of the draft might be seen as a major thrust to move the military toward the occupational model. The selective service system was premised on the notion of citizen obligation—a "calling" in the almost literal sense of being summoned by a local draft board—with concommitment low salaries for junior enlisted personnel. Furthermore, it is estimated that about half of the "volunteers" in the peacetime pre-Vietnam Army were draft motivated. Even though the termination of the draft in 1973 has been the most visible change in the contemporary Army, it must be stressed that an all-volunteer Army in and of itself need not be correlated with an occupational model. It is only that the architects of the present AVF have chosen the occupational model as their paradigm.

Traditionally, the military has sought to avoid the organizational outcome of the occupational model—this in the face of repeated governmental commissions and studies advocating that the armed services adopt a salary system which would incorporate all basic pay, allowances, and tax benefits into one cash payment, and that they replace the "pay by rank" system with one based on "pay by skill" (which is a euphemism for pay by shortage). Despite certain exceptions, the traditional system of military compensation reflected not only the so-called "X-factor"—the unusual demands of service life—but the corporate whole of military life.

The military institution is organized "vertically," whereas an occupation is organized "horizontally." People in an occupation tend to feel a sense of identity with others who do the same sort of work and who receive about the same pay. In an institution, on the other hand, it is the organization in which people live and work which creates the sense of identity that binds them together. Vertical identification means that one acquires an understanding and sense of responsibility for the performance of the whole and, ideally, a respect for those above and below in the hierarchy. In the armed forces the very fact of being part of the service has traditionally been more important than the fact that military members do different jobs. The organization one belongs to creates the feeling of shared interest, not the other way around.

The argument about the proper relationship between the soldier's vertical ties with the Army and his horizontal ties to those outside the Army—between institutional and occupational ties—will never reach a clear-cut choice. Most soldiers' preference, most of the time, will be for a diagonal. But influential members of Congress and certain independent commentators have been trying to get across to the manpower analysts in the Office of the Secretary of Defense that the tilt to the horizontal has gone too far, even as the Labor Department in 1983, for the first time, counted military personnel as part of the nation's "labor force."

Worried commanders have also been alert to the Pentagon's post-Vietnam shift to a more occupational mentality. In the 1980s, the Army, along with the other services, was renewing its emphasis on the distinctive "professional" and "institutional" features of life in uniform. In order to enhance unit cohesion, the Army took steps to move toward a "regimental system," with unit rotation replacing individual replacements along with a permanent home base for each regiment to which its component units will return after a tour in South Korea or Germany.[20] The Army was also trying to reduce personnel turnover in units, notably among officers commanding companies and battalions. The Army wanted more housing, more service-in-kind, not just more pay, to bind its soldiers closer together.

The future of the Army enlisted man will continue to reflect the tensions between institutional versus occupational tendencies in the Army, tendencies which in the American context overlap with distinctions between citizen-soldier and economic-man views of military manpower. The key variables to watch can be dichotimized as supporting citizen-soldier versus marketplace principles: (1) low versus high recruit pay, (2) salary linked to rank rather than to skill, (3) more of compensation in kind and deferred versus in salary and up-front, (4) more active duty military members in first term than in the career force, and (5) more of the total force in reserves than on active duty.

Two truths emerge from this overview of the Army enlisted life. One is that the enlisted experience has moved much more toward the occupational direction than most people are aware. The other is that institutional traits persist, or are reconstituted, to a much greater extent than econometric approaches can explain. Both truths operate in such a way that the future of the Army enlisted man is best understood as the interplay between citizen-soldier and marketplace trends.

NOTES

1. Of the approximately thirty million living veterans in 1985, about twenty million served as Army enlisted men, the large majority as draftees.
2. The classic World War II study on Army enlisted men is Samuel A. Stouffer, et al., *The American Soldier: Adjustment During Army Life*, Vol. 1; *The American Soldier: Combat and Its Aftermath*, Vol. 2 (Princeton, NJ: Princeton Univ. Press, 1949). For the Vietnam and all-volunteer Army eras, see Charles C. Moskos, *The American Enlisted Man* (New York: Russell Sage, 1970), and Moskos, "The Enlisted Ranks in the All-Volunteer Army," in *The All-Volunteer Force and American Society*, John B. Keeley, ed. (Charlottesville, VA: Univ. of Virginia Press, 1978), pp. 39–80. A historical overview of enlisted men is Richard N. Kohn, "The Social History of the American Soldier," *American Historical Review*, 86 (June 1981):553–567.
3. See, for example, Morris Janowitz and Charles C. Moskos, "Racial Composition in the All-Volunteer Force," *Armed Forces and Society, 1* (Fall 1974):109–123; Alvin J. Schexnider and John S. Butler, "Race and the All-Volunteer System," *Armed Forces and Society, 2* (December 1974):421–432. A particularly comprehensive and balanced account is Martin Binkin and Mark J. Eitelberg, *Blacks and the Military* (Washington, DC: Brookings Institution, 1982).
4. For example, about 35% of white military entrants fall into Categories I and II compared with about 10% of blacks.
5. H. Wallace Sinaiko, ed., *First-Term Enlisted Attrition* (Washington, DC: Smithsonian Institution, 1977); H. Wallace Sinaiko et al., eds., *Military Personnel Attrition and Retention Research in Progress* (Washington, DC: Smithsonian Institution, 1982).
6. Inasmuch as ability differences are partly individual and partly due to contextual factors, it is the interaction between individual potential and group processes which account for soldierly performance. Yet nearly all studies on soldierly performance seek to correlate individual aptitudes with that same individual's performance, thereby neglecting social psychological or group variables. Among the most detailed and notable treatments of the subject are Juri Toomepuu, *Soldier Capability-Army Combat Effectiveness—SCACE* (Ft. Benjamin Harrison, IN: Soldier Support Center, 1981); David J. Armor et al., *Recruit Aptitudes and Army*

Job Performance (Santa Monica, CA: Rand, 1982); J. Richard Wallace, "The Gideon Criterion: The Effects of Selection Criteria on Soldier's Capabilities and Battle Results," USAREC Research Memorandum 82-1 (Fort Sheridan, IL: U.S. Army Recruiting Command, Jan., 1982).

7. John S. Butler, "Inequality in the Military," *American Sociological Review 41* (October 1976):807–818.
8. Other major Army posts in the continental United States are Fort Carson, CO; Fort Lewis, Washington, Fort Ord, CA; and Fort Riley, KN.
9. The effects of the "peace movement" in Western Europe, as well as the terrorist actions directed against military installations and high-level military officers, on attitudes of American soldiers stationed in Europe deserve examination. I predict the short-term results will be an increase in unit solidarity; in the long run, however, the consequences will more likely be deleterious to morale.
10. For relevant studies on race relations, see Charles C. Moskos, "Minority Groups in Military Organization," in *Handbook of Military Institutions*, ed. Roger W. Little (Beverly Hills, CA: Sage, 1971), pp. 516–535; K.L. Wilson and John S. Butler, "Race and Job Satisfaction in the Military," *Sociological Quarterly 19* (Fall 1978):626–638; Richard O. Hope, *Racial Strife in the U.S. Military* (New York:Praeger, 1979); Binkin and Eitelberg, *Blacks and the Military*; John D. Blair, Richard C. Thompson, and David R. Segal, "Race and Job Satisfaction in the U.S. Army," in *Changing U.S. Military Manpower Realities*, ed. Franklin D. Margiotta, James Brown, and Michael J. Collins (Boulder, CO: Westview, 1983), pp. 129–154.
11. For a conceptual as well as programmatic treatment of cohesion and the military organization, see John H. Johns, *Cohesion in the U.S. Military* (Washington, DC: National Defense Univ. Press, 1984).
12. For accounts of enlisted life in the all-volunteer Army given by field researchers, see David Gottlieb, *Babes in Arms* (Beverly Hills, CA: Sage, 1980); James H. Powers, *The Volunteer Soldier—A Self Portrait* (Carlisle Barracks, PA: Army War College, 1980); David L. Cole, *The Mid-Term Soldier—A Self-Portrait* (Carlisle Barracks, PA: Army War College, 1982); and Larry H. Ingraham, *The Boys in the Barracks* (Philadelphia, PA: ISHI, 1984). For research based on survey data, see Jerald G. Bachman, John D. Blair, and David R. Segal, *The All-Volunteer Force* (Ann Arbor, MI: The University of Michigan, 1977); David R. Segal, Barbara A. Lynch, and John D. Blair, "The Changing American Soldier," *American Journal of Sociology 85* (July 1979):95–108; Stephen R. Wesbrook, "Sociopolitical Alienation and Military Efficiency," *Armed Forces and Society 6* (Winter 1980):170–189; David R. Segal, "Military Service in the 1970s," in *Manning the American Armed Forces* eds. A.R. Millett and A.F. Trupp (Columbus: Mershon Center of Ohio State University, 1981), pp. 43–63; and David R. Segal et al., "Institutional and Occupational Values in the U.S. Military," in Margiotta et al, *Military and Manpower Realities* (note 10) pp. 107–127.
13. John H. Faris, "The Military Occupational Environment and the All-Volunteer Force," in Millett and Trupp, *Values in the U.S. Military*, pp. 31–42; John D. Blair and Robert L. Phillips, "Job Satisfaction among Youth in Military and Civilian Work Settings," *Armed Forces and Society 9* (Summer 1983):555–568; Charles Dale and Curtis Gilroy, "Determinants of Enlistments," *Armed Forces and Society 10* (Winter 1984):192–210.
14. The "dual market" concept of Army recruitment is outlined in Maxwell R. Thurman, "Sustaining the All-Volunteer Force 1983-1993." Paper presented at the conference on the All-Volunteer Force, Annapolis, MD, October, 1983. See also Timothy W. Elig et al., "The 1982 DA Survey of Personnel Entering the Army."

Personnel Utilization Technical Area Working Paper 83-24 (Alexandria, VA: Army Research Institute, 1983); Denis L. Benchoff, "Analysis of Recruitment Incentives Survey." Unpublished paper. U.S. Army War College, 1983. Also relevant are proposals for a dual track enlisted personnel system distinguishing between a "citizen soldier" and a "career soldier": Charles C. Moskos, "Making the All-Volunteer Force Work," *Foreign Affairs 60* (Fall 1981):17–34; and Moskos and John H. Faris, "Beyond the Marketplace" in *Toward a Consensus on Military Service*, eds. A.J. Goodpaster, et al., (New York: Pergamon, 1981), pp. 131–151.

15. For the manner in which patriotic sentiments impinge on military service see James S. Burk with John H. Faris, "The Persistence and Importance of Patriotism in the All-Volunteer Force," USAREC Special Report 82-6, U.S. Army Recruiting Command, Dec., 1982. See also John H. Faris, "Economic and Noneconomic Factors of Personnel Recruitment and Retention in the AVF," *Armed Forces and Society, 10* (Winter 1984): 251–275. A major theoretical statement is Morris Janowitz, *The Reconstruction of Patriotism* (Chicago: Univ. of Chicago, 1983). Also relevant is Morris Janowitz and Stephen D. Wesbrook, eds., *The Political Education of Soldiers*, (Beverly Hills, CA: Sage, 1983).

16. The relevant sociological literature on combat motivation in World War II is Stouffer, Vol. 2, *The American Soldier* (note 2); and Edward A. Shils and Morris Janowitz, "Cohesion and Disintegration in the Wehrmacht," *Public Opinion Quarterly 12* (Summer 1948):280–315. A retrospective on the Stouffer volumes from the vantage of an original collaborator is Robin B. Williams, "Field Observations and Surveys in Combat Zones." Paper presented at the annual meetings of the American Sociological Association, August, 1983, Detroit, Michigan. On the Korean War, see Roger W. Little, "Buddy Relations and Combat Performance" in *The New Military*, ed. M. Janowitz (New York: Russell Sage, 1964), pp. 195–223. On the Vietnam War, see Moskos, *American Enlisted Man*, 1970, pp. 134–156; Kurt Lang, "American Military Performance in Vietnam," *Journal of Political and Military Sociology 8* (Fall 1980): 269–286; Moskos, "Surviving the War in Vietnam," in *Strangers at Home*, eds. C.R. Figley and S. Leventman (New York: Praeger, 1980), pp. 71–85. Valuable syntheses of research on combat motivation are David H. Marlowe, "Cohesion, Anticipated Breakdown, and Endurance in Battle" unpublished paper, Walter Reed Army Institute of Research, 1979; Elliot P. Chodoff, "Ideology and Primary Groups," *Armed Forces and Society 9* (Summer 1983):569–594; W. Daryl Henderson, *The Human Element* (Washington, DC: National Defense Univ. Press, 1984); Overviews of the literature on combat motivation are found in Sam C. Sarkesian, ed. *Combat Effectiveness* (Beverly Hills, CA: Sage, 1980); and Anthony Kellett, *Combat Motivation* (Boston: Kluwer, 1982). For an insightful comparison of the combat potential of contemporary Russian and American soldiers, see Richard A. Gabriel, *The Antagonists* (Westport, CT: Greenwood, 1984).

17. Survey results of soldiers' attitudes in the all-volunteer Army toward hypothetical combat situations are Charles W. Brown and Charles C. Moskos, "The American Volunteer Soldier: Will He Fight?" *Military Review, 56* (June 1976):8–17; William C. Cockerham, "Volunteering for Foreign Combat Missions," *Pacific Sociological Review 24* (Summer 1981):329–354; and David R. Segal and Joseph J. Lengermann, "Professional and Institutional Considerations," in S.C. Sarkesian, ed. *Combat Effectiveness*, pp. 254–285.

18. Treatments of organizational trends in the AVF are found in Charles C. Moskos, "The Emergent Military," *Pacific Sociological Review 16* (April 1973):255–280; Moskos, "From Institution to Occupation," *Armed Forces and Society 4* (Fall 1977): 41–50; David R. Segal and Mady W. Segal, "Change in Military Organiza-

tion," *Annual Review of Sociology 9* (1983):151–170. Broader reformulations of the institution/occupation thesis are Frank C. Pinch, "Military Manpower and Social Change," *Armed Forces and Society 8* (Summer 1982):575–600; and Charles A. Cotton, "Institution Building in the All-Volunteer Force," *Air University Review 34* (Sept.–Oct., 1983):34–49. On the reserve components, see Robert L. Goldich, "Historical Continuity in the U.S. Military Reserve System," *Armed Forces and Society 7* (Fall 1980):88–112.

19. *Report of the President's Commission on the All-Volunteer Force* (Washington, DC: U.S. Government Printing Office, 1970).

20. The best treatment of the institutionalization of the Army's efforts to move toward a regimental system is Thomas E. Kelly, "The Army Develops a New Personnel System." Paper presented at the conference of the Inter-University Seminar on Armed Forces and Society, Oct., 1983, Chicago.

4

The Continuing Debate:
Women Soldiers in the U.S. Army*

Martha A. Marsden

HISTORICAL ROOTS

From World War I to the present, women in the U.S. Army, all volunteers for duty, have served their nation with distinction under varying conditions of war and peace. From officers to enlisted personnel, nurses to mechanics, clerk-typists to truck drivers, they have experienced the unique challenges, accomplishments, and hardships which are a part of membership in the Army. Although always officially regarded as noncombatants, women soldiers have also shared the risk, and occasionally the actual experience, of combat conditions.

[For as long as American women have participated in Army activities, whether in war or in peace, there has been debate among civilian policymakers, military leaders, and the general public concerning the proper roles for female soldiers. Over time, these debates have been kindled by numerous arguments and counter-arguments about the nature of military life, warfare, and combat; differences between the capabilities of men and women; lessons from history; and powerful societal values.

For enlisted women in the Army, a major outcome of these continuing debates has been the tendency for policymakers to see female soldiers collectively as a problem which requires a host of special policy solutions.]The thesis of this chapter is that[Army policies regarding female soldiers, often shaped by controversy, uneasy compromise, and ambiguity, affect significantly the

*Author's Note: I am grateful to Romana Danysh, Nora Scott Kinzer, Dennis M. Kowal, Mary J. Mayer, and Harry J. Thie for providing background information. The opinions expressed in this chapter are the author's and not to be construed as official or reflecting the views of the Department of the Army or the Department of Defense. Portions of the chapter are from the author's doctoral dissertation.

quality of life experienced by enlisted women and the contributions they are permitted to make to the nation's defense.]

Although the focus of this discussion is on enlisted Army women, certain material on women officers, including nurses, is also presented. Historically, U.S. experiences with military nurses both paved the way for subsequent utilization of women in other military roles and provided a long-term model for examining women's capabilities under various types of wartime conditions. Some references to female line officers are also included in relation to their positions as role models and advocates for enlisted women.

⚹ Before World War II

Although women's direct participation in activities of the Army dates at least as far back as the Revolutionary War, until World War II the nature and extent of that participation were extremely limited.

During the Revolutionary War, some number of "women of the Army" did cooking, washing, and nursing for the soldiers and sometimes followed husbands and fathers almost literally onto the battlefield.[1] A few accounts of individual women who performed soldiers' duties in wartime have also been documented.[2] Additionally, there have been several recorded cases of women who, disguised as men, served as soldiers.[3] In the Civil War and the Spanish–American War, female civilian nurses worked with diligence and skill under extremely difficult conditions.[4] In 1901, to improve coordination and control of Army nursing activities, Congress created the Army Nurse Corps as a quasi-military organization. It did not attain full Army status until 1944.[5]

During World War I, close to 10,000 Army nurses were assigned to hospital units in Europe, where at various times they were

> threatened by poison gas attacks, forced to seek shelter from shelling, consistently exposed to the same communicable diseases that afflicted the soldiers (especially influenza), subjected to squalid and verminous living conditions, and, perhaps more intensely than the combat troops, required to witness the pathetic results of the physical violence of modern warfare.[6]

As for having women serve in other kinds of Army jobs, General Pershing and his field commanders made numerous requests to the War Department for uniformed women as telephone operators, stenographers, typists, and clerks—traditionally female jobs in which women's skills far surpassed men's. Despite the Army's critical need for these skills, the successful experience of the British Women's Auxiliary Army Corps, and the U.S. Navy's action to enlist women, the War Department maintained, with regard to a proposal for a women's corps in the Army, that it was not convinced of "the desirability or feasibility of making this most radical departure in the conduct of our military affairs."[7]

With the war's end and military demobilization, the issue of women's roles in the Army, excluding nursing, slid into virtual dormancy to remain unresolved until the rumblings of the next war over twenty years later.

World War II

By 1941, as the active participation of the United States in World War II drew near, the likelihood of developing a women's corps in the Army increased, spurred on by the support of the Army Air Corps, Eleanor Roosevelt, Congresswoman Edith Rogers, and the Army Chief of Staff, General George Marshall. Having become convinced of the great need for women's skills in the Army, the general declared in late November, "I want a women's corps right away and I don't want any excuses!"[8]

Less than two weeks after the bombing of Pearl Harbor, military and congressional "plans for a women's corps moved with a speed unequaled in the past decades,"[9] but not without considerable debate, ambivalence, and eventual compromise. On the floor of the House of Representatives, for example, heated emotional arguments reflected the widespread uneasiness about the proposal:

> I think it is a reflection upon the courageous manhood of the country to pass a law inviting women to join the armed forces in order to win a battle.
> Take the women into the armed service, who then will do the cooking, the washing, the mending, the humble homey tasks to which every woman has devoted herself?
> Think of the humiliation! What has become of the manhood of America?[10]

The proposed Women's Army Auxiliary Corps (WAAC) was to be "not a part of the Army but it shall be the only women's organization authorized to serve *with* the Army, exclusive of the Army Nurse Corps."[11] This quasi-military status, which was somewhat similar to that of the Army Nurse Corps, would soon lead to major legal and administrative problems. As Congresswoman Rogers' authorizing bill moved quickly through the House and Senate, War Department planners worked with great speed to make the numerous necessary preparations for implementing the WAAC, which was to become law in May of 1942. Oveta Culp Hobby, newspaper publisher, lawyer, and civic leader, was selected as Director of the WAAC.

First-year personnel projections for the new WAAC originally called for 10,600 "auxiliaries" (so-called because they were not true enlistees *in* the Army) and 340 officers. Due to a sizable underestimate of the Army's need for WAAC skills, these figures turned out to be 600% too low.[12] This initial miscalculation proved to be a harbinger of future problems throughout the war, in which the demand for women's skills continually outstripped supply. By the end of 1943, for example, the Army estimated that over 1.3 million Waacs could be used to fill approximately two-thirds of its non-combat jobs in administration, one-eighth in motor transport, one-fifth in radio operation, and one-third in supply.[13] Such demand created impossible recruiting pressures on a voluntary corps whose wartime strength was never able to exceed 100,000 at any given time.[14] These pressures were further exacerbated by the high mental and "moral" standards which prospective Waacs (later Wacs) were consistently required to meet, except during a brief period in early 1943.[15]

Due to legal and administrative problems created by the quasi-military auxiliary status of the WAAC, Congress passed a new bill in late June of 1943 which converted the WAAC to the WAC (Women's Army Corps), whose members would serve directly *in* and not merely *with* the Army. Although this conversion did alleviate some of the problems concerning the legal status and command coordination of Army women, it neither intended nor accomplished any full integration of the small female Army into the large male Army. Administered and housed in separate WAC companies, women soldiers were to be assigned in groups of varying size, generally no fewer than fifty, to integrated non-combat Army units, both in the United States and in the overseas theaters.[16] Thus, in one sense women were a part of the real (i.e., male) Army, while in another sense they were not. The ambiguity of this situation continued to raise questions throughout the war. Should women soldiers be treated differently from male soldiers because they are women? Or should they be treated the same because they are soldiers? As subsequent history was to show, these questions would still remain partially unanswered, even after the official disestablishment of the WAC in 1978 and the full integration of women into the Army.

Regarding the Army's difficulty in meeting its continually rising wartime quotas for the new women's corps, the conventional wisdom of the time was that "if the women of the nation knew the Army's need for their services they would respond at once."[17] According to a mid-1943 nationwide Gallup poll of military-eligible women and their parents, 86% said that they were aware of the Army's need for more women. Given the generally patriotic mood of the nation, why then wasn't the response greater? The major reasons appeared to be apathy, fear of Army life (too physically rigorous and regimented), misunderstanding of the jobs Army women held (almost one-third thought kitchen police was the main one), negative attitudes of relatives and friends, and perceived Army opposition to the new women's corps.[18]

In a similar vein, a different poll of Army men conducted several months earlier reported that only 25% of the men said they would advise a sister or girlfriend to join the women's corps, 35% were undecided, and the remaining 40% said they would not advise a sister or girlfriend to do so.[19] Reasons for the last response included:

"Women are more help in industry, defense work, farm"; "better off at home"; "Army no place for a woman"; "too close contact with soldiers"; "too hard a life"; "don't like Army life and wouldn't want her to be in anything similar."[20]

In addition to these relatively mild expressions of negative attitudes toward women's service in the Army, the first half of 1943 also witnessed the spreading of a number of highly publicized rumors about the alleged low morals and scandalous behavior of women soldiers. These rumors, which were later found to be groundless, soon escalated into a virtual "slander campaign" in several cities. According to a subsequent Army investigation, the rumor spreaders included officers, enlisted men, Army wives, civilian women, gossips, fanatics, and Army women who were dissatisfied or who had been discharged.[21] The effect of these rumors on efforts to recruit women and to maintain morale among the women currently in the Army was chilling.

One important implication of these poll responses and the rumor campaign is that wartime patriotism, military personnel needs, and the Army's newly found positive interest in womanpower were insufficient forces to counteract the powerful influences of a long history of female exclusion from the military and the deeply held belief that being a woman was incompatible with being a soldier.

In contrast to this belief and these findings, however, is another interesting report from late 1943, in which

> the American public seemed to be solidly behind the idea of drafting women. Gallup polls showed that 73 percent in October of 1943 and 78 percent in December believed that single women should be drafted before any more fathers were taken. Single women of draft age themselves endorsed their draft by a 75 percent majority, although stating that they would not voluntarily enlist so long as the Government did not believe the matter important enough to warrant a draft. Every section of the nation had large majorities favoring the drafting of women.[22]

The findings from these polls were a reflection of the American public's concern over the Army's growing manpower crisis as the war developed and the acceptance, however reluctant, of the value of drafting single women for the large number of noncombat jobs which needed to be filled. In this light, the Army's 1943 plans for drafting women, which were far more serious than those considered the previous year, made eminent sense.[23]

The extent of the Army's need for women soldiers was clearly reinforced by its leaders. By early 1944, the Army Chief of Staff, General Marshall

> went so far as to authorize release to the general public of the precedent-shattering statement that, for American women, "aside from urgent family obligations, *enlistment in the military takes precedence over any other responsibility*." He added, "It is important that the general public understand the Army's urgent need for women to enable the military effort to go forward according to the schedule of operations in prospect."[24]

Taken together, the attitudes and arguments for and against military women, the progression of events during the war, escalating personnel requirements, and the nation's inexperience with using women soldiers all combined to form a complex situation marked by ambivalence and doubt.

During World War II, some 143,000 enlisted women and 7,000 women officers in the WAC served in the Army's major Air, Ground and Service Forces in the United States; and over 12% of the women served in overseas theaters, primarily in Europe and the Pacific.[25] Especially in Europe, the heavy needs of troop supply and support created a great demand for Wacs; it was argued "that one Wac typist could replace two men while eating only half as much."[26] Although the majority of Army women held female-traditional jobs (e.g., administration, telephone operation, health care), a sizable proportion of female soldiers worked in a large range of nontraditional areas as well. They served as specialists in electronics, cryptography, anti-aircraft artillery, chemical warfare, physical and military training, and control tower operation. They were also mechanics, draftsmen, truck drivers, photographers, and parachute riggers.[27]

Throughout the war, Army women served under conditions which were frequently tedious, sometimes physically and emotionally difficult, and occasionally exhilarating. Some 5,500 Army women served in the Southwest Pacific Area, primarily in Australia, New Guinea, and the Philippines.[28] Of their service, which took place under especially rigorous conditions, General Douglas MacArthur later noted:

> I moved my Wacs forward early after occupation of recaptured territory because they were needed and they were soldiers in the same manner that my men were soldiers. Furthermore, if I had not moved my Wacs when I did, I would have had mutiny . . . as they were so eager to carry on where needed.[29]

Through the nation's experience with comparatively large numbers of military women in World War II, much valuable information was gained concerning the capabilities, issues, and problems surrounding the use of female soldiers in a wartime Army. The Army's official history of the Women's Army Corps during the war, finely written by Mattie E. Treadwell, provides extensive and well-documented data on a range of issues which remain relevant for the Army of today and the future. Included are analyses covering the recruitment, training, leadership, and job assignment of Army women, and also reports concerning their physical and psychological health, discipline, pregnancy, relationships with fellow soldiers of both sexes, job satisfaction, and military performance.[30] When all circumstances are taken into account, perhaps the most important lesson from World War II is that women soldiers performed very well. As summed up by Major General Willard S. Paul in 1946,

> American women, through their services in the Women's Army Corps, showed that, contrary to dogmatic opinion, the previously untapped potentiality of womanpower could be directed into the channel of personnel power with positive results. The record shows that their contribution erased any doubt as to the ability, adaptability, and stability of American women in time of national crisis.[31]

Post World War II Through Vietnam

One result of the nation's experience with women in the wartime Army, as well as in the other military services, was the passage in 1948, after much congressional debate, of the Women's Armed Services Integration Act:

> With inadequate male enlistments to maintain total strength levels, the armed forces viewed women as an important alternate source of supply.
>
> Institutionalizing the role of women would also attain other objectives: it would provide a trained nucleus that would facilitate expansion of the service in a national emergency; it would economize by using women in jobs—the "feminine" occupations—for which they were considered better suited than men; and it would make it easier to determine, through experience, how best to utilize women in the military. . . .
>
> Though signifying a major breakthrough for women, the 1948 legislation also sowed the seeds of sex discrimination that were to persist for two decades. . . .[32]

This law required women's minimum age at enlistment to be higher than men's. It severely limited their military career opportunities, and it mandated that husbands and children demonstrate their dependency on female servicemembers before normal military family benefits would be provided. A ceiling of 2% of total enlisted force strength was placed on the number of enlisted women allowed, and the proportion of female officers (excluding nurses) was not permitted to exceed 10% of female enlisted strength. The highest attainable rank for women was temporary colonel (or captain in the Navy), which only one woman from each service could hold at a given time.[33]

In an important provision of the 1948 law, Congress spelled out a combat exclusion policy for women in very explicit statutory terms for the Air Force and the Navy (and, by extension, the Marine Corps); it chose not to do so, however, for the Army. The intent of Congress to exclude Army women from combat was clearly the same. However, the presumed difficulty of distinguishing combat areas from noncombat areas on the Army battlefield, contrasted with the apparent ease of doing so in the other services (i.e., distinguishing combat aircraft and ships from noncombat ones), led Congress to delegate responsibility for making such decisions to the Secretary of the Army.[34] Accordingly, while female combat exclusions in the Air Force and Navy became solidified in statute (10 U.S.C. Sections 8549 and 6015, respectively), those in the Army became embodied in Army regulations which, theoretically at least, were more open to modification and changing interpretations of combat. (Over thirty years later, this lack of a clearly defined statutory prohibition, combined with the influence of the women's movement, the great expansion of Army women's numbers and roles, especially into combat-related areas, and prevailing resistance to the notion of women on the battlefield, would precipitate intense debate, followed by the decision to close certain combat-related jobs to women which had been previously open.)

Another difference between the postwar military services was the Army's decision to continue its separately administered Women's Army Corps, while the Navy, Air Force, and Marine Corps moved to integrate women fully into their regular forces. Several months after the passage of the Women's Armed Services Integration Act, the WAC shrank to less than 3,300 enlisted members and 700 officers.[35]

With the Korean War, largely unsuccessful attempts were made from 1951 through 1952 to expand women's strength in all the armed forces from 28,000 to 112,000. A strength of only 46,000 could be reached, and the WAC actually decreased from 12,000 to 10,000 in 1952.[36] With the exception of nurses, no military women served in Korea during the war. Many factors contributed to the armed forces' failure to meet recruitment goals for women. Probably the most salient were the unpopularity and ambiguity of this war itself and the nation's weariness from the strains of World War II. As to what was learned,

> The Korean War experience reinforced the lesson that should have been taken from World War II: the mobilization of large numbers of women through volunteer means is not possible.[37]

For the rest of the decade and through the mid–1960s, the status of women in the military languished. According to Jeanne Holm, who was to become Director of Women in the Air Force (WAF) and later a major general:

> The accepted wisdom of all the services was that, because of the normal patterns of women's lives and general public disapproval of military careers for women, recruiting women in peacetime in significant numbers was not feasible, except at prohibitive recruiting costs and at an unacceptable sacrifice of quality.[38]

By the mid-1960s, American military involvement in Vietnam was rapidly escalating, accompanied by anti-war and anti-draft responses by certain segments of the American public. It was also a time of heightened prominence for civil rights issues, the emerging new feminist movement, and the growing participation of women in the labor market. Such forces, as they related to current and projected military manpower problems, stimulated in 1967 several significant changes regarding military women. These changes were summarized ten years later:

> Provisions of the [1948] law that limited the career opportunities available to women officers were altered, first to allow them to hold permanent grades up through colonel (captain in the Navy) and to be appointed to general or flag officers and, second, to remove existing differences between men and women with respect to retirement provisions. The 1967 law also struck down the 2 percent limitation on female enlisted strengths that had been in effect since 1947. Nevertheless, women constituted less than 2 percent of total military strength for the remainder of the decade; and if it were not for changing social mores and military expediency, that would probably still be the case today [1977].[39]

By the end of American combat involvement in Vietnam, about 7,500 military women, the majority of them nurses, had served in Southeast Asia. No more than 500 Wacs had duty in Vietnam.[40]

THE ALL-VOLUNTEER FORCE

In 1973 the draft was ended, and the All-Volunteer Force (AVF) was born. With this major shift, Congress and defense planners had to face changing manpower needs, projections of a declining pool of military-eligible young adults, and a social environment in which women were playing larger and more diversified roles. Because of these factors, and the critical need to recruit sufficient numbers of qualified personnel to fill the increasingly technical jobs in the AVF, the decision was made to expand greatly the use of women in all the military services. While in 1972 some 45,000 women accounted for 1.9% of the total force, by 1976 the figure had risen to 108,000, or over 5%. By the end of Fiscal Year 1982, the total female strength had reached 190,000, or 9% of the total force.[41] In the Army, in FY 1972, 12,350 enlisted women comprised 1.8% of its total enlisted force; by the end of FY 1982, the figures had climbed to 64,250, or 9.6%.[42]

In addition to these substantial numerical increases, by 1976 several notable personnel policy changes were occurring in all the services.

(1) permitting women to command organizations composed of both men and women, (2) allowing women to enter aviation training and military academies, (3) eliminating policies that require automatic discharge of pregnant women and those with minor dependents, (4) equalizing family entitlements for married servicemen and servicewomen, (5) giving women access to a wider range of training opportunities . . .

With respect to the nature of women's service opportunities and [A]part from training, changes have taken place in the kinds of jobs to which women can be assigned . . . prior to the 1972 expansion, only 35 percent of all military enlisted job specialties were opened to women. Following an initial reassessment in 1972, over 80 percent of the specialties were opened to women; and by 1976 they could be used in all but the combat-associated specialties.[43]

By the end of FY 1980, enlisted Army women had become eligible for 95% of all enlisted military occupational specialties (MOS), including some involving combat support.[44] In 1982, however, the Departments of the Army and Defense decided to exclude women further from combat-related MOS by reducing the total number of MOS open to female soldiers to 83%. In late 1983 this figure was changed to 86%.[45]

Attitudes Toward the Roles of Women in the Army

Two of the most heated areas of debate concerning military women are the issues of combat and the draft.[46] Although these issues pertain to women in all the military branches, Army women are more often the focal point of debate because of the Army's traditional direct reliance on the draft, especially in wartime, to meet its large personnel needs and its well-known, male-identified combat mission epitomized by the rifle-carrying infantry foot soldier.

Despite arguments that the two issues of women in combat and women and the draft are separate and involve different considerations, these topics are commonly treated as interrelated because of the fairly widespread acceptance of the assumption that the purpose of the draft is to induct citizens for explicitly combat jobs in the armed forces. From this assumption comes the argument that women should be excluded from the draft because, under present law and policy, they are barred from combat jobs. Critics of this assumption maintain, however, that the purpose of the draft is to induct citizens for *all* kinds of necessary military jobs. Since many of these are noncombat jobs for which female citizens have the requisite skills, they can and should be subject to the draft as men are, in accordance with prevailing law and policy concerning female exclusions from combat.[47] As for the counterargument that enough women would voluntarily join the military in wartime to make a female draft unnecessary, the experiences of World War II and the Korean War, as discussed earlier, strongly suggest otherwise.

Such debates over the basic purpose of the draft, differing opinions regarding the relationship between draft registration and actual reinstatement of the draft, and the expression of certain anti-war sentiments by both men and women were all heard in reaction to former President Jimmy Carter's unsuccessful attempt in 1980 to include women in his draft registration proposal to Congress. After much debate, Congress approved registration of males only, an action which prompted a U.S. District Court to rule on a pending 1973 case (Goldberg vs. Rostker) that a male-only registration was in violation of the Fifth Amendment to the Constitution. In 1981, however, the Supreme Court overturned this ruling on the grounds that Congress has overriding constitutional authority to "raise an army" and, therefore, may choose to exclude women from conscription.[48]

In addition to opinions expressed by Congress and the courts, those of the American public and the military community regarding these issues are also important to an understanding of the social context in which Army women live.

In a 1971 Roper poll, 71% of the civilian respondents disagreed with the statement that "women should have equal treatment regarding the draft."[49] Response differences by sex were not noted. Nine years later a similar question was asked in the Gallup Poll of American civilians between the ages of 18 and 24: "If a draft were to become necessary, should young women be required to participate as well as young men, or not?"[50] Overall, 50% responded that they should, 47% that they should not. Analysis of the responses by sex showed, interestingly, that 61% of the men, but only 39% of the women, believed that women should be required to participate in the draft.

A follow-up question in the Gallup Poll pursued the issue of women in combat: "If women are drafted, should they be required to take combat roles as men are, should they be given combat roles only if they volunteer for them, or should they not be eligible for them?" The response patterns are presented in Table 4.1.

Table 4.1. Attitudes Toward Women in Combat Roles

	All Respondents (%)	Men (%)	Women (%)
Given combat roles as men	10	12	9
Only if they volunteer	68	61	74
Not eligible	21	26	16

What is especially striking about responses to this latter question is the strong endorsement, particularly by females, that women should be allowed to volunteer for combat duty although they definitely should not be compelled to do so.

As for the opinions of Army people themselves regarding combat roles for women, two large 1974 surveys indicated that between 50 and 60% of the respondents were against the idea. Women, however, were significantly less opposed than were men.[51] In another large 1974 survey, male and female officers and enlisted personnel were asked to rate the appropriateness of twenty-four different military jobs for women. The most striking finding from this study was that

of all the jobs listed, only one (rifle-carrying infantry foot soldier) was consistently judged by the majority of the respondents to be *in*appropriate for women. All other jobs, including one that requires exercising command authority over men (company commander in a mixed-sex company) and several that potentially involved physical danger or violence (e.g., MP guard duty, helicopter pilot, bomb disposal specialist) were judged appropriate for women by the majority of respondents of both sexes.[52]

Taken together, these polls and surveys suggest considerable uncertainty, resistance, and ambivalence, both in the military community and in the general society, concerning the issues of women in combat and the draft. This conclusion is reinforced repeatedly by comments from Army people and others who have firsthand familiarity with the issues. While it is impossible to weigh how typical the following varied remarks are, they all illuminate viewpoints which are fairly commonly expressed.

First, some women soldiers themselves.

A 22-year-old decontamination specialist, whose job would place her in forward battlefield areas in war, noted, "I have mixed feelings about this . . . I know I can do the job. But I also know some men wouldn't obey a woman leader in combat." A female private in the same field added, "I'd be prepared to die for the country, but it would be disruptive to society. I don't think the country could handle it."[53] A medical specialist remarked, "If I had to fight, I could." But she added, "Women shouldn't have to. We have a different sense of life and death from men. The men are taught to be aggressive and demanding. But I'd like to save someone's life."[54] A different opinion was expressed by a sergeant who had been mistakenly detailed to an artillery unit for over two years. She noted, "That whole time I was wandering around doing a man's job. I did rather well. I even got a commendation. I don't think women should be excluded. It's my country as well as yours."[55] From a female 20-year-old helicopter mechanic, "I know my job, I know my helicopter and it's my unit. It's like you're a member of the team, but when it's really important, then the Army says women can't go."[56]

And what about the opinions of Army men, whose overwhelming dominance in numbers and positions of leadership shapes the quality of life experienced by female and male soldiers alike?

In 1980, Major General David E. Grange, Jr., then commander of Fort Benning, home of the infantry, said of Army women, "They remind me of the little guy on the baseball team—they try harder and they do a good job." Although the general believed that women should be subject to the draft for noncombat duties, he was clearly against combat roles for them. "What you're talking about is a plane unloading at Andrews [Air Force Base] with disfigured gals. The bottom line is a fourth floor in a VA hospital for girl paraplegics. I just don't want to see gals in the front lines." He was also concerned about the impression that such a situation would present to the world. "It would bother me to have gals up there in the front lines with a bayonet and a rifle taking on a big Russian. What would the Russian general staff think?"[57] Regarding this latter comment, it is noteworthy that the Soviet Union now appears to be mounting a fairly extensive media campaign to recruit more women for its noncombat military jobs. At present, however, it is estimated that there are only 10,000 to 30,000 women, accounting for less than 1% of total strength, in the combined Soviet armed forces.[58]

Moral outrage and strong adherence to traditional chivalry marked the views of a male West Point-educated captain regarding the Army's expanded use of women in traditionally male jobs which approach combat roles:

> I am worried about the government's reasons for legislating this change onto us. I think this is trendy, an attempt to rectify the recruiting problem, a high visibility social demonstration. I don't sense caution. . . . It seriously bothers me as an American that this whimsical plunge has been taken, and it is truly immoral to play with something so important. People have a moral twinge at the thought of women or thirteen-year-old boys or fifty-eight-year old men going out to fight. We keep them out, which means we discriminate by sex and by age—*but we are keeping them out of the meat grinder*. What use is it to defend a nation that sends its women to the meat grinder? What are we defending? And what right do people have telling me I need to be resocialized, change my ideas? . . .[59]

When asked about the possible problem of male soldiers risking their own safety and jeopardizing their unit's mission to protect female comrades in battle, a colonel who commanded an infantry brigade replied:

> I'm going to protect a wounded male soldier as much as a wounded female soldier. But is that the mentality of the guys in this brigade? I doubt it. I'm also

not going to say that all females should have the opportunity to live like a hog in the field and be able to join the infantry.[60]

The viewpoints of civilian experts also reflect concern and ambivalence on these issues.

In 1980, William Clark, then head of Army manpower programs, observes:

> The whole battlefield—rear areas and all—are going to be extremely lethal in any next major war. Women will be killed, wounded, captured in the next war. . . . [W]omen are doing a superb job in the Army. We're far passed the point where they are an experiment.
> But units engaged in close combat are principally in a dirty, filthy business that is extremely violent. The fundamental objective of the Army is to be prepared and there's a lot we still don't know about women in the military.[61]

Martin Binkin, coauthor of a major report on women in the military[62] and a retired Air Force colonel, offered related comments:

> For too long, we've ignored the question, because people don't want to meet it head-on. . . . Combat in this day and age is not that clearly defined and it differs among the services, but I think the burden of proof is on people who say that the introduction of women would not harm unit effectiveness.
> There isn't enough scientific evidence that's going to lead to the right answer. . . . The question will turn on moral and political issues.[63]

In 1980, however, then Deputy Assistant Secretary of Defense for Equal Opportunity, Kathleen Carpenter, pressed to find such evidence while there was still time.

> Women have always been the resource of last resort. . . . We need to learn in peacetime what the capability of this nation would be without precluding 51 percent of our populace out of hand.[64]

Even when these most volatile issues—of women in combat and women and the draft—are not the specific focus of attention, Army women are still subjected to intense scrutiny and frequent criticism in their daily lives. Much of this negative attention is related to the continuing fundamental discomfort of American society, even in the 1980s, with the notion of women as soldiers. And then there is the simple but critical factor of numbers, of which Army women are constantly reminded.

A female lieutenant observed that

> Women are so few and so visible that any one woman represents all of them. Men already have their place in the military. If you have some schmuck and they discharge him, nobody pays attention. If one woman has problems, suddenly all the men start saying women don't belong in the Army. We haven't established ourselves, and that makes it a nonstop struggle.[65]

A captain who was the only woman instructor at the Army's infantry school at Fort Benning added

> I'm the token female in this school. . . .
> I'm pro-Army and I like my job. . . .

My whole purpose in this school is to leave an impression that female soldiers have a place in the Army and don't require special favors. My main motivation is to be a credit to female soldiers . . .[66]

Another captain described her experiences in a virtually all-male Army environment where traditionally male jobs were the norm:

There were four females and one hundred and fifty men. They didn't know what to do with us. Some of the gals used their femininity to get out of certain jobs in the motor pool, because they didn't want to be greasy and dirty. And permissive NCOs let them, so the guys were furious. As more women arrived, the men learned how to deal with it. . . .[67]

In a related comment about life in this kind of Army setting, a female major bluntly noted:

Those jobs with the greatest numbers of men have the lowest grade men, the ones who ventilate the greatest hostility toward women. So the women experience a great deal of hardship to add to the dirty job. Of course they'll leave if they're not welcomed.[68]

Even if other issues could be put aside temporarily, this very basic fact of an overwhelmingly skewed sex ratio in the Army contributes heavily to many of the observed situational problems involving male and female soldiers. The work of sociologist Rosabeth Moss Kanter with civilian organizations would suggest that women soldiers, because of their very small numbers relative to men, are so highly visible in the Army that they are subject to excessive job performance pressures. Moreover, as members of the majority male group exaggerate differences between themselves and the minority female group, social boundaries between the two groups becomes more rigid, and assimilation is thwarted. Finally, because their numbers are so few and their isolation from the dominant male Army culture is so great, women soldiers tend to be viewed by their male peers, superiors, and subordinates less as unique individuals and more as common female stereotypes.[69]

A 25-year-old sergeant remarked, "The Army tries to tell us that we're soldiers first and then women, but I think they believe we're women first and then soldiers."[70] A private added that it is "hard to be a mother, a wife and a soldier all at the same time. There are just so many roles a woman can play."[71] Women soldiers, like this Specialist 5, have often commented that they feel as if they're being tested all the time. "You are constantly having to prove yourself. . . . You have to show you're better than Joe, that you're not a lesbian, that you aren't sleeping with officers."[72]

A 26-year-old lieutenant elaborates:

Your're watched every minute as soon as you come in . . . to determine what sexual category you belong in. It's make it or break it right away. . . . I feel sad for those who don't make it. It's not their fault. There aren't a lot of women who can take it.[73]

Retired Air Force Major General Jeanne Holm has explained further the dilemma faced by military women who must live with the still existing, demoralizing stereotype that female soldiers are either whores or lesbians.

> Women do play a double game. . . .
>
> They have a real need to show that they are women, and there are no role models for them yet among the officers because the numbers of enlisted personnel have increased so fast.
>
> They watch television with its current [sexual] emphasis and they think that's what you do to be attractive. The military women walk a very delicate line between what may be taken for a come-on and just wanting to be attractive. It's difficult for a young girl to sort out.[74]

Sometimes volatile and sensitive situations escalate into confrontations between female and male soldiers, problems in unit functioning, and volleys of charges and countercharges regarding prejudice, discrimination, and sexual harassment.

Regarding the latter problem, Holm observes:

> Deep down there's this feeling that women who join the military are asking for it. . . . There's still this feeling that this is a man's Army. I don't think that's going to go away for a long time.[75]

In late 1979 and 1980, the problems of sexual harassment of military women, especially in the Army, gained national prominence.[76] Since that time, all of the military services have taken major steps to try to eliminate the problem.[77] As for other kinds of harassment encountered by women soldiers, a determined female captain offered advice:

> I've been picked on and burst into tears. But you have to fight it. I sit there with tears in my eyes and think: . . . you're not going to make me cry. You just have to change your habits, . . . fight instead of crying to Daddy. The system is set up to fight prejudice—if only people will make it work.[78]

Taken collectively, the remarks quoted in this section give the strong impression that Army life is unpleasant for female soldiers, especially those working in traditionally male fields. Such an impression, while true for some women, is not the case for others, who may find Army life exciting, worthwhile, or at least tolerable. The main point is that because of the way American society creates its Army, defines its sex roles and soldier roles, and channels its collective attitudes into public policies, situations faced by women soldiers are very likely to be difficult. Under these circumstances, the fact that most Army women are able to do their jobs satisfactorily and maintain adequate levels of personal well-being becomes an impressive accomplishment.

CURRENT ARMY POLICIES

Based on policy decisions made during the administration of President Jimmy Carter, Department of Defense projections in 1980 called for continuing the expansion of female strength in all the services to reach 223,000, or about 12.5% of the total force, by 1985-1986.[79] In 1981, however, the individual branches of the armed forces, "to varying degrees . . . expressed concern about being able to achieve these increased goals and the effect of the increased number of military women on mission capability."[80] In particular, this concern focused on certain female-specific issues, such as pregnancy and the statutory and policy combat restrictions; as well as on other issues which, in practice, were often considered female-specific—even though they pertained to personnel of both sexes—such as single-parent responsibilities and physical strength requirements for certain jobs.[81]

About this time, Army policymakers announced publicly the decision to "pause temporarily" at a level of 65,000 enlisted women rather than proceed with the Defense Department directive to reach 87,500 by 1986.[82] The reason given by the Army was that the rapid increase in women's numbers (from 1.8% of the enlisted force in 1972 to 9.1% at the end of Fiscal Year 1980) had occurred "without adequate analysis and planning."[83] Accordingly, in mid-1981 the Women in the Army Policy Review Group (WITAPRG) was formed to assess the situation and make recommendations.

The group decided to focus on two major issues related to female utilization in the Army: (1) Military Occupational Specialty (MOS) Physical Demands Analysis, and (2) Direct Combat Probability Assessment.

The first issue, which pertains to soldiers of both sexes but affects women disproportionately, involved an extensive analysis of all duty positions in the 351 MOS, which were then classified into five categories, ranging from "light" to "very heavy" physical demands placed on incumbents. Over three-fourths of all duty positions were judged either "heavy" or "very heavy." The Army's concern was that, according to its records, over 50% of its current enlisted women were working in these two heavy categories of positions, but only about 8% of Army women were judged sufficiently strong to perform the required tasks. In contrast, about 72% of male soldiers were judged capable of meeting the physical demands of "heavy" and "very heavy" jobs.[85]

To remedy these apparent soldier/job mismatches, WITAPRG recommended that a physical test battery, already developed and being validated in 1982-83, be incorporated into standard Army enlistment processing and job assignment for all personnel, male and female alike.[86] Thus, an enlistee wanting a particular duty position which was classified "heavy" would be required to pass the physical demands test battery for that level.

This test battery became operational in early 1984. Army policymakers decided, however, to use it as a job counseling tool rather than a mandatory screening tool. For example, an enlistee who wants a specific "heavy" job but is not able to meet the required physical demands would be counseled about this problem, presented with alternative choices, but still permitted to be considered for the job if he or she so desired. This compromise decision was probably motivated by the desire of policymakers to avoid additional criticism from influential groups still reacting to other Army policy changes discussed below and to avoid possible legal suits regarding adverse impact on women.

The second issue addressed by WITAPRG concerned the Army's dissatisfaction with its combat exclusion policy for women:

> Though the current . . . [p]olicy proscribes the assignment of female soldiers to MOS that routinely engage in direct combat, it fails to address the numerous duty positions within an MOS requiring the incumbent to share virtually the same risk as infantrymen, armor crews, scouts, and field artillery personnel.[87]

Accordingly, the Policy Review Group recommended that the Army broaden its operational definition of direct combat to include "MOS duties, unit mission, battlefield location and tactical doctrine."[88] Anticipating this recommendation, the Army had developed a Direct Combat Probability Code, ranging from P1 (high) to P7 (low), to classify all jobs within all MOS. 302,000 (53%) of the total number of enlisted jobs were judged P1.[89] Since approximately 1,300 enlisted women were found to be working in certain P1 jobs, the Army announced in August of 1982 that the number of MOS closed to enlisted women due to high combat risk would be increased from 38 to 61.[90] As the Policy Review Group noted, however

> This action will not mean that female soldiers will never be in combat, for a fluid battlefield will dictate otherwise. What it does mean is that the probability of their being engaged routinely in direct combat will be reduced. The Army will implement the new combat probability codes by contracting new accessions into appropriate skills and by reclassifying and retraining existing personnel when they reenlist to new skills that do not have a high probability of direct combat.
>
> Existing enlistment and reenlistment contracts will be honored.[91]

In October of 1982, Assistant Defense Secretary Lawrence J. Korb announced that, within these new guidelines, the Army would increase its female enlisted strength from 65,000 to 70,000 by 1987. He added, "No qualified woman is going to be turned down. In other words, if a lot of women qualify for these jobs, we'll continue to take them, even if it means going above 70,000."[92]

These decisions, to exclude Army women from twenty-three additional combat-related MOS and to increase only minimally the female enlisted strength, quickly stimulated much criticism from individuals and organizations favoring expanded roles for military women.[93] In reaction to this criticism and in light of manpower needs in some of the recently closed MOS, the Army decided in late 1983 to reopen to women thirteen of the disputed MOS and to increase 1987 female enlisted strength projections from 70,000 to 72,700.[94]

OVERVIEW

By highlighting the history of Army women, the attitudes of the American people toward them, and the major policy decisions governing their roles as servicemembers, this chapter attempts to sketch what life is like for female soldiers. A major theme of this discussion is that there has always been and still is much uneasiness in American society regarding appropriate roles for the nation's women soldiers. This ambivalence, coupled with the Army's increasing need for skilled personnel and the expanding roles of women in the larger society, has resulted in Army policies which undeniably open new opportunities to women soldiers but which, when problems arise, also tend to look to the women rather than to the Army organization itself as the primary source of trouble. In this context, policymaking becomes very difficult, especially when it is the already conceptually unclear and emotionally charged issues of combat roles for women and the draft which are pressing for sound policy decisions.

For the present and very near future, and in the absence of extremely urgent defense needs, it seems likely that the U.S. Army women soldiers will remain excluded, at least in formal policy, from explicit combat roles. The draft question, if argued convincingly as being separate from the combat issue, seems more likely to witness the inclusion of women with men, if conscription is reinstated. The passage and ratification of a resurrected Equal Rights Amendment would also have major implications for the expansion of women's roles in the armed forces.[95]

In the meantime, given the current situation of the all-volunteer force and a strong commitment to make it successful, the nation's leaders would be wise to examine carefully ways of making even more extensive and diversified use of women's capabilities under various military conditions. As retired Major General Jeanne Holm observes,

> To fail to tap the pool of young women volunteers will inevitably drive up recruiting costs at a time when the President is trying to hold down the federal budget; drive down the quality of the force at a time when the requirement has never been greater for intelligent, educated, trainable people; divert scarce male resources from combat skills to fill jobs women could perform as well or better; and, in the end, make it more difficult to maintain the armed forces without a draft. Indeed, the ability of the President to keep his commitment to build the nation's defenses without conscription may very well turn on the question of women.[96]

NOTES

1. Linda K. Kerber, *Women of the Republic* (Chapel Hill: Univ. North Carolina Press, 1980), pp. 55–58. Thanks to Janice E. McKenney, " 'Women in Combat': Comment," *Armed Forces and Society* 8 (Summer 1982): 686, for noting this source.
2. McKenney, "Women in Combat," pp. 688–689.
3. Linda Grant De Pauw, "Commentary," *Military History of the American Revolution*, The Proceedings of the Sixth Military History Symposium, United States Air Force Academy, 10–11 October 1974, Washington, DC, 1976, pp. 175–176.
4. Jeanne Holm, *Women in the Military* (Novato, CA: Presidio Press, 1982), pp. 6–9; Philip A. Kalisch and Margaret Scobey, "Female Nurses in American Wars:

Helplessness Suspended For the Duration," *Armed Forces and Society, 9* (Winter 1983): pp. 217–218.
5. Kalisch and Scobey, "Female Nurses," pp. 218, 232.
6. Ibid., p. 219.
7. Mattie E. Treadwell, *The Women's Army Corps*, United States Army in World War II, Special Studies (Washington, DC: Office of the Chief of Military History, Department of the Army, 1954), p. 7, citing primary sources.
8. Ibid., p. 22, citing primary sources.
9. Ibid., p. 24.
10. Ibid., p. 25, citing primary sources.
11. Ibid., p. 19, citing primary sources. (Italics Treadwell.)
12. Ibid., p. 28.
13. Ibid., p. 93, citing primary sources.
14. Ibid., pp. 543, 765, citing primary sources.
15. Ibid., pp. 173–184, citing primary sources.
16. Ibid., p. 543, citing primary sources.
17. Ibid., p. 186.
18. Ibid., p. 186, citing primary sources.
19. Ibid., p. 171.
20. Ibid., p. 171.
21. Ibid., pp. 191–218, especially p. 206, citing primary sources.
22. Ibid., p. 247, citing primary sources.
23. Ibid., pp. 95–96, 246–247, citing primary sources.
24. Ibid., p. 250, citing primary sources. Italics Treadwell.
25. Ibid., pp. 766, 773, citing primary sources.
26. Ibid., p. 384, citing primary sources.
27. Ibid., pp. 288–292, 299–304, 308–338, citing primary sources.
28. Ibid., p. 410, citing primary sources.
29. Ibid., p. 423, citing primary sources.
30. Ibid.
31. Ibid., pp. 752–753, citing primary sources.
32. Martin Binkin and Shirley J. Bach, *Women and the Military* (Washington, DC: Brookings Institution, 1977), pp. 10–11, citing primary sources.
33. Ibid., p. 11.
34. Ibid., pp. 26–27, citing primary sources; U.S. Department of Defense, Office of the Assistant Secretary of Defense (Manpower, Reserve Affairs, and Logistics), *Background Review: Women in the Military*, October 1981, Washington, DC, pp. 38–39.
35. Holm, *Women in the Military*, p. 128.
36. Ibid., pp. 150–153.
37. Ibid., p. 157.
38. Ibid., p. 158.
39. Binkin and Bach, *Women and the Military*, p. 12, citing primary sources.
40. Holm, *Women in the Military*, pp. 206, 214.
41. Binkin and Bach, *Women and the Military*, pp. 14–15, citing primary sources; U.S. Department of Defense, Office of the Assistant Secretary of Defense (Manpower, Reserve Affairs, and Logistics), *Military Women in the Department of Defense*, April 1983, Washington, DC., p. 1.
42. DoD, *Background Review*, pp. 102–103; DoD, *Military Women*, p. 18.
43. Binkin and Bach, *Women and the Military*, p. 17.
44. DoD, *Background Review*, p. 32.
45. U.S. Department of the Army, Office of the Deputy Chief of Staff for Personnel, *Women in the Army: Policy Review*, 12 November 1982, Washington, DC, pp. 4–

17 to 4–20, 5–6; David Wood, "Army to Close 23 Job Categories to Women," *Los Angeles Times*, August 27, 1982, Part II, p. 16; "Army Reopens 13 Jobs to Women," *Los Angeles Times*, October 21, 1983, Part I, p. 11.
46. See, for example, "Draft Women? The Arguments for and Against," *U.S. News and World Report*, April 6, 1981, pp. 30–31; and Nancy Loring Goldman, ed., *Female Soldiers—Combatants or Noncombatants? Historical and Contemporary Perspectives* (Westport, CT: Greenwood Press, 1982). Of particular relevance in this volume are selections by Goldman, "Introduction," pp. 3–17; George H. Quester, "The Problem," pp. 217–235; Jeff M. Tuten, "The Argument Against Female Combatants," pp. 237–265; and Mady Wechsler Segal, "The Argument for Female Combatants," pp. 267–290.
47. "Draft Women? The Arguments for and Against;" Holm, *Women in the Military*, pp. 347–378.
48. Aric Press and Diane Camper, "Uncle Sam Says 'Men Only;' " *Newsweek*, July 6, 1981, pp. 64–65; Holm, *Women in the Military*, pp. 371–378.
49. Binkin and Bach, *Women and the Military*, p. 39.
50. "Women in the Armed Forces," *Newsweek*, February 18, 1980, pp. 34–42.
51. Joel M. Savell, John C. Woelfel, and Barry E. Collins, "Attitudes Concerning Job Appropriateness for Women in the Army" (Research Memorandum 75-3). Rosslyn, VA: U.S. Army Research Institute for the Behavioral and Social Sciences, 1977. Cited by David R. Segal, Nora Scott Kinzer, and John C. Woelfel, "The Concept of Citizenship and Attitudes Toward Women in Combat," *Sex Roles 3* (1977):473.
52. Joel M. Savell, John C. Woelfel, Barry E. Collins, and Peter M. Bentler, "A Study of Male and Female Soldiers' Beliefs About the 'Appropriateness' of Various Jobs for Women in the Army," *Sex Roles 5* (1979): 41–50.
53. Robert S. Dudney, "Women in the Army—End of a Honeymoon," *U.S. News and World Report*, October 4, 1982, p. 51.
54. Helen Rogan, *Mixed Company* (New York: G.P. Putnam's Sons, 1981), p. 289.
55. Dudney, "Women in the Army," p. 51.
56. Sandra G. Boodman, "Equality in the Trenches: An Emotional War," *The Washington Post*, January 27, 1980, p. A-2.
57. Ibid.
58. Allen E. Carrier, "Soviets Begin Media Push to Get Women in Military," *Navy Times*, January 31, 1983, p. 40.
59. Rogan, *Mixed Company*, p. 22.
60. Boodman, "Equality in the Trenches," p. A-2.
61. Ibid.
62. Binkin and Bach, *Women and the Military*.
63. Boodman, "Equality in the Trenches," p. A-2.
64. Ibid.
65. Rogan, *Mixed Company*, p. 241.
66. Sandra G. Boodman, "They Enlist for Same Reasons Men Do," *The Washington Post*, January 28, 1980, p. A-4.
67. Rogan, *Mixed Company*, p. 242.
68. Ibid.
69. Rosabeth Moss Kanter, "Some Effects of Proportions in Group Life: Skewed Sex Ratios and Responses to Token Women," *American Journal of Sociology 82* (1977): 965–990; *Men and Women of the Corporation* (New York: Basic Books, 1977).
70. Boodman, "Equality in the Trenches," p. A-2.
71. Dudney, "Women in the Army," p. 52.
72. Ibid.

73. Karen Hosler, "Army Recruits Most Open to Abuse," *The Sun* (Baltimore), December 17, 1979, p. A-2.
74. Ibid.
75. Sandra G. Boodman, "Women GIs Cite Sexual Harassment at Army Bases," *The Washington Post*, January 29, 1980, p. A-6.
76. See, for example, Karen Hosler, "Women Say Sexual Harassment is Driving Them Out of the Army," *The Sunday Sun* (Baltimore), December 16, 1979, pp. A-1, A-2; Hosler, "Army Recruits"; Boodman, "Women GIs"; and Jay Finegan, "End to Sexual Harassment Ordered," *Army Times*, January 14, 1980, pp. 1, 39.
77. U.S. Department of Defense, Defense Advisory Committee on Women in the Services (DACOWITS), *Proceedings of Fall Meeting*, November 7–11, 1982, Fayetteville, North Carolina, Tab F.
78. Rogan, *Mixed Company*, p. 182.
79. DoD, *Background Review*, p. 1; Tom Philpott, "Services Want to Enlist Fewer Women Until Impact on Readiness is Known," *Navy Times*, January 19, 1981, pp. 1, 28.
80. DoD, *Background Review*, p. 1.
81. Ibid., pp. 74–86; Philpott, "Services Want to Enlist Fewer Women."
82. DoD, *Background Review*; Philpott, "Services Want to Enlist Fewer Women"; Kathy Sawyer, "Pentagon Reassessing Impact of Women in the Armed Forces," *The Washington Post*, May 13, 1981, pp. A-1, A-2.
83. DA, *Women in the Army*, p. 2.
84. Ibid., Appendix A, A-1.
85. Ibid., pp. 2-36, 2-37; Dennis M. Kowal, "Physical Capacity Screening for Job Selection and Classification," in Nancy H. Loring, ed., *Women in the United States Armed Forces* (Chicago: Inter-University Seminar on Armed Forces and Society, 1984), p. 206.
86. Ibid., p. 3-22; Dennis M. Kowal, "Physical Capacity Screening."
87. DA, *Women in the Army*, pp. 4-15.
88. Ibid., pp. 4-12.
89. Ibid., pp. 4-17.
90. Ibid., pp. 4-17 to 4-20, 5-6.
91. Ibid., p. 10.
92. Dudney, "Women in the Army," p. 53.
93. Allen E. Carrier, "DACOWITS Rips Army Women Study," *Army Times*, November 22, 1982b; Pete Earley, "Army Fails To Prove its Claim on Women Dropouts," *The Washington Post*, November 9, 1982.
94. "Army Reopens 13 Jobs To Women," *Los Angeles Times*, October 21, 1983, Part I, p. 11.
95. Martha Lynn Craver, "Myths Harmful to Military Women, Panel Told," *Navy Times*, November 21, 1983a, p. 14; Craver, "Senate Panel Hears Pro-, Anti ERA Testimony," *Navy Times*, November 21, 1983b, p. 17.
96. Holm, *Women in the Military*, p. 392.

5

Prime Hand to Petty Officer: The Evolution of the Navy Noncommissioned Officer*

James F. Downs

FORCE STRUCTURE OF THE NAVY

Military organizations are generally viewed as pyramids, with fewer people in each ascending level exercising greater authority over those in the lower levels. The modern U.S. Navy departs from this model. A detailed examination of enlisted force structure reveals that there are more noncommissioned (petty) officers authorized to exercise military line authority over subordinates than there are subordinates. Table 5.1 shows the distribution of enlisted personnel by rank in 1980 and clearly shows that there are "more chiefs than Indians."

This ratio of rated to non-rated personnel—those with and without line authority—contrasts sharply with previous periods of naval history in this century as well as in the nineteenth century. Until the post World War II period there were always more non-rated people than there were petty officers.[1] All petty officers are at the same time technical specialists and military noncommissioned officers and are expected by law, regulations and custom, to act in both capacities.[2] There are no specialists without line authority as in the Army and Air Force.

For at least the past decade, there has been a general feeling within the Navy that petty officers were not performing their military roles as leaders and managers as effectively as had petty officers in the past. This was most frequently expressed on an unoffical and informal basis, but the concern of the Navy is demonstrated in the fact that by 1978, 157 courses or course

*Author's Note: The research upon which this paper is based was supported in large part by Office of Naval Research contract number N0014-80-C-0198 between that agency and Development Research Associates of Reston, VA. Preparation of the manuscript was supported by University Research Corporation, Chevy Chase, MD.

Table 5.1.　Active Duty Navy Males by Rank and Length of Service (1980)*

Rank		Length of Service		
		Less than 4 years	4 or more years	Total
Nonrated	(E1-3)	155,183	8,659	163,842
P.O. 3	(E-4)	60,606	23,829	84,435
P.O. 2	(E-5)	71,946	63,351	75,291
P.O. 1	(E-6)	23	65,212	65,235
CPO	(E-7)	0	30,298	30,298
SCPO	(E-8)	0	8,377	8,377
MCPO	(E-9)	0	3,257	3,257
Total		227,758	202,983	430,735

*Source: Naval Military Personnel Command, Navy Military Personnel Statistics (MILPERS 15655), June 1980.

segments devoted to leadership and/or management were being offered in various training contexts. In that year the navywide Leadership and Management Education and Training program was developed, and its implementation begun.

This chapter will provide data to support the contention that modern, compared to past, petty officers are not performing as effectively in their military roles. To explain this phenomenon, I will discuss the development of the current enlisted rating structure and argue that the present situation is a consequence of combined historical, environmental, operational, and "social" factors.

The Present Rating Structure

The enlisted force of the U.S. Navy is divided into three major subgroups: non-rated, rated, and "chiefs". The first two groups are each divided into three classes. In the chief petty officer group, there are four classes or levels of responsibility.

Non-rated people are classified in six general apprenticeships: seaman, fireman, airman, constructionman, dentalman and hospitalman. Each of these groups is vertically divided from recruit, at the bottom, to "man". A sailor then can be classified as a seaman recruit or a fireman apprentice before being advanced after approximately one year's service to the highest non-rated pay grade—in these cases, seaman or fireman.

In the rated groups there are also three classes: petty officer third, second, and first. Like non-rated men, petty officers (after the Navy's short-lived attempt to dress all hands in the same style uniform) wear the traditional bell bottom jumper style uniform and are included in the general "folk" classification of "white hats." There are eighty specialties into which petty officers are divided, each identified by a special insignia or rating device. A rated man may be referred to by either rating or rate: petty officer first class Jones or boatswain's mate first class Jones.

Chief petty officers advance through four levels of authority: chief, senior chief, master chief, and command master chief petty officer. This fourth level carries the same pay grade as master chief petty officer. Selection is from among the most senior enlisted, and selectees serve as advisors on enlisted matters to various commands. The Master Chief Petty Officer of the Navy is the senior enlisted person in the service. This group is the only rated community not associated with an occupational specialty.[3]

About 70% to 80% of any recruit cohort goes directly from recruit training to technical training, or an "A" school, where the recruits are trained in the basic technical duties of a petty officer third class and are officially designated as strikers (one who is preparing for advancement to petty officer). The remaining 20% to 30% of each cohort are assigned to apprentice training courses and are taught the basic skills of either deck seaman, fireman or airman. They are then assigned to general duty, usually afloat. Apprentice graduates may strike for ratings through on-the-job training and correspondence courses. While strikers may be assigned the technical duties of third class petty officers, they do not exercise military line authority.

Advancement through the petty officer classes is accomplished, after serving prescribed periods at each level, through correspondence courses, on-the-job training, possible additional schooling, and passing a navywide examination which establishes eligibility for advancement. Chief petty officers advance to master chief by the same process as that used for promoting officers: selection boards making determinations based on reviews of service records. Each year a small number of first class, chief, senior chief or master chief petty officers are promoted to the commissioned ranks of chief warrant officer or limited duty officer.

In the enlisted force, rate governs pay, educational opportunity, living accommodations, messing, working conditions, privileges, and responsibility. Rating, which plays an enormous social and psychological role in naval life, is as important as rate. One's rating determines with whom one will work and with how many people, the amount of supervision he or she will experience, types of assignments, opportunity for advancement, and the acquisition of skills marketable in the civilian world. Over the years folklore has grown up around each of the ratings providing stereotypes about the kinds of people in each rating group, their presumed intelligence, and general demeanor. An individual's personal identification and self-image are largely determined by his or her rating. From the moment young sailors become designated strikers, they have entered a special, identifiable community within which, in all likelihood, they will remain throughout their naval careers. Advancement, and thus acquisition of military authority, is dependent on performance in a technical field. There is no official structural role for the powerful and persuasive person who is technically inept. Nor, officially, is there a place for the accomplished technician who has no talent or liking for the responsibilities of leadership and management.

The question at hand is whether or not petty officers of today effectively perform their leadership role, which is to use Navy jargon, the maintenance of "discipline and good order." Table 5.2 shows the rate of non-judicial punishment cases brought to captain's mast in sixty ships over an eighty year period, examined every ten years from 1900 to 1980. It is immediately clear that the "old Navy," especially in the pre-World War I years, was rather long on discipline and short on good order. On the other hand, the year 1940 reports exceptionally low nonjudicial punishment rates.

If we assume that fewer cases brought to captain's mast means that a greater number of problems were resolved by petty officers or actually prevented by them, the petty officers of 1940 appear to have been head and shoulders above their predecessors and their successors. But before we can safely make such a comparison, we must determine whether or not the term petty officer and the roles accorded to petty officers were the same at different periods. To do this we must review briefly the development of the present system of universal dual responsibility for all petty officers.

Early History: The Nineteenth Century

The year 1820 is used as a starting point because it was prior to the advent of steam, and because the records are easily accessible.[4] Table 5.3 presents the pay and rations of petty officers, as defined in 1820. All other jobs on board were assigned to seamen, ordinary seamen, landsmen, marines, or boys. It is difficult to determine the degree of authority held by petty officers. Pay schedules did not necessarily represent seniority in the nineteenth century. Boatswain's mates are mentioned frequently in memoirs and fiction, and most certainly they had day-to-day control of the non-rated people who made up

Table 5.2.   Navy Non-Judicial Punishment (NJP) Rates (1900-1980)

Year	NJP Rate
1900	200 + %
1910	85
1920	105
1930	55
1940	25
1950	53
1960	60
1970	80
1980	75

Source: James F. Downs, Judith Cobart, and Constance Ojile, *Naval Personnel Organization* (Reston, VA: Development Research Associates, 1982).

Table 5.3. Navy Monthly Pay and Rations by Rating (1820)

Rating	Pay ($)	Rations
Master's Mate	20	
Captain's Clerk	25	
Boatswain's Mate, Carpenter's Mate	19	1
Coxswain, Quarter-Gunner, Quartermaster, Master-at-Arms, Armourer, Steward, Cooper, Cook	18	

Source: Navy Register: 1820

the bulk of the crew. It was the boatswain's mates, by means of their voices or their pipes (or, properly, calls), who passed orders throughout the ship. Many of them carried "starters," short pieces of rope used to urge sailors to greater effort. The use of the starter was clearly not considered a punishment, inasmuch as the right to award punishment was, and still is, the sole prerogative of the commanding officer.

Another petty officer mentioned frequently was the master-at-arms, who served as the ship's police officer, assisted by non-rated ship's corporals. His responsibility was to enforce order below the main deck and supervise the cleanliness in all parts of the ship.

Pay differentials suggest higher status, if not more authority, for the captain's clerk and the master's mate. Other petty officers were, in the main, specialists or artisans who worked alone or with only a few helpers. In day-to-day practice, general military authority appears to have been the jealously held prerogative of the commanding officer, who delegated it to junior officers as his representatives. As noted above, punishment could be awarded only by the captain. During the Civil War, many volunteer officers tended to ignore this stricture and to award punishment on their own authority which, at least occasionally, resulted in court martial and dismissal for "abuse."

In part, the historic authority of the boatswain's mate stemmed from the fact that it was he who wielded the cat when men were ordered flogged by the captain. The master-at-arms was most frequently the petty officer who re-. ported the infractions which brought a man to mast and to the flogging gratings. One gets the distinct impression, however, that the master-at-arms was viewed by the crew as a spy and informer who worked for the captain rather than a petty officer exercising authority in his own right.

Until the 1840s there were no insignia to distinguish petty officers from the rest of the crew. The boatswain's mate carried his call and the master-at-arms perhaps brandished a nightstick, but both wore the same uniform as all other enlisted men. This suggests that the number of petty officers was relatively small in a crew of four hundred, enabling everyone on board to know them on sight.[5]

Petty officers held their positions at the pleasure of the commanding officer, who recruited his own crew. If a commanding officer was relieved, all petty officers were reduced to seaman until the new captain confirmed their appointments or appointed new petty officers. If a man was transferred to another ship he was disrated.

Naval service in the early nineteenth century was only one of the alternatives open to seafarers, who might also work on merchant ships. Until the 1850s, many merchant vessels carried guns; and, of course, the working of a sailing vessel did not differ because of the use to which she was put. From the point of view of the Navy, a year before the mast was a year before the mast. Experienced seamen and petty officers were shipped into the Navy directly in what today we would call an advanced pay grade program. It was the practice of the time to decommission ships in port in the United States and send the officers and warrant officers home on half pay until another berth was available. Enlisted people were simply returned to the maritime labor market to find a berth. It is not surprising that men recruited and dismissed in such a fashion were not, in the main, accorded military authority.

In general, enlisted military authority appears to have been exercised only by the master-at-arms and, to a lesser extent, by the boatswain's mates as personal representatives to the commanding officer who appointed them. Specific occupational authority was delegated to enlisted men in order to carry out assigned tasks, but no petty officer exercised authority in his own right.

In the 1840s, a number of jobs which had been those of "prime hands" (i.e., experienced seamen, captains of the forecastle and top, captain of the hold) were elevated to petty officer status. The captain's clerk became a yeoman whose pay depended on the size of the ship. Master's mate, which had been a route from the berth decks to the wardroom, was abolished. Ship's corporals had become petty officers. A band master rating was established. Below the petty officers were seamen, ordinary seamen, boys, and two new ratings: first and second class musicians.

In this same period, special insignia for petty officers was authorized. Here most certainly we see the foreshadowing of policy which accords authority by rank as well as skill level. The insignia did not indicate rate or rating, all petty officers wearing an anchor, star, and eagle on their left arm. This can only mean that there was little or no official precedence between petty officers save that accorded by the nature of their jobs. The officers' corps had always been exceedingly conscious of and sensitive to the most minute gradations of rank and precedence. Their failure to symbolize such differences between enlisted people can only mean that it was not yet considered an important issue.[6]

Between the 1840s and 1880s a number of new ratings were created, particularly in the artificer and engineering branches, but there appears to have been no official shift in the attitude toward enlisted authority. In the 1880s, however, major changes did occur. They represented those occurring in naval technology and led to a distinct change in the role of enlisted personnel. See Table 5.4 for the rating structure of 1884.

Table 5.4.   Navy Occupational Structure: Rate, Rating and Pay (1884)*

Rating/Pay Seaman branch		Rating/Pay Artificer branch		Rating/Pay Special branch	
Rated as first class petty officers					
Chief Boatswain's		Machinist	$70	Master at arms	$65
mate	$35			Engineering Yeoman	$60
Chief Quartermaster	$35			Apothecary	$60
Chief Gunner's mate	$35			Paymaster's Yeoman	$45
				Writer	$45
				Band master	$52
				Schoolmaster	$45
Rated as petty officer second class					
Boatswain's mate	$30	Boilermaker	$60	Ship's corporal	$28
Gunner's mate	$30	Armourer	$45	Cook	$35
Quartermaster	$30	Carpenter's mate	$40	Chief Musician	$36
Coxswain to C-C	$35	Sailmaker's mate	$40		
		Water Tender	$38		
Petty Officer Third Class					
Captains:		Printer	$40	Captain:	
Foretop	$30	Painter	$40	of the hold	$30
Maintop	$30	Oiler	$30		
After guard	$27				
Coxswain	$30				
Quarter Gunner	$27				
Nonrated					
Seaman Gunner	$26	Fireman 1/c	$35	Lamplighter	$25
Seaman	$24	Carpenter's mate	$25	Jack-o-dust**	$22
Sea. App. 1/c	$24	Caulkers	$25	Buglers	$33
				Musician 1/c	$32
				Tailor	$30
				Barber	$30
Seaman Second Class					
Ord. Seaman	$19	Fireman 2/c	$30	Bayman***	$18
Sea. App. 2/c	$19			Musician 2/c	$30
Seaman Third Class					
Landsman	$16			Coal Heavers	$22
Sea. App. 2/c	$11				
Sea. App. 3/c	$10				
Boys	$10				

*Source: Navy Register, 1884
**Traditional title of the sailor in charge of stores.
***Sick bay attendant.

This elaboration of the rating structure provided, for the first time, a clear cut military precedence quite separate from title or job or pay. It also corresponds with the beginnings of the steel Navy of the United States and a period of unparalleled pomp and ceremony in naval life. Aside from the Russo-Japanese and the Spanish-American wars, the major naval events of the period were world cruises and reviews, which continued until the very eve of World War I.

This was the period in the United States during which agitation for an all-American Navy began. Our merchant service was in decline. The Navy could no longer recruit trained seamen. The complex steel warship, moreover, was entirely different from a merchant vessel. Naval seamen needed to be trained in Navy ships. There was increased concern about attracting and keeping sailors. Guaranteed four-year enlistments were initiated and incentives established for continuous service. The apprentice program, which accepted boys from fourteen to eighteen to serve until their twenty-first birthday, was established to encourage American youths to enter the Navy.

Beginnings of the Modern Navy

The mid-1890s saw the establishment of the basic outlines of the modern rating structure. The rate of Chief Petty Officer was established in 1893. These senior enlisted men were authorized to wear an officer-type uniform (a privilege previously accorded first class petty officers), display distinct hat ornament, and, above all, enjoy separate and much better messing and berthing. By 1899, a thirty-year nondisability retirement system for enlisted had been established to encourage continued service. The old sailing-Navy ratings were disestablished and new ones useful in the steam Navy established. A new precedence was created, with the designation of the master-at-arms, now shifted into the seaman branch, as the senior rating. The old term for seaman ratings, "petty officer of the line," was abandoned and the term "petty officers" used to indicate those of the seaman branch. All other petty officers were referred to as "petty officers of the artificer and special branches." The Bluejackets Manual (BJM), first published in 1902, makes a clear distinction between these two types of petty officer in matters of authority and responsibility. The seaman branch wore rating badges on the right arm, all others on the left. The design of the badges followed the pattern established in the 1880s: chevrons, an eagle, and a speciality mark for each rating. The same manual for 1907 spells out the differences between right and left arm rates quite clearly:

> All CPOs of the seaman branch must be leading men, thoroughly familiar with the duties of their ratings, able to handle and instruct recruits and trained men, direct a gun crew, a company of infantry or section of artillery.

On the other hand:

> Chief Machinists, Carpenters Mates, Boilertenders should be experts in charge of men at their duties, controlling and best employing their force and maintaining discipline.

Subsequent editions of the BJM indicate the gradual shift in attitude toward both right and left arm petty officers. By 1916 it was made quite clear that all petty officers had military responsibilities. Left arm CPOs, for instance, were expected to be able to handle an infantry squad.[8] It was made equally clear that right arm ratings were senior to left arm. Officers were cautioned to avoid putting left arm CPOs in charge of groups of men containing right arm petty officers. If this was unavoidable, the right arm petty officer was to be considered senior in all military matters. It should be remembered that at this time artificer and special branch petty officers could be recruited directly from civilian life, and in some ratings even chief petty officers might have had no previous naval experience. Seaman branch petty officers, on the other hand, were promoted from nonrated status after at least one enlistment. Nonetheless, ordering precedence by rating rather than by rate created a structural tension in an organization so concerned with rank. Officers were cautioned to avoid the situation if at all possible.

Advanced pay grade recruitment was virtually abandoned after World War I. Inexperienced apprentice seamen were enlisted and trained in school or on the job for promotion to the lowest petty officer ratings. Thus petty officers of the artificer and special branches, after about 1920, generally had as much naval experience as did their seaman counterparts.

As a result, the older precedence system was abandoned and all petty officers were accorded seniority by rate. Within a class, however, rating precedence was continued, so that Chief Boatswain's mates were the senior enlisted men. All other chief petty officers were ranked below them, with the right arm rates, which by 1920 numbered five, being senior. Master-at-arms was disestablished in 1920 and police functions were delegated to right arm petty officers, generally boatswain's or gunner's mates.

World War II and Beyond

The situation described above remained in effect until the late 1940s. During this period training manuals and other material increasingly emphasized the military responsibilities of all petty officers and made it clear that these, rather than technical responsibilities, were the most important. Recruits were constantly reminded (if such a mild word is suitable) to turn to their petty officer for all advice and guidance, to adhere strictly to the chain of command from its lowest link, and to obey petty officers with the same alacrity that they would commissioned officers. Petty officers, on the other hand, were enjoined to enforce regulations not only in their spaces and divisions, but everywhere afloat and ashore. They were held strictly accountable for the behavior of those under them and were expected to represent their subordinates and demonstrate concern for their welfare. This, then, was the authority environment of 1940, when nonjudicial punishment rates were at an all time low. Elsewhere I have discussed a number of factors which combined to create this situation.[9] Twenty years of emphasis on the role of the petty officer, combined with a recruiting and training system which put somewhat older and more experienced people in charge, made it the era of the ideal petty officer.

During World War II the number of ratings expanded from approximately thirty in 1940 to over fifty. Perhaps a more important effect of the war was the need to change the training system. Wartime demands called for large numbers of skilled sailors at sea at once. Prior to the war, seamen and firemen were not eligible for technical training until they had served at sea; however, during the war a very large proportion of recruit training graduates went directly to schools. In many cases the highest 10% of each school class were promoted to petty officer third class, and another 20% promoted to seaman first class. Throughout the postwar years greater and greater numbers of recruits have gone to technical training before serving at sea. In the 1960s and 1970s, educational doctrine combined with "cost effectiveness" philosophy dropped military training from the "A" school environment and shortened the recruit training period. The entire process suggested very strongly to young sailors that technical rather than leadership competencies were the most important.

This view was supported by the changes in enlisted classification which took place in the late 1940s. Under the aegis of the new Department of Defense, the distinction between left and right arm ratings was abolished. All rating badges were shifted to the left arm. Although previous practice was not immediately abandoned, the precedence of ratings gradually fell into disuse and was finally officially removed from regulations. The determination of seniority became cumbersome and difficult, causing no small amount of confusion in the enlisted force. Although officially charged with responsibility for maintaining good order and discipline in any context, fewer and fewer petty officers seemed to be willing to do so outside of their own division or "gang," or other situations where they had been assigned responsibility.

This situation has been exacerbated by the creation of a number of ratings or collateral duties to perform tasks that in the past were considered a normal part of the petty officer's job. Career counselling, for instance, which was formerly almost entirely in the hands of divisional CPOs, has become the responsibility of the Navy Counselor rating.

The creation of the senior and master chief rates in the 1960s in effect reduced the chief petty officer's status. Thus many young sailors did not associate with a role model who represented the top of the enlisted structure, there being relatively few master and senior chiefs and many of those few being assigned to staff positions.

At the time these rates were established it was the Navy's intent to abandon the ranks of warrant and chief warrant officer (following the example of the Royal Navy), dividing their duties between the senior enlisted on one hand and junior limited duty (ex-enlisted) officers on the other. No new warrant officers were appointed for five years, after which time the Navy reinstituted the warrant officer program. This has created an aura of confusion about the responsibilities of three groups of people who are peers in age, experience, and time in service.

There have been many ways to account for the apparent decline in petty officer performance. They range from blaming poor education and permissive schools to according former Chief of Naval Operations Admiral Elmo E. Zumwalt complete responsibility for the collapse of the Navy (although the problems which he is credited with creating were well recognized before he became CNO).

ATTEMPTS TO FIX THE SYSTEM

Most attempts to solve the problem have involved increased training in management and leadership or wholesale attempts to "get tough" in a manner considered to be analogous to the "old Navy." One possible approach, which to my knowledge has not been officially or systematically addressed, recognizes that authority rests not in intensive training or naive imitation of the past but rather in structured personal relationships as they are affected by the total Navy environment. The effective use of authority depends on the opportunities afforded a petty officer to exercise authority and the subordinates to obey. What then are the naval vessel environments in which authority can be exercised? I suggest they can be categorized as work/watch standing, berthing, messing, and liberty.

Work Watch

Throughout the period under study, petty officers have exercised authority within the context of their specific jobs. However, the environments of different jobs require different methods. Boatswain's mates, then and now, direct the work of relatively large numbers of semi-skilled newcomers to the Navy as they perform routine and often repetitious tasks. The same description is accurate for machinist's mates or boiler tenders in the engineering departments or aviation petty officers on the flight deck. Many of the artificers and artisans of the past did not, and high tech ratings of the modern Navy do not, control large numbers of juniors. They may work alone or in a gang containing perhaps one or two other petty officers. In one context, a petty officer is indeed a leader or driver; in another, a co-worker with his authority derived from technical expertise. In both cases, the senior men have been specifically assigned by the division officer or department head. The increase in the number of ratings requiring high levels of technical training and expertise has meant that more and more petty officers are working in the co-worker environment. In many cases they have reported to their first assignment after many months of technical training during which the military aspects of naval service have not been emphasized. Some may have already earned promotion to petty officer third class, or will very shortly after reporting on board. Their careers do not provide an opportunity to acquire leadership skills and generally emphasize their technical expertise rather than their military position.

Messing

Mealtimes have always been an interlude wherein petty officer authority could be exercised in an other-than-work context. In the nineteenth century, the crew was divided into messes of ten to twenty men each. Each group selected one among them to be mess cook. The mess cook, under the supervision of the ship's cook, would prepare the meals for his mess mates and serve them on the berth deck. The senior man in the mess was responsible, under the general control of the master-at-arms, for the behavior of the members of the mess.

In most cases men ate under the controlling eye of the same petty officers who directed their work on deck, a strong reinforcement of the omniscience of the petty officer. The master-at-arms and the yeoman generally ate in a separate mess symbolic of their exalted positions and their authority and power over all the crew. These eating arrangements remained unchanged except for the installation of collapsible tables which were suspended from the overhead and lowered into place at mealtimes. The senior man at the table was responsible for cleanliness, good behavior, and table manners, although his standards were perhaps not those of the drawing room. Generally men at the mess table were served in order of seniority, a thrice daily reminder of the power of rate.

Eating in the berthing compartments continued in some ships until after World War II, but the old system of having the mess cook prepare meals for his mess mates was replaced by the institution of the general mess. Rated ship's cooks were responsible for food preparation for the entire crew. Mess cooks were nonrated men appointed by the division officer (in fact the CPO) to assist the cook in preparing food and serving it either from a cafeteria line or by bringing food to the berth decks in specially designed pannikins. Changes in ship design made eating in berthing compartments less and less practical. Modern ships with great compartmentation for watertight integrity did away with the vast open gun or berth deck. Hammocks, which were taken up each morning, leaving berthing compartments available for messing, were abandoned in favor of bunks. The alternative was to design special messing compartments. Inasmuch as no ship could have a mess deck sufficiently large to feed the entire crew at once, cafeteria style eating was adopted. The role of the petty officer at the head of the same tableful of men at each meal disappeared. Order on the mess decks was maintained by the master-at-arms force, often a special mess-deck master-at-arms who also supervised the mess cooks. In many ships a special table was reserved for petty officers first class, who were also accorded the privilege of going to the head of the chow line, a singularly important demonstration of their status. As the senior enlisted present, they were still held responsible for maintaining order and providing an example. They also collected funds to purchase extra condiments for their own use, which again provided a special and important symbol of the privileges and powers of rate.

In an effort to enhance the prestige of the senior petty officers, many ships developed a further practice of setting aside a totally separate compartment for first class petty officers' messing and off-duty lounging. The consequence, however, was to remove the first class petty officer from the messing environment and reduce the opportunity for exercise of authority or demonstration of status and power. To the petty officer it conveyed a subtle message that he was not responsible for his juniors in the messing hours.

Berthing

When men slept in hammocks on the gun decks, the petty officer in charge was the master-at-arms, assisted by his corporals. They assured that regulations were observed, suppressed gambling and disorderly behavior, and directed the crew in cleaning the area. They were assisted to some degree by the boatswain's mates, who passed orders and were responsible for rousing the men from their hammocks in the mornings. Greater compartmentalization, as noted earlier, caused the disappearance of the berth decks housing most of the crew under the eyes of the master-at-arms. The crew became dispersed throughout the ship in smaller compartments. Day-to-day responsibility for cleanliness was shifted to the senior petty officer in each berthing compartment. In some large divisions a special compartment petty officer was assigned to stand responsible for supervising the nonrated compartment cleaners. Until at least the 1950s, standard practice was to assign bunks by seniority. When a new petty officer came on board, he was permitted to eject anyone his junior from the bunk of his choice.

In World War II, in order to avoid losing all the men of a division or rating, the practice of mixed-rate berthing was instituted in most ships. The principal of rate seniority was still observed, but the senior man might well be a different rating group or division than others in the compartment. Thus the importance of rate over rating was again emphasized.

In recent years some ships have set aside special first class berthing which, like the separate messing facilities, effectively removed senior petty officers from yet another environment wherein authority might be exercised. In the 1970s and 1980s, increases in military pay and the greater number of married enlisted (54%) have resulted in many sailors' living ashore whenever their ship was in home port. In general, liberty is granted in the United States five nights out of six, which means that many sailors do not remain under the eyes of their petty officers more than one night a week, further reducing the opportunity for leaders to lead or followers to follow.

Liberty

In the early days covered by this study, shore liberty was not common. Ships did not spend much time in U.S. ports, and fear of desertion discouraged the practice of granting liberty in foreign ports of call. When men were allowed ashore, however, the Navy generally did not extend its control with them. Miscreants were brought back to naval authorities by civilian police and their punishment was awarded in the context of naval justice. Although granting liberty became more common as the nineteenth century progressed, the issue of behavior ashore remained essentially the same. The cruise of the Great White Fleet in 1907-1908 changed this attitude. Under extreme pressure from President Roosevelt to avoid unpleasant incidents in foreign ports, the Navy instituted a shore patrol, composed of petty officers under the command of a shore patrol officer, to supervise enlisted off-duty behavior. By 1940, in many regular Navy ports, civilian authorities had, with apparent willingness, permitted the Navy to handle its own problems, at least those of a minor nature. In other places where sailors were not popular, the shore patrol served not only to enforce uniform regulations and suppress disorderly conduct but also to protect sailors against civilian police. In early years shore patrolmen were generally selected from among the right arm rates, but the great numbers of men to be supervised, the manifest unfairness to the right arm rates, and the problems of having too many duty petty officers ashore combined to expand eligibility for shore patrol to all ratings. By World War II, all ratings were represented in the shore patrol, although it was uncommon to see yeomen, cooks or storekeepers in these roles. Initially shore patrol was maintained by requiring that each ship in port provide a party of petty officers each night. During World War II, permanent detachments of shore patrol were established in major Navy ports, and in some cases detachments of Armed Forces Police made up of noncommissioned officers from all services were established.

By 1940 and into the war years, the environments in which petty officers might legitimately exercise authority had been expanded to include not only work and watch, berthing and messing aboard, but also free time on liberty ashore.

In the post-war years, particularly after the late 1960s, the practice of assigning ships' petty officers to shore patrol in the United States was abandoned. Either permanent Armed Forces Police detachments were established or the sailor was left to the jurisdiction of civilian authority. Although the Armed Forces Police are composed largely of noncommissioned officers, their power stems from their assignment as police and the authority represented by the police badge they wear, rather than from their rating badges. In today's Navy sailors are policed more frequently by "policemen," either civilian or military, than by the petty officers they know, once again reducing the areas within which petty officer authority can be realistically exercised.

A second area in which petty officer authority was regularly demonstrated in relation to liberty was in the issuance of liberty cards. This practice, instituted in the 1920s, permitted only those men holding a liberty card to go ashore. The cards were, in most ships, turned in on the quarterdeck at the expiration of liberty and given to the division CPO or leading petty officer. Men requesting liberty had to report to their petty officers to obtain their cards. Although it was not authorized, a petty officer could withhold the card if the man was not performing properly. A sailor could demand his card, but at the risk of being put on report and going to captain's mast, thus losing at least one night's liberty even if acquitted.

Before going on liberty, a sailor had to be inspected to see if his uniform was regulation and clean. This was performed on the quarterdeck by the officer of the deck or the boatswain's mate of the watch. The sailor had, in many cases, already been inspected by his chief or leading petty officer when reporting for his card.

Liberty cards were abandoned in the 1970s. At the same time, enlisted men were authorized to keep civilian clothes on board and wear them ashore. This effectively eliminated liberty as an authority environment. It also eliminated the regular display of rating symbolism. Inasmuch as dungarees had, since World War II, become the standard working uniform, and the change to the officer style uniform had done away with the undress blue uniform which had been worn in the evening by the duty section, many sailors went for months without wearing any uniform except dungarees.

In summary, in the early nineteenth century petty officer authority was limited to working situations and not exercised as general military authority. This gradually changed during the next one hundred and twenty years until World War II, when all petty officers were charged with general military authority and exercised it in a number of contexts. This was accompanied by a clear cut precedence between ratings which allowed both subordinates and superiors to determine who was responsible in any given situation. Since World War II the opportunities to exercise military control over subordinates or gain experience in leadership have, for a number of reasons, been reduced.

Despite the official position which supports general petty officer authority and the efforts made to improve enlisted leadership performance and petty officer prestige, statistics suggest that petty officer performance has declined since World War II. This parallels a period in which technical expertise has been a major emphasis in enlisted career development.

At this point we should perhaps ask why the Navy in the late nineteenth century and the first decades of the twentieth century began to emphasize enlisted leadership and authority.

AUTHORITY CHANGES IN THE ENLISTED FORCE

Early twentieth century changes in recruiting practices, which brought the majority of sailors into the Navy at an early age and trained them from the lowest ranks, altered the nature of the enlisted force. It became increasingly composed of men in all rating groups who had much experience in the Navy and who had opportunity to develop leadership skills. One cannot discount the fact that the percentage of native-born American citizens was increased. In 1900 20% of the enlisted force were noncitizens and another 20% foreign born. The decision to recruit native-born Americans changed these figures dramatically within a few years. It is possible that the officer corps simply felt more comfortable according greater authority to Americans.

Three other factors have impacted on the decision to delegate greater degrees of authority to enlisted personnel. One of these was a continued attempt on the part of some naval officers in the last quarter of the nineteenth century and the early years of the twentieth to have the marine detachments removed from naval vessels.[10] To justify this proposal the anti-marine faction needed to demonstrate that the landing party function of the marine detachment could be carried out by sailors and that the traditional police function of the marines could be handled by Navy petty officers. The willingness of naval officers to assume this military role may have been a consequence of the introduction of infantry training at the Naval Academy in the 1870s. A review of disciplinary records for the early 1900s suggests that removal of the marines would have meant a reduction in disciplinary problems, inasmuch as marines appear in records of captain's mast in disproportionate numbers.

Linked to this internal struggle was the nature of naval operations in the late nineteenth century and the first forty years of the twentieth. To put it simply, a professional naval officer or sailor was much more likely to see combat ashore, operating as infantry, than he was at sea as member of a gun crew. From the end of the Civil War, during which naval personnel fought ashore on several occasions, no action at sea was experienced until 1898. From the end of the Spanish–American War until 1940, with the exception of World War I, sailors again fought more frequently ashore than afloat. This period saw a naval expeditionary force land in Korea and sailors go ashore in Cuba, Puerto Rico, the Philippines, Haiti, Nicaragua, Trieste, Greece, Turkey, to the relief of the legations at Peking, and on numerous occasions in China in the 1920s and 1930s. Naval detachments operated railway guns on the western front in World War I and operated as infantry in northern Russia and Siberia. Of the sixty-eight Congressional Medals of Honor awarded to graduates of the Naval Academy, twenty-five were awarded for valor fighting as infantry in the naval brigade at Vera Cruz in 1914.[11] Fighting as infantry requires organization into squads, platoons, companies and battalions lead by noncommissioned officers, particularly at the platoon and company level. Until at least the 1950s, every ship had as part of its organization a landing party with regular assignments of officers, petty officers and sailors to an infantry formation. *The Landing Force Manual* was the standard guide for such formations and for all the skills required for operations ashore. Since that time the Navy has been relieved of this responsibility, at least officially, and the manual withdrawn from circulation.

A third and less aggressive operational issue has its origins in the Great White Fleet. In all ports of call the fleet staged a parade which required the organization of sailors into infantry formations. For many years afterward, the naval marching party was a part of civic celebrations in all coastal cities where naval vessels were ported or to which the Navy could be persuaded to send a ship.

While it can be cogently argued that a ship underway or in port can be effectively managed through the exercise of occupational authority, except in a few general police functions, large groups of men ashore, either marching, providing disaster relief, or fighting, do require a more traditional military organization with its attendant delegation of military authority to the lowest organizational levels. The willingness (and eagerness) of naval officers to take on a role ashore may stem in part from the fact that fighting ashore was part of the very earliest experience of many of the senior officers of the 1890s and 1900s. Their vision of acceptable naval operations and organizations could hardly fail to be shaped by their first—and for many their only—action in the Civil War when, as midshipmen, they took part in the storming of Fort Fisher, North Carolina.

THE DIFFUSION OF AUTHORITY

The legal basis for the exercise of military authority by Navy enlisted personnel has remained the same: petty officers have been granted the authority necessary to carry out their assigned duties. Nonetheless, in the one hundred and sixty-four years covered by this study the structure and exercise of authority in the enlisted force has changed considerably. From a situation in which there were only a handful of petty officers in a crew of several hundred, the Navy has developed into an institution with 61% of its personnel rated as petty officers. If recruits and apprentices in training are excluded, the petty officer/nonrated ratio in operational contexts is even greater.

Along with this development we have seen great variance in the effectiveness of petty officers in maintaining good order and discipline. There appears to be a positive correlation between effective petty officers' peformance and the degree to which their military responsibility is emphasized over their technical performance. In addition it would appear that a clear-cut precedence of ratings is related to effective performance.

The policies and procedures which provided the widest opportunity for petty officers to exercise authority in a wide variety of contexts—working/watch standing, messing, berthing, and liberty—have been examined as they interacted with the structural situation. The introduction of steam power required more people with a technical background. Technicians (artificers in the language of the time) had automatically been accorded petty officer status (armorer, cooper, carpenter's mate, etc.), and thus engine room ratings began to appear. They were, however, accorded lower precedence than the deck petty officers, just as engineering officers were junior to deck officers. This relationship between the deck and technical ratings remained essentially unchanged until the turn of the century. At that time, many of the expressions of naval "smartness"—sail handling, rowing, and manning the yards—had disappeared. They were replaced by military "smartness"—parades, infantry formations, etc. And, despite the stated purposes of our growing fleet to fight naval battles at sea, the most common "action" seen by sailors and naval officers had been and continued to be operations ashore as expeditionary forces, in disaster relief, or in ceremonial marching parties. In modern terminology, "power projection" was far more frequent than "sea control" as a naval mission.

The demands of World War II required that much training shift from the ships to shore installations and emphasized rapid acquisition of occupational skills rather than the slower development of military leadership experience. And while the stated official position of the Navy did not change—petty officers were both technical experts and military noncommissioned officers—many shifts in structure and procedure made it difficult to realize this goal in practice. Changes in technology, naval architecture, training philosophy, and personnel procedures, as well as attempts to bolster the prestige of petty officers, symbolically combined to reduce the opportunity for the exercise of authority.

The abandonment of the "right arm/left arm" distinction and the basing of enlisted precedence entirely on rate, rather than a combination of rate and rating, made it difficult to determine who was in charge except in the technical work center. In short, authority was diffused throughout the enlisted force perhaps beyond the organization's needs for authority roles. Attempts to improve petty officer leadership through additional training have not been unqualified successes. Such training without a suitable authority environment cannot achieve institutional goals.

Post-World War II reorganizations which established undifferentiated authority by rate throughout the enlisted force may have been a critical factor in the erosion of petty officer performance. Until that time, there had been a clear if unspoken distinction between petty officer with full military authority and those whose military authority was less widely or less often exercised. In short, the Navy had developed a system analogous to that of the Army and Air Force which distinguished between line and technical or specialist noncommissioned officers, thus focusing military leadership functions while recognizing necessary technical expertise. It is possible that some such system is the element missing in modern naval organization.

NOTES

1. See James F. Downs, Judith Cobart, and Constance Ojile. *Naval Personnel Organization: A Cultural Historical Approach.* Technical Report 0001 AD, August 1982, Reston, VA: Development Research Associates.
2. The terms rate and rating are confusing to those outside the Navy. Rate is used to describe the level of line authority and is synonymous with rank. Rating refers to technical speciality. A nonrated man may have a rating but all rated men have both rate and rating. In very recent times E-1 through E-3 have been designated "rates". Day-to-day usage does not yet reflect this. The official position appears to further erode petty officer status.
3. Enlisted insignia denote both rate and rating. Nonrated people wear short angled stripes in white, red, green or blue to denote their general apprentice field. Some may also wear a rating device to indicate that they are designated strikers. Petty officers wear one, two, or three chevrons designating class, surmounted by an eagle or "crow". The rating device is worn in the angle of the chevrons. Chief petty officers add an arc or "rocker" to their badges, joining the arms of the upper chevrons. Senior chiefs wear a single star above the eagle, and master chiefs two stars. The Master Chief Petty Officer of the Navy wears three stars. He and all command master chiefs replace their former specialty mark with a star. All rating badges are now worn on the left arm.
4. Harrod has recorded the dynamics of rating development from 1865 to 1940: see Frederick S. Harrod, *Manning the New Navy: The Developments of the Modern Naval Enlisted Force 1899–1940* (Westport, CT: Greenwood Press, 1978). For subsequent years see Downs et al, *Naval Personnel Organization*.
5. James E. Valle, *Rocks and Shoals: Order and Discipline in the Old Navy, 1800–1861* (Annapolis, MD: Naval Institute Press, 1980).
6. Peter Karsten, *The Naval Aristocracy* (New York, NY: The Free Press, 1972).
7. *Blue Jackets' Manual*, published irregularly since 1902.
8. The gradual assignment of military authority to left arm rates, particularly those of the engineering divisions, may well have been indirectly influenced by the assumption of line authority by engineering officers who were, in effect, staff officers until they were taken into the line in 1899.
9. James F. Downs, "Environment, Communications and Status Change Aboard an American Aircraft Carrier," *Human Organization 17* (31), 1959.
10. Harrod, *Manning the New Navy*.
11. Downs et al, *Naval Personnel Organization*.

6

From Yeomanettes to WAVES to Women in the U.S. Navy

Patricia J. Thomas

WOMEN IN THE NAVY

Navy women were the first American women to don enlisted military uniforms and apply their skills in other than a nursing role. As the United States prepared to enter World War I, Josephus Daniels, Secretary of the Navy, recognized that since the Naval Reserve Act of 1916 referred solely to "citizens," he could enlist women. The yeoman (F) rating was quickly created to include duties performed by clerks, telephone operators, translators, camouflage designers, and fingerprint experts. Approximately 13,000 young women served with the Navy or Marine Corps between 1917 and 1919. Some even saw duty in France, Puerto Rico, and the Panama Canal Zone.[1] At a time when women were not permitted to vote, the experience must have seemed quite adventurous. In 1925, the loophole in the law was closed by the insertion of "male" into the reserve act, effectively delaying the entry of women into the Navy when World War II broke out. On July 30, 1942, however, the Navy established the WAVES (Women Accepted for Voluntary Emergency Service), which differed in a very significant way from the Army's two-month-old WAAC (Women's Army Auxiliary Corps): Navy women were given full military status whereas Army women were members of an auxiliary.[2] During the height of mobilization, 55% of all uniformed personnel in Navy Department offices and installations in Washington, D.C., were women. All naval aviators trained between 1943 and 1945 received aerial navigation instruction in Link trainers from enlisted women. When peace came in 1945, 94,000 women were serving in the WAVES. While their numbers would drop abruptly and the acronym would pass into history, women were permanently to be members of the U.S. Navy.

GENDER DIFFERENCES IN BACKGROUND
AND CAREER BEHAVIOR

The selection criteria for Navy enlisted women historically have been higher than those for men, although supporting statistics from before 1971 are sketchy. Part of the reason for the difference is due to laws and regulations applied solely to women, and part to the fact that the supply of qualified female applicants exceeds the number accepted for enlistment. Until 1974, women had to have reached the minimum age of twenty-one in order to enlist without the written consent of their parents. Prior to 1983, women, unlike men, had to possess a high school diploma and score high enough on the aptitude battery to be eligible for a technical school. These age and educational factors have been shown to be important in the numerous studies conducted on samples of male personnel.[3] Among enlisted men, for example, low aptitude and educational levels are associated with unauthorized absences (UA) and attrition. Among enlisted women, mental level is not correlated with UA rates,[4] and those who leave the Navy before the expiration of their four-year contract have significantly higher aptitude scores than do those that remain.[5] Moreover, at the U.S. Naval Academy, both aptitude and high school achievement are negatively related to completion of the four-year program for female midshipmen, but not for males.[6] These findings contradict not only those obtained for military men in the same environments but also those obtained for civilians in training programs—suggesting that aspects of the military affect women in a unique way.

During the past decade, the increased reliance on women to make up for shortages of men has led to several Navy studies contrasting the career behaviors of the two genders. Some of these investigations revealed an unexpected degree of similarity between the sexes, while others identified important gender differences. These differences highlight the potential advantages or disadvantages of substituting women for men. On the positive side, women are less apt than men to be involved with the abuse of hard drugs,[7] to engage in behavior leading to a court-martial,[8] and to lose time during duty hours.[9] On the negative side, women account for a disproportionate amount of hospitalization,[10] have lower reenlistment rates than men,[11] and are more frequently referred for psychiatric assessment than men.[12] Obviously, these differences affect the return to investment experienced by the Navy. In the 1981 DoD study of women in the military, life-cycle costs of enlisted women and men were contrasted, and the following conclusions were drawn:

> Comparisons of expenditures for personnel over a 20-year career showed that, within all services, women are slightly less expensive, but the differences are small. . . . Viewed in terms of the return of trained manyears to initial investment,

with the exception of the Navy, females appear to have a lower return to initial investment than males during the first five years of service. (Italics are the author's.)[13]

A cost-effectiveness assessment conducted on all personnel enlisting in 1975 supported the conclusion that Navy women cost less than men during their initial tour of duty.[14] The variables included in the analysis were the cost to the military of dependents (for housing, medical care, and travel), UAs and desertions, medical inpatient care, and recruiting. By enlisting 5,984 women in 1975 rather than an equal number of men, the Navy saved $5,104,352 for these variables.

MOTIVES AND ATTITUDES OF NAVY WOMEN

Motivation for Enlisting, Reenlisting and Leaving the Navy

Why do women join the Navy—a tradition-bound, traditionally male organization that exists for the sole purpose of national defense? Undoubtedly, some women feel that it is adventurous, but the majority of them do not. Yet, even though the Navy makes no effort to recruit women, there are consistently two to three times more women wanting to enlist than can be accepted. Despite popular belief to the contrary, women enlist for the same reasons that men do—to make something of their lives, to acquire new skills, and to travel and meet people.[15]

Do women expect to be employed in the same manner as Navy men? Probably not, for the occupational values of the two genders are different. Women enlisting in 1975 reported that they did not want jobs that focused on printed material or data rather than people, involved physical risk, followed a set routine, or were machinery-oriented. Instead, they were searching for work that they felt would make the world a better place to live in, and they valued intrinsic rewards more than financial ones. Approximately 20% of the almost 1,000 women in the sample, however, subscribed to work values considered nontraditional for their gender.

Why do women leave the Navy before completing their first enlistment? Not for the same reasons nor under the same circumstances that men do, although the numbers are very similar. The survey sample mentioned above, (the 1,000 women who enlisted in 1975) was followed for four years to determine whether women's work behavior differed from men's. A highly significant finding was that, of sample members discharged, 80% of the women were discharged under honorable conditions, compared to 31% of the men.[16] It naturally follows that the reasons for releasing women and men from their enlistment contract must also differ. Forty-one percent of the women who left during the first two years (10% of the sample) were pregnant. Since the Navy permits a woman to have her child and remain in uniform, these women were asked why they requested a discharge. A quarter of the sample stated that they wanted to become full-time mothers, and an additional 20% reported that they felt combining a Navy job and motherhood would be too difficult. Because three out of every four married Navy women have a spouse who is also in the service, the prospect of separation from their husbands also influenced many women to leave. Women being discharged who were not pregnant cited three sources of job dissatisfaction as critical: insufficient training, lack of challenging work, and dislike for the geographic location where assigned. The most frequently mentioned sources of personal dissatisfaction were lack of privacy, regulation of one's life, not being treated with respect, the military lifestyle, and difficulty in remaining feminine. Since the complaints of women and men who remained in the Navy were not solicited, it is difficult to determine how much importance to attach to these factors.

What influences women to reenlist in the Navy or to return to civilian status at the end of their first enlistment? Although proportionately fewer women than men reenlist, their reasons for doing so are the same.[17] Career potential and educational opportunities are the primary incentives for both genders, followed by job satisfaction, security, fringe benefits, and travel. Women and men gave different reasons for not reenlisting, however. Over half of the women cited role or personal stress and better opportunities in the civilian world. The sources of stress for married women were not job-specific but due to separation from husband or children and the difficulties inherent in being in the Navy and simultaneously fulfilling a domestic role. Men, by contrast, tended to leave because of inadequate pay and opportunity.

Frequently, when women's motives for leaving the Navy are discussed, the question of the types of job assignments they held is raised. It is believed that women in the military and civilian sector experience role conflict and become dissatisfied in jobs that are nontraditional for members of their sex, and that this dissatisfaction influences their work behavior in terms of attrition, change of occupation, and retention. The DoD classifies all military jobs into nine categories. Two of these categories, administrative/clerical and medical, are considered to be traditional for women; and the remainder, nontraditional. On the basis of this definition, the research sample of women and men enlisting in the Navy in 1975 was dichotomized according to their job assignment and compared across gender and job type in terms of attrition, satisfaction, advancement, reenlistment, and migration rates. Surprisingly, no significant differences were obtained with the women's sample, but several were found with the men's.[18] That is, women's satisfaction, attrition, advancement, and reenlistment were not related to whether they were working in a traditionally feminine or a traditionally masculine job. However, men in jobs that are traditionally masculine had higher attrition and advancement rates and lower reenlistment rates than did those in traditionally feminine jobs. The major reason for this finding is probably not because of the work itself but, rather, because of where it is performed. The majority of men in their first enlistment who are assigned to traditionally masculine jobs are often on sea duty, where the quality of work life is inferior to that ashore. Very few women in these jobs were serving aboard a ship from 1975 through 1979. Thus, attrition rates were high and reenlistment rates were low among men in sea-going ratings—a trend that enhanced the advancement opportunities of the survivors. Interestingly, job satisfaction did not differ significantly by job type for either gender. Migration from one job to another was so infrequent that meaningful comparisons by job or gender could not be made.

Desire for Equal Treatment

Another question that is often raised when military women are discussed is the degree of equality they want or should be accorded. Many people believe that women want to be protected from the rigors and dangers associated with filling an unrestricted role in the armed forces. If this premise is correct, the present oversupply of female applicants to the Navy would decrease if current laws and regulations enacted to prevent women from being thrust into combat were voided. Thus, surveys are periodically conducted to determine how such a change would impact on (1) the applicant pool, (2) women currently in the military, and (3) military men. Not surprisingly, the results are mixed. As with the Equal Rights Amendment, feelings toward equal responsibility and op-portunity for women in the Navy vary as a function of age, education, and the amount of personal benefit or detriment anticipated to occur.

In December 1977, a nationwide sample of young adults of prime recruiting age was queried about their interest in joining the Navy under the policy then in effect regulating assignments of women—limiting them to shore duty—and under three alternative policies or options: (1) women would be assigned to a wide range of jobs but not to ships or aircraft, (2) women would *have to* serve on some support ships, support aircraft, and more overseas locations, and (3) women and men would be assigned without regard to gender, resulting in equal exposure to combat and equal opportunity for jobs and advancement.[19] The percentages of female respondents interested in joining the Navy under these four conditions were 7.9 (present policy), 11.1. (Option 1), 8.5 (Option 2), and 8.4 (Option 3). Although the assignment policy in 1977 was actually the same as that described in Option 1, 40% more women were interested in enlisting in the Navy when told of the opportunities available to them. If there is ever a need to increase the number of female applicants to the Navy, it is obvious that an informational campaign would be effective. The assignment policy for women today (1985) is somewhere between Options 1 and 2; that is, women may serve aboard noncombatant ships and aircraft, but not many are so assigned. If they all had to serve on such ships, the number of applicants would still be higher than under the typical "no information" condition and the characteristics of the female applicants would be different. To illustrate, women interested in enlisting under the 1977 policy came predominately from the South Atlantic states and indicated that they preferred to work with people rather than machines. However, as the possibilities for a greater variety of jobs and assignments to combatant ships were introduced in the survey questions, half of the original group lost interest. They were replaced by women who tended to come from the Pacific states, were better educated, and were more likely to expect to work full time throughout their lives. The effect upon men's enlistment propensity of changes in policies affecting women was also measured. Under 1977 conditions, 16% of the male sample exhibited interest in enlisting, compared to 20% if gender were no longer a factor in assignment and women assumed an equal risk (Option 3).

In 1977, women already in the Navy were surveyed to determine their attitude toward a gender-free assignment policy.[20] The 380 enlisted women in the sample were dichotomized into those in ratings where women have traditionally been assigned and those in traditionally masculine ratings to investigate any differences in the opinions of the two groups. While a majority of both groups felt that women should be allowed to serve aboard ships, compete with men for command, and perform in any job they are capable of handling, those in traditionally masculine ratings were more contemporary in their orientation than those in traditional ratings. On the critical question of how they would react if *required* to serve at sea, 10% of these enlisted women, regardless of rating, would try to get out of the Navy.

The opinions of women actually serving on sea duty have also been measured. A sample of about 200 nonrated (E-1 through E-3) women and a control group of 1,000 nonrated men assigned to eight of the first ten ships to be gender-integrated were surveyed before they reported aboard ship and after they had been in the crew a year.[21] In completing the statement, "Being assigned to sea duty has made me feel_____", far fewer women than men were neutral. That is, more female sailors serving on their first sea tour evaluated the experience positively than did their male peers (31% versus 26%); also, more women than men were negative (46% versus 32%). Large differences were found between the eight crews in the orientation of their women. In the original survey almost half of these women indicated that sea duty was an assignment they wanted. Of greater importance, there was *no* difference in the opinions of the groups of women being assigned to the eight ships.[22] It seems obvious that experiences intervening between the administrations of the two surveys had significantly affected the feelings of these women toward serving aboard a Navy ship.

DISADVANTAGES TO THE NAVY OF UTILIZING WOMEN

If women of high quality are in plentiful supply and are willing to assume full responsibility as members of the armed forces, why are the services reluctant to accept them? The most compelling argument is that women might render the fighting forces of the United States ineffective. Such an outcome is predicated upon the undeniable facts that women, on the average, possess less physical strength than men and are the sex that becomes pregnant. Adding to the power of these facts are the strongly held beliefs that a gender-integrated military would convey a message of weakness to our enemies and threaten male bonding. Additionally, because the military is androcentric, or geared to men, the changeover to a more heterogeneous force would be expensive and would require coming to grips with problems that are unique to women or have been successfully ignored in the past. These points have merits, some of which are discussed in the following paragraphs.

Biologically Determined Sex Differences

Enduring issues which military managers must confront when attempting to substitute women for men focus on the unarguable differences between the sexes. They include anthropometric (body size and proportions), physiological (functioning of bodily parts), and psychological differences associated with gender. Few would argue with the statement that women tend to be smaller and physically weaker than men but the impact of such differences on the armed forces has not been established. The military avoided coming to grips with the issue for many years by establishing a low ceiling on the number of women in uniform. By keeping the numbers small, the impact on the group of a few "inferior" members was of little consequence. Other ways of coping are to: (1) restrict women's assignments to jobs all women are physically capable of performing; (2) determine the physical requirements of military jobs and adopt a selection procedure that screens people on their physical abilities; and (3) redesign jobs or equipment to be compatible with the female physique. Each of these solutions has been applied to some degree in the Navy.

The Women's Armed Services Integration Act of 1948 restricted enlisted women to 2% of the enlisted male population of each service and women officers to 10% of the enlisted female strength.[23] At that time, there was no reason to believe that women were incapable of performing in virtually all military billets, for indeed, they had worked in many traditionally masculine occupational specialties in World War II. Thus, when the military's personnel requirements skyrocketed during our involvement in Vietnam, Congress repealed this section of the act and the Secretary of each service was allowed to determine the number of women in uniform in that service. Since that time, the fate of women as members of the military has been sensitive to the vagaries of the political climate and the beliefs of those temporarily occupying high military and civilian positions. During the relatively liberal period under President Carter, goals were established for each of the services that were expected to culminate in 233,600 enlisted women in uniform by the end of fiscal year 1986 (12.5% of the force).[24] The early 1980s, however, brought a period of reevaluation, either because of the election of a more conservative government or because of the changes caused by the no-longer-inconsequential numbers of women. All of the services, except the Navy, expressed doubt about the wisdom of meeting the goals, particularly in view of the unknown effect of so many women on mission accomplishment. The Navy reaffirmed its intention to include 45,000 women in its enlisted component—an increase of 157% in just a decade.[25]

After World War II and prior to the mid-1980s, women's assignments were usually restricted to those jobs not involving strength. This practice became less frequent when conscription of men ended and the pressure to provide women equal employment opportunities began to be felt. In 1973, for example, 89% of all Navy enlisted women were concentrated in five occupational fields—health care, administration, communication, supply, and data processing, compared to 84% in 1977 and 75% in 1984, the most recent date for which figures are available.[26]

As women were assigned to jobs in which few of their gender had previously served, problems concerning strength, stamina, and person/equipment mismatch began to emerge. Women in the aviation branch of the Navy, particularly in the ordnance and structural mechanic ratings, were unable to lift the heavier armament or equipment to the heights required. Those working as mess cooks had difficulty in lifting 100-pound sacks of flour and reaching the high shelves on which staples were stored. Women assigned to general detail duties aboard floating drydocks could not control the sand blaster with one hand, carry five-gallon cans of paint up ladders, or erect scaffolding. Supervisors had several options in handling these inadequacies, all of which had drawbacks. If they refrained from assigning women to the physically demanding tasks, men had to shoulder the additional work and would express resentment. If they let women work in pairs, the amount of work accomplished decreased. If they attempted to treat men and women identically, injuries to the women were apt to result. Thus, as the numbers of women in traditionally masculine jobs increased, the problems multiplied. The fact that women were smaller in stature and had less strength than men not only made life difficult for supervisors but had the potential for endangering the lives of others. For example, emergencies aboard ship can require that the wounded be rapidly evacuated up steep ladders or that heavy water-tight doors be secured. Firefighting at sea or ashore involves the use of pumps and hoses weighing over 100 pounds. Although not everyone in the unit is usually required to participate in every emergency, it could be critical if someone "in the right place at the right time" were unable to react appropriately.

The second and most equitable solution to the strength problem is also the most difficult and time consuming; that is, to accurately match people to jobs without regard to gender. This approach requires that all important physical demands of each military job be identified, the anthropometric requirements of each of these tasks be determined, and tests to measure the capability of people to meet these requirements be developed. This problem in the military is complicated by the following factors: (1) the large number of different jobs performed and the variety of tasks within a specialty, (2) the need for people to participate in general activities (firefighting, loading supplies, etc.), and (3) the variability in the physical fitness of those being tested at the entry point. Since 1977, Navy researchers have been engaged in a long-term project to gather the data needed to establish a physical screening procedure for enlisted personnel. To date, they have determined that approximately 75% of all Navy ratings do not involve activities that cannot be performed by most women.[27] The majority of those tasks identified as being muscularly demanding utilize upper body strength, an attribute on which men are decisively superior to women. Women do increase their strength during physical training. Since the same is true for men, however, the differences between the two genders remain large.

The third solution to the problem of physical inferiority is to redesign jobs, tools, or equipment. Military human factors engineers design equipment and systems for men whose size and strength falls within the 5th and 95th centiles; that is to fit 90% of all men. Unfortunately, the size and strength of about one-fourth of all women in the Navy are below those of men at the 5th centile.[28] Jobs are frequently made more manageable by incumbents, however, sometimes in ingenious ways such as breaking down large packages into smaller ones, rolling equipment too heavy to carry on a dolly, and extending pedals beyond the reach of short legs.[29] Tool and equipment redesign are usually expensive, not only in terms of human engineering research but also in replacing hardware that fits the vast majority of those required to use it.

Along with the issues of strength and size, physiological gender differences impinge on the management of women. Some male supervisors originally had difficulty deciding how to treat women suffering from menstrual distress, but this syndrome is rarely viewed as a problem today. Pregnancy, however, remains a management dilemma that is all the more difficult to solve because of the balance that must be achieved between the legitimate needs of the individual and those of the organization. Although pregnant women cannot be placed in an environment or given tasks that could damage or abort the fetus, any restrictions on their assignments must not appear to be punitive or showing favoritism. From management's viewpoint, pregnancy is disruptive because of the personnel transfers that are often involved. If the woman is ashore, her reassignment usually can be accomplished within her department or command; when the woman on sea duty becomes pregnant, however, her billet may be vacant for several months before a replacement arrives.

In addition to the logistical problems, there are emotional overtones associated with pregnancy. Since being pregnant is a sufficient reason for obtaining a discharge, it is looked upon as an easy way of voiding one's military contract—particularly by men, who do not have such a means available. More-over, pregnant women who remain in the Navy are given paid time off for prenatal medical care—even though they may not be ill—and up to six weeks of prepartum and postpartum leave. Thus, those who are so inclined can argue that benefits or advantages are bestowed selectively upon a small group of women. Pregnancy is costly in terms of turnover, lost time, and manage-ment attention required. On balance, however, it is probably no more costly than the unauthorized absences of men.

Restrictions on Utilization

Another major disincentive for using women is that their assignments are restricted. In other words, men may be assigned where needed, while women are limited to shore duty in the United States, some overseas locations, and a handful of ships. On the surface, this ruling would seem to provide considera-ble flexibility and ample opportunity for as many women as would care to affiliate with the Navy. At any one time, however, almost half of all men in the regular Navy are afloat. Since personnel are rotated back to shore duty after a sea tour, the majority of shore billets must be reserved for men. Prior to the modification of Section 6015 in 1978, the maximum number of enlisted women who could be accommodated in the Navy was 30,000. Under the present interpretation of the Federal Code, 45,000 enlisted women can be incorporated into a force of 490,000. Currently, women may be assigned for duty aboard major auxiliaries (destroyer tenders, submarine tenders, repair ships), minor auxiliaries (salvage ships, fleet ocean tugs, submarine rescue ships), research ships (guided missile test ships, deep submergence support ships), oceanographic units, and training aircraft carriers. While not all of such ship types are yet integrated, over 3,000 women are serving at sea. The seven-year plan developed by the Chief of Naval Operations in 1983 allows for 5,000 enlisted women and almost 200 women officers to be assigned for permanent duty afloat by the end of fiscal year 1985. However, since the total afloat force is expected to number 216,000 by 1985, women will make up a bare 2.4% of those on sea duty.

Restrictions to women's assignments also exist in service regulations. Preg-nant women may not serve aboard a ship, nor may a married Navy couple. Women in the Pacific Fleet must go in pairs to nonintegrated ships for training or to repair a piece of equipment. Enlisted women may not be assigned, even temporarily, where bathroom facilities external to the male berthing area are not available. Thus they frequently cannot accompany their divisions on sea trials or maneuvers of even a few days. Obviously these rulings create prob-lems for detailers, commanding officers, male peers, and supervisors. When one woman officer needs a particular type of instruction to become surface-warfare qualified, her commanding officer may have to release another woman to accompany her to a combatant ship. When the maintenance crew of a squadron goes aboard a carrier for a two-week maneuver, up to 40% of the crew might have to stay behind because of their gender. If such maneuvers occur with any frequency, men will be working overtime and spending a considerable amount of time at sea while technically on shore duty. When a woman in a ship informs her command that she is pregnant, she must be assigned to shore duty immediately. When a couple aboard ship announce they have married, one of the pair must be reassigned. Since these problems were nonexistent when only men occupied such billets, the inevitable reaction to the burden of complying with gender-specific regulations is to blame women.

New Problems

A third disadvantage to increasing the proportion of Navy women is the novel problems that must be faced, issues rarely or never addressed with a predominately male force. One such problem is the need for privacy. Boys in our society experience much more physical exposure than girls during their formative years and generally find modesty in their own gender puzzling. Many girls, by contrast, are uncomfortable with nudity. Thus, the influx of women into the Navy required not only the separation of the sexes to the degree protected by the Constitution, but also some concern over how much privacy is reasonable and can be accommodated. These issues reached their zenith when plans were first developed to assign women to ships. Curtains were hung around shower stalls and bunks, and doors were installed inside the heads (restrooms) of the women's berthing area. To prevent men from crying "favoritism," similar changes were made to their quarters.

A novel problem that arose when women were assigned to ships was overt heterosexuality. While strictures against homosexuality have existed for many years, there was no need to control encounters between members of the opposite sex. As plans for integrating ships became public, concerns about the effect of male/female relationships on "good order and discipline" were voiced. Those expressing reservations mentioned rivalries among men, the inability of a superior to supervise an attractive subordinate objectively, and the demoralizing effect upon the Navy wife. Each commanding officer established his own policy regulating what became known as "public displays of affection." In recognition of the legitimate concern of the Navy wife, meetings were held to allay their fears. These meetings were poorly attended, suggesting that such fears were highly overblown. As a matter of fact, a survey of over 400 Navy wives revealed that they were no more opposed to their husband's serving aboard a ship with women than they were to his serving ashore with women in a location where the family could not accompany him.[30] Many Navy women viewed these concerns with amusement. After an orientation, I overheard one confide in another, "I can't understand why any woman would think I'd be interested in her fat little old chief when there are all these guys my own age around." The concern has persisted, however, but in retrospect there is now evidence that assignment to an integrated ship may place more stress on a woman's marriage than on a man's.[31] While the proportions are small, 20% of the men and 26% of the women in eight of the first ten ships to be integrated stated that their assignment had created problems with their spouse or girl/boyfriend. This difference was statistically significant.

Logistical problems, while usually temporary, presented management with additional reasons to regret the transition to a gender-integrated force. Government quarters had to be found for unmarried enlisted women (women officers generally live in civilian housing). In some cases, existing bachelor quarters could be modified by dedicating one floor or wing to women. In other locations, whole buildings were designated or constructed for female occupancy. The former arrangement appeared to work more smoothly and, surprisingly, provide women with greater security than the latter. When women were housed alone, particularly on a base where transient personnel are numerous, the building became a focal point for male sailors. Women sometimes found they had to run a gauntlet of vocal males to reach the entry hall and needed escorts after dark.

Availability and appropriateness of uniforms created frustration for management, wearers, and suppliers alike. Enlisted women's work uniforms proved to be impractical aboard ship and in an industrial environment. The fabric was not sturdy and required ironing and the shoes were flimsy and a hazard. Moreover, no "official" dress blue slack existed to meet the needs of women on watch or standing inspection aboard ship.[32] When the regulation requiring the discharge of pregnant women was voided, maternity uniforms had to be designed. The resistance to the adoption of such a uniform (by which, implicit approval was given to pregnancy in the Navy) was soon overcome because of the confusion caused by women in civilian clothes.

In addition to the provision of quarters and uniforms, barbers had to be trained to cut women's hair, low calorie foods needed to be added to menus, and washer/dryer combinations purchased to handle lingerie that would have been shredded by the Navy laundry. While this list is far from exhaustive, the accompanying impact is obvious. In the opinion of many, such changes cost money that could have been better spent and required the attention of people who would have been otherwise (better) employed.

One final concomitant to the increase in proportions of women in the Navy should be discussed. It is the emergence of family issues that had been ignored for decades. Women are not unique in having marital or parental roles, but they experience more role conflict than men when they attempt to combine the realms of work and family. In our society, the female partner usually has the primary responsibility for the care and welfare of children, even though she may be fully employed. Working women also are expected to defer to the needs and aspirations of husbands when their careers conflict. Although these "truths" are being questioned and exceptions exist, those who fail to conform to society's expectations often suffer. Thus, as the number of women in the military grew, so did the need to accommodate the natural desire of couples to be assigned in the same geographical area and to have child care facilities provided on military bases. Such changes benefit men as much as women. Every military couple has one male member, and in terms of sheer numbers there are more male parents in the Navy than female parents. Such arguments ring hollow in the ears of policymakers, however, because if there were only a few women in uniform, the problem of co-locating military couples would be manageable and child care would never have become a concern of the Navy.

DIFFICULTY OF FUNCTIONING
IN NAVY ENVIRONMENT

Most predominately male organizations contain a cadre of homosocial members—men who prefer the company of other men. If accused of misogyny, such men would protest that they love women—and they probably do in that other part of their lives that is divorced from work. In the male organizational setting, however, they follow customs and behaviors that exclude women. These behaviors, which seem to be a reaction against the moralizing influence of the significant females in men's lives (mothers, teachers, wives), may include use of excessive profanity, crude sexual joking, hard drinking, participation in vigorous sports, and even condonation of extralegal, extramarital pursuits. When women gain entrance into predominantly male organizations, such behaviors may increase. This phenomenon has been called "boundary heightening" by Rosabeth Kantor, who saw it as an exaggeration of the common male bond to emphasize to women that they are outsiders.[33]

Women in the military are required to function in an androcentric environment to a greater degree than women in any other traditionally masculine setting (with the possible exception of police or fire departments). Because the armed forces continue to view themselves as populated by male personnel, women must adapt to the military rather than expect the military to adapt to a gender-integrated force. Because so many fail to accept that women and men differ in other than the obvious physiological, anthropometric ways, a very small group is saddled with an unreasonable burden—a burden that is often cavalierly dismissed with the attitude of, "If you can't stand the heat, get out of the kitchen." The price women pay in personal terms is rarely made public because of the emphasis in the military on being team-oriented.

The U.S. Naval Academy and auxiliary ships are two recently integrated Navy environments with a long tradition of exclusive male participation, and they exemplify these difficulties. Incidents occurring at and attitudinal data collected from these environments attest to the existence of homosociality, boundary heightening, and the necessity for women to adjust to the situation rather than change it. While the solution to the last problem would seem to be within the scope of management, the backlash from men has often caused delay and second thoughts. At the Academy, for example, any change in a tradition or standard was viewed as evidence of deterioration and blamed on gender integration even when the impetus for change was unrelated to women.

In some respects, ships are an even more difficult milieu to integrate than the USNA. Naval lore as presented in fiction, song, and documentary is strongly masculine and predates the founding of our nation. Moreover, the completely circumscribed physical environment aboard a ship at sea has led to the development of a unique lifestyle affecting personal space, language, status, recreation, and even behavior when temporarily ashore. Some of the appeal of the Navy, for at least a portion of its members, is the periodic escape to sea from certain responsibilities and all feminine influence. Nevertheless, pragmatism dictated that women be assigned to ships if they were to relieve the Navy's personnel shortage.

During the first year of integration (1978–1979), 396 enlisted women and 53 officers reported for duty aboard ten navy noncombatant ships. The number in each case, ranging from about 60 to 100, was determined by the size of the berthing compartment that had been modified for female habitation. The ratio of women to men ranged from a low of 8% on one of the larger ships and a high of 22% on a smaller one. As part of an evaluation effort, research was undertaken to describe and interpret the integration process from the perspective of those involved.[34] Surveys were developed and administered to the ships' crews before the women reported aboard and from one to two years afterwards. In addition, naval reservists were assigned to the ships for two-week periods to act as participant/observers. Analysis of the preintegration form of the Navy in Transition Survey, responded to by almost 2,000 men and over 350 women, yielded the following results.

1. Men in departments having parallels ashore where Navy women have traditionally worked (i.e., medical, dental, supply, administration) expressed the most favorable attitudes toward having women in the crew. Men in aviation, weapons, and engineering departments, where the work is physically strenuous and experience with female coworkers more rare, expressed the most opposition to gender integration.

2. Male attitudes differed significantly between the various pay grades. Nonrated men (E-1 through E-3) anticipated preferential treatment of women, particularly in assignment to jobs and disciplinary matters. Yet, more than any other group, they felt they would like having women in the crew. Chief petty officers and commissioned officers expected that women would have very little impact on the ship and crew but regretted the demise of the exclusively male environment at sea.

3. The crews of the ships held significantly different opinions about integration. Women being assigned to these ships held very similar opinions.

The results of the postintegration survey, administered to almost 5,000 officer and enlisted personnel, highlighted differences between groups with respect to attitudes toward and experiences in a mixed-gender ship.[35] Some of these differences represented a solidification of earlier opinions. Men in the departments and ships that anticipated adverse consequences were the least positive of any groups afterwards. Their attitudes, which may have been vocalized or manifested in behavioral ways, seem to have affected the adjustment and morale of the women with whom they worked. While no differences had been found in the predispositions of the women prior to their reporting to the ships, a significant difference existed one to two years after integration. Women assigned to the ship and the department with the largest majority of pessimistic men reported more problems and dissatisfaction than did any other women.

During their initial year aboard the ships, the majority of women indicated that they were experiencing problems with the lack of privacy (87%), boredom (60%), men's behavior toward women (56%), tasks requiring physical strength (54%), profanity (54%), women's behavior toward men (52%), and having to prove themselves (51%). Only the first two issues were cited as sources of difficulty by a majority of men on their first sea tour. The women who made the adjustment to sea duty most easily were single, had been in the Navy ten or more years, were not working in the aviation or engineering departments aboard ship, and had participated in a good workshop preparing them for the experience.

FUTURE DIRECTIONS

The number of women in the Navy probably will increase, even after the theoretical limit has been reached. The young males available for recruiting through the year 2000 have already been born and each year for the next ten years fewer and fewer will reach the age of seventeen. By the mid-1990s, the decline will bottom out at 23% below the pool of 1979. It is doubtful whether the number of births will ever again rise to previous levels. Coincident with the decrease in recruitable males is the increase in the number of people needed. A 600-ship Navy requires 620,000 personnel to operate it, in contrast to the 1982 force of 560,000. Obviously, women are not the only answer to the problems of personnel shortfalls. Other options are being investigated, but women appear to be the least expensive plentiful human resource available to the Navy.

There is a catch to increasing the number of women—Catch 6015, as it is known. Many believe that only repeal or reinterpretation of Title 10 U.S.C., Section 6015 can open more billets to women after the maximum of 45,000 is reached in 1985.[36] After all these years, one might wonder what circumstances are likely to cause this to occur. People at the top of the organization who believe that change is in the best interest of the Navy could support repeal of the statute or realize the same outcome by fiat. If a buildup of forces should occur in response to a national threat, Navy management would want the flexibility of assigning women wherever they were needed and might choose this course. Another impetus for change could come from the women themselves. United States District Judge John L. Sirica ruled in 1978 that Title 10, Section 6015 is unconstitutional. If women were to file suit to force compliance with that decision, all barriers to their serving on ships would be apt to fall.

However, the future will also include a labor market in which women are more competitive and sought after than ever before. Technological change is already affecting the civilian work force by placing less reliance on strength and stamina factors. Increased use of robotics eliminates many heavy production jobs and creates a need for those with different skills, particularly skills associated with the electronics industry. Today women outnumber men in the assembly of electronic equipment and probably will continue to do so. Moreover, as the demand for their services translates into better wages, the armed forces will lose an attraction for women—compensation equal to that of men.

A change occurring along with the anticipated increase in jobs for women is a diminished supply. While a great deal of discussion has centered on the decline in the number of young men available to the military, it is seldom recognized that the number of women is also declining. The civilian labor force will be able to adjust to the decrease in the number of people entering it by encouraging older workers to remain employed longer, reducing the number of jobs through automation, and making greater use of foreign labor. The military force, however, is dependent upon a constant input of 17-to-21-year-olds, the majority of whom serve only four years. Retention of more of these individuals for a second enlistment would be difficult when civilian employment is very high. Efforts to delay the retirement of those who have served twenty years would meet with great resistance. Enlisting foreign nationals, with the exception of Filipinos, is prohibited by law. Although women have always come forward in the past, the future may be an era in which they are no longer willing to be the military's resource in time of need.

NOTES

1. Captain Joy Bright Hancock, USN (ret) served as a yeoman (F), was a civilian employee at the Bureau of Aeronautics (Navy Department) for many years between World Wars I and II, became one of the first women commissioned as an officer in the WAVES in 1942, and culminated her career as Assistant Chief of Naval Personnel for Women (1946-1953). Her book is an insightful account of

these years. See Joy Bright Hancock, *Lady in the Navy, a Personal Reminiscence* (Annapolis: Naval Institute Press, 1972).

2. Public Law 110, which gave the Army 90 days to dissolve the Women's Army Auxiliary Corps and enlist or commission women into the Women's Army Corps, was signed by the President on 1 July 1943. For a description of the debate over granting women membership *in* the Army, versus serving *with* the Army, see Mattie E. Treadwell, *U.S. Army in World War II: Special Studies—The Women's Army Corps* (Washington, DC: Office of the Chief of Military History, Department of the Army, 1954):pp. 95–99, 113–121.

3. See, for example, John A. Plag and Jerry M. Goffman, "The Prediction of Four Year Military Effectiveness from Characteristics of Naval Recruits," *Military Medicine 131* (August 1966):720–735; John A. Plag, *A Decade of Research in the Prediction of Naval Effectiveness*, Report No. 70-21 (San Diego: Navy Neuropsychiatric Research Unit, 1971); or Robert F. Lockman, *Chances of Surviving the First Year of Service*, Study 1068 (Arlington: Center for Naval Analyses, 1975).

4. Anne Hoiberg and Patricia J. Thomas, "The Economics of Sex Integration: An Update of Binkin and Bach," *Defense Management Journal 18* (Second Quarter 1982):18–25.

5. Patricia J. Thomas, *Factors Influencing First-term Reenlistment of Women and Men*, Special Report 80-21 (San Diego: Navy Personnel Research and Development Center, 1980).

6. Idel Neumann and Norman M. Abrahams, *Validation of Naval Academy Selection Procedures for Female Midshipmen*, Technical Report 82-54 (San Diego: Navy Personnel Research and Development Center, 1982).

7. Marsha Olson and Patricia J. Thomas, *Preenlistment Drug Experiences of Navy Women and Men*, Technical Report 78-35 (San Diego: Navy Personnel Research and Development Center, 1978).

8. Susan W. Conway, *Effects of Race and Gender on Rates of Court-Martial*, Special Report 83-20 (San Diego: Navy Personnel Research and Development Center, 1983).

9. Marsha S. Olson and Susan S. Stumpf, *Pregnancy in the Navy: Impact on Absenteeism, Attrition and Workgroup Morale*, Technical Report 78-35 (San Diego: Navy Personnel Research and Development Center, 1978).

10. Anne Hoiberg, "Sex and Occupational Differences in Hospitalization Rates Among Navy Enlisted Personnel," *Journal of Occupational Medicine 22* (October 1980):685–690.

11. Office of the Assistant Secretary of Defense, *Background Review: Women in the Military* (Washington, DC: Manpower, Reserve Affairs and Logistics, 1981).

12. Marc A. Schuckit and E.K. Eric Gunderson, "Psychiatric Incidence Rates for Navy Women: Implications for an All Volunteer Force," *Military Medicine 139* (July 1974):534–436.

13. Office of the Assistant Secretary of Defense, *Background Review*, p. 60.

14. Hoiberg and Thomas, "The Economics of Sex Integration."

15. The popular myth is that women join the military to get away from the small towns in which they are living and the influence of their families. Few females or males enlist for these reasons. See Patricia J. Thomas and Kathleen P. Durning, "The Young Navy Woman: Her Work and Role Orientation," *Youth and Society 10* (December 1978): 135–158.

16. Patricia J. Thomas, "Attrition Among Navy Enlisted Women," *Defense Management Journal 16* (Second Quarter 1980):43–49.

17. Thomas, *Factors Influencing*.

18. Patricia J. Thomas, Marilyn J. Monda, Shelley H. Mills, and Julie A. Mathis, *Navy Women in Traditional and Nontraditional Jobs: A Comparison of Satisfaction, Attrition, and Reenlistment*, Technical Report 82-50 (San Diego: Navy Personnel Research and Development Center, 1982).
19. Jules I. Borack, *Intentions of Women (18-25 Years Old) to Join the Military: Results of a National Survey*, Technical Report 78-34 (San Diego: Navy Personnel Research and Development Center, 1978).
20. Patricia J. Thomas and Kathleen P. Durning, *Role Affiliation and Attitudes of Navy Wives*, Technical Report 80-10 (San Diego: Navy Personnel Research and Development Center, 1980).
21. Patricia J. Thomas and Carol S. Greebler, *Men and Women in Ships: Attitudes of Crews One to Two Years After Integration*, Technical Report 84-6. (San Diego: Navy Personnel Research and Development Center, 1984).
22. Carol S. Greebler, Patricia J. Thomas and Judy D. Kuczynski, *Men and Women in Ships: Preconceptions of the Crews*, Technical Report 82-57 (San Diego: Navy Personnel Research and Development Center, 1982).
23. This act did not apply to women in the Nurse Corps.
24. Office of the Assistant Secretary of Defense, *Background Review*.
25. Ibid.
26. Department of the Navy, *Navy Military Personnel Statistics* (Washington, DC: Naval Military Personnel Command, 1973, 1977, and 1982).
27. David W. Robertson, *Development of an Occupational Strength Test Battery (STB)*, Technical Report 82-42 (San Diego: Navy Personnel Research and Development Center, 1982).
28. Ross L. Pepper and Mark D. Phillips, *Naval Architectural Research for Women Aboard Ship*, Technical Report 658 (San Diego: Naval Ocean Systems Center, 1981).
29. One would think that the adaptations made by foreign military personnel of small stature (Southeast Asians, Iranians, etc.) to the American equipment purchased by their governments would be applicable to this issue. When the author has raised this possibility as worthy of investigation, it has been dismissed as being inappropriate because makeshift conversions are "unsafe" and small men are stronger than the average military woman.
30. Thomas and Durning, *Role Affiliation*.
31. Thomas and Greebler, *Men and Women in Ships: Attitudes*.
32. Commanding Officer, USS SANCTUARY, *Report on the Evaluation of the Assignment of Women to the USS SANCTUARY (AH-7)* (Letter to the Chief of Naval Personnel of 19 November 1973).
33. Rosabeth M. Kanter, "Some Effects of Proportions on Group Life: Skewed Sex Ratios and Responses to Token Women," *American Journal of Sociology 82,5* (March–April 1975): 965–990.
34. Greebler, Thomas, and Kuczynski, *Men and Women in Ships: Preconceptions*.
35. Thomas and Greebler, *Men and Women in Ships: Attitudes*.
36. According to some analysts, the Navy used very conservative estimates in arriving at its figures. They suggested that 100,000 billets could be filled by female sailors. See Martin Binkin and Shirley J. Bach, *Women and the Military* (Washington: The Brookings Institution, 1977), pp. 106–107.

7

The View From the Top: Oral Histories of Chief Master Sergeants of the Air Force

Jacob Neufeld and James C. Hasdorff

THE MOST SENIOR NCOs

Primarily because of prodding by Congressman R. Mendel Rivers, who insisted that each of the military services have a top ranking noncommissioned officer (NCO) at the highest possible level, the position of Chief Master Sergeant of the Air Force (CMSAF) was established in 1967. Paul W. Airey became the first incumbent on April 3, 1967. The chief master sergeant is "the senior enlisted member of the U.S. Air Force." His responsibilities and tenure are entirely at the discretion of the Air Force Chief of Staff, a four-star general.

The perspectives of the chief master sergeants of the Air Force provide in microcosm a unique portrait of enlisted affairs. As principal spokesmen for this military segment, their views are valuable not only from the standpoint of their own personal experiences but also because they were in a position to work toward improving the lot of their fellow enlisted men and women. The reminiscences of these former CMSAF are especially poignant because, through the medium of oral history, they are presented with a richness, color, and candor that is unique to the tape-recorded interview. All six of the former ranking NCOs were interviewed by members of the USAF History Program—the authors, Hugh N. Ahmann and Captain Mark C. Cleary. The results of the interviews form the primary basis of this chapter.

THE EARLY YEARS

Of the six former chief master sergeants of the Air Force considered in this study, three served on active duty during World War II. Paul W. Airey, the first CMSAF, enlisted in the Army Air Corps in November 1942 and flew combat as a B-24 radio operator-aerial gunner while based in North Africa and Italy. During his twenty-eighth mission over Vienna, Austria, in July 1944, Airey's B-24 was shot down by anti-aircraft fire and he was incarcerated in Stalagluft 4 for the remainder of the European conflict.[1] Donald L. Harlow, the second CMSAF, is also a World War II veteran. He entered military service in August 1942 and served as an instructor in the Aircraft Armament Ground School and later in the personnel career field. Unlike Airey, who served continuously until his retirement in 1970, Harlow left active duty in February 1946 and remained in the Air Force Reserve until his recall during the Korean War in August 1950.[2] Richard D. Kisling entered the Army in July 1944. He saw combat with the Third Infantry Division in the Spring of 1945 and earned a battle star in the southern Germany–Austria campaign. After the war Kisling worked as a clerk in divisional headquarters G-2 section where he was involved with the repatriation of displaced persons.[3]

Thomas N. Barnes, the fourth, Robert D. Gaylor, the fifth, and James M. McCoy, the sixth CMSAF, all entered the Air Force prior to or during the Korean conflict. Barnes, the only black who has served as CMSAF, entered the service in April 1949 and received basic training in one of the Air Force's last segregated units. Of the five individuals, Barnes is also the only one to have served in Korea during the war. He was based in Japan with the Fourth Troop Carrier Wing and performed as both a flight engineer and a hydraulic specialist there, and in Korea on a temporary duty basis.[4] Gaylor entered the Air Force in September 1948 and was assigned to the security police field,[5] while McCoy, who entered the service in January 1951, initially served as a radar operator and instructor with the Air Defense Command.[6]

Race Relations

Barnes's reflections reveal that the segregated situation he encountered at Lackland Air Force Base (AFB), Texas, left an indelible impression on him. After departing his native Pennsylvania, Barnes befriended several white recruits while the group travelled to San Antonio for basic training:

> But then I got the shock of my life, I guess, at that point in arriving at San Antonio, being picked up from the train station and trucked out to Lackland, and ran into a segregated basic training situation. Today, when I talk about that, I find many people look very strangely and say, 'Well, I never knew the Air Force was like that.' But it was. I was one of the last flights in that year that experienced a complete and total segregation of basic training. So the friends I had gone with I lost.[7]

Gaylor, who had undergone basic training some eight months before Barnes, also commented on the segregated conditions at Lackland. He noted that a training flight of blacks "would catch everyone's attention," as they marched "much better than we did" with their impressive cadence and strut.

Gaylor had never questioned why they were not integrated. He regarded it simply as "a way of life, you accepted it, you took it for granted." Then, in mid-1949, while at his first duty station at Waco, Texas, Gaylor recalled that a rumor began to spread that the blacks were going to be moved in with the whites. Another rumor had it that "if anyone felt because of their upbringing that they could not live with a black person, all they had to do was to go to the orderly room and ask to be discharged." The second rumor proved false and short-lived for Gaylor's commander soon announced that integration would indeed take place. "Anyone who cannot live with blacks, or does not attempt to get along with them, will be court-martialed and severely punished," was the edict.[8]

After integration was initiated in 1949 Gaylor saw a degree of tension on the part of both blacks and whites. "There was an adjustment, a feeling-out, a getting-acquainted-with period." Suddenly, Gaylor found that many sounds and sights began to change in the barracks. To the music of Tommy Dorsey and Hank Snow were added the strains of Dinah Washington and Count Basie, and the musical clash readily lent itself to some potentially volatile situations.[9]

Gaylor felt that this had been the start of his education in the ways of race relations, since he had seen blacks only from afar before the experience at Waco. For the most part, he found that blacks were a decent group of people to live and work with; and he realized that it was a historically momentous period in which he played a small part. Gaylor believes that this early education helped him through the years in working out racial problems. This was especially true during the 1970s when the Air Force "really began to address . . . and talk openly about some of the racial differences."[10]

Although integration had become an accomplished fact, Barnes found that many racial problems persisted. After completing technical school, his greatest aspiration was to become a flight engineer. But it was there that he ran into a "blockage of unwillingness . . . based purely on race." There were no black crewmembers in the organization, and no effort was being made to change the situation. No opportunity existed to return to the United States for schooling, and only a slight chance existed to acquire this skill through on-the-job training. Barnes, however, regarded this as a challenge and he determined more than ever to become a flight engineer.[11]

The first real opportunity presented itself when Barnes assisted a "rough, gruff" crew chief in changing an actuating cylinder on a C-54 aircraft. It was a difficult and time-critical task. Barnes not only worked through the night, but he also employed an ingenious shortcut to expedite matters. The crew chief appreciated his extra efforts in getting the plane into commission, and this episode resulted in the two men becoming fast friends. It was through this friendship that Barnes got the opportunity to fly during his off-duty time. By observing the crew chief and the other specialists on board—electricians, mechanics, and propeller specialist—Barnes learned the basics of being a flight engineer. In his words, "I flew and I worked, and I slept when I could, literally."[12]

Unfortunately, learning the job was not the only obstacle that the budding flight engineer was to face. He still required formal certification which included a check ride with an engineering officer. Following a period of heart-breaking refusals, a happenstance event occurred when all of the unit's flight engineers were engaged in "mission essential duties," and Barnes was called to stand in for a test flight. The officer with whom he flew had refused to certify him previously, and Barnes noted that

> here is where he and I came to grips in that airplane on a test flight, getting it ready to put into a mission lineup. . . . Often in the face of [doing] things for the country . . . come some other things. It came [about] that realization in the air, doing engine featherings, doing retractions, doing some free falls, doing stalls, where his dependence upon me doing what I should have done made the safety of that flight what it was. . . . There grew an interdependence in that situation. We got on the ground; he looked me straight in the eye, and he said, "I had no intent for your certification, but after today's workout up there, I see no way to deny that." And he pinned the certification for my flight engineer status on.[13]

Living and Working Conditions

While he had not confronted the same circumstances as Barnes, Gaylor vividly recalled his first assignment at Waco AFB. After arriving and signing in, he reported to a corporal for a career field assignment. Much to his chagrin the only options available were the fire department, food service, or the military police. Gaylor reluctantly opted for the military police field and reported to the base provost marshal. His "first official performance as a cop" consisted of walking a tour around the finance building from one to five o'clock on Christmas morning. On top of everything else, it was a bitterly cold day and he thought himself to be "the most lonely, homesick, frustrated young man, asking, 'How did I get into all this?' " However, soon after this experience Gaylor volunteered to serve as a gate guard. This assignment greatly improved his outlook, and he earned a reputation as "the friendly gate guard" which stood him well at promotion time.[14]

Because of his harrowing experience during basic training at Lackland AFB during the frigid winter of 1951, McCoy later sought to enter the training field. The Korean War brought an influx of thousands into the facility and the newly arrived trainees were crowded into tents. When a severe ice storm struck the San Antonio area, the improper shelter and clothing provided the new recruits resulted in a tremendous outbreak of sickness and an eventual congressional investigation. As a result of what he had experienced and witnessed, McCoy decided "to make sure that what happened to me didn't happen to anybody else." He did not get his wish initially—he was shuttled off to Keesler AFB, Mississippi, to become a radar operator. But within six years he found himself a technical sergeant supervising training instructors at Lackland. By the time McCoy arrived there, he found "a lot more organization in basic training" than there had been during his initial stay in 1951.[15]

With regard to living facilities for single airmen, all of the former chief master sergeants of the Air Force encountered nearly the same situation with the typical open-bay barracks and communal baths and latrines. Particularly in the 1950s, however, the Air Force made a special effort to improve living facilities for its enlisted force. As separate rooms began to replace the open bays, Gaylor noted:

> All I'd ever lived in was open-bay barracks, thirty men to a room, no privacy. You knew everything that everybody owned, said, and did. Lights on all night. Noises that you learned to live with. Your buddy borrowing your freshly laundered shirt to go on a date while you were in the shower. You know, the open-bay was a lifestyle that, unless someone has lived it, could never appreciate it. As a matter of fact, believe it or not, initially I missed it. When they put us in rooms, two to a room, I was lost. I said, 'Where are my buddies?' I'd go out into the hall looking for someone to talk to. I couldn't imagine this confinement. I was used to four years of living in community lifestyle. And now we had locked lockers, a sink in our room. I just couldn't imagine this luxury.[16]

Most single enlisted airmen appreciated the physical improvements, but a seemingly more important matter to them was the perception that they were subjected to inspections and additional duties that their married brethren were often able to avoid. Airey agreed that this was an irritant with single airmen, that married personnel frequently did not have to stand inspection and "got away from a lot of the so-called nitpicking things."[17]

Recreational opportunities appeared to vary from one base to another. The older, established installations, quite naturally, had better facilities—with gymnasiums, tennis courts, and swimming pools—than the newly opened bases such as Laredo AFB, Texas. When Gaylor arrived at Laredo in March 1952 he found no living or dining facility and nothing in the way of onbase recreation. Eventually, the living and recreational facilities were built, but Gaylor noted that for black enlisted men the base afforded them their only opportunities for social activity through sports. Blacks had no social opportunities in the city of Laredo and had to go across the border to the "boys' town" section of Nuevo Laredo.[18]

Although racial matters were a major issue, there were other problem areas as well. One of these was the practice of promotions via filling a unit vacancy. This offered opportunities for abuse. Kisling recalled an episode in which a colonel wanted to promote a certain technical sergeant to master. First the colonel asked Kisling, who was the first sergeant, to accept another position—thereby creating the desired "vacancy." Then, in relatively short order, the colonel's candidate was nominated and approved as first sergeant. To the colonel's chagrin, at the time of promotion his new first sergeant was in jail charged with drunk driving. Unit-vacancy promotions ended in 1953. Efforts to improve the system led to the restriction of promotions to certain grades, first to the major commands and then to centralized Air Force-wide management. But these "reforms" led to closed selection boards and frozen career fields.[19]

CHANGING TIMES: THE 1960s AND 1970s
Promotion Policy

By the 1960s the Air Force was receiving numerous complaints from its enlisted ranks concerning its promotion system. When he became CMSAF in 1967, Airey encountered this issue at every installation he visited.[20] Promotions were frozen in certain "softcore" career fields, such as food service and transportation. Thus, individuals might be in the same grade for twelve years or more without a chance for promotion.[21] The practice was to promote in career fields with vacancies in the pay grade concerned. If there were no vacancies, or if a surplus existed, no promotions were made. Consequently, people in career fields with the greatest number of turnovers received the most promotions, while those in the most stable fields received the fewest. In this way the Air Force used promotion as a means of retention.

That it did not work was evident from the reenlistment statistics. In January 1966 first-term-airmen retention was the lowest it had been in twelve years. Although some tried to blame the unpopularity of the Vietnam War for the decline, most acknowledged that a combination of factors—low military pay, remote duty assignments, better opportunities in the civilian sector—turned the airmen away. But the poor promotion system was the major culprit. In the 1967–1968 period, when no promotion opportunities existed for the lower grade airmen, the "headquarters solution" was to redesignate the airman position to sergeant. Kisling regarded this as a mistaken policy in that the new designation did nothing to change the nature of the airman's job.[22]

Compounding the problem was the existence of "special" promotion systems, such as the Strategic Air Command's "exceptionally well qualified" or EWQ promotion category. This provided SAC with more than an equitable share of enlisted ranks. Airmen also looked enviously at the Army—which, because it had a higher turnover rate than the Air Force, offered more promotions; and which, unlike the Air Force, had kept the warrant officer program. The Army was able to lure away senior Air Force enlisted men by offering to make them warrant officers.[23] This was especially true in the Air Force's security and personnel fields, where little opportunity for promotion existed.

As a result of the Air Force's promotion policy, Congressman L. Mendel Rivers (D-S.C.), chairman of the House Armed Services Committee, received between 15,000 and 20,000 letters each year. Indeed, the pressure for change came from Congress, as Airey noted that Air Force Personnel did not face up to the problem until it was forced into it.[24] In October 1967 Rivers's committee called the chief master sergeants of the military services to testify. The committee severely criticized the Air Force's promotion policy.

One of the major reforms in this area was the establishment of a new Weighted Airman Promotion System (WAPS). It was devised by a group of "pretty smart people," including two colonels and chief master sergeant; as CMSAF, Airey "had a certain basic input." All of the former chief master sergeants of the Air Force were unanimous in lauding the new system. One called it "by far the fairest, best, most equitable system of any of the armed forces for the enlisted man."[25] Likewise, others described it as "the best promotion system ever devised, without question," "probably the most well understood promotion system that we have today," and "the best system we have ever come up with."[26] Barnes called WAPS very successful because "it places the burden of responsibility directly on the shoulders of the individual, the necessity to prepare for the testing," and he added that in all but a few cases the weighted factors are "directly at the control of the individual."[27] Undoubtedly WAPS has been fully accepted by the enlisted force in the light of both Airey's and Harlow's comments that instead of the previous thousands of letters received annually by Congress, "They very seldom get any."[28]

Drug Abuse

Drug abuse was still another tough problem that the Air Force faced. Like the other military services, the Air Force refused at first to acknowledge the problem. Officially, drugs were regarded as a "civilian problem" and the Air Force would not tolerate anyone who was even remotely connected with drug use. This position soon proved unrealistic as evidenced by the fact that there were not reliable tests to measure the extent of the problem. Eventually, the drug problem was attacked through drug rehabilitation centers at the local level. Kisling credits the Air Force with the best handling of the matter among the military services. A "typical" program would last about six weeks and might employ the help of medical personnel, psychologists, and enlisted people.[29]

Both drug and alcohol abuse were serious issues with which senior enlisted advisors had to contend. Gaylor, while serving as the senior enlisted advisor to the United States Air Forces in Europe (USAFE), traveled to various bases in the company of a man named Cal Espinoza. Espinoza, a former convict and drug user, proved extremely effective in getting across the message about the dangers of alcohol and drug abuse to young, impressionable airmen. Gaylor felt that Espinoza was indispensable in this regard and credits General Jones, the USAFE Commander, with the foresight of having hired this man:

He [Espinoza] stood up on the stage with a hand mike, no training aids, and really told it like it was in gutter language, right off the street, four-letter words, prison talk, and really made an impression on those airmen. It opened their eyes and their mouths, 'Wow!' you know, 'this guy is telling it like it is.'[30]

Race Relations in the 1970s

The frustrations experienced by black airmen at Laredo AFB reached a boiling point in the early 1970s when a number of them barricaded themselves inside a dining hall and refused to leave until their grievances had been redressed. Barnes, who was the senior enlisted advisor for the Air Training Command at that time, noted that the problem affected primarily single black airmen who attempted to patronize local business establishments. Invariably, a policeman would appear whenever a group of young blacks congregated. The police stood by until the blacks left the premises. Barnes remarked that this was "kind of depressing when you are going to eat with some guy standing around you with a gun and a stick." It was always readily evident, he added, that the policeman appeared after they got there "because the management called him."[31] This type of harassment was not experienced by black families:

> Where there was, say, a little older guy, maybe with a wife, he posed no threat. He walked in with a wife and two kids and he ate. Then when the question got asked, 'Do you have any problem in town?' 'No. I go to eat at such and such place. I never have any.' But there is that difference, you see. This is the kind of guy that gets identified by younger blacks, or more militant ones, as an Uncle Tom.[32]

Because the base authorities would not act on this kind of willful treatment, the black airmen occupied the base dining hall, as Barnes said, "not with the intent to hurt anyone, but to make a point.[33]

When the situation at the dining facility reached an impasse, Barnes was asked by the Air Training Command staff to go to Laredo and attempt to talk with the militants. After he arrived, Barnes observed that the situation had deteriorated further. The blacks inside learned that communications had been cut off and that they would be unable to air their grievances with military or political officials. The occupants also believed that an armed force was positioned outside and this "had frightened them to death to come out."[34]

After arriving on the scene, Barnes had the good fortune of being recognized by one of the militants and allowed to enter the dining hall through a window. Barnes encountered an angry and frightened group, but one that was neither armed nor bent on destruction. Since the group had no spokesman or leader, it was difficult to address their problems. Barnes convinced the militants that they had made their point. They had made the Air Force aware, and the civilian world knew about their plight through coverage in the newspapers and on television. He then stressed that if they persisted in denying people "who have nothing to do with your situation from eating in this facility," then the matter would be placed in an entirely different category. Barnes told them that they were "beginning to impede mission capability, . . . something larger than you wish to bargain for." He convinced the airmen to continue their effort elsewhere and the sit-in finally came to a close.[35]

Gaylor also believes that General Jones was ahead of his time in dealing with the racial unrest that was manifest in the Air Force during the early 1970s. Jones was the first to launch a "race relations" training program that was mandatory in the USAFE command. The mandatory training basically consisted of "how to live and get along with the black man." Initially, it set the scene for some volatile outbursts "and things were coming out that had never been said or come out before."[36] But, despite the program's early flaws and detractors, it was soon instituted throughout the Air Force.

Along with the emphasis on racial problems came a growing awareness of the discrimination and harassment directed against female members of the Air Force. In 1960, while assigned to a women's basic training squadron at Lackland AFB, Gaylor learned that women were limited to five career fields: administrative, medical, dental, supply, and stewardess.[37] Harlow commented on the discriminatory practice of not allowing female service members to claim their civilian husbands as dependents and thereby receive quarters allowances and other benefits. Additionally, Harlow noted that women's barracks were at first not only separate, but also located in areas behind fences to further ensure seclusion.[38]

THE ROLE OF THE CMSAF

Air Force Regulation (AFR) 39-2 establishes the position of Chief Master Sergeant of the Air Force (CMSAF) and the incumbent "automatically becomes the senior enlisted member of the U.S. Air Force and takes rank and precedence over all other enlisted members" during his or her tenure in the position. This regulation also establishes the selection procedure for the CMSAF, which is accomplished "under criteria set by the Chief of Staff"; and tenure is presently "at the discretion of the Chief of Staff." Initially, this was a two-year tour of duty, but a 1980 revision established the present indefinite policy.[39] Additionally, the incumbant CMSAF is allowed "a special pay rate," with retired pay computed accordingly.

Harlow recalled that the service chiefs of staff (four-star general officers) were against the concept of a chief master sergeant position. Congressman Rivers, nevertheless, warned "they were going to have a top NCO whether they wanted one or not." According to Kisling, "Rivers—more than anyone else—deserves the credit for creating the position and bringing enlisted people's issues to public attention." Airey vividly recalled his experience as the first CMSAF:

> You would be surprised how many officers rebuffed or were against the Chief Master Sergeant of the Air Force position. The only way you won out over some of these people is when they retired. You weren't going to convince them.[40]

General John P. McConnell, the Air Force Chief of Staff at the time, was not initially in favor of the CMSAF position. But after only a few months, Airey remembers, "I couldn't have asked for a better supporter."[41] Subsequent CMSAFs have undoubtedly benefitted from the groundwork laid by Airey during the infancy of this position. .

By regulation the CMSAF advises the Secretary of the Air Force and the Chief of Staff "on matters affecting the morale, health, and welfare of enlisted members." However, such an open-ended directive has allowed for a great deal of diversity from one CMSAF to another. After assuming the position, Gaylor did not regard himself as simply a replacement for his predecessor. Rather, he felt that it was "a job where you move in and do your own thing."[42] Gaylor's successor, McCoy, noted that some of the CMSAFs worked extensively with the Air Staff in the Pentagon, while others concentrated their efforts on the field units. McCoy believed that each CMSAF had to set his own agenda and priorities when assuming the job. In his case McCoy attempted to balance travel and staff work, while also finding the time to sit on eleven different boards that dealt with enlisted affairs.[43]

Despite their diversity in approach and style, all of the CMSAFs faced the prospect of bridging a "credibility gap" with the enlisted constituency they were attempting to serve. Airey encountered a number of people who were convinced that the CMSAF position was going to be a "phony" arrangement, simply a tool of the Air Staff.[44] Barnes faced the added burden of being the first black CMSAF and knew that some people perceived his selection as mere tokenism:[45]

> I knew there were people watching to see just what would happen. I knew there were people who felt now will come a flood of things for blacks. The time will be spent with blacks on visits to installations and that the whole thing will advance to the Chief of Staff, information that was more beneficial to blacks. All of those things were made.[46]

Similarly, Harlow found his first six months on the job particularly difficult because he had to establish credibility with the young airmen.[47] McCoy said that he "took a lot of hits" from people who did not agree with what he was trying to do,[48] and Gaylor found that the CMSAF job was not for the "thin-skinned people because some [of them] will let you know immediately that they are not too caught up with your position."[49]

Senior Enlisted Advisors

By a strange twist, the Senior Enlisted Advisor position was created independent of and *after* the establishment of the Chief Master Sergeant of the Air Force (CMSAF) in 1967. Barnes felt that the creation of the CMSAF opened the door for the advent of the senior enlisted advisors, since the former proved indispensable in dealing with the entire range of matters affecting the enlisted force. Also, while some enlightened commanders—like General Jones—were utilizing sergeants-major,[50] Gaylor recalled how one key officer at Second Air Force called him in one day and bluntly said that he was against it. The officer railed that a sergeant-major, or an enlisted advisor was "a waste of time and space."[51] Eventually, however, Air Force commanders found the position useful. Barnes remarked that "it was inevitable that its acceptance and subsequent well-working at lower echelons had to come about."[52]

In creating the Senior Enlisted Advisor position, the Air Force sought yet another means to redress problems of its enlisted force. The advisors were to serve as conduits between the commander and enlisted personnel on a variety of matters. (Originally the position carried the old Army title of sergeant-major.) In 1970 Gaylor served as one of the first senior enlisted advisors to the then commander of Second Air Force, Lt. Gen. David C. Jones. In establishing the position, Jones wanted someone to "feel the pulse [and] improve communications" with the enlisted personnel. At the time that Gaylor was selected, Strategic Air Command, of which Second Air Force was a part, did not itself have such a position. It would get one five years later.[53]

Once the notion of an enlisted advisor was established, a dispute arose over exactly what title to use for the position. Some favored retaining the title of sergeant-major, but Gaylor and others felt that this was too much an Army term. On the other hand the title Senior Enlisted Advisor did not appeal to some because it suggested that a "junior" advisor existed. Instead, Harlow preferred prefixing the name of the command on to the title as in SAC Enlisted Advisor, and so on.[54] Airey did not care for the term at all, referring to it as a "nonmilitary, namby-pamby nondescript, stupid title" that did not befit a senior Air Force noncommissioned officer. He favored the title "Chief Master Sergeant of SAC," for example.[55] Gaylor was so outspokenly against the title that he declared, "As long as I am in this job [CMSAF], there will never be that title."[56] Air Staff members opposed use of the title because they believed that it would be too confusing.[57]

More important than the argument over titles was the fact that many commanders questioned the need for the position. Initially, several commanders refused to accept the idea, but as some commands incorporated the position and it proved successful, most commanders came to accept it.[58] During the early stages, Barnes stressed, the advisors were used differently from one command to the next and since many commanders did not support the program, it did not always succeed.[59]

Gaylor related how one commander grudgingly accepted the idea of an enlisted advisor provided that twelve chief master sergeants instead of one be assigned to fill the position! This commander declared that no one enlisted advisor could answer all of his questions; therefore, he wanted different individuals with specialized expertise to advise him. These "twelve apostles," as they came to be known, remained in place until a new commander took over and appointed one enlisted advisor.[60]

MANPOWER AND PERSONNEL PROBLEMS

Pay and Benefits

The complex of enlisted airmen's problems resulting from the promotion-stagnation dilemma, discrimination, extended temporary duty assignments, and the erosion of benefits ultimately led to an increased demand for unionization in the military services. The situation reached a climax in 1977 when approximately 35% of the Air Force's enlisted force expressed an interest in joining a union.[61]

Gaylor discerned a direct correlation between the eroding benefits and the rise of unionism. Following "a couple of pretty decent pay raises" and the restoration of some previously lost benefits, however, the Air Force managed to defuse the issue, and the desire of airmen to join a union waned. Gaylor adamantly opposed unionization, believing that the military simply could not exist in such an environment.[62] Barnes termed it "truly ridiculous to even consider . . . that a unionized military would work; . . . there is no place in our military structure for a union."[63]

One situation that particularly galled many airmen was the inequity in travel and baggage allowances between officers and enlisted personnel. Gaylor lamented that a chief master sergeant with many years of service and a large family was authorized to ship far less in the way of household goods than a single or newly married second lieutenant who probably did not even need the additional weight allowance. Gaylor also thought that the accompanied baggage allowance of 225 pounds for single enlisted people reassigned within the United States was unrealistic, since many of them owned stereo equipment, cameras, and additional clothing that almost always exceeded this limit. A more realistic figure, he believed, was a minimum of 500 pounds.[64] Additionally, enlisted personnel questioned the inequities in per diem, hazardous duty pay, and "pro-pay,"[65] as well as their plight overseas, where some junior enlisted people were forced to accept relief packages from German churches.[66]

These inequities and deteriorating benefits, plus a severely weakened dollar caused by inflation, produced an exodus of skilled enlisted personnel. Hundreds left the Air Force for better paying jobs in the private sector. Gaylor placed the primary blame on the Carter administration because it "did not do the things they should have done until they were literally forced to do it."[67] McCoy held the view that numerous skilled NCOs left the service because the pay differential between themselves and first-term recruits was only three to one as opposed to a rate of seven to one during the 1960s. The increased pay for first-term airmen was aimed at encouraging reenlistment, certainly a necessary aim. But McCoy noted that "it sure hurt the hell out of the senior NCOs." If a staff sergeant's pay approximates that of a senior master sergeant (E-8), or a chief master sergeant (E-9), what incentive, McCoy asked, was there for him "to stay on and become a chief master sergeant?"[68]

Another controversial issue among the enlisted ranks was the matter of special pay for critical Air Force Specialty Codes (AFSCs). This was controversial, according to Gaylor, "because if you pay one person and tell him he is 'critical,' and tell another he is not, you have a problem right there."[69] McCoy thought it would be a tragic mistake for the military structure ". . . to change the pay system based upon complexities of the job or how many people you supervise" since only a limited number of people would then be entitled to draw so-called "superior performance pay." A more realistic and less demoralizing approach, he thought, was through the selective reenlistment bonus program. "That is a bonus," he noted, "not a monthly perk so you can compare your paycheck with my paycheck."[70] Gaylor, however, found that this program was not entirely successful, as he encountered numerous airmen who "were getting out while staring at a $4,000 bonus." Likewise, Barnes observed that the bonus "has not necessarily held people in" because so many of their other benefits had been eroded.[71]

A survey taken in 1977 revealed that enlisted personnel did not consider pay nearly as important as they did "dependable medical care." The survey also showed that today's young enlisted people "feel they are pawns in efforts to reduce defense spending [and were] sick and tired of the piecemeal erosion of their earned benefits."[72] Barnes emphasized that the Uniformed Services Health Benefit Plan (USHBP) and the Civilian Health and Medical Program of the Uniformed Services (CHAMPUS) under it, had "definitely not" proven satisfactory. He attributed this failure primarily to red tape which had caused CHAMPUS participating physicians to drop out in increasing numbers—"They are tired of fighting the Government for their money."[73] Gaylor agreed that the basic problem with CHAMPUS was in its administration, but he also noted that while some service personnel had experienced difficulties, others were quite pleased with the program.[74]

Middle Management Crisis

In 1967 the Air Force initiated a program called the Top Three—for chief, senior, and master sergeants. The program aimed at closing the communications gap with young airmen and sought to improve first-term reenlistments. On the surface, Barnes noted, there was nothing wrong with the concept of senior NCOs talking directly to the airmen. But what really occurred was an almost total alienation of the middle-manager NCOs, the technical, staff, and "buck" sergeants, who had been bypassed in this process.[75] Gaylor blamed the loss of responsibility and authority for NCOs on the increasing tendency of the officer corps to assume leadership roles that had traditionally been held by NCOs. Decisions were now consistently being made at increasingly higher levels, and by the time one reached down the chain of command to the NCO "nobody asks him anything anymore."[76]

Two of the former CMSAFs cited the Total Objective Plan for Career Airmen Personnel (TOPCAP) as a contributing factor to the middle-manager crisis. The "high year of tenure policy" of TOPCAP was instituted in 1968 to flatten out the "Korean hump," which occurred when career enlisted personnel had entered the Air Force in large numbers and were all projected to leave the service at about the same time. The TOPCAP program forced the retirement of various NCO grades at regular intervals—staff at twenty years, technical at twenty-three, master at twenty-six, and so forth—to remedy the expected mass exodus and to avert "promotion program stagnation." Airey thought that TOPCAP had accomplished its objectives but also felt that "it has long since outlived its usefulness." He was pleased that modifications were made in the program and that commanders were allowed to grant waivers in some instances.[77] Barnes considered that TOPCAP had caused some key NCOs to leave the service and that it caused a "noticeable drop in experience" in some critical career fields.[78]

While enlisted personnel learned the technical aspects of their jobs, their knowledge of military responsibilities was sadly lacking. Kisling traced this middle manager crisis to the creation of the centralized base personnel office (CBPO) in the mid-1960s. Traditionally, each squadron handled its own personnel records. For example, an airman started out as a clerk and through on-the-job training (OJT) rose to chief clerk. In the process he was involved in all aspects of the job. With the establishment of the CBPO, however, the learning opportunity was removed and an individual would rise to the position of first sergeant without learning all of his military responsibilities. As a corrective, Kisling noted, he helped to establish a first-sergeants course at Keesler AFB.[79]

The middle-manager NCO crisis also affected the first sergeant positions throughout the Air Force. Barnes emphasized that first sergeants were "noticeably affected" by a loss of authority as the squadron disciplinarians and, consequently, "got out by the droves." He felt that the introduction of the E-8 and E-9 grades particularly undermined their status since they were no longer the ranking NCOs in the squadrons. As most of the chief master sergeants in the Air Force were in the maintenance field, Barnes described a typical scenario:

> Here is a line chief who is a chief and a first sergeant who is a master, and here is Joe Doaks who screwed up at the barracks this morning and who the first sergeant has got by the collar, but the line chief has hollered, 'Turn him loose. I

need him down here," and the commander is caught in the middle. You know, is his bread and butter getting the airplane launched or getting Joe Doaks' shoes shined under his bed? More often than not he favored the line chief, and the first sergeant found the frustration.[80]

Gaylor recalled that the first sergeant situation reached a point around 1970 where the Air Force came "within a half-inch" of doing away with the position altogether. He noted that there were many who felt that a first sergeant had become "a glorified clerk" and that this old Army position was no longer needed. In 1974 it was decided to retain the first sergeant position; but by then, Gaylor said, the damage had been done. The "first sergeants bailed out and found other jobs." He lamented, "We hung the first sergeant out and literally let go of him, then we tried to woo him back into the field." Many refused to return and some were actually forced to become first sergeants; the Air Force has experienced shortages in this area ever since.[81]

CONTRIBUTIONS OF THE CMSAF

In reviewing the contributions made by each of the CMSAFs, some common threads emerged from their viewpoints. Airey, who laid the groundwork as the first incumbent, considered his relationship with the Air Staff of great importance because that was the group that could best help him accomplish his job of representing the enlisted airmen.[82] Likewise, Harlow felt that his long experience in the Pentagon enhanced the role of the CMSAF and gained greater acceptance of the position by the Air Staff and major commanders. Gaylor felt that he had contributed the most by continuing "to bridge the gap between the enlisted men and the officer ranks." He credits this to his close working relationship with members of the Air Staff.[83]

Kisling considered his most important contribution the opening of "the chain of communications" between the enlisted ranks and the highest levels of authority in the Air Force, civilians and officers. The lack of communications, he believed, had resulted in the enlisted forces not having a voice in their destiny and thinking that their commanders did not care. These deficiencies involved instances of insensitivity and ignorance. An example of the former was the concept of "mass punishment," punishing an entire group for the misdeeds of an individual. An example of ignorance occurred when officers on a mixed officer–enlisted aircrew were unaware that the temporary duty (TDY) pay allowance was lower for the enlisteds than for the officers.[84]

McCoy also noted that he was able to "build tremendous rapport with the Air Staff."[85] Finally, Barnes thought that his access to this top planning body was "really unbelievable initially" and very helpful in bringing about "the solidification of the program of enlisted inclusion in the planning process."[86]

All six of the former top Air Force NCOs considered their tours as CMSAF the high points of their careers. Gaylor fondly reminisced about his advent into the position at a 1977 meeting of the Air Force Sergeants Association:

So it was a night of standing ovations and hugs and tears and best wishes for success. You know, you're on top of the world. I know how 'most valuable players' feel, and Miss America, and the President. I'm not saying my position was at those levels, but in my own way I experienced the same feelings, the exhilaration, the feeling that you've arrived.[87]

Harlow saw his CMSAF role as an "opportunity to enhance the position [and] build the image of the enlisted corps," which he termed his "greatest satisfaction."[88] Barnes felt honored to have held the Air Force's highest enlisted position, especially since he was the only incumbent to receive two unprecedented extensions.[89]

In reflecting over their terms, each of the CMSAFs considered the position to be of vital importance not only to enlisted men in particular, but also to the Air Force in general. Kisling believed that the position provided a means of communication to bring the concerns of the enlisted force to the attention of Air Force leaders.[90] Gaylor recollected that in years past a senior NCO would "have been lucky to get an audience with a colonel," but now he and major command enlisted advisors were participating in conferences in Washington with top ranking military and political leaders on a regular basis.[91] Barnes felt honored to have had the opportunity "to wholly represent the Air Force in testimony at the House and Senate Armed Services Committees,"[92] while Harlow noted the increased acceptance of the CMSAF position as the incumbent "is involved in more things" such as council meetings and high-level briefings.[93]

The increasing acceptance of the role of Chief Master Sergeant of the Air Force since its inception in 1967 augurs well for its continued existence in the foreseeable future.

NOTES

1. Department of the Air Force, "Biography of CMSAF Paul W. Airey," Secretary of the Air Force/Office of Information, Washington, DC, 1967.
2. Department of the Air Force, "Biography of CMSAF Donald L. Harlow," Secretary of the Air Force/Office of Information, Washington, DC, 1969.
3. Interview of CMSAF Richard D. Kisling by Jacob Neufeld, 15 and 29 July, 1 and 15 September 1983, Washington, DC [Hereafter, Kisling interview.]; Department of the Air Force, "Biography of CMSAF Richard D. Kisling," Secretary of the Air Force/Office of Information, Washington, DC, 1971.
4. Department of the Air Force, "Biography of CMSAF Thomas N. Barnes," Secretary of the Air Force/Office of Information, Washington, DC, 1976.
5. Department of the Air Force, "Biography of CMSAF Robert D. Gaylor," Secretary of the Air Force/Office of Information, Washington, DC, 1978.
6. Department of the Air Force, "Biography of CMSAF James M. McCoy," Secretary of the Air Force/Office of Information, Washington, DC, 1980.
7. Interview of CMSAF Thomas N. Barnes by James C. Hasdorff, 11–12 November 1980, Ft. Worth, TX, p. 14. [Hereafter, Barnes interview.]
8. Interview of CMSAF Robert D. Gaylor by James C. Hasdorff, 16–17 January 1981, San Antonio, TX, pp. 14-15. [Hereafter, Gaylor interview.]

9. Ibid., pp. 15–16.
10. Ibid., p. 16.
11. Barnes interview, pp. 27–28.
12. Ibid., pp. 29–30.
13. Ibid., pp. 31–32.
14. Gaylor interview, pp. 11–12.
15. Interview of CMSAF James M. McCoy by Captain Mark C. Cleary, 25–26 February 1982, Omaha, NE, pp. 10–26. [Hereafter, McCoy interview.]
16. Gaylor interview, pp. 22–23.
17. Interview of CMSAF Paul W. Airey by Hugh N. Ahmann, 23–24 March 1981, Panama City, FL, p. 153. [Hereafter, Airey interview.]
18. Gaylor interview, pp. 35–37.
19. Kisling interview.
20. Airey interview, p. 90.
21. McCoy interview, p. 19.
22. Kisling interview.
23. In May 1958 PL 85-422 (85th Congress) created two new enlisted grades, E-8 and E-9. On 1 September 1958 the Air Force promoted their first E-8 group and on 1 December 1959 their first E-9s. The Air Force had eliminated the warrant officer program in early 1959.
24. Airey interview, pp. 90–91.
25. Ibid.
26. Gaylor interview, p. 182; McCoy interview, p. 180; Interview of CMSAF Donald L. Harlow by Hugh N. Ahmann, 9–10 December 1980, Washington, DC, p. 138. [Hereafter, Harlow interview.]
27. Barnes interview, p. 134.
28. Airey interview, p. 90; Harlow interview, p. 139.
29. Kisling interview.
30. Gaylord interview, pp. 84–85.
31. Barnes interview, p. 69.
32. Ibid.
33. Ibid., p. 70.
34. Ibid., pp. 70–71.
35. Ibid., pp. 71–72.
36. Gaylor interview, pp. 101–102.
37. Ibid., p. 53.
38. Harlow interview, pp. 259–260.
39. Department of the Air Force, AFR 39-2, HQ USAF, Wash., DC, 3 January 1980.
40. Airey interview, p. 77; Harlow interview, p. 86.
41. Ibid., p. 94.
42. Harold D. Newcomb, "Follow the Leader," *Airman*, January 1978, p. 9.
43. McCoy interview, pp. 126–127.
44. Airey interview, pp. 83 and 125.
45. Harold D. Newcomb, "The New Chief Master Sergeant of the Air Force . . . No Stranger to Problems," *Airman*, April 1974, p. 16.
46. Barnes interview, p. 154.
47. Harlow interview, p. 127.
48. McCoy interview, p. 147.
49. Gaylor interview, p. 159.
50. Gaylor interview, p. 75.
51. Ibid., pp. 81–82.

52. Barnes interview, p. 90.
53. Gaylor interview, pp. 75–76.
54. Ibid., p. 197.
55. Airey interview, p. 126.
56. Gaylor interview, p. 197.
57. Harlow interview, p. 181.
58. Ibid., p. 182.
59. Barnes interview, p. 90.
60. Gaylor interview, p. 196.
61. Barnes interview, p. 83.
62. Gaylor interview, pp. 142–143.
63. Barnes interview, pp. 125–126.
64. Gaylor interview, pp. 145–146.
65. "Enlisted TDY Pay: The Question of Equity," *Air Force Times*, June 28, 1976, p. 2; Harlow interview, pp. 230–231.
66. Richard Barnard, "Plight of EM Overseas Hit," April 10, 1978, p. 27.
67. Gaylor interview, pp. 147–148.
68. McCoy interview, p. 192.
69. Gaylor interview, p. 165.
70. McCoy interview, pp. 167–169.
71. Barnes interview, p. 128; Gaylor interview, p. 165.
72. Jim Parker, "EM Put Medical Care Ahead of Pay," *Air Force Times*, July 11, 1977, p. 21.
73. Barnes interview, p. 131.
74. Gaylor interview, pp. 166–167.
75. Barnes interview, p. 77.
76. Gaylor interview, pp. 175–176.
77. Airey interview, p. 115.
78. Barnes interview, pp. 80–81.
79. Kisling interview.
80. Barnes interview, pp. 80–81.
81. Gaylor interview, pp. 173–174.
82. Airey interview, p. 102.
83. Gaylor interview, p. 156.
84. Kisling interview.
85. McCoy interview, p. 133.
86. Barnes interview, pp. 118–120.
87. Gaylor interview, p. 126.
88. Harlow interview, p. 256.
89. Barnes interview, p. 119.
90. Kisling interview.
91. Gaylor interview, p. 157.
92. Barnes interview, p. 126.
93. Harlow interview, p. 159.

8

"It's Not What I Expected": The Young Enlisted Air Force Woman Overseas

Constance S. Ojile

OVERSEAS DUTY

The more than 55,000 enlisted women in the U.S. Air Force in 1984 represented over 11% of that force,[1] up from about 2% in 1972.[2] During this time the occupational distributions of enlisted women also increased dramatically; of the 230 job specialties in the Air Force, women are now excluded from only four.[3] One consequence of women's increased participation in the military is that more women are serving at overseas duty stations. In 1983, 27% of Air Force enlisted women were stationed overseas.[4] The majority of Air Force women can expect overseas duty at some point, often early in their association with the Air Force. Since "the recent expansion of roles and numbers of military women involves primarily those just entering the services, who are likely to be between the ages of 18 and 23," we can expect to find a large group of relatively young enlisted women stationed overseas doing a wide variety of jobs.[5]

The opportunity for young women to be stationed overseas presents a challenge and the potential for adventure. For most, the assignment brings many professional and personal rewards and is generally viewed as a positive experience. Others express disappointment and dissatisfaction with the circumstances, however. They suffer from physical and emotional ills, describing themselves as feeling confined, isolated, and alienated from other Americans and host nationals. Many of the problems of overseas duty are also problems for male military personnel and dependents; that is, they seem not to be gender related but due to the nature of the closed military community overseas. Some may, in fact, not be unique to overseas stations. My data were collected from Air Force women in Europe, but the findings are not necessarily limited by region.

Living in a military community, particularly in a foreign country without the support system of family, friends, and familiar surroundings, heightens one's sensitivity and susceptibility to problems that in another context may

134

not seem so traumatic. While many of the problems associated with overseas duty are similar to those experienced in stateside assignments, their intensity is magnified.

Although the majority of young enlisted Air Force women stationed overseas are well adjusted and experience successful tours of duty, there is much to be learned from those who experience difficulty. The problems they describe may interfere with job performance and may, therefore, have organizational, policy, and managerial implications. Additionally, exploration of their concerns may enhance the effective utilization of women in the military, a goal recognized to have direct implications for overall military readiness. By examining the problems encountered by these women, we may discover solutions to problems facing the increasing numbers of women in the military and perhaps the majority of military personnel, male and female, stationed overseas.

FIELD RESEARCH

I collected information on young Air Force enlisted women from 1977 through 1980 while teaching anthropology and women's studies in the European Division of the University of Maryland University College. During this assignment I lived on NATO bases in Germany, Spain, Iceland, and Turkey, most of which were supervised by the U.S. Air Force. As an anthropologist, I found it a unique opportunity to live and work with these young women stationed abroad, as most of them lived on base and some were also my students.

More than 100 female Air Force enlisted personnel were interviewed throughout Europe during the three-year period. They were primarily between the ages of 18 and 23, single, and in the lower ranks. I used formal and informal settings as opportunities to discuss the effects of overseas duty on these enlisted women. The data-collection methodology included participation in routine and periodic events and informal conversations in barracks, laundry facilities, recreation centers, at parties and social gatherings, at the enlisted club, and anywhere else that presented the opportunity to have a conversation either one-on-one or in a small group. I used no questionnaires, although I did follow an interview schedule, or outline of topics that I was interested in exploring. I used open-ended questions when asking about adjustment to overseas duty. It was not my intent to catalog responses but rather, following ethnographic fieldwork methodology, to be a participant observer and to be involved in as many activities as possible.[6] After interviewing a woman or attending an event or social gathering, I recorded my impressions and observations. Often during the activity I would leave the area to write notes while the statement or event was still fresh in my mind.

To all of the women I spoke with I conveyed my interest in them and my intent to record events; all gave me their permission to be quoted anonymously in future work.

THE WOMEN'S CONCERNS

As in many other institutions or organizations, complaining is a popular and accepted pastime which serves to vent anger and provide a degree of group cohesiveness, i.e., "we're all in this together." This held true for young enlisted women. When asked to describe their life overseas they consistently described what was troublesome. With further questioning, they would add that, in addition to various discomforts, they also experienced times of great enjoyment—traveling, meeting new people, learning about foreign customs, and gaining more work experience. Therefore, even though I have chosen to make the most-frequently described problems the focus of this chapter, it should not be assumed that the women were as a whole an unhappy, troubled group unable to cope.

Successful adjustment and satisfactory work performance were affected by the women's interpretations of their personal problems and by the alternatives selected to cope with those problems within the closed military overseas community. The dissatisfaction expressed by these women was not attributable to a single source. Rather, their frustrations and disappointments were the result of a combination of several factors. Many of the problems described by women are undoubtedly experienced by men also. To understand the women's perspectives and the problem-solving choices they made, it is instructive to examine specific problem areas. These areas were selected for inclusion here because of the importance assigned to them by the women themselves.[7]

When interviewed, women tended to begin the description of their lives with comments about problems related to predeparture preparation, climate, location, mobility, financial resources, recreation, housing, and the host country. These problems were viewed as about equal in importance. The interviewees then went on, however, to reveal that issues related to work, health, and social life were of greatest concern and constituted the sources of the most significant and persistent problems.

Predeparture Preparation

Most of the problems women faced occurred after they arrived at their overseas duty stations. Yet a significant and often overlooked experience occurs before the women arrive overseas. During the predeparture phase, expectations for the overseas assignment are established. These expectations, if formed on limited or inaccurate information, may hinder initial adjustment overseas. The Air Force gives predeparture courses, but women also rely on friends who have been stationed overseas for information—which commonly consists of shopping, eating, or recreational tips and fails to stress the nature and extent of problems or to suggest coping strategies and skills. Consequently, there may be a gap between expectation and reality which can be followed by disappointment and frustration.

The following comment is typical of complaints on lack of preparation: "I knew where to buy the best nutcrackers but couldn't deal with my German landlord." A Navy-sponsored study on the problems of women serving overseas points out that "almost two thirds of the sample (65%) reported one or more problems relating to the adequacy of preparation."[8]

The lack of adequate predeparture preparation can set a tone of dissatisfaction which may persist and eventually affect positive long-term adjustment. "The success-rate of overseas adjustment among Americans is not nearly as high as it might be. If left to luck, your chances of having a really satisfying experience living abroad would be about one in seven."[9]

In addition to the lack of specific preparation, many of the young women lacked extensive travel experience. Overseas assignments often represented the first time the young women had traveled abroad, or even very far from home. Because of their youth, their life experiences were limited as well, which resulted in difficulty coping with their new living and working environments. Under these circumstances, some withdrew and expressed feelings of inadequacy. Although there was a sponsor program available, with a person already on-site acting as an informal advisor to an incoming individual to facilitate transition and ease the difficulties encountered during relocation, many women complained that their sponsor did not pay enough attention to them. "I could die over here, and who'd know?" was one expression of the loneliness that frequently accompanied the initial immersion in the overseas environment. It is not unusual to experience some degree of "culture shock" or alienation in a foreign environment. Women who had the most difficulty adjusting reported high and often unrealistic predeparture expectations which neither they, the Air Force, nor the host country could meet.

Climate, Location, and Mobility

Sometimes such factors as the local weather and the geographic location served to increase the sense of isolation. In Turkey, at Incerlik NATO Base, torrential downpours, high heat, and extreme humidity limited mobility because "it's just too hot to do anything but breathe." During the nearly six dark winter months in Keflavik, Iceland, heavy snows and gales could result in closed roads, the restriction of personnel to quarters (the workplace, club, commissary or wherever one happened to be when Charlie condition—the worst weather—was called), and the development of "cabin fever."[10] The rain, fog, and overcast skies common at Hahn, Bitburg, and Spangdahlem Air Force Bases in Germany were the foundation of many local jokes about the location's being inappropriate for flying and conducive to depression.

Additionally, the women interviewed wished for access to urban centers with their cultural and recreational opportunities. Where easy access to these areas was prohibited by rural or otherwise remote base locations, the sense of confinement increased. One joke about Keflavik reflects this: "They say Ice-

land is at the edge of the world. That's not true. But you *can* see the edge from
here!"[11] There was no public transportation to urban centers from Hahn,
Bitburg, or Spangdahlem, all of which were remote locations. Since young
women rarely owned their own cars overseas, they were dependent on friends
with cars or military transportation if they wanted to leave the bases. Recent
research has shown that feelings of isolation, particularly cultural isolation,
are common among men deployed away from home as well.[12]

When the factors of inclement weather and long or difficult trips to urban
centers were coupled, many women expressed a feeling of being trapped or
stuck on base. It was easier to stay in the barracks than to face heat, cold or
rain, or to make sometimes complicated travel arrangements. In some instances, this climatic, geographical, or self-imposed restriction to base produced such side effects as increased consumption of food and, in particular,
alcoholic beverages. For instance, women in Keflavik complained about
weight gain and expressed concern about the amount of alcohol which they
and their peers consumed daily. Those who complained often blamed this
increased consumption on "the weather."

Financial Resources

In addition to weather and distance, lack of funds or some other financial
problem formed the basis of some of the most common complaints. Careful
budgeting was a goal not always achieved, largely because the responsibilities
of financial management were a relatively new experience for most young
women. Although there were many complaints about the base exchange and
commissary (centering around their shortage or lack of "favorite" items),
women cited base stores as their primary shopping outlets. Frequently, mail-
order houses and friends or family in the United States supplied goods unavailable locally.

Although the Air Force provided for basic necessities, the base exchange
and shops on the local economy tempted personnel to spend money on
stereos, cameras, and the local specialty items. Then the most common form
of complaint was that it was "impossible to save any money."

Women interested in finding a source of supplemental income found the
task very difficult. Part-time work for pay was scarce and, when available,
usually consisted of typing or child care for other military personnel. Entry
into the host country's work force was rarely available; when it was, lack of
language skills, contacts, or working papers not readily given to Americans
stood in the way.

Another limit to mobility or adaptation to the host culture was the fact that
moving about in the local area required knowledge of foreign currency and the
rate of exchange. Although many commercial establishments adjacent to military bases accepted dollars as well as local currency, American personnel who

lacked skill in dealing with foreign currency tended to feel confined. The familiarity and comfort with local currency was summarized by one woman in this way: "I never carry marks around. I don't need to, and besides, they're like funny money to me."

Lack of funds, discomfort with local currency, problems presented by the weather, and the inaccessibility of urban centers frequently added up to a decision to remain with the familiar surroundings of the facilities on base. This decision hampered positive adjustment to the host country and increased feelings of isolation. Women who were comfortable with leaving the base rarely complained of boredom and found that it helped them adjust more readily to overseas duty.

Recreation

Complaints about the quality and availability of entertainment sources were often connected to feelings of boredom and dissatisfaction. One joke reflects this by asking, "What's the difference between a tour in Iceland and a trip on the Titanic?" The answer was, "The Titanic had a better band." Although many on-base facilities offered ways to fill off-duty time, women were reluctant or unwilling to participate. For instance, the enlisted club was viewed as the scene of drinking and fighting.[13] "The club is okay for happy hour or with a group, but you don't want to go alone" was the warning of one woman who explained that being at the club ensured that derogatory rumors would "fly around by morning." Thus, although the club could have been a place for young women to gather and socialize in activities which could reduce their sense of isolation, most women avoided it. Because they could rarely find a replacement environment, they chose to socialize in the barracks. Peer pressure and social network composition influenced recreational choices. The woman with limited social skills, or who lacked resourcefulness, was often left out of group activities. While a woman with social handicaps might be left behind, however, she was rarely alone. One aspect of military life described by these women was that "there always seem to be people around." This was especially true of living quarters.

Housing

On base the young enlisted single women lived in the barracks. These rooms were double or triple occupancy. Everyone had, or expected to have, a room-mate. Lack of privacy was the source of the strongest complaints about housing, followed by incompatibility of personalities and schedules of room-mates. The lack of privacy was an issue raised in every discussion of barracks life. Rooms could be inspected at any time, and women reported cases where supervisors entered to inspect without knocking. People were coming and going at all hours. It was almost always noisy. "Stereo wars," parties, and general traffic were described as extremely upsetting to shift workers trying to sleep. It was difficult to establish a sense of "home" when people and noise were nearly constant intruders. Often the living conditions characteristic of barracks life presented little refuge. One woman expressed the sentiment of many when she observed, "I live there, but it's not home."

Generally, women felt resigned to the lack of privacy as part of the overall circumstances. Some liked the fact that "it's like living in a dorm, you know what's happening to everybody." Others took the first opportunity to move into local housing with friends, as it more clearly separated working and living spaces and offered a more private and quiet environment. However, the cost of alternative living and Air Force restrictions on moving more often than not forced women to remain in the barracks.

The Host Country

The young women's willingness to explore the host country and to seek interaction with host nationals can be described by grouping their behaviors and attitudes into four categories.

Group One—"most closed"—is the category of women who were reluctant or unwilling to explore the host country and interact with host nationals. During nearly all of their stay overseas, some women were able to avoid carrying local currency, visiting local scenic or cultural points of interest, or meeting host nationals in an informal setting.

Group Two—"somewhat closed"—is the category of women who were willing to leave the base but usually went to places frequented by other Americans—where they could go by military or public transportation, the proprietors spoke English, and dollars were accepted. They were also the group most likely to take the base recreation center's country tours.

Group Three—"somewhat open"—describes young women who actively sought local color and experiences and reported enjoying contact with host nationals. This was the best prepared group for intercultural encounters. They were aware of, and respected, foreign customs. They traveled more and were more willing to take risks. One woman reported her willingness to take risks by describing how she confronted the language barrier: "I always try to speak Spanish because I had it in high school, and I don't care if they laugh at me." They were cautious about their personal possessions and demonstrated awareness of personal safety concerns when traveling.

Group Four—"most open"—is the category of women who expressed the fewest fears about intercultural contact. These women took the most travel and communication risks, sometimes disregarding caution altogether. They were the most willing to explore areas away from tourist zones and meet host nationals. They described their trips as "unplanned" and "spontaneous."

The majority of the women I interviewed, 52%, were in group two. This form of behavior was convenient. It allowed them to visit the country and still feel comfortable because they were surrounded by Americans. Group three women formed the next largest representation with 27% followed by group four, 12%, and group one, 9%.[14] Women generally agreed that their willingness to interact with the host country increased during their stay. The degree of change, however, was difficult to assess. Some women could be categorized as group two types at the beginning of their overseas tour and group three nearer the end. As they adjusted to their environment and developed confidence and basic communication skills, they were more willing to take risks tempered by caution.

Groups one and four reported the highest degree of dissatisfaction. Group one had the lowest incidence of cross-cultural experience and the strongest negative stereotypes about host nationals. They believed many of the horror stories about leaving the base, thus confirming predetermined stereotypes and increasing their fears. While group four women were eager to go exploring, they usually went unprepared to cope with intercultural or travel challenges. Initially they were the most adventuresome group, but many withdrew from travel because of experiences such as getting lost or having their valuables stolen. Their lack of culturally relevant information left these women the most vulnerable to misunderstandings with host nationals.

The establishment of close personal ties with host national families or individuals was rare for all of the women. Women repeatedly said that the host nationals' negative stereotypes about American women in general, and American military women in particular, prevented the formation of friendships. In making this point, the Air Force women revealed that they had also formed stereotypes about the host nationals. When the negative characterizations on both sides could be transcended and ties formed, however, the resulting friendships offered an avenue to understanding the host country's culture and customs.

Women who felt dissatisfied with barracks life or base activities and turned to local attractions for recreation reported fewer feelings of isolation than those who remained with the familiarity of the base. Some women clearly needed more preparation, encouragement, and support before they could take advantage of activities away from the base.

Work

Nearly all of the women interviewed, 98%, experienced some problems at work. The problems were primarily interpersonal: usually gender- and sometimes race-related. Although male and female host nationals were employed on the bases, women said they experienced fewer work-related problems with this group and repeatedly identified American military men as the source of difficulty. Though the severity of problems varied, all women felt that these problems had a negative effect on their job performance.

They reported problems of sexual harassment, hostility, differential treatment, needing to prove themselves, and tokenism. While many of the women felt these were the same problems they experienced in the United States, most felt the problems were intensified by the nature of the closed military overseas community. As one woman observed, "I think I'm more sensitive to it over here than I would be at home." They felt that the unbalanced male/female ratio, lack of support or problem-solving resources, the stress of being away from home, and isolation were among the contributing factors.

Sexual harassment was primarily verbal rather than physical and ranged from forms of teasing to threats and abuse. Hostility arose in work situations when men expressed strong feelings about women's capabilities (physical and mental) or resented perceived and actual preferential treatment. Differential treatment took the form of patronization of women or not according women a full range of responsibilities. One woman who worked with heavy equipment in a flight line maintenance shop explained that she felt lucky to have a good crew chief who gave her the same tasks as everyone else; but, nevertheless, she said, "I get a lot of hassle about the big tool box, and the damn thing's on wheels."[15] Many young women said they had to work doubly hard to prove themselves. Some said that tokenism was present when they were given favorable evaluation reports or, the reverse, when they thought they were not being promoted as quickly as their male peers because they had been "shuttled off to some unit that needed a woman to meet its quotas."[16]

The formal military hierarchy places young enlisted women in the same subordinate role as their male peers. Yet women described an "informal hierarchy" which they said placed them below men of the same age and rank. They complained about feeling and being treated as subordinate to men who were theoretically their equals. Thus, they saw themselves separated from not only their superiors but also their male peers in their work environment. As a result, they perceived their peer group as limited to other women their age and rank. This form of exclusion led to further isolation and presented additional fodder for frustration and anger.

The women interviewed described various methods for coping with feelings aroused by what was perceived as inequitable treatment at work. Some said they coped by ignoring it because "there was nothing you could do about it anyway." Others tried confrontation but, as one woman pointed out, "that gets you nowhere fast" and may only lead to increased hostility. Other women suggested "rolling with the punches" or not letting it "get to you." For some, the upsetting events at work affected their health and, consequently, their work performance. Symptoms such as headaches, upset stomachs, and in one case a skin rash were ultimately diagnosed as related to work stress.

In general, the women performed well at work, received good evaluation reports and, for the most part, liked their jobs. Yet, those who voiced strong complaints said that their position in the formal and informal hierarchy left them with little power over disturbing work-related events.

Health

More than 90% of the women interviewed reported having been sick one or more times since their arrival overseas. The type, degree, and length of illness varied. (Illness is common among male military personnel as well.[17]) Women's complaints included irregular periods, more intense cramps, facial blemishes, rashes, urinary tract infections, vaginal infections, concerns about contracting venereal disease, concerns about the availability of abortions, feelings of depression, suicidal ideation, and head and body aches and pains. Many women said that the development of these problems coincided with their overseas duty and insisted that these were "problems I never experienced or thought much about before coming here."

Women explained these outbreaks by saying that their bodies were expressing tension or that they were reacting to local drinking water and viruses. One woman summarized her feelings by saying, "It's like I don't know what to expect next. I got warts, my face is breaking out, my cramps are worse—it's like my body is revolting or something." The reactions of the women to these experiences included fear, bewilderment, and increased anxiety about their physical and mental well-being. They complained of feeling helpless or powerless over the things happening to them.

When they turned to the medical facilities and staff available to them, they often encountered more frustration. One woman reported going to the hospital several times over a six-week period complaining of stomach problems. She was seen by a physician's assistant (PA) who repeatedly asked her if she was having trouble with her boyfriend or if she could be pregnant. She finally demanded a pregnancy test to convince the PA that she was not pregnant and that he should look elsewhere for the cause of her problems.

Concerns about the quality and availability of medical staff and facilities were supported by the experiences of other women. Pap tests for cancer frequently had to be sent to another location, and sometimes another country, for processing. Abortion counseling was minimal. In some hospitals, LaMaze and prenatal courses were offered, but birth control and sex education courses were not.

Women, especially those with limited knowledge about their bodies, dreaded the prospect of visiting overworked gynecologists. They complained about the impersonal nature of their treatment (being rushed through exams and feeling intimidated about asking questions), about the lack of written material on health problems, and about the shortage of female gynecologists. Similar complaints came from pregnant women, some of whom would have preferred to give birth at a civilian hospital but were deterred from doing so by high cost and/or language barriers. A few even tried to arrange trips to the United States to coincide with delivery, but lack of leave time and funds and the reality of work responsibilities usually prevented this.

Though some of the problems would have been the same if the women were stationed in the United States and some may have existed prior to overseas transfers, the women's reactions to their problems were largely reflective of the limitations present in the overseas context. These limitations transcended problems associated with the military medical staff and facilities. Without the supportive network of family or close personal friends, many women felt isolated and tried to handle their problems, as one woman put it, "all on my own." The potential for exaggeration was increased by real fears for their health. When these fears were taken to professionals for confirmation or dismissal, the women felt that their concerns were trivialized, and they often left the examination feeling rejected and more confused. Women who did not have bad experiences themselves knew of and retold the experiences of frightened or disappointed friends.

Complaints of depression arose more than any other problem of emotional or mental health. The symptoms of depression reported by these women included lack of appetite, sleeping longer and more often than they normally would, lethargy, withdrawal, overeating, insomnia, and nervous anxiety. Some of the causes to which women attributed their depression were loneliness, work pressures, separation from family and longtime friends, a sense of inadequacy or failure, and troubled relationships with male and female friends.

Drugs and Alcohol

Some troubled women found relief by talking with friends, counselors, or chaplains. Others used drugs, both prescription and illicit, and/or alcohol to self-medicate. The drugs were available through military medical facilities, civilian doctors, and the black market. Alcoholic beverages also were available, reasonably priced, and in general more socially acceptable. Excessive alcohol consumption and erratic alcoholic behavior were somewhat expected of or tolerated from young men but were viewed as unacceptable for young women. Therefore, women concealed the amount and frequency of their drinking or turned to chemical depressants such as valium or darvon as a substitute for alcohol. Women who avoided drinking in public might drink to intoxication in private settings, among peers, or alone.

Use of marijuana and stimulants also was reported. Marijuana was used to enhance relaxation, while "uppers" were used to get through shift work or recover from depressant use. Many women habitually used diet pills containing high amounts of stimulants and were often unwilling to correlate their irritability, restlessness, and depression with the drug.

Women using or abusing drugs and alcohol frequently displayed the characteristics associated with chemical dependency. Denial, avoidance, and rationalizing accompanied most discussions of drug (including alcohol) abuse. The most common explanation was that this use/abuse was temporary and would diminish or be eliminated once they returned to the United States. This "situational dependency" is not limited to young women in the Air Force. Environmental factors are often invoked as explanations for drug dependency by the user. Yet it is important to note that the women using or abusing drugs and/or alcohol consistently related their usage to their environment rather than attributing it to a desire to experiment, comply with peer pressure, or rebel.

Though perceived as temporary and functional, this usage often led to deeper states of depression and a vicious cycle of increased dependency. One woman who viewed her usage as medicinal stated, "It (valium) helps me cope. I just know I won't be able to sleep tonight without it."

Continued drug or alcohol use served to mask feelings such as hurt, resentment, anger, fear, and rejection. The young women with these problems frequently lacked knowledge of alternatives or were unwilling (and eventually unable) to seek help. There seemed to be a social blindness at work among both women and those around them. Although a few were able to evaluate or confront their usage on their own, the majority of abusers went undetected and untreated.[18]

Social Life

The social life of young enlisted women presented more complications than many women were used to or prepared to handle. Those who reported enjoying their social life also said that they were generally satisfied with other areas, i.e., climate, mobility, host country, etc., with the exception of work and health. One woman described herself as having "blossomed from the wallflower I was before I got here." Complaints about social life varied in degree more than any other topic. Yet regardless of the severity, problems associated with men and problems attributed to gossip formed the focus of discussions about social activities.

Women were outnumbered by men in every social setting and were aware that men were competing for them. Men who viewed women as undesirable in the workplace reversed their attitudes in social settings and saw women as desirable company. Young enlisted women were approached, followed, courted; some reported being "hassled by men." Initially, all this attention was flattering, but eventually it became a source of irritation and resentment.

One common complaint was the "goldfish bowl syndrome," a feeling of constantly being observed and evaluated. One woman said, "I feel like every time I move someone's taking notes." Women said that their intentions and

actions were frequently distorted and misunderstood. For instance, an inno-
cent action, such as going to lunch with a man, could be interpreted by others
as having an affair. Women were often surprised and hurt to find themselves
the subject of rumors and gossip.

Gossip existed in both the social network and the workplace. One woman
summarized the feelings of many women when she said, "I can't wait to get to
work on Monday to find out what a great time I had this weekend." Persistent
teasing by male coworkers embarrassed and sometimes angered women. If
women denied the rumors or defended their actions, they found that they had
only stimulated further teasing and indirectly legitimized the accusations. "If
there wasn't anything to the rumors, why was she so steamed?" was the
unspoken question. This cycle of teasing-anger-teasing created a social trap.
Frequent and intensive teasing could result in women's choosing to withdraw
socially to avoid accounting for themselves. One woman, referring to her lack
of interest in socializing with coworkers, said, "I go to work and when 4:30
p.m. comes, I'm gone!" Women who did not withdraw explained that they
felt a strong need to control their behavior in an attempt to avert misunderstanding. The nature of the closed military community seemed to intensify
these interactions. Most women were able to maintain a sense of humor, tease
back, and ignore or shrug off gossip; yet they still commented that the frequency of the cycle of teasing-anger-teasing was higher than in their stateside
assignments or previous civilian work environments.

Young enlisted women were perceived by others as "suitable" partners for
their male peers, superiors, and even "tabooed" officers. Yet their own perception of the availability of relationships with others, both male and female,
was much more circumscribed. They avoided socializing with male coworkers,
saying that this caused tension at work. Enlisted women who dated officers
said they had to sneak around, since the woman rather than the officer would
be reprimanded if they were caught.[19] Single women said they were excluded
from the social circles of female married personnel and dependent wives by
their lack of common interests. The effects of being in competition with other
women both at work and socially resulted in further alienation. Those who
lacked experience with personal relationships were unprepared to deal with
many of the social pressures. Nowhere was this more evident than in their
relationships with men on temporary duty—of a few days to a few months—
away from their permanent assignment.

TDY: A Special Case

For many military personnel, TDY (temporary duty) is a time when "everything goes but nothing counts," a time to abandon responsibilities and
disregard social sanctions. The myth is that men on TDY literally and symbol-

ically abandon their normal roles. Husbands remove wedding bands and pursue women; the quiet, responsible guy gets drunk, starts fights, and spends his money; and so forth.[20] This TDY attitude is not limited to men actually on TDY. Some men are reported to see their whole overseas tour as one long TDY. Young enlisted women said they were attracted to men on TDY because these men spent money on them and took them to places where they were not likely to run into a lot of people from base. As one woman stated, "The good thing about TDY guys is that they aren't cheap; they'll take you out to places nobody else goes." So in addition to having a good time, women found in these men an opportunity to escape the base community and gossip mill. They usually chose men older than themselves and described these men as "understanding, mature, and trustworthy."

Although some women glamorized their relationships with men on TDY, others presented a dramatically different view. These women claimed that relationships with men on TDY could only result in the woman's being subjected to emotional abuse and frustration. One woman said, "It happened to my roommate. She was seeing this pilot. First off he's an officer! . . . so I told her to be careful. Well, he dumps her, goes away, and now she mopes around and I'm the one who has to live with it. But I told her and she just went, hook and all; all he had to do was reel her in!" If an enlisted woman had doubts about a man on TDY who, for instance, said he wasn't married, she had few avenues for verification of her suspicions. One woman explained: "They all stick together. One is not going to tell on the other. It's like a code of silence." Even if the woman managed to find out that the man was married and confronted him, she experienced further frustration. One woman said, "I spent the whole evening listening to him tell about his unhappy marriage and how he's really almost divorced." Separating truth from fiction in these matters "could become a full-time preoccupation," was one observation.

The young woman's choice to get involved with a man on TDY usually depended on her degree of alienation from those around her and her previous experiences with men.[21] The most vulnerable women were those who had little previous experience with intimate male–female relationships or those who saw these relationships as their sole source of happiness. If she was unhappy with her work or social setting, the man offered a refreshing change and a brief escape from her problems. The attention and affection enhanced her self-esteem and was a welcome contrast to work-related stress. Yet the temporary nature of the relationship presented its own problems. Women interested in a short-term relationship with few commitments were seldom disappointed.

However, many women—including some of those who initiated the relationship with few expectations—reported feeling "used" when the relationship terminated with the man's departure at the conclusion of his TDY. Those who denied the impermanence of the relationship were most likely to make attempts at prolonging it after the man had departed. They reported writing letters, making telephone calls, and trying to get transferred to the man's duty station.

One woman, recovering from an abortion with complications, fondly looked back on her affair. She felt the relationship had been ruined because she and her lover were both in the Air Force. She explained that it was only the Air Force which kept them apart, and she planned to visit the man during her next leave. Her friends reminded her that he was married, that he had rejected her, and that, despite her efforts, she had not heard from him since he left. She responded by defending his actions and supporting her hypothesis that he was only doing this in her best interest.

Certainly, young women do not have to be stationed overseas to feel rejected and hurt by their relationships. These situations arise for civilian and state-side-military women (and men) as well. However, when women reflected on their overall circumstances, they repeatedly identified the closed nature of the community and the unavailability of support systems as contributing factors which they said left them more vulnerable than they might otherwise have been. Thus, many women identified themselves as "victims of their situation" and were more willing to blame their troubles on the Air Force than to assume responsibility themselves.

OVERVIEW

The majority of enlisted Air Force women stationed overseas adapt well to their assignment. Nevertheless, it is necessary to take a serious look at the content of problematic issues that affect the adjustment of personnel and to examine the related processes at work in a closed overseas military community.

When young enlisted Air Force women stationed overseas described their environmental adjustment problems, the areas of concern they focused on were predeparture preparation, climate, location, mobility, financial resources, recreation, housing, and the host country. They also identified problems related to their work, health, and social life which they considered more important and not well under their control.

Although the details of events described by women varied, concerns for the same subject areas and, more importantly, the same processes were repeated from Air Force base to Air Force base. One of the major problems was the women's inability to clarify what was troubling them, to express these concerns, and to get satisfactory resolution. It is tempting to identify poor weather, location, housing, or lack of funds as the key to feelings of discontent. Complaints about these subjects are real and need to be addressed in their effect on the quality of life; but for the most part these are peripheral issues, symptomatic of underlying concerns. As one woman observed, "The weather doesn't make people fat." Rather, it was the women's perception of their problems, and their thwarted attempts at resolution, which led to dysfunctional behavior and poor adjustment to overseas duty. The combination of their perceived and real lack of preparation, recourse, and support formed the foundation for the majority of problems.

Women who said they felt unprepared also said they had few alternatives when confronted with work, health, or social problems. They described their situation as hopeless and themselves as helpless. This was most apparent when extremely sensitive issues such as homosexuality, unwanted pregnancies, and sex or racial discrimination arose.

Some women told of taking their concerns to higher authorities, only to be rejected. Consequently, they became apathetic and convinced that their side of a story would ultimately be dismissed or trivialized. Women who experienced frustration and difficulties with adjustment also often complained of depression and anger. This anger was primarily directed toward the Air Force, which they held responsible for their being "stuck in Turkey, separated from close friends, gaining weight, getting sick," or being generally unhappy.

Because there were few outlets for their hostility, some women masked their feelings with drugs or alcohol and/or withdrew. Sometimes this led to a desire to leave the Air Force, and the women tried to obtain an early release. At the end of Fiscal Year 1981, "the Air Force had the highest number of 'unsuitability discharges' for apathy."[22] Further investigation on the correlation between women's adjustment and their discharge rates may yield implications for retention potential.

The troubled young women repeatedly described themselves as living and working in a system which they said offered little support, either from within the formal military hierarchy or through their social contacts. Work, health, and social problems blended into one another because the way they dealt with problems, regardless of content, remained the same for most women and too often yielded unsatisfactory results.

The neglect of these problems by the Air Force had clear organizational implications. Untreated problems and unresolved issues affected the woman's job performance and her attitude toward the Air Force. A more formal investigation on overseas adjustment would be necessary before specific program evaluations and recommendations could be offered. However, the general categories and descriptions of problems identified by those having difficulty provide a starting point for further investigation.

To assist in solving the problems outlined in this chapter, the programs already in place—predeparture, recreational, intercultural, health education, financial management, and others—need to be restructured and enhanced by revision or expansion. It would seem that predeparture training should include some basic socialization skills as well as more effective training in economic realities, language proficiency, and the positive aspects of the host country. It might be interesting and useful to investigate how positive adjustment is related to education level and background. A comparison of the degree of adjustment experienced by male enlisted personnel and officers might also yield information which could be used to enhance already existing programs. Issues related to self-awareness and health education might be incorporated into programs, since problems in these areas appear to affect positive adjustment.

Strengthening the quality and availability of services, promoting positive communication among coworkers, and developing viable support systems and a truly functional grievance mechanism could lessen the degree of dissatisfaction expressed, increase the potential for more productive overseas tours, and ultimately result in a longer association with the Air Force. As more and younger women enter the Air Force and choose the military as their career, it becomes increasingly important to recognize them as the valuable labor force they represent and to utilize them in the most efficient and effective manner.

The effective utilization of women in the military has direct implications for overall maximum readiness. In a 1982 memo to the armed services secretaries, Casper Weinberger, Secretary of Defense, stated: "Women in the military are a very important part of our total force capability. Qualified women are essential to obtaining the numbers of quality people required to maintain the readiness of our forces. This Administration desires to increase the role of women in the military, and I expect the Service Secretaries actively to support that policy."[23]

If this is to happen, it will be necessary to look beyond job assignments and other work-related issues to see the role of women in a larger, more holistic context. The Air Force is more than a job or career field. It represents a whole subculture of which overseas communities are a part. Disturbing events, problems, and conflicts within these communities have a significant impact on an individual's ability to adjust to overseas duty and to the Air Force as well. Careful consideration of identified problem areas could lead not only to solutions for current problems but also to prevention of such occurrences in the future for the majority of military personnel, male and female, stationed overseas.

NOTES

1. Defense Manpower Data Center Report No. 3035, 30 September 1984. Washington, DC: Office of the Assistant Secretary of Defense (Manpower, Installations and Logistics).
2. Ellen C. Collier, *Women in the Armed Forces*. Issue Brief No. IB79045, The Library of Congress Congressional Research Service, update of 6/29/82: Appendix.
3. On the basis of the U.S. code relating to combat missions (Title 10, Sections 6015 and 8549), the excluded occupations for women are: Security specialist involved in

base defense; combat pararescue specialist who picks up downed pilots behind enemy lines; serial gunner on B-52s; and tactical air command and control specialist.

4. U.S. Air Force Military Personnel Center, *USAF Strength by Grade and Command.* Report PMC-P264, Randolph AFB, San Antonio, TX, September 1983.
5. Mady Wechsler Segal, "Women in the Military: Research and Policy Issues," *Youth and Society 10* (1978):101.
6. For an explanation of ethnographic fieldwork techniques, see R.N. Adams and J.J. Preiss, *Human Organization Research: Field Relation and Techniques* (Homewood, IL: Dorsey Press, 1960).
7. This presentation is not intended to represent Air Force or Department of Defense policy, all enlisted women, or every duty station. An effort was made to select the concerns which arose most frequently in interviews, with the understanding that the order of priority varied from person to person.
8. S. Mumford, "Navy Women and the Cross-Cultural Experience," *HRM Journal* (Spring/Summer 1983).
9. R. Kohls, *Survival Kit for International Living* (Chicago: International Press, 1979).
10. Alpha, Bravo, and Charlie conditions refer to the degree of inclement weather and were used to designate the degree of mobility accorded personnel in Keflavik. Charlie was the worst and required that all personnel remain where they were until it was lifted.
11. Many complaints were couched in humor. This allowed the expression of dissatisfaction when more direct forms were inappropriate or were viewed as detrimental to one's social or professional standing.
12. See for example Jesse J. Harris and David R. Segal, "Observations from the Sinai" *Armed Forces and Society 11* (February 1985): 235-248.
13. The atmosphere, food, and entertainment in enlisted clubs varied from base to base. Yet women complained about the high probability that fights would occur, and they repeatedly mentioned their discomfort with going to the club alone.
14. The percentages for each group are approximations based on the results of field interviews. No questionnaires were administered.
15. The Air Force has a "physical strength testing program in which both men and women must meet certain physical requirements in order to be assigned a job with physically demanding tasks." See B. Oganesoff, "Is it Really a Matter of Human Power?" *Government Executive* (February 1982): 22.
16. Complaints about transfers based on the need to fill "female quotas" were reported more often during the earlier years of the interviews. By 1980 this issue seemed to diminish in importance. No details on numbers or frequency of transfers were available at this writing.
17. See, for example, Joseph M. Rothberg et al., "Illness and Health of the U.S. Battalion in the Sinai MFO Deployment," *Armed Forces and Society 11* (Spring 1985): 413-426.
18. The statistics on the number of drug and alcohol-related incidents for women were unavailable at the time of this writing and may present an area for further investigation.
19. Although formal rules regarding the fraternization between officers and enlisted personnel were acknowledged, an informal interpretation of these rules was practiced.
20. This represents a generalization of what was described and observed as typical behavior of men on TDY.

21. Women who became involved with men on TDY seemed to express high expectations for sexual solutions to their problems.
22. P. Smith, "Discharge Policies Differ in Each Service, DoD Finds," *Navy Times*, April 12, 1983. The Air Force percentage of persons discharged short of completing their full enlistment because of "unsuitability—apathy" was 15.3%; corresponding percentages for the other services were: Army, 6.6%; Navy, 1.7%; Marine Corps, 4.9%; and all other DoD, 7.4%.
23. Oganesoff, "Matter of Human Power," p. 45.

9

The Leathernecks: A Few Good Men ... and Women

Michael L. Patrow and Renee Patrow

MARINE CORPS ROLES AND MISSIONS

We fight our country's battles in the air, on land and sea . . . .

This line from the Marine Corps Hymn highlights the unique character of the Marine Corps as a military force which is ready to engage in air, land, and naval warfare. This diverse character of the corps stems from its mission as established in Title 10 of the United States Code, Section 5013 which reads in part:

(a) The Marine Corps, within the Department of the Navy, shall be organized as to include not less than three combat divisions and three air wings, such other land combat, aviation, and other services as may be organic therein. The Marine Corps shall be organized, trained, and equipped to provide fleet Marine forces of combined arms, together with supporting air components, for service with the fleet in seizure or defense of advanced naval bases and for the conduct of a naval campaign. In addition, the Marine Corps shall provide detachments and organizations for service on armed vessels of the Navy, shall provide security detachments for the protection of naval property at naval stations and bases, and shall perform such other duties as the President may direct. However, these additional duties may not detract from or interfere with the operations for which the Marine Corps is primarily organized.

(b) The Marine Corps shall develop in coordination with the Army and the Air Force, those phases of amphibious operations that pertain to the tactics, technique, and equipment used by landing forces.

The naval character of the Marine Corps is clearly established by its mission to seize and defend advanced naval bases, participate in naval campaigns, provide marines for service aboard naval vessels, and provide security for naval stations and bases. In connection with these missions, the enlisted marine may frequently find himself serving with the United States Navy. He may be temporarily embarked aboard ship as a member of a large marine air-ground task force which could range in size from 2,400 to 46,000 marines.[1] An enlisted marine might also serve aboard a navy ship as a member of a permanent marine detachment. Detachments vary in size from about twenty to fifty marines, and their mission involves ceremonial duties, providing the ship with internal security, and serving as the ship's landing party. Another instance in which marines serve with the Navy is at marine barracks aboard naval bases. Guard duties, ceremonies, and preparation for these functions take up most of the working day for a marine who is assigned to a barracks.[2]

In addition to its role as a naval service, the Marine Corps has also been given the mission to maintain its own aviation component. The corps is tasked by law to maintain three air wings and provide the fleet marine forces with supporting air components. Because of this mission, approximately one out of every five enlisted marines is trained and assigned in an aviation related skill.[3]

Finally, the role of the Marine Corps as a ground combat force stems from its mission to maintain three combat divisions, provide forces for the seizure and defense of advanced naval bases, and develop landing force doctrine for amphibious operations. In addition to these tasks, the mission statement also contains the catchall phrase, ". . . and shall perform such other duties as the President may direct." This phrase has resulted in the marine's mission to provide security guards at United States embassies. The phrase has also imposed some unusual missions on marines such as the evacuation of American civilians from Saigon during the fall of South Vietnam in April 1975, and the use of marines as part of the multinational peace keeping force which was sent into Lebanon during 1982.

DEMOGRAPHY OF THE ENLISTED FORCE

Who are the enlisted marines? The Marine Corps is the smallest of the four American military services. Its officer-to-enlisted ratio is 1 to 9.4: the smallest of the four services. The corps also has the largest proportion of its enlisted force (over 55%) in the bottom three paygrades. At an average age of 23, enlisted marines tend to be younger than the enlisted personnel of the other services, and somewhat less well-educated. Although the corps is predominately white, the minority population in the corps' enlisted force (29.9%) is substantially larger than the proportion of minorities in the United States population which, according to the 1980 census, is 16.8%.[4] The corps, along with the other services, is also predominately male. Although approximately 51.4% of the United States population is female, the proportion of women in the enlisted forces of the four services is only 9% with the Marine Corps having the smallest proportion of women, 4.1%[5] Another distinguishing characteristic is that the corps has the lowest proportion (5.7%) of enlisted personnel with some college education.

THE ENLISTED MARINE—MORE THAN A TECHNICIAN

All enlisted marines start out in the corps with the common experience of recruit training which is followed by training and assignment in a primary military occupation specialty (MOS). Although a marine's career potential depends to a great extent on his achieving and maintaining technical proficiency in his primary skill, he is also expected to maintain a battery of general military skills (e.g., marksmanship, physical fitness, and drill) and to exercise sound leadership of his subordinates with his promotion to higher grades.

This concept of the marine as being more than just a technician is also evidenced by the corps' policy of using marines from all MOSs to fill certain special duty assignments. These jobs are referred to as "B-billets" and they include assignments such as recruiting duty, training recruits as a marine drill instructor, serving at a marine barracks on a naval base, duty with a marine detachment aboard a naval ship, or serving at one of the many United States embassies throughout the world as a member of a marine security guard detachment.[6] All enlisted marines, from infantrymen to electronics technicians, are eligible to be considered for assignment to a B-billet. A cook or an administrative clerk is just as likely to spend a tour of duty as a marine drill instructor as is a tank driver or rifleman.

In addition to working in his primary MOS and serving one or two tours of duty in a B-billet, most enlisted marines also receive additional training during their career. This includes advanced training in their primary skill and professional military education. (Professional education is conducted at noncommissioned officer schools and staff noncommissioned officer academies and is designed to prepare the marine to assume increased responsibility by expanding his professional knowledge of the corps and developing his leadership and managerial skills.[7])

Another characteristic of the enlisted force, which emphasizes the importance of leadership as well as technical expertise, is the designation of first sergeants and sergeants major at the grades of E-8 and E-9 respectively. When a marine is promoted to the grade of E-8, the second highest grade in the enlisted grade structure, he is designated as either a first sergeant or a master sergeant. The marine who is promoted to master sergeant continues to work in his primary skill, whereas the marine who becomes a first sergeant assumes a new role. As a first sergeant, the primary duty of the marine is to serve as the senior enlisted advisor and assistant to the commanding officer of a unit. Upon promotion to E-9, the first sergeant becomes a sergeant major and continues his role as a senior enlisted advisor, while the master sergeant who is promoted to E-9 continues to fill senior supervisory billets in his primary MOS as a master gunnery sergeant. All marines, regardless of their primary skill, can aspire to the position of first sergeant or sergeant major. When selecting individuals for these grades, the corps looks for marines with all-around professional competence and proven leadership ability. According to Marine Corps policy, the most important prerequisites for designation as a first sergeant or sergeant major are "outstanding leadership combined with an exceptionally high degree of professional competence in troop leadership and the ability to act independently as the principal enlisted assistant in all administrative, technical, and tactical requirements of the organization."[8]

From the fledgling marine private who has just finished boot camp to the veteran sergeant major or master gunnery sergeant, the expectation of the corps is clear and unchanging: the senior marine takes charge. He must therefore, regardless of MOS, have the leadership ability and the basic military skills to do so.

BOOT CAMP

". . . the most precious thing . . . our most fragile thing . . ."

If any of the U.S. armed services has a reputation for being the most military, the most physically demanding, the most austere, or the most of a host of other adjectives setting it apart from the others, that service is the Marine Corps. Some call it an elite force, that is, the choicest segment of the U.S. military. Others find fault with it as an institution representing the purest form of militarism in a free democratic society. Some even call for its abolition. Yet almost all, whether friend, foe, or disinterested party, will agree that the Marine Corps is conspicuous among U.S. armed services. To what does it owe this degree of fame or infamy?

When searching for a difference between the marines and the other services, the subject of recruit training always turns up. Other characteristics of the marines that seem to make them unique are their emphasis on marksmanship, and the enforcement of stringent physical fitness and weight standards. There are other traits too that set the Marine Corps apart. But recruit training is the preeminent discriminator, for it is the fountainhead of an enlisted marine's unique identity.

Marine Corps recruit training, or "boot camp," is not unlike recruit training in the other services in its basic purpose of indoctrinating young civilians into the mysterious ways of military organizations. Each service has its own variation of this theme, but the theme is common to all. Yet Marine Corps boot camp, whether by design or chance, has become much more than a military indoctrination. It is more a rite of passage—a prerequisite to the title, "Marine."

How it got to be this way is obscure. From 1911 until the establishment of the recruit training depots at Parris Island, South Carolina, in 1915,[9] and at San Diego, California, in 1923,[10] recruit training had been conducted at several installations on the east and west coasts.[11] Before 1911, recruits were trained at the marine barracks nearest their place of enlistment.[12]

Although the curriculum changed frequently in content and duration over the years, consolidation of recruit training at these two sites established an element of stability necessary to make the boot camp experience a common one to which every enlisted marine could relate and reflect upon with pride of accomplishment.

The subjects taught in boot camp are not the determining substance of the experience. The subjects do not differ much from what the basic soldier in any army must know. As early as 1927, an anonymous writer in the *Marine Corps Gazette* expressed concern that marines would have trouble explaining the difference between the product issuing from marine recruit training and that exiting Army boot camp. To make sure there was a difference, he claimed that swimming and the handling of small boats had been introduced into the schedule to cement, once for all, that the marine was not a soldier, but a sea-soldier.[13]

Brigadier General Dion Williams, writing two years earlier, argued somewhat more cogently for a Marine Corps-unique flavor to boot camp:

> Recruit training must include . . . instruction in the tradition and history of the Corps in order that the young man joining the Corps may at the outset of his Marine career gain some of the pride and esprit in his chosen service . . . which has always been one of the great assets of the Marine Corps.[14]

General Williams further suggested that only through "strenuous and exacting" recruit training could the Marine Corps live up to the high standards which had been previously established and which had "made the Corps popular with the people of the country and with the Congress."[15]

Hints of the real or perceived importance of the boot camp experience to the very identity of the Marine Corps appear frequently in the *Marine Corps Gazette*, the unofficial professional publication for marines. Lieutenant Colonel Robert Heinl, Jr., a prolific writer of Marine Corps history and frequent commentator on the health of the corps, referred in 1946 to the ubiquitous belief that boot camp is the most critical event in a marine's career.[16]

Eight years later Lieutenant Colonel Heinl, now convinced his previous observation was a true one, refers to boot camp as "the seed-bed" of Marine Corps attitudes and then draws this analogy which eloquently captures the impression of boot camp on a new marine:

> Like a sensitized plate, the Marine recruit will take only one clear exposure, and that first exposure will be printed on him throughout his service. Recruit depot, so to speak, is the camera which affords and regulates that initial exposure.[17]

There is probably no scientifically valid process that could establish beyond doubt that boot camp is the source of the spirit of the Marine Corps. But if ever perception gave birth to reality, the belief among marines that marine boot camp is the bedrock foundation of the corps is such a case.

How did this phenomenon come about? The answer is not clear, for recruit training today differs significantly from that in the early years of the two recruit depots. Over time, the length of recruit training has varied from twenty-four days to twelve weeks.[18] Subjects have changed. Even the role of the drill instructor has changed. The two recruit depots enjoyed substantial degrees of autonomy until 1944, when strict training schedules first appeared.[19] The two depots today are required by Marine Corps order to use syllabi which are identical save for some minor modifications required by physical differences in the depots' facilities or geographical constraints. Nevertheless, each depot prides itself on doing the best job turning out basic marines.

Not surprising, however, were the findings of an objective survey conducted by Headquarters Marine Corps in 1981. The purpose of the survey was to ascertain how well recently graduated recruits had learned many of the skills taught in boot camp. Immediate supervisors or leaders of these new marines completed the questionnaires. When the sample of recruits was separated by depot and results analyzed, statistically significant differences in skill levels appeared in only seven of the sixty skills rated. Parris Island graduates got higher ratings on four objectives. San Diego graduates fared better on three. The report concludes, "The pooled overall average performance ratings for all objectives combined were virtually identical for both depots' graduates.[20]

In his work *Warriors: A Parris Island Photo Journal*, Richard Stack, himself a 1963 graduate of Parris Island, hints about the subtle workings of the boot camp experience. The recruit is

> taught Marine Corps history and tradition. He is told how the Marines have always been the best, never losing a battle; he's told that the Army's soldiers, doggies, as they are called, aren't too much on the ball. It seems to work. It seems to give him a type of pride that's hard to define.[21]

This pride is what's important even if it is attained at the expense of a selective reading of Marine Corps history and unwarranted denigration of the American soldier—who in his recruit training no doubt hears some unflattering stories about marines. To highlight this pride, Stack prints some responses to a question he asked graduating recruits on what graduation meant to them. Pride in self was the most common and was expressed best, solecism and all, as follows: "I've made it as a Marine. The best military personal [sic] in the world."[22] Replies from the same group to the question, "Who and what are the marines?" again ooze pride if not arrogance. A characteristic one: "An elite group of men in a world of boys."[23]

William Manchester, another former marine and an accomplished contemporary historian, records in *Goodbye Darkness* the feelings aroused in his 1942 boot camp experience.

> How could I enjoy this? Parts of it, of course, I loathed. But the basic concept fascinated me. I wanted to surrender my individuality, curbing my neck beneath the yoke of petty tyranny. Since my father's death I had yearned for stern discipline, and Parris Island . . . gave it to me in spades. Physically I was delicate,

even fragile, but I had limitless reservoirs of energy, and I could feel myself toughening almost hourly. Everything I saw seemed exquisitely defined—every leaf, every pebble looked as sharp as a drawing in a book. I knew I was merely becoming a tiny cog in the vast machine which would confront fascism, but that was precisely why I had volunteered. Even today, despite the horrors which inevitably followed [battles in Pacific], I am haunted by memories of my weeks as a recruit. It is almost like recalling a broken marriage which, for one divorced partner, can never really end.[24]

Pulitzer prize winning reporter Jim Lucas found himself at Parris Island earning the title "Marine" before heading to the Pacific as a combat correspondent. He describes his experience in a humorous, self-deprecating vein. But his account of rifle qualification, the acme of recruit training, reflects the personal pride boot camp can elicit in a young man.

On the final round, at 500 yards, I needed a 48 out of 50 to qualify. Eight bull's eyes and two fours. Nothing less would do. Somehow I did it. I shall never forget that last shot. I worked for five minutes before squeezing it off, and was rewarded with [a bull's eye]. . . . My pals were lined up back of me, praying and pulling. A successful candidate for the presidency never got such an ovation, and certainly never strutted more nobly.

I was, at last, a Marine.[25]

Richard Wheeler was a member of the company that raised the flag at Mount Suribachi, Iwo Jima, on February 19, 1945—a moment in history immortalized in a photograph by Joe Rosenthal of the Associated Press. Wheeler's detailed account of the battle of Iwo Jima includes his thoughts of the significance of boot camp to himself and his fellow marines.

The building of the Marine *esprit de corps* began with boot camp, which was painfully tough. No Marine ever forgot his boot camp hitch. It was common for Marines to split up after boot camp, go through several campaigns, then meet again and barely mention their campaigns in their eagerness to reminisce about boot camp. . . .[26]

Speaking of the end result of this difficult training period, Wheeler says:

What had begun in deep anguish ended in high pride . . . They [the recruits] had qualified themselves for admission into a highly capable outfit with worthy traditions. They had become full-fledged United States Marines![27]

Successful Completion of Boot Camp

The foregoing anecdotal and philosophical accounts of the effects and benefits of boot camp, taken mostly from World War II experiences, have recently been shown to have some scientific validity among today's Marine Corps recruits.

A five-year study tracking a sample of marine recruits from time of enlistment to completion of enlistment period was conducted by the University of South Carolina during the years 1976-1981.[28] The study investigated differences in three groups of enlistees: those who failed to complete their enlistments, those who completed their enlistments and then separated, and those who reenlisted.

The study discerned a trend among several variables which could be surrogates for measures of pride and motivation. There was a pronounced peaking of the intensity of these surrogates at recruit graduation, followed by either a gradual or a precipitous declension depending upon the subgroup (reenlistment, separation after completing enlistment, premature separation). These measures included (1) intention to complete one's enlistment, (2) intention to reenlist, (3) identification with military role, and (4) satisfaction.[29]

The final report of this project summarizes: "completion of basic training elevated attitudes toward the military to their highest point for nearly all leaver and stayer groups."[30] To explain this result, the report suggests, several "socialization dimensions" come into play: training that is formal, group oriented, sequential, and done on a fixed time schedule; the use of role models, such as the drill instructor; the divestiture of recruits' identities at the outset of training thereby allowing a new identity to be formed.[31]

Many recruits who begin recruit training never become marines. Since 1979 attrition during boot camp has been between 12% and 15%.[32] What are the differences between those who succeed in training and those who do not?

Within the military manpower community, it has become almost trite to mention the performance gap between high school graduates and high school nongraduates. (In marine boot camp, the attrition rates for the two groups averaged 11% and 19% respectively for the fiscal years 1979 through 1981.)[33] Less well known are the findings of research dealing with stress on recruits conducted at the San Diego Recruit Depot by the University of Washington.[34] This comprehensive project showed that recruits who complete boot camp tend to

> [have] lower levels of thoughts related to failure, upset, and worry and more readily perceive the training experience as challenging. Attriters are more inclined to perceive themselves negatively and are less motivated to succeed in training.[35]

Along the same theme, the report concludes that "recruits graduating from training were characterized by higher self-appraisals and higher motivation than attriters."[36]

An earlier report from this research at San Diego discussed the concept of locus of control. Locus of control refers to a person's belief that rewards are contingent upon personal effort and skill (internal locus of control), or conversely, that rewards are not under personal control but result instead from luck, chance, fate, or powerful others (external locus of control).[37] As one would expect, those recruits evidencing a strong internal locus of control had much lower loss rates in recruit training than their external-locus-of-control counterparts.[38]

As we have seen, for those 85% to 90% who succeed in becoming marines, the thrill of recruit-training graduation ranks high among life's positive emotional events. Over thirty years ago, Lieutenant Colonel W.M. Kessler described the state of a new marine leaving Parris Island for his first duty assignment.

> The Parris Island recruit draws down discipline from portal to portal. No other part of his training is more greatly stressed. But remember, recruit training does not give long immunity to the red flag. His military discipline like his beard is easily removed. For 10 weeks he has been drilled, lectured and guided, and his ears were accustomed to the yammer of an authoritative voice from reveille to taps. Suddenly, the uproar ceases, his instructor is gone, he stands expectantly waiting—waiting for someone to tell him what to do.[39]

The illustration holds true today.

The DI

The marine drill instructor, or DI—the yammering authoritative voice—is the magician who deliberately orchestrates this ten-week transition of an anxious mob of civilians into a proud unit of marines. His role is as difficult as it is critical. The job of DI demands a lot of the young noncommissioned or staff noncommissioned officer. For some it demands too much. The interaction between the DI and his recruits within the recruit training environment exposes the Marine Corps' Achilles' heel. But before we explore this vulnerability, the drill instructor warrants a closer look.

In 1936, a prescient marine lieutenant, Wallace M. Greene, Jr., claimed that training recruits was the hardest job in the Marine Corps. He was not happy with many of the noncomissioned officers (NCOs) being assigned as recruit instructors. Lieutenant Greene claimed that although they had excellent previous records, many NCOs failed as recruit instructors because they could not study, could not handle recruits, could not teach what they knew, or would not work hard.[40]

Lieutenant Greene then identified the critical role of the NCO recruit instructor: "Every platoon which passes through training under his guidance will mirror his ability and efforts for the remainder of its time in the Marine Corps."[41]

One of the reasons for Lieutenant Greene's later success in the Marine Corps—as General Greene he was the Commandant of the Marine Corps from 1964 to 1967—was that he recommended sound solutions to problems. To remedy the deficiencies among recruit instructors, he posited the following:

1. Establish a standard school for NCOs assigned to train recruits;
2. Give special duty pay to recruit instructors;
3. Allow meritorious promotions to recruit instructors;

4. Guide each platoon through the entire basic training syllabus and marks-manship detail (then six weeks) by one team of instructors.[42]

All four of his recommendations are now in effect and have been for some time.[43]

Richard Wheeler's comment, quoted earlier, points out marines' propensity to reflect on their boot camp experience. The drill instructor is the personification of that experience. One would search far and wide for any former or active duty enlisted marine who could not immediately recall the name of his recruit training platoon's senior drill instructor. The articulate Lieutenant Colonel Heinl wrote in 1946

> If recruit training is considered the most important period in a Marine's career, the men who make it so are the drill instructors. Ask any veteran of Parris Island or San Diego . . . the question: 'What single person exerted the greatest influence on your Marine Corps career?' Nine times out of ten, the answer will be, 'My drill instructor.'[44]

Lieutenant Colonel Heinl then argued that drill instructors be appointed only from the "very cream and elite of all our noncommissioned officers, selected on a Corps-wide basis."[45] As with Lieutenant Greene's suggestions of a decade earlier, Lieutenant Colonel Heinl's recommendation is now practice.[46]

Training Tragedies

Heinl unwittingly foreshadowed a recruit training tragedy ten years hence when he wrote that the drill instructor accomplished his solemn duty of making marines "by precept, by appearance, by example, sometimes by main force."[47]

Those words, "by main force" would never be written by any responsible marine officer after April 1956. On the night of April 8, 1956, an overzealous Parris Island drill instructor, for disciplinary motives, took his platoon on an unauthorized night march. He led his seventy-four recruits into Ribbon Creek, a tidal creek behind the rifle range. As the platoon reached a pothole in the creek's bottom, panic swept the unit. Six recruits drowned.

The Marine Corps and the nation were shocked by the tragedy: the Marine Corps' process of training recruits would never again be considered strictly the Marine Corps' business.

Marine Corps and congressional investigations followed. Debate raged within the corps and in the press to either defend or condemn training methods. Ribbon Creek brought hasty and major reforms to recruit training. Commissioned officer supervision of training increased. The workload on drill instructors decreased.[48]

The issue of brutality in boot camp, catapulted into the public eye at Ribbon Creek three decades ago, remains to this day as an active volcano.

Sometimes it rumbles; sometimes it erupts; usually it rests dormant, deceiving the unwary of its awful potential.

In 1971 the volcano rumbled. Two journalists from WINS Radio in New York City published their book, *See Parris and Die*. The book, as its title suggests, is replete with hyperbole. It sets forth, with no credible supporting evidence, several hypotheses that only the most vitriolic of Marine Corps critics could contrive or accept (e.g., that an undercurrent of latent homosexuality pervades the Marine Corps;[49] that marine fathers impose excessively harsh discipline on their children[50]). Yet the book's main theme, brutality in boot camp, is supported by some cases that seem plausible and which, if accurately portrayed, were clearly inexcusable. This book and other critical articles written years after the Ribbon Creek incident had faded into history caused no significant public or congressional outcry—just a transient yelp in some book reviews.[51] Marines were being trained and the Marine Corps, in the eyes of the public, was doing its job well.

In December 1975, almost twenty years after the drownings in Ribbon Creek, the volcano erupted again. Within a one-month period, two recruit maltreatment incidents, one at each depot, raised the question of Marine Corp recruit training methods once more to the level of congressional inquiry.

On December 6, 1975, at San Diego Recruit Depot, Private McClure, a recruit assigned to a "special motivation platoon" (explained below) was beaten unconscious in a pugil stick bout.[52] He died three months later. At Parris Island, less than a month after the fatal pugil stick bout, a drill instructor who was trying to frighten a recruit in a mock execution, inadvertently shot the recruit in the hand.

The external pressure brought on the Marine Corps to correct a training system that would allow such abuses was less vocal than in 1956. It was, however, of similar intensity as the Commandant and several of his generals who sat before angry congressional committees would aver.

A *New York Times* editorial suggested that, even after the Ribbon Creek tragedy and supposed reforms, the additional recent incidents "indicate that not all Marines have yet learned to draw the line between toughness and sadism."[53]

Changes were made. Again the essence of the changes was to provide for more direct supervision of training by commissioned officers and to reduce the workload on drill instructors.[54]

The drill instructor's autonomy, almost total before 1956, has been greatly reduced today. Some marines trained under the old system complain that recruit training has been degraded in effectiveness by reining in the drill instructor. However, the product of the training does not substantiate that claim. Young enlisted marines are still proud and still perform admirably.

The similarity of the corrective actions taken after both the 1956 and 1975-1976 training accidents point to a possible cause of indiscretion by drill instructors. In each case, efforts were taken to reduce the workload on drill instructors. In 1956, two weeks were added to the training course with no new subjects, giving drill instructors 20% more time to do the same job. The number of drill instructors per platoon (about seventy-five recruits) was doubled from two to four, and subsequently reduced to three. A motivation platoon was also established as a repository for problem recruits who threatened the discipline and degraded the performance of a drill instructor's platoon.[55] Ironically, Private McClure was assigned to the motivation platoon when he sustained his fatal beating.

In 1976, sixty-four training hours were eliminated—about a 15% reduction—without any reduction in course length. And a normal daily routine from 0700 to 1700 was established. Again, the workload on the drill instructor was being reduced. (The motivation platoon, now seen as part of the problem rather than part of the solution, was abolished.)[56]

Stress on the DI

Although the high-stress nature of the drill instructor's job had long been recognized, only recently has a true picture of the magnitude of that stress and its debilitating effects become available.

The University of Washington research cited above started out as a study of stress on recruits. While pursuing that end, the researchers soon recognized that stress experienced by drill instructors was a topic equally worthy of study.

> Our interest in the drill instructor has two key sources. In certain recruit-focused research projects . . . we have discovered strong training unit influences on recruit performance and attrition. Since the drill instructor team shapes the training unit (i.e., platoon) environment, the importance of studying the drill instructor became more salient . . . A second reason for the interest in drill instructors is that in the course of our recruit stress research we were often told by drill instructors that we should study them. In a variety of formal and informal interviews, drill instructors informed us of the stressful nature of their job and disclosed aspects of personal difficulty that they attributed to job stress. In our process monitoring of recruit training, our observations of drill instructors and their tasks were consistent with the concerns that they reported.[57]

Upon the researchers' recommendation, the Office of Naval Research and the Marine Corps expanded the scope of the project to include drill instructors. Initial findings of the study have been enlightening.

First, both self-reported information and physiological changes indicated that drill instructors experience increased stress during their first year on the job after graduation from Drill Instructor School. Second, performance evaluations of drill instructors by their superiors are related to self-reported stress. People who say they experience high stress tend to be poor performers. The report of these results cites, as an important finding, the increase in scores that measure "the time urgency behavior . . . of the Type-A pattern . . . [which] involves the tendency to become irritated and to lose one's temper."[58]

Whether or not stress was a factor in the 1956 and 1975-1976 incidents cannot be established. Perhaps those drill instructors involved were cool and unexcitable but plagued by poor judgment and bad luck. Nevertheless, it cannot be denied that there is potential for abuse of recruits in an environment that produces significant and quantifiable increases in stress measurement over time in certain types of personalities. A more thorough understanding of this process should result in better ways of preventing the potential for recruit abuse.

Clearly, the Marine Corps must perform a delicate balancing act with its boot camp. It must create an authoritarian aura without inviting authoritarian abuse. General Robert H. Barrow, a former Commandant of the Marine Corps (1979-1983) and himself a product of boot camp, has best articulated the relationship of recruit training to the organization:

> It is at once the most precious thing we have in the Marine Corps, and it's our most fragile thing . . . We can't let the DIs screw it up and we can't let the policy makers screw it up . . . This thing is the guts of the Marine Corps.[59]

Recruit training creates the unique identity of the enlisted marine, and the enlisted marine is the identity of the Marine Corps. This is so if for no other reason than that so many marines believe it to be so. Yet to accomplish its end, recruit training must establish a milieu with some unique characteristics. The first such characteristic is an authority figure, the DI who establishes and enforces a strict discipline foreign to that ever experienced by most recruits. Second is a demanding training schedule which pushes the recruit beyond his preconceived limits of abilities so that he may gain self-confidence and be encouraged to seek a higher level of performance than he thought himself capable of. Third is the establishment of a mutual bond among members of the training unit by demanding a high degree of interdependence to achieve certain platoon objectives.

The environment necessary to do these things is one that will always possess the potential for abuse of recruits by drill instructors who are working under documented high stress conditions. If it lacks vigilance in regulating boot camp, the Marine Corps could jeopardize a most precious and fragile ingredient.

ENLISTED WOMEN MARINES

Women marines are relative newcomers to the corps, inasmuch as women did not serve in the corps until World War I and did not become a permanent part of the Marine Corps until after World War II. A review of the history of women marines reveals that the corps was reluctant to admit women to its ranks in 1948, and controversy still exists within the corps concerning the appropriate role for women marines. The account of women marines which follows not only chronicles the experience of women in the corps, it also reveals how the Marine Corps has been affected by and has adapted to one of the most significant social movements in recent American history—the changing role of women in American society.

World War I

In the summer of 1918, the 4th Marine Brigade was heavily engaged in the fighting in France as the Allied forces repulsed a German attack and then took the offensive against the German army. Because of high casualties, replacement troops were urgently needed in France, and it became evident that one source of replacement personnel was the sizeable number of trained, able-bodied marines in the United States who were filling clerical and administrative jobs. To free these marines for the fighting in France, the Commandant of the Marine Corps requested the authority "to enroll women in the Marine Corps Reserve for clerical duty at Headquarters Marine Corps and at other Marine Corps offices in the United States where their services might be utilized to replace men who may be qualified for active field service."[60] In view of the all-out war effort in the country, enrolling women in the Marine Corps was not a bold move by the corps. Out of necessity, American industry and business were already using women to replace the men who had volunteered or been drafted to serve in the armed forces. Also, the Navy had started enlisting women as yeomen as early as March 1917, just before the United States entered World War I in April 1917.[61] The Secretary of the Navy readily approved the Marine Corps' request on August 8, 1918, and within days, Marine Corps recruiting offices throughout the country were swamped with women seeking to enlist.[62] Between August and November of 1918, 305 women were enlisted in the corps.[63] Recruiters were instructed to enroll only women with business or office experience who possessed such skills as stenography, bookkeeping, accounting, typing, etc.[64] Although a few women served at various Marine Corps recruiting offices throughout the country, most of the women reservists were stationed at Headquarters Marine Corps in Washington, D.C. They were assigned primarily to the offices of the adjutant and inspector, the paymaster, and the quartermaster, where they worked as secretaries, clerks, and messengers. Women marines received the same pay as men of the same grade, and the highest grade held in the Marine Corps by a woman during World War I was sergeant.[65]

The tenure of women in the Marine Corps during World War I was very brief. With the end of the war on November 11, 1918, the women reservists were no longer needed. Accordingly, on July 15, 1919, the Commandant directed that all of the women reservists were to be transferred to inactive status by August 11, 1919.[66]

World War II

Women remained outside the corps until World War II when, once again, it became necessary to enlist women to replace male marines who were needed for combat duty in the Pacific. When the proposal of admitting women was initially presented to the Commandant, Lieutenant General Thomas Holcomb, he opposed the idea, believing that women could serve no useful purpose in the Marine Corps.[67] However, the urgent need to release men for operations in the Pacific caused the proposal to be reconsidered, and on November 7, 1942, a Women's Reserve was officially authorized as a branch of the United States Marine Corps Reserve.[68]

During the course of establishing the Women's Reserve, the corps implemented policies which were designed to ensure that the women would be regarded as full-fledged members of the corps. The women reservists were to be called "Marines." Nicknames or acronyms similar to the use of "WAVES" (Women Accepted for Volunteer Emergency Service) in the Navy would not be used. Also the uniform would be the traditional forest green color of the Marine Corps "with suitable differences being made in the material and in the cut of the uniform to conform to the convenience and smart appearance of women, but sufficiently like the marine uniform to permit no possibility of doubt as to the branch of service to which the Women Reservists are attached."[69]

The role of women in the corps during World War II was distinctly different from that of the World War I women marines. A much larger number of women served in World War II in a wider variety of skills and at many more duty stations. By June 1944, the Women's Reserve had reached a strength of 18,838.[70] Unlike the World War I women marines, who performed only clerical jobs and were assigned primarily to Marine Headquarters in Washington, the Women Reservists in World War II were assigned to all major Marine Corps duty stations in the continental United States, to Hawaii at the Pearl Harbor Naval Base, and to the Marine Corps Air Station at Ewa.[71] World War II women marines were assigned in over two hundred different occupational specialties, which included many traditionally masculine jobs such as radio operator, motor transport driver, control tower operator, and automotive mechanic.[72] Women were commissioned as marine officers for the first time during World War II, with the highest grade being that of colonel. Enlisted women were no longer restricted to the grade of sergeant as they were during World War I. During World War II, enlisted women marines were promoted up to the highest enlisted pay grade, E-7.[73]

Formal training for women was also instituted in World War II. Initially, enlisted women recruits were trained at the U.S. Naval Training School (WR), which used the facilities of Hunter College in the Bronx, New York.[74] In July

1943, recruit training was moved to Camp Lejeune, New River, North Carolina.[75] Subsequent to recruit training, which lasted about four weeks, women with skills which could be immediately used and those who would receive on-the-job training were sent on to their permanent duty stations. Others attended specialist training in a variety of skills such as paymaster, parachute rigger, aerographer, control tower operator, aerial gunner instructor, celestial navigation radio operator, auto mechanic, and aviation supply.[76]

With the large number of women in the corps during World War II, the Marine Corps had to deal with the issues of marriage and dependents of women marines. When the Women's Reserve was formed in February 1943, a married woman could enlist provided she had no children under 18 years of age and was not married to a marine. Additionally, a single woman who joined the Corps could not marry a marine while in the service.[77] In March 1943, this policy was modified to allow women in the Marine Corps to marry another marine after completion of their initial training (either recruit training or officer candidate school). Later in 1943, the policy was changed again to permit wives of marines below the grade of second lieutenant to enlist. However, the Marine Corps warned each married enlistee that "the probability of being stationed with her husband is very slight, and that consideration cannot be given to personal desires in the matter."[78]

With the surrender of the Japanese on V-J Day, September 2, 1945, the corps made plans to completely demobilize the Women's Reserve by September 1, 1946.[79] In the directive which announced the demobilization, the Commandant acknowledged the contribution made by women marines during the war while also recalling the reservations that existed in the corps when the Women's Reserve was initially created.

> It was with some hesitation that the Marine Corps admitted women to its ranks in February 1943, but during the intervening years they have made a most valuable contribution to the Corps. . . . As the time comes to release them, I am reminded again of the important part they have played in support of our combat Marines while the actual fighting was in progress.[80]

The performance of the women marines during World War II even won over Lieutenant General Thomas Holcomb who, as Commandant, had been opposed to admitting women to the corps. In contrast to his earlier belief that women couldn't serve any useful purpose in the Marine Corps, General Holcomb stated in 1943:

> There's hardly any work at our Marine stations that women can't do as well as men. They do some work far better than men. . . . What is more, they're real *Marines*. They don't have a nickname, and they don't need one. They get their basic training in a Marine atmosphere, at a Marine post. They inherit the traditions of Marines. They are Marines.[81]

Post World War II

Although women marines had proven their usefulness in a wartime Marine Corps, the leaders of the corps after World War II were adamant in their belief that women did not belong in the corps during peacetime. This attitude was plainly stated in October 1945 by Brigadier General C.G. Thomas, Director of the Division of Plans and Policies at Headquarters Marine Corps, who stated:

> The opinion generally held by the Marine Corps is that women have no proper place or function in the regular service in peace-time. . . . The American tradition is that a woman's place is in the home. . . . Women do not take kindly to military regimentation. During the war they have accepted the regulations imposed on them, but hereafter the problem of enforcing discipline alone would be a headache.[82]

As it turned out, however, the plan to completely disband the Women's Reserve was never carried out. While the Marine Corps proceeded with its demobilization of the Women's Reserve after the end of the war, both the Navy and the Army were making plans to retain a large number of women on active duty in their peace-time forces. Recognizing that some sort of permanent role for women in the U.S. armed forces was soon to become a reality, the Marine Corps acquiesced slightly by proposing a plan for women to participate in the Volunteer and Organized component of the Reserve. A small cadre of women reserves, forty-five officers and twenty-three enlisted women, would be assigned to active duty to administer the program. However, no woman would be allowed to remain on active duty more than four years.[83] Additionally, summer training, which has always been an important feature of the reserve program, was not considered to be necessary for the women reservists.[84] The limited scope of this program was a clear statement of the reluctance of the corps to have women on active duty in peacetime.

Legislation to establish the reserve program was introduced in the second session of the 79th Congress, but the bill died in committee when the 79th Congress adjourned.[85] During the 80th Congress, legislation concerning women in the Army, Navy and Marine Corps was again introduced. However, this legislation not only provided for a Women's Reserve, it also authorized women to become members of the regular component of each of the services.[86] Integration of women in the regular establishment was strongly supported by the Army and Navy, but it was something that the Marine Corps did not want and had sought to avoid. At the Senate subcommittee hearings on the legislation, two distinguished World War II flag officers, General of the Army Dwight D. Eisenhower and Fleet Admiral Chester W. Nimitz, gave strong endorsements to the legislation. General Eisenhower declared:

Not only do I heartily support the bill to integrate women into the Regular Army and Organized Reserve Corps, but I personally directed that such legislation be drawn up and submitted to this Congress.[87]

Later in the hearing, Admiral Nimitz stated:

The Navy's request for the retention of women is not made as a tribute to their past performance. We have learned that women can contribute to a more efficient Navy. Therefore, we would be remiss if we did not make every effort to utilize their abilities.[88]

In contrast to the enthusiastic support of the Army and the Navy, Colonel J.W. Knighton, the Marine Corps representative at the hearings, made a brief statement:

The previous witnesses have expressed the views of the Commandant; the Commandant of the Marine Corps is in favor of the bill and trusts that it will be enacted as soon as possible.[89]

On June 12, 1948, President Truman signed the Women's Armed Services Integration Act, which became Public Law 625. In addition to integrating women into the regular Marine Corps and the Marine Corps Reserve, Public Law 625 also contained a number of restrictions. Regular women could not exceed 2% of the strength of the regular Marine Corps. Also, women could not be assigned to duty in aircraft engaged in combat missions or in vessels of the Navy other than transport and hospital ships.[90] Although this last restriction only referred to the presence of women aboard combatant aircraft and vessels, it implicitly prohibited women from being used in any form of combat, to include land combat as well as naval and aviation combat. By including this restriction, Congress intended to ensure that women would not serve in combat roles.

Even though the leadership of the Marine Corps had been opposed to having women in the regular establishment, they had also recognized that the women's legislation would eventually be enacted, and as early as December 1947 a board was convened at Headquarters Marine Corps to determine how many regular women the corps could effectively use. The board recommended a regular women marine strength of 65 officers and 728 enlisted.[91]

There was a strong desire among many marines to have the corps return to an all male club, but some of the opposition in the Marine Corps to having women in the peacetime force was based on practical consideration. Unlike the Army and the Navy, which could use a large number of women in their medical corps as nurses, medical and dental assistants, and laboratory technicians, the Marine Corps did not have a large number of billets in its supporting establishment which could easily be staffed with women because the Navy provides that support. At the time that the women's legislation was being debated, the Marine Corps had demobilized from its huge wartime strength and was limited by Congress to a total active duty strength of 100,000.[92] This meant that for every woman on active duty, the Marine Corps must give up a male marine who could be trained for combat and deployed if necessary. Moreover, having women on active duty decreased the rotation base of nondeployable billets for male marines. Nondeployable billets are those jobs in which a person would not be sent to combat.[93] Every woman on active duty meant one less nondeployable billet into which a male marine could be assigned periodically to give him a respite from the arduous duty and family separation usually associated with deployable billets. Erosion of the rotation base for male marines had the potential of resulting in such adverse effects as decreased morale among male marines and lower reenlistment rates. Primarily because of the combat restrictions on women's assignments and the problem of maintaining a rotation base for male marines, the Marine Corps restricted the number of women on active duty to 1% of the Marine Corps strength, even though by law the limit was 2%. Because of this self-imposed constraint, the number of women marines remained low for many years. Between the Korean and Vietnam Wars, the number of women declined from a high of 2,728 in September 1953 to 1,281 in December 1964.[94]

Even though the number of women remained small, the corps authorized women to serve in a wide variety of its occupational fields. Between Korea and Vietnam, twenty-seven of the forty-three enlisted occupational fields were open to women.[95] These twenty-seven fields were based on a 1951 study of the use of women during the Korean War. There appeared to be general agreement that the effectiveness of women in a period of mobilization would be increased if they were trained and used in a wide variety of skills during peacetime.[96] Despite the wide variety of skills open to them, women marines became concentrated in a small number of skills which were administrative and nontechnical in nature. For instance, in March 1958, approximately 42% of the women were assigned in administration, followed by 23% in supply, 7% in communications, and 5% in disbursing.[97] Furthermore, during the years between Korea and Vietnam, very few women marines received formal skill training after boot camp. The scope of the problem as of December 1964 was outlined by the Director of Women Marines:

> Seventy percent of our women Marine recruit graduates are between the ages of 18 and 20 and, in most instances, have come directly from high school into the Marine Corps with little or no work experience. These young women are bright, capable trainees, but we are actually expecting them to be proficient in a specific MOS with only eight weeks of basic training. During calendar year 1963, 771 women Marines completed recruit training and only five were ordered directly from recruit training to a service school.[98]

The waning strength of women marines and the lack of skill training, as well as ineffective utilization and general mismanagement of women marines, eventually led to the Woman Marine Program Study Group which was convened in August 1964. As a result of this study, women marines were to be assigned and trained in a larger number of occupational fields; the number of duty stations for women was also increased.[99]

The Era of Equal Opportunity

The changes to and improvement of the status of women in the Marine Corps in the decades of the 1950s and 1960s were, in general, initiated by and within the Marine Corps as an institution. In the decades of the 1970s and 1980s, the role of women in the corps would undergo still more changes, often in response to pressure from organizations which were external to the Marine Corps, such as the Department of Defense, Congress, and the Supreme Court. The 1970s can be characterized as the era of equal opportunity in American society, and during the decade this movement had a great impact on all of the U.S. armed services.

Early in the decade of the 1970s, the Secretary of Defense directed each of the services to develop affirmative actions plans by November 30, 1972, to promote equal opportunity for minorities and women. In response to this directive, the Marine Corps formed an ad hoc committee to develop a plan of action to eliminate discrimination based solely on sex and to increase opportunities for women marines. The final report of the committee contained recommendations for an increase in women marines to 3,100 by June 30, 1977, the opening of more occupational fields to women, and—most surprising of all—the opening of Fleet Marine Force (FMF) assignments to women.[100]

Heretofore, women had never been assigned to FMF organizations because, in theory, all FMF units were deployable in combat. However, as a result of the ad hoc committee's recommendations, the corps began a pilot program in 1974 to assign women to FMF billets which would not be included in the assault echelon of the command should the unit be sent into combat.[101] This new policy was designed to allow women marines much wider assignment opportunities without violating the combat restriction implied in the law. Soon after FMF assignments were opened for women in 1974, the career opportunities for women were expanded even further when the Commandant opened all occupational fields to women with the exception of four fields which were directly related to combat: infantry, artillery, tanks and amphibian tractors, and flight crews.[102] The wider variety of occupational fields available for women, and the assignment of women to the FMF, paved the way for the decision to significantly increase the total number of women in the corps. In March 1977, during an appearance before the House Armed Services subcommittee, the Commandant announced that the Marine Corps was planning to increase its women marine strength to 10,000 by 1985.[103]

Another important advance for enlisted woman marines which occurred during the 1970s was the selection of the first women for the grades of first sergeant (E-8) and sergeant major (E-9). These grades had been created in 1955 for the purpose of providing marine commanding officers with a senior enlisted advisor and assistant.[104] When the designations of first sergeant and sergeant major were created, women were precluded from holding them on the grounds that the senior NCO in a unit must be able to lead the unit in the field or when in a combat situation. In 1960 a brevet system was established which allowed women in the grades of master sergeant (E-8) and master gunnery sergeant (E-9) to be temporarily appointed as first sergeants and sergeants major respectively when they were filling positions in women's units which were designated as first sergeant or sergeant major billets. When the women left these jobs, they reverted back to their permanent grade of master sergeant or master gunnery sergeant. The brevet system continued until 1972, when the policy was changed to allow permanent appointments for women to the grades of first sergeant and sergeant major.

One of the strongest advocates for this change was the corps' top enlisted man, the Sergeant Major of the Marine Corps, Joseph W. Daily. In a memorandum to the Commandant in November 1971, Sergeant Major Daily discussed the unfairness of the policy and also related that 95% of the staff NCOs attending a recent symposium had voted in favor of having women marines promoted to the grades of first sergeant and sergeant major. Sergeant Major Daily concluded his memo by strongly recommending that "Women Marines be given the same opportunity as Male Marines in our promotion system and that it should commence with the Fiscal Year 1972 Board. . . ." An additional impetus for a change in the policy also came from the Assistant Secretary of Defense for Manpower and Reserve Affairs, who issued a memo directing the services to eliminate such inequalities. As a result of these events, women marines were considered for selection to the grades of first sergeant and sergeant major during the 1972 E-8/E-9 promotion board.[105]

The 1970s also witnessed the end of women's units in the corps. Ever since World War II, when large numbers of women served in the corps, women marines had been organized into women's units. Enlisted women at Marine Corps posts and stations usually had their own barracks, which they maintained themselves. Although the women worked in different offices and units throughout their duty station, they were organized for administrative purposes into companies and battalions or squadrons which were commanded by women officers.[106] This practice resulted in having a separate chain of command for men and women. Whereas a male marine was commanded by the unit for which he worked, a woman marine who worked in the same office or shop was under the command of the woman marine company or battalion.

By the 1970s, the policy of maintaining women marine units appeared to be contrary to the goal of equal treatment for women marines because it singled them out for special treatment. Accordingly, the Commandant directed all commanders to review the requirement for separate women's units.[107] By

June 1977, all but three women's units had been deactivated.[108] At most major posts and stations, women continued to be housed in a separate barracks but were attached for command and administrative purposes to the unit for which they worked.

Marines as Wives and Mothers

In addition to the expanding career opportunities for women marines, the policy on marriage and motherhood of women in the corps also underwent great change during the decade of the 1970s. A study of these changes reveals that they closely paralleled and reflected the changing attitude toward working wives and mothers which occurred in American civilian society during the 1970s. In the period from 1949 until the Vietnam era, an enlisted woman marine who married could request and receive an administrative discharge provided she had completed one year of service beyond her basic training. In 1964, this policy changed when the corps stopped automatically discharging married women marines upon their request. A joint household policy was established which, in general, granted discharges for marriage only when the corps was unable to station the individual woman at or close enough to the domicile of her husband to permit the couple to maintain a joint residence. With the joint household policy in effect, the Marine Corps was in a position to require married women marines to complete their enlistment contracts.[109]

Significant changes were also made in the laws concerning the dependency status of civilian husbands of women of all the services. Based on the provisions of the Women's Armed Services Integration Act of 1948, a civilian husband was not considered a dependent of a service woman unless he was actually dependent on her for his "chief support."[110] Accordingly, the civilian husband was not issued a dependent's ID card and, therefore, was considered a visitor when he came on a Marine Corps base. Unlike the civilian wife of a male marine, who has access to all base activities such as the service club, commissary, exchange, golf course, swimming pool or theater, the civilian husband of a woman marine could only use these facilities when accompanied by his wife as her guest. He was not entitled to dependent medical care, nor was the couple eligible for family housing. In terms of pay and allowances, the woman marine with a civilian husband was treated as if she were single. If she was authorized to be paid basic allowance for quarters, it was at the single rate. Also, she was not entitled to travel and transportation allowances for her spouse or any of the other special allowances authorized for married male marines. The distinction between the dependency status of the spouse of male and women marines was changed in May 1973 when the Supreme Court ruled in the case of *Frontier vs. Richardson* that service women were eligible for all benefits, privileges, and rights granted servicemen under the same circumstances.[111]

Marine Corps policy regarding pregnancy and motherhood of women marines also changed radically during the 1970s. The following statement from a study group which met in 1948 to consider proposed regulations on the discharge of servicewomen summed up the attitude toward motherhood of servicewomen which prevailed at the time women were integrated into the regular Marine Corps:

> It is believed that pregnancy and motherhood *ipso facto* interfere with military duties. . . . It is believed that a woman who is pregnant or a mother should not be a member of the armed forces and should devote herself to the responsibilities which she has assumed, remaining with her husband and child as a family unit.[112]

This attitude formed the basis of Marine Corps policy on motherhood of women marines until 1970. From 1948 until 1970, a woman who acquired natural, adopted or foster children, or stepchildren was automatically discharged.

This policy was strictly enforced until 1970, when Headquarters Marine Corps announced it would consider granting waivers for women marines who were stepparents or had personal custody of or adopted a child. In 1971, another important precedent was set when the corps allowed two women marines who became natural mothers, a gunnery sergeant and a major, to remain on active duty. (In the case of Gunnery Sergeant Frances I. Gonzales, the only work days missed due to pregnancy had been charged to annual leave or to travel time associated with a change of duty station.) Both of these waiver cases were considered on their own merits, the primary criteria being the woman's record and her ability to care for the child while remaining on active duty.[113] In 1975, the Marine Corps policy of deciding each case on its own merits was brought to an end when the Department of Defense (DoD) published a policy which precluded the involuntary separation of service women solely on the basis of pregnancy. On the basis of the new DoD regulations the Marine Corps revised its policy, providing women who became pregnant the option of being retained on active duty or requesting discharge. This new policy, however, also warned women marines who chose to remain on active duty that they would be guaranteed no special consideration in duty assignments or duty stations based solely on pregnancy or the fact that they had children. The women were also advised that they could be discharged if they failed to maintain themselves reasonably available for duty and productive as marines subsequent to their becoming a parent.[114]

Women Marines in the 1980s

A look at the enlisted woman marine force during the 1980s reveals the impact of the changes which occurred during the three previous decades. At the end of fiscal year 1981, enlisted women marines numbered 7,091, which accounted for 4.1% of the total enlisted force. Although the proportion of women in the enlisted force remains small, the number of women has grown significantly since 1948 when the corps planned to have an enlisted women's component of only 728. Women marines are also more widely dispersed throughout the corps' occupational fields. Table 9.1 compares the distribution of women marines by occupational field in March 1958 with the distribution as of December 1982.

Between 1958 and 1982, the number of occupational fields to which women were actually assigned rose from twenty-two to thirty-five.[115] Table 9.1 also reveals that the Marine Corps was living up to its advertised policy of using women in all skills except those related to combat. It is to be noted, however, that the women were still concentrated in the same two skills (administration and supply) in 1982 as they were in 1958; but the proportion of women in these two fields has declined somewhat from approximately 65.2% in 1958 to 47% in 1982. The information in Table 9.1 indicates that the assignment of women marines is shifting slightly from the clerical fields, such as administration and supply, to the more traditionally male jobs, such as motor transport and military police, and to the more technical fields, such as the aviation-related skills. Finally, in the 1980s it is not uncommon to see active duty women marines who are married and have children, whereas in previous decades most women marines were single and the few who were married had no children.

The current official attitude toward women in the corps appears to be very supportive. In a 1980 letter to all Marine Corps commanders, the Commandant expressed his commitment concerning equal and fair treatment for women marines.

> Women Marines and male Marines serve side by side in our ranks. They are equal in every sense. They are Marines. They deserve nothing less than outstanding leadership, equal treatment, and equal opportunity for professional development.[116]

Despite the official policy, however, opinions of individual marines, expressed in unofficial forums such as professional journals, indicate that there is still controversy within the corps concerning the role of women marines. In the July 1981 issue of the *Marine Corps Gazette* a marine major criticized the policy on pregnancy of women marines. He bemoaned the lost time incurred by the corps due to pregnancy and the physical limitations of pregnant women marines which restricted their performance of some duties. The author expressed his belief that "pregnancy damages the acceptance of women by male marines. . . . Males resent the increased workload that often results when a pregnant co-worker is absent or unable to perform certain duties."[117] Another area of controversy is FMF assignments for women. In an article entitled "No

Table 9.1. Distribution of Enlisted Women Marines by Occupational Field
as of March 1958 and December 1982*

OF	Title	% March 58	% December 82
01	Personnel & Administration	42.4	23.7
02	Intelligence	.1	.4
03	Infantry**	—	—
04	Logistics	.1	1.8
08	Field Artillery**	—	—
11	Utilities	—	1.9
13	Engineer	—	1.1
14	Drafting, Surveying & Mapping	.6	.2
15	Printing & Reproduction	.1	.3
18	Tank & Amphibian Tractor**	—	—
21	Ordnance	—	1.2
23	Ammunition and EOD	—	.5
25	Operational Communications	7.3	8.8
26	Signals Intelligence	—	1.2
28	Data Communications Maintenance	.1	3.2
30	Supply	22.8	13.3
31	Transportation	.8	1.6
33	Food Service	.1	5.0
34	Disbursing	5.1	4.3
35	Motor Transport	.4	6.0
40	Data Systems	3.5	2.8
41	Marine Corps Exchange	3.2	.3
43	Public Affairs	1.1	1.2
44	Legal Services	—	1.6
46	Audio Visual Support	1.1	1.6
55	Band	—	1.3
57	Nuclear Biological & Chemical Defense	—	.1
58	Military Police	—	2.2
59	Electronic Maintenance	—	.9
60	Aircraft Maintenance — (Fixed Wing)	.6	3.2
61	Aircraft Maintenance (Helicopter)	—	.2
63	Avionics (Organizational)	—	1.9
64	Avionics (Intermediate)	—	1.4
65	Aviation Ordnance	—	.5
66	Aviation Electronics***	.5	—
68	Weather Services	.5	.3
69	Aviation Training Devices***	.2	—
70	Airfield Services	.9	1.2
72	Air Control/Support	—	.1
73	Air Traffic Control	.6	.9
98/99	Identifying & Reporting MOS's	8.0	3.8

*1958 data developed from Administrative Assistant, Office of the Director of Women Marines memo
(Washington, DC: Headquarters U.S. Marine Corps, 6 June 1958). 1982 data developed from
Monthly Report of Women Marines by Occupational Field, HQ-1080-37 (Washington, DC: Head-
quarters U.S. Marine Corps, 31 December 1982).
**Women are excluded from these skills because they are directly related to combat.
***Not a separate occupational field in 1982.

Place for Women," a marine lieutenant colonel advocated returning to the policy of excluding women from all FMF assignments. He argued that when FMF units are embarked aboard navy ships, the women in these units have to be replaced, thereby causing personnel turbulence which erodes unit integrity and reduces combat readiness. The author also surmises that in spite of the official policy which allows women to serve in rear echelon FMF units, the corps will pull women out of these units in wartime rather than run the risk of having women killed or wounded. In addition, the author sees other benefits to excluding women from FMF units.

> Problems regarding fraternization and sexual harassment would be minimized in the operating forces. Problems regarding privacy and separate sanitary facilities in field conditions would be eliminated. Commanders would be relieved of the mental gymnastics of determining appropriate FMF working conditions for women. How many women stand solitary guard posts in the middle of the night? How many are allowed even to work alone in office spaces after regular working hours? Marine training is oriented toward, among other things, achieving group cohesion. The presence of females—and the inevitable liaisons that develop—fractures the cohesion so vitally necessary to good morale and fighting efficiency. A conservative exclusion policy would minimize such problems in the units in which the maintenance of cohesion and unity of effort is a paramount concern.

The author goes on to say that an "FMF exclusion would facilitate a termination of the present absurdities in pursuit of amorphous social goals" and concludes his essay by asserting: "The presence of women in the Fleet Marine Force undermines the battleproven axiom that 'every Marine is first and foremost a rifleman.' "[118]

These comments exemplify some of the adverse attitudes faced by women in the corps as well as some of the very real problems which the Marine Corps must still resolve. The successful resolution of these issues and the future of women in the corps is likely to depend on several factors. Of primary importance will be the continued commitment of the corps' leaders to fair treatment and effective use of women marines. The corps can also expect to be persistently pushed and prodded to expand the role of women marines by forces such as the women's rights movement. However, the primary impediment to expanding the number of women marines and the scope of their assignments is the combat restriction contained in the law. Until the American people express their will via Congress to lift the restriction on using women in combat, the number of women marines is not likely to be increased beyond current goals. Finally, the future of women in the corps will depend on the women themselves. As women marines individually and collectively fulfill the corps' high standards of performance, appearance, conduct, and leadership, their place in the Marine Corps will become increasingly steadfast and sure.

NOTES

1. U.S. Marine Corps, *NAVMC 2710, Marine Air-Ground Task Forces* (Washington, DC: Headquarters U.S. Marine Corps [Code PL]), pp. 6 and 10.
2. U.S. Marine Corps, *MCO P1200.7D, Military Occupational Specialties Manual* (Washington, DC: Headquarters U.S. Marine Corps, 17 December 1979), par. 10003.
3. U.S. Marine Corps, *Enlisted Personnel Availability Digest (EPAD)*, HQ-1300-2 (Washington, DC: Headquarters U.S. Marine Corps, Apr. 1982). The approximate number of Marines in aviation skills was calculated from data in the EPAD. The sum of the actual inventory in occupational fields 59 through 73 was divided by the total Marine Corps actual inventory.
4. U.S. Bureau of the Census, *Population Profile of the United States: 1981*, Current Population Reports, Series P-20, No. 374 (Washington, DC: GPO, September 1982), p. 20.
5. "Latest Profile of American's People," *U.S. News and World Report*, 14 September 1981, p. 26.
6. *MCO P1200.7D*, par. 10002-10003.
7. *MCO P1200.7D*, par. 10002.7a.
8. U.S. Marine Corps, *MCO P1400.29B, Marine Corps Promotion Manual* (Washington, DC: Headquarters U.S. Marine Corps, March 1977), par. 3010.2.
9. U.S. Marine Corps, Headquarters Marine Corps, Historical Branch, G-3 Division, *A Brief History of the Marine Corps Recruit Depot, Parris Island, South Carolina 1891-1956* (Washington, DC: Headquarters U.S. Marine Corps, 1960 [Revised]), p. 3.
10. U.S. Marine Corps, Headquarters Marine Corps, Historical Branch, G-3 Division, *A Brief History of the Marine Corps Recruit Depot, San Diego, California* (Washington, DC: Headquarters U.S. Marine Corps, 1960 [Revised]), p. 8.
11. *A Brief History of the Marine Corps Recruit Depot, San Diego, California*, p. 8.
12. Paul Van Riper, Michael W. Wyde, Donald P. Brown, *An Analysis of Marine Corps Training* (Newport, RI: Naval War College Center for Advanced Research, 1978), p. 247.
13. "Professional Notes—Recruit Training," *Marine Corps Gazette*, 27 September 1927, p. 193.
14. Dion Williams, "Marine Corps Training," *Marine Corps Gazette*, December 1925, p. 137.
15. Ibid., pp. 137-138.
16. Robert Heinl, Jr., "Our Future DIs," *Marine Corps Gazette*, March 1946, pp. 31-32.
17. Robert Heinl, Jr. "NCO's—A Challenge from Within," *Marine Corps Gazette*, November 1954, p. 47.
18. *A Brief History of the Marine Corps Recruit Depot, Parris Island, South Carolina 1891-1956*, p. 7.
19. Kenneth W. Condit, Gerald Diamond, Edwin T. Turnbladh, *Marine Corps Ground Training in World War II* (Washington, DC: Headquarters U.S. Marine Corps, 1956), pp. 170-172.
20. [Michael L. Patrow], *A Report: Field Commands' Impressions of the Recruit Training Program of Instruction* (Washington, DC: Headquarters U.S. Marine Corps [Code MPI-20], 1981), p. 7.
21. Richard Stack, *Warriors: A Parris Island Photo Journal* (New York: Harper and

Row, 1975), 6th page of section entitled, "The Background" (pages are not numbered).

22. *Warriors: A Parris Island Photo Journal*, 5th page from the end of the book (pages are not numbered).

23. *Warriors: A Parris Island Photo Journal*, 3rd page from the end of the book (pages are not numbered).

24. William Manchester, *Goodbye Darkness* (Boston: Little, Brown and Company, 1980), pp. 122–123.

25. Jim Lucas, "Boot Camp Days," in *The United States Marine Corps in World War II*, ed. S.E. Smith (New York: Random House, 1969), p. 81.

26. *Iwo* (New York: Lippincott and Crowell, 1980), p. 41.

27. Ibid., p. 43.

28. The study was conducted under the Navy All Volunteer Force Manpower Research and Development Program of the Office of Naval Research under contract N000-14-76-C-0938 with the University of South Carolina. The study began in1976. The final report (TR-13) was published in October 1981.

29. Stuart A. Youngblood et al., *Organizational Socialization: A Longitudinal Analysis of Attitude Change, Turnover, and Reenlistment in the Military*, TR-13 (Columbia, SC: Univ. of South Carolina, 1981), pp. 17–35.

30. Ibid., p. 40.

31. Ibid., p. 40.

32. U.S. Marine Corps, Recruit attrition statistics reported in Jul. 1982 by Headquarters U.S. Marine Corps (Code MPI-20), Washington, DC.

33. U.S. Marine Corps, Recruit attrition statistics.

34. The research is being conducted under the Navy Manpower Research and Development Program of the Office of Naval Research under contract N00014-77-C-0700 with the Univ. of Washington.

35. Gregory L. Robinson, Raymond W. Novaco, Irwin G. Sarason, *Cognitive Correlates of Outcome and Performance in Marine Corps Recruit Training*, Technical Report AR-005 (Seattle: Univ. of Washington, 1981), p. 20.

36. Ibid., p. 22.

37. Thomas M. Cook, Raymond W. Novaco, Irwin G. Sarason, *Generalized Expectancies, Life Experiences, and Adaptation to Marine Corps Recruit Training*, Technical Report AR-002 (Seattle: Univ. of Washington, 1980), p. 11.

38. Ibid., p. 30

39. W. M. Kessler, "Here's Your Recruit," *Marine Corps Gazette*, November 1948, p. 23.

40. Wallace M. Greene, Jr., "Selection and Training of Recruits," *Marine Corps Gazette*, November 1936, p. 13.

41. Ibid., p. 13.

42. Ibid., pp. 10–14.

43. U.S. Marine Corps, *MCO 1326.6A*, Subj: Selection Screening and Preparation of Enlisted Marines for Assignment to Drill Instructor, Recruiter and Independent Duty (Washington, DC: Headquarters U.S. Marine Corps, 2 June 1980), Encl. (1) and (5).

44. Heinl "Our Future DIs," p. 31.

45. Heinl "Our Future DIs," p. 32.

46. *MCO 1326.6A*

47. Heinl "Our Future DIs," p. 32.

48. Van Riper et al., *Analysis of Marine Corps Training*, pp. 257–259.

49. H. Paul Jeffers and Dick Levitan, *See Parris and Die: Brutality in the U.S. Marines* (New York: Hawthorne Books, Inc., 1971), pp. 35–36.

50. Ibid., pp. 70–71.
51. Robert Sherrill, *The New York Times Book Review*, 30 May 1971, p. 17. In his review, Sherrill harshly criticized the authors for failing to recommend major reforms to the military justice system which failed to adequately punish those responsible for alleged brutalities in boot camp. Sherrill also challenged the authors' accepting the premise that in joining the military, citizens necessarily must waive some basic constitutional rights.
52. Robert J. Moskin, *The U.S. Marine Corps Story* (New York: McGraw-Hill, 1977) p. 933.
53. "Training the Marines," *New York Times*, 14 April 1976, p. 38, col. 1-2.
54. Van Riper et al., *Analysis of Marine Corps Training*, pp. 275–276.
55. Ibid., p. 259
56. Ibid., p. 275
57. Raymond W. Novaco, Irwin G. Sarason, Gregory L. Robinson, Frank J. Cunningham, *Longitudinal Analysis of Stress and Performance Among Marine Corps Drill Instructors*, Technical Report AR-ONR-007 (Seattle: University of Washington, 1982) p. 1.
58. Ibid., p. 14. Novaco describes Type A behavior, or coronary-prone behavior as being characterized by time-urgency, competitive drive, and generalized hostility, and as being associated with heart disease.
59. Moskin, *Marine Corps Story*, p. 935.
60. Linda L. Hewitt, *Women Marines in World War I* (Washington, DC: History and Museums Division, Headquarters U.S. Marine Corps, 1974), p.4.
61. Ibid., p. 3.
62. Ibid., p. 4.
63. Ibid., p. 9.
64. Ibid., p. 3.
65. Ibid., pp. 25 and 28.
66. Ibid., p. 40.
67. Pat Meid, *Marine Corps Women's Reserve in World War II* (Washington, DC: Historical Branch, G-3 Division, Headquarters U.S. Marine Cops, 1968), p. 2.
68. Ibid., p. 3.
69. Ibid., p. 7.
70. Katherine A. Towle, "Lady Leathernecks," *Marine Corps Gazette*, February 1946, p. 3.
71. Ibid., pp. 4 and 6.
72. Meid, *Women's Reserve in World War II*, p. 28.
73. Ibid., p. 63.
74. Ibid., p. 14.
75. Ibid., p. 16.
76. Ibid., pp. 20–21.
77. Ibid., p. 40.
78. Ibid., p. 41.
79. Towle, "Lady Leathernecks," p. 7.
80. Meid, *Women's Reserve in World War II*, p. 53.
81. Ibid., p. 64.
82. Mary V. Stremlow, *A History of Women Marines 1946-1977*, working draft (Washington, DC: History and Museums Division, Headquarters U.S. Marine Corps, March 1979), p. 1.
83. Ibid., pp. 3 and 5.
84. Julia E. Hamlet, Director, Marine Corps Women's Reserve, statement before the Committee on Civilian Components, 5 March 1948, p. 9.

85. Stremlow, *History of Women Marines*, pp. 17-18.
86. U.S. Congress Senate, Subcommittee of the Committee on Armed Services, *Hearings on the Women's Armed Services Integration Act of 1947*, 80th Cong., 1st sess., 2 July 1947 (Washington, DC: GPO, 1947), p. 1.
87. *Hearings on the Women's Armed Services Integration Act of 1947*, p. 10.
88. *Hearings on the Women's Armed Services Integration Act of 1947*, p. 13.
89. *Hearings on the Women's Armed Services Integration Act of 1947*, p. 68.
90. U.S. Congress, *Public Law 625*, 80th Cong., Chapt. 449, 2d sess., S. 1641, (Washington, DC: GPO, 1948) Title II, secs. 210 and 213.
91. U.S. Marine Corps, Division of Plans and Policy memo for the Commandant, Subj: Requirements for Regular Women Marines, (Washington, DC: Headquarters U.S. Marine Corps, 26 October 1948).
92. Stremlow, *History of Women Marines*, p. 17.
93. Examples of nondeployable billets are: Instructors at Marine Corps Schools, personnel at Marine Corps bases who operate and maintain base facilities, recruiters, personnel assigned to Headquarters Marine Corps, etc.
94. Stremlow, pp. 66–67 and 79.
95. U.S. Marine Corps, Marine Corps Memorandum, No. 41–52, Subj: MOS's appropriate for enlisted women Marines (Washington, DC: Headquarters U.S. Marine Corps, 17 April 1952).
96. Stremlow, *History of Women Marines*, pp. 61–62.
97. U.S. Marine Corps, memo from the Administrative Assistant, Office of the Director of Women Marines, Subj: Current assignments and approximate strength of women Marines (Washington, DC: Headquarters, U.S. Marine Corps, 6 June 1958).
98. Stremlow, *History of Women Marines*, p. 74.
99. Ibid., pp. 76–78.
100. Ibid., pp. 97–98.
101. Ibid., p. 104.
102. Ibid., p. 99.
103. Ibid., p. 98.
104. For a detailed explanation of the grades of first sergeant and sergeant major, see "The Enlisted Marine—More than a Technician."
105. Stremlow, *History of Women Marines*, pp. 150–152.
106. Towle, "Lady Leathernecks," pp. 4–5.
107. U.S. Marine Corps, CMC White Letter, No. 5-76, Subj: Women Marines (Washington, DC: Headquarters U.S. Marine Corps, 23 June 1976).
108. Stremlow, *History of Women Marines*, p. 142A.
109. Ibid., p. 153.
110. *Public Law 625*, Title II, secs. 211 and 213.
111. Stremlow, *History of Women Marines*, pp. 157–158.
112. Ibid., p. 154.
113. Ibid., pp. 154–155.
114. U.S. Marine Corps, *MCO 5000.12*, Subj: Marine Corps Policy and Procedures for women Marines who are Pregnant (Washington, DC: Headquarters U.S. Marine Corps, 16 July 1975).
115. The number of fields (i.e. 22 to 35) which is based on the information in Table II does not include occupational fields 98 and 99 because these fields are only used for manpower accounting purposes and do not represent job skills.
116. U.S. Marine Corps, CMC White Letter, No. 18-80, Subj: Leadership and Responsibilities Pertaining to Women Marines (Washington, DC: Headquarters U.S. Marine Corps, 2 December 1980).

117. R.N. Roman, "Pregnant Marines," *Marine Corps Gazette*, July 1981, pp. 19–20.
118. David Evans, "No Place for Women," *United States Naval Proceedings*, November 1981, pp. 54–56.

10

Enlisted Family Life in the U.S. Army: A Portrait of a Community*

Mady Wechsler Segal

ENLISTED COMMUNITIES

This chapter provides a description of life in an enlisted family housing community on one Army post, focusing on the community atmosphere, the residents' feelings about their life-style, their informal social support, and their use of formal Army services. The selected community is probably fairly representative of many other Army post housing areas whose residents are soldiers in the middle enlisted ranks and their families.

The pattern and intensity of demands that the military places on the life-styles of its personnel are different from those of other work organizations. Among these requirements are: frequent moves, isolation from extended family, frequent and sometimes prolonged periods of separation of service members from their spouses and children, residence in foreign countries, and the potential for violent injury and death. While other occupations share some of these demands, military life has a unique combination of them. Each require-

*Author's Note: This research was conducted while the author was in the Department of Military Psychiatry of the Walter Reed Army Institute of Research (WRAIR), initially on an Intergovernmental Personnel Act appointment and later as a Guest Scientist and on an Army Summer Faculty Research appointment. I am grateful to David H. Marlowe, Chief of the Department, for his support and encouragement. I appreciate the research assistance of Edgar N. Marshall, Richard Pickle, Donna M. Ross, and Katherine Swift Gravino. Joseph M. Rothberg provided helpful comments on an earlier version of this paper. I thank the post personnel who gave so graciously of their time and insights and the respondents from the community who welcomed us into their homes and shared their thoughts and feelings with us. The opinions or assertions contained herein are the private views of the author and are not to be construed as official or as reflecting the views of the Department of the Army or the Department of Defense.

ment that becomes an actuality places stress on service members and their families, both by its nature and because its timing is often not under the control of those involved. While the pressures vary in degree and frequency between services (and between organizational units within services), most military families experience all of them at some point in their careers.

Successful coping with these stressors has been fostered in the past by a tightly knit military community. The essential nature of this community is not geographical but psychological, with its sense of shared experience and understanding, mutual dependence, and informal social support among members. However, the physical proximity on a military post and the isolation from the larger civilian society certainly have contributed to a psychological sense of closeness, whether in the barracks or in family housing areas.

The consensus of observers appears to be that this sense of community, at least in the Army, has deteriorated; it is less clear when the erosion began or what its causes are. Moskos and Faris discuss the recent movement out of the barracks to off-post civilian housing by single enlisted personnel as well as the increasing proportion of married junior enlisted people living off-post. They cite the All-Volunteer Force's "large salary raises for junior enlisted personnel" as the cause of "the ebbing of barracks life. What barracks life remains tends to be vulnerable to social fragmentation."[1] (See also Moskos, chapter 3.)

In the mid-1960s, Coates and Pellegrin observed a decline in community feeling even on post. They noted that the growing size of the military installation following World War II had "led to a depersonalization of relationships within the military community and to a reduction in the social solidarity among base personnel and their families."[2] They also discussed the need for formal military programs to help families deal with the demands of their life-style and resulting problems: "While military families once depended on informal mutual aid from friends and close associates in time of need or trouble, today the impersonal nature of the military community makes it necessary that more formal and impersonal aids be provided."[3] Coates and Pellegrin described the Family Services Program of the Air Force at that time, a program not unlike those established later in the other services, including the service-wide Army Community Services and the various post-level community representation systems. These authors viewed such programs as attempts "to recapture in a formally organized way some of the feelings of community and identification with the service that have eroded as the military community has expanded and assumed many secondary group characteristics," as well as "to meet some of the most pressing problems of military family life."[4]

Until the late 1970s, empirical research on military families tended to focus on families with problems, either those who came for help to clinical services or those in special problem circumstances, such as the families of prisoners of war.[5] Since that time increased attention has been paid to military families by

military policymakers, the press, and social scientists.[6] There has been pressure from military families themselves for changes in organizational demands
on them and for support to help them adapt, as evidenced by such occurrences as the establishment of the National Military Wives Association (renamed the National Military Family Association) and the volunteer-organized
first Army Family Symposium (in 1980). Attention by policymakers in the
Department of the Army is evidenced in many ways, including official support
of the second and third Army Family Symposiums and policy initiatives such
as the establishment of the Family Liaison Office and the development of a
Family Action Plan.

Despite the attention to military families, not many empirical studies have
been published that convey the flavor of military communities and the life-
style of their residents.[7] This chapter is intended to help fill this gap in our
knowledge and understanding of Army family life.

EDEN GARDENS

Eden Gardens is one of ten family housing areas on a large post in the
South.[8] Each of these areas has a name, recognizable boundaries, and an
Army unit (of varying size and type) assigned to provide support to its community activities. One officer from the unit is in charge of providing such
assistance in addition to his regular duties. The residents of each area come
from all of the units on post, not necessarily from the unit which supports it.
Eden Gardens is supported by a brigade. This study was initiated in response
to a request for help in dealing with community problems from the officer
with responsibility for Eden Gardens.

Each family housing community on-post has a representative elected by the
residents. These community representatives meet together regularly to com-
municate residents' views to post facilities personnel. Each representative is an
unpaid volunteer who resides in the housing area and is the civilian spouse (in
all actual cases, a wife) of an officer, noncommissioned officer, or enlisted
person (depending on the rank of soldiers living in the area). Most housing
areas have other volunteers who help the community representative—for example, by coordinating specific activities (e.g., welcoming newcomers) or by
serving as advisors on governing boards of specific post agencies (e.g., PX,
commissary, schools).

There are 500 housing units in Eden Gardens, which make it one of the
largest of the family housing areas on post. Each family occupies a two-story
townhouse unit in a building comprised of five to eight such quarters. The
buildings are arranged around a court of two to four buildings (i.e., ten to
thirty-five family units). Each of the twenty courts has its own parking lot.
Front doors face the center of the court, which is either the parking lot or a
large area of grass. Most courts have sidewalks in front of the houses with a
small garden area between the house and the sidewalk. Back doors open onto

individual backyards, beyond which lie large grassy areas, many of which have playgrounds.

The houses in Eden Gardens were built in the late 1950s. About half of the units have been substantially renovated and the other half have not. A large grassy area divides the renovated and unrenovated sections. Although they share a single name and representation on post, the two sections might really be considered two communities. There are certainly major differences in the quality of the quarters and in the residents' attitudes about their housing.

The quarters in both sections have three bedrooms and a bathroom upstairs. The main level of the unrenovated quarters has a living room and a kitchen with no table area; therefore, one end of the living room serves as a dining area, making the living room area small. The renovated quarters have been extended out the front and the kitchens redesigned to include a table space (with a window facing the front) and an area with doors for a clothes washer and drier (though residents must provide their own). Each unit also has a new half-bath on the main floor; a dishwasher and a garbage disposal; new floors, appliances, plumbing fixtures, and roof; air conditioning and a chain link fence in the backyard—all of which are lacking in the unrenovated quarters area.

FIELD RESEARCH

Eden Gardens was studied over a period of almost two years using several different methods. First, the author conducted interviews with post personnel who provide services to families and/or deal with family or community problems. Those interviewed included post command personnel, chaplains, provost marshall personnel, social workers, psychiatrists, psychologists, the child care center director, community representatives (from all housing areas), and personnel from Army Community Services, the housing office, recreation services, and the post community representation program.

The second method was personal interviewing of residents of Eden Gardens. Two family units from each court were selected at random. The name of the service member living in each of the selected quarters was obtained from the name plate on the door. (If there was no name plate, the next house to the right was substituted. In almost all cases when there was no sign, it was because the family had moved in very recently.) A personally addressed, typed letter was sent to each husband and wife selected in the sample, explaining that this was to be a study of family issues and stating that the interviewers would be in the community during a certain week and would come to the house to ascertain whether the person was willing to be interviewed. Confidentiality was assured.

Contact was then made at the quarters in person and appointments for interviews made with those who consented. A total of sixty-three individuals in thirty-three families (approximately 80% of the families selected) were interviewed. There was no significant difference between the respondents and the nonrespondents on either rank or race. The husband was the soldier in thirty-two of the families; in thirty of them both the husband and the wife were interviewed, while in two families only the wife was interviewed.[9] One of the families consisted of a divorced enlisted woman and her children.

Interviews were conducted at the homes of the respondents, for husbands and wives separately and simultaneously by two interviewers. Each interviewing team consisted of one man and one woman. The author was a member of one of the teams. The other three interviewers were Army behavioral science specialists (one with E-4 rank and two with E-6 rank). For some interviews, interviewer and respondent were matched on gender, whereas for some they were cross-gender matched. The interviews consisted primarily of open-ended questions, were tape-recorded (and later coded from the tapes), and generally took between one to two hours to complete.

A pre-test had been conducted with a sample of twenty-four individuals representing sixteen families, as well as follow-up interviews with six pretest respondents (four families) to explore the process of social integration of newcomers into the community. The pretest and follow-up interviews are not reflected in the quantitative results reported in this chapter, but they did affect the author's insights into and conclusions about the community.

In addition to interviewing support personnel and residents, the author attended various community events as an observer. These included formal meetings of the community representatives with officials of post agencies and various activities of Eden Gardens (town meetings and a Christmas party) held at the community building. The author also met informally with four successive Eden Gardens community representatives and got to know two of them well through repeated contacts. The transition of leadership from one representative to the other was of particular interest.

A PORTRAIT OF THE RESIDENTS

Eden Gardens is officially defined as family housing for soldiers of rank E-4 to E-6 (i.e., the three middle enlisted pay grades which include Specialists 4 and 5, Sergeant, and Staff Sergeant). Army regulations specify the number of bedrooms that must be provided as a function of the number of family members and the children's ages and genders. These policies have a direct impact on the distribution of certain demographic characteristics of the residents. This is obvious with respect to rank and closely related variables (such as years in the Army and age), and less obvious but no less important for other variables that have an impact on the life-style in the community. The housing design combines with these policies to create a neighborhood of young families with a high density of small children.

Table 10.1 shows the distributions of respondents on selected background characteristics. The typical family in Eden Gardens consists of a husband and wife in their late 20s and two or three children. The husband is in his second or third enlistment. The wife does not work outside the home. The oldest child is less than 8 years old and the youngest is less than 4. Extrapolation of the full distribution of ages of children in the interview sample can be used to describe a "typical" Eden Gardens court of twenty-four families. In such a court, there would be 54 children, 42 of whom are under eight years of age (and only one of whom is over age 14). There are always small children underfoot and within earshot. In each court, there are children and/or tricycles on the sidewalk, in the parking lot, and on the grass (sometimes in neighbors' garden areas). Drivers must use extreme caution in the area. This density of small children has consequences for relationships between neighbors, as will be discussed later.

Only 28% of the wives work outside the home, though 34% more say they used to be employed. Those who work are generally in minimum-wage jobs, though a few are clerical workers and nurses. In almost all families where the wife is employed, the major reason given is financial, though some also mention self-satisfaction or boredom. The major reasons given for wives not working outside the home are to be with the children, inability to find a job, husbands not wanting wives to work, problems finding reliable babysitters or the cost of child care, and problems with or expense of transportation. The costs of transportation and child care combined with the low pay in the available jobs for which they qualify mean that it makes more sense for them to stay home with the children. About one-third of the women do volunteer work.

Eden Gardens is fairly homogeneous with respect to education as well as life cycle stage. The vast majority of the residents have at least a high school diploma. More than one-third of both husbands and wives have some additional education, mostly college level but no degree. A few respondents are currently going to school; the vast majority of the others indicate a desire for more education. What almost all the men see as an obstacle to further education is lack of time, which they ascribe primarily to the requirements of their jobs but also to the desire to have some time with their children. (Several reported registering for classes but having to drop out because of late duty hours and field duty.) The women are as likely to cite, as impediments, lack of money as lack of time.

On other demographic variables, the community is diverse. Most notable is the racial/ethnic distribution: 52% are black, 40% white, 6% Hispanic, and 2% Oriental. This racial/ethnic composition makes Eden Gardens (and other housing areas like it throughout the Army) very different from typical working-class civilian communities, which tend to be racially segregated or at least predominantly of one race. It is also likely that the residents grew up in racially segregated neighborhoods, so that the social experience in their army housing represents an important change for them.

Table 10.1. Selected Background Characteristics of Respondents

Pay Grade/Rank of Service Member	Number of Families
E-4 (Specialist 4)	4
E-5 (Specialist 5 or Sergeant)	14
E-6 (Staff Sergeant)	13
E-7 (Sergeant First Class)	2
Total	33

Number of Years in the Army	Number of Service Members
2-3	3
4-6	13
7-9	7
10-15	7
16-18	3
Total	33

Number of families where service member has had a break in service: 8

		Age of Wife				
		20-24	25-29	30-34	35-45	Total
Age	20-24	3	3	0	0	6
of	25-29	0	11	1	0	12
Husband	30-34	0	4	4	1	9
	35-39	0	0	0	3	3
	Total	3	18	5	4	30

Number of families where wife is older than husband: 14
Number of families where wife is at least three years older than husband: 5

Duration of Marriage	Number of Couples
1-3 years	7
4-6	8
7-9	10
10-15	7
Total	32

Number of husbands who have been married before: 5
Number of wives who have been married before: 10
Number of families with children of the wives from previous marriages or relationships living with them: 9

Age of Oldest Child	Number of Families	Age of Youngest Child	Number of Families
2-4	6	0-1	13
5-7	12	2-4	10
8-9	9	5-6	4
11-13	4	10-11	3
15-17	2		
Total	33		30

The regions where the respondents grew up cover the entire United States and a few other countries. The largest number (about half) come from the South, which has traditionally been overrepresented in the American military. About one in seven of the men and the women spent their high school years within about 100 miles of the post; increasing the radius to about 200 miles includes about one-fourth of the residents. In most of the couples, the husband and wife grew up in the same or an adjacent region, though about one-third come from widely disparate regions. The sizes of the places where the residents grew up are equally varied.[10]

An interesting finding, with potential implications for interpersonal relations in the community, is that a strong relationship exists between race and place of origin. The black respondents are much more likely to be from the South than the whites. About two-thirds of the black men and women are from southern states, compared to only one-fifth of the white men and one-third of the white women. Fully two-fifths of the black men and women grew up within about 200 miles of post, compared to none of the white men and only one out of fifteen white women. This difference in region of origin adds another cultural difference to the racial dissimilarities between neighbors.

One background characteristic shared by many of the residents is having come from a relatively large family: more than three-fifths of the respondents have three or more siblings, including about one-third who have five or more siblings. This is above the national average on family size for the respondents' generation and has been observed in at least two other studies of Army family members.[11]

The vast majority of respondents have a religious preference. In most couples, the husband and wife have the same preference. Common affiliations are Baptist, Catholic, and Pentacostal. Most respondents attend religious services infrequently if at all, though about one-fifth are more than routinely involved in religious activities. Of the respondents who attend church, most go to chapel on post at least some of the time. There is a strong relationship between the frequency of religious attendance of husbands and wives.

Eden Gardens is a transient community. Half of the families have been there for less than one year (58% for one year or less); 63% have been in their current quarters for one year or less. If the current residents are any indication, the community turns over almost completely every three years (88% of them have been there three years or less). This undoubtedly reflects the Army's assignment policies. Given this transience, it would not be surprising to find a lack of symbolic identification with the community or a lack of closeness with neighbors. The nature of Army personnel assignment policies forces a temporary sense of residence in any community. Soldiers are periodically reassigned to new locations. Most Eden Gardens residents can expect to move again within a year or two, making it difficult for them to view the community as "home." Furthermore, even if they expect to stay longer, they know that most of their neighbors will not. Therefore, they know that any close friendships they form cannot be sustained by continued interaction. They may also feel that interpersonal problems with neighbors do not have to be resolved, since the neighbors or they themselves will be likely to move away soon. When the community atmosphere is discussed later, the effects of this perceived lack of stability in the neighborhood will be examined.

VIEWS OF THE RESIDENTS

Attitudes about Housing

The residents' feelings about their quarters depend partly on whether they are in renovated or unrenovated units. Not surprisingly, those in the newer units, especially the women, are much more satisfied with their houses. Feelings of relative deprivation are expressed by residents in the older units. (Such feelings are expressed in about three-quarters of those households.) The post housing policy is that a family is assigned to the first available housing unit for which it is eligible. Some residents resent it when newcomers to the post, or lower ranking personnel, get to move into the nicer houses. They think they should be allowed to move into the newly renovated units and the newcomers should move into their vacated, unrenovated quarters. Recognizing the financial reasons for Army policy against this, some expressed willingness to bear the cost of the move themselves (that is, to move themselves, to forfeit the usual temporary housing allowance, and even to paint the quarters they vacate).

Those living in renovated quarters especially like the kitchen (with its dishwasher, garbage disposal, and laundry area), the air conditioning, the fence in the backyard, and the extra half-bath. Not having these amenities is the source of the dissatisfaction expressed by those in the unremodeled units. Most residents of both sections are pleased with the responses they get from the civilian contract agency responsible for repairs and maintenance.

Residents of both sections generally see their quarters as better than what they could afford in the civilian community, especially on their Army housing allowance. Many of the residents had to live off post for a while before moving into Eden Gardens, and they do not want to have to live again in such housing, typically trailer parks or small apartments. They also like the convenience of living on post, which saves them money and time. Since most of the families have one car at most, being near the service member's work gives the wife more mobility. She can easily drive her husband to work, or he can get a lift with friends or neighbors, so that she can have the car during the day.

On the other hand, some residents would prefer to own their home but cannot afford to do so. Some would even prefer to rent housing off post and remain on post only for financial reasons. They would like to have more privacy than is possible in Eden Gardens and to get away from the regulations on post (such as those governing how short they must cut the grass or when they may run their heat or air conditioning). In a majority of households, at least one of the partners would prefer to live off post. Although the percentage is almost the same in unrenovated and renovated quarters, the pattern of responses of husbands and wives is very different in the two areas. In unrenovated houses, about two-fifths of both husbands and wives would prefer to live off post, whereas in renovated houses, a little more than half of husbands but less than one-fifth of wives would like to off post. The latter figure reflects the very high level of satisfaction of wives in the remodeled housing units.

Daily Life

In many ways, the daily lives of Eden Gardens residents resemble those of young nonmilitary families. However, there are also ways in which being in the Army affects their family and community life. Most notable are the effects of duty requirements on the soldiers' schedules and the geographic separation from their relatives and life-long friends.

The residents' schedules and leisure activities vary, but there are some typical patterns. The most common weekday schedule is characteristic of families in which the wife does not work outside the home and the children are young (which describes the majority of Eden Gardens households). On days with required physical training (three to five per week), the husband rises about 5:00 A.M. and leaves shortly thereafter. He returns, showers, has breakfast, and goes to work. Whether or not he has PT that day, he is usually gone by 8:00.

Meanwhile, the wife has been taking care of the children, getting the older ones off to school. Some make breakfast for their husbands. Many of the mothers wait at the bus stops with the young children. Most of those with school age children also have preschool children (many are infants), so they have at least one child at home with them all day. When the weather is nice, many children play in the front yards, in the backyards, or on the sidewalks. Many of the mothers are either outside with the children or keeping an eye on them from inside (though some respondents complain about neighbors' not adequately supervising their young children). Most of the children are frequently on the move between inside and outside.

Common activities for the mothers during the course of the day include household chores (e.g., cleaning, laundry, cooking), making lunch for children and husband (some come home for lunch), taking the children to a playground, other activities with children (e.g., reading to them), chatting outside with neighbors, having coffee with friends or neighbors, talking on the phone with friends, and watching television. In most of the houses there is a television set in the living room and it is on for most of the day. Sometimes no one is watching, sometimes the children are watching alone, sometimes the mother is watching with the children. Soap operas are popular with the women; sometimes they watch alone, sometimes with the children, and sometimes with friends and neighbors.

The soldiers' schedules vary and for many there is a lack of predictability. That is, they expect to be home at a certain time but last-minute duty requirements may make them late. The majority of the men report that they work more than fifty hours in a typical week (if PT is included). Almost all report working more than forty hours. These figures do not represent weeks when they are away from home, which is quite often. Asked how much temporary duty (TDY) or field duty they have had in the past year, a majority of the soldiers indicate at least thirty days. More than one-quarter of the sample spent ninety days or more away from home. During the month before the interviews, about one-quarter of the soldiers had been away at least seven days; in five families the husband was away for fourteen or more days.

When they are not away on field duty, most of the soldiers arrive home around 5:00 in the afternoon. In many of the families, the husband will then spend some time with the children. At least in warm weather (when we were there), it is common for the men to come home and drink a beer (or more). In some of the families, the men fall asleep in front of the television, either before or after dinner. This pattern probably reflects their early rising time as well as the physical demands of their jobs.

Common leisure activities (besides watching TV) of the men are reading, activities with the children, physical activity (such as going to a gym on post), going to the movies, and spending time with friends. The most frequently mentioned leisure activities of the women are reading, watching television, activities with the children, crafts (e.g., sewing, knitting, ceramics), work around the house, time with friends, going to the movies, and bowling.

The majority of families seem to spend their weekends together most of the time. Common outdoor activities include working on cars, mowing the grass for which they have responsibility, and taking the children to a park or playground. Some of the families have members involved in athletic activities (e.g., softball, bowling). Most of the men (three in five) say they play ball with the children. Often the family will shop together, for groceries and other things; going to an indoor mall is a common family outing on evenings and weekends. Evenings, both during the week and on weekends, are often spent watching television, including pay-TV channels. Other common activities with children are playing games, reading to them, and working on hobbies with them.

The children are occasionally left with babysitters. Those mothers who are employed have regular babysitters, mostly neighbors or the post child-care center or both. Most of the others will leave their children for short periods with a neighbor or other friends while they go shopping, run an errand, or participate in leisure activities. They, in turn, often look after friends' and neighbors' children. Such arrangements are without pay and appear to be very informal (without the accounting of hours used in more formal babysitting pools). About one-third of the families with children too young to be left alone have used the post child-care center at least three times; less than one-quarter, including those who use it when they work, use it regularly.

The life-styles of the wives reflect their stage in the life cycle as mothers of young children. Unlike their contemporaries in civilian families, who are more likely to be employed, they are at home most of the time. Their daily lives appear similar to those of other women with small children who do not work outside the home. However, because of their husbands' Army assignment, they are less likely to live near close relatives and long-term friends. Their husbands are also more likely to work long hours and to be away from home for days, weeks, or even months at a time.

These characteristics of army life have important potential consequences for the women's quality of life and social support. In general, women's friend-ships are very important to them; they tend to be long-lasting and more intimate than men's friendships.[12] Close friendships are particularly important for social support and a sense of self to mothers of young children. The more their husbands live separate lives, the more important close friendships are to the wives. Working-class women are more likely than middle-class women to have friends from their neighborhood rather than from organizations to which they belong. Furthermore, married working-class women tend to maintain close ties with relatives and long-term friends. The women in Eden Gardens are young working-class wives living apart from their relatives and life-long friends, and their husbands are frequently away from home. Therefore, we would expect them to look to the community as a source of close personal relationships and social support. Their husbands, who spend much of their time on their jobs (often in the field), have potential friends in their units. Thus, the psychological sense of community for the women may be different from that of their husbands and the neighborhood atmosphere is likely to be more important for the women. We will consider this in the next section.

Community Atmosphere

When asked about geographic boundaries, most respondents saw their court as their "neighborhood." Some (one-third of husbands, one-quarter of wives) also saw the court as their "community," though about as many (one-third of husbands and wives) saw Eden Gardens as their community.

Relationships with most neighbors tend to be characterized as polite but not close. Most residents, especially the wives, have one or two neighbors they consider to be friends, and to whom they look when they need a favor or just want to talk. A few respondents expressed feelings of social isolation and loneliness or said the neighbors do not care about each other. A substantial minority of the men have no close relationships with neighbors, and most of them do not express concern about this.

Respondents were asked about their friends. Fully 70% of the women named at least one neighbor as one of their closest friends. Of the 30% who did not name any neighbors as friends, 80% named at least one neighbor when asked specifically whether they were close with any of their neighbors. For the majority of the women, at least half of their friends were residents of Eden Gardens. In contrast, only 33% of the men named at least one neighbor as a friend. Of the rest, half named a neighbor as close when specifically asked. For 24% of the men, at least half of their friends are residents of Eden Gardens.

Although most of the women considered a neighbor or two to be among their closest friends, these friendships may not be very intimate and psychologically supportive. Of necessity, all of these relationships are of rather short duration. A friendship can become close in a short period of time, and some army family members may learn how to foster such closeness. However, the knowledge that interaction is transitory may prevent strong bonds from forming. Some women specifically mentioned during the interviews the difficulty of developing close friendships and the pain they felt when a close friend moved away.

The residents were asked what kinds of things they do with neighbors. The most common responses were: "talk," watch each other's children, visit at each other's homes to talk, drink coffee, play cards, or other games, watch children together, do yard work together, go shopping, and participate in such post activities as bowling, scouting, and Tupperware parties. These activities are primarily done with the one or two neighbors with whom they are the friendliest. In a few of the courts, mowing the grass is done as a group, with all (or most) of the residents of the court contributing, rather than by each family mowing only the part of the grassy area for which it has responsibility.

Given the transient nature of the community and of Army life, being welcomed when one moves in may be important to adjustment and to one's feeling about the friendliness of the neighborhood. Asked whether anyone came to their quarters to welcome them when they moved in, 61% of the families said at least one neighbor did, while in 39% neither the husband nor the wife indicated having been greeted by anyone.

Residents also reported the number of families they had met in their court. The women, not surprisingly, have met more neighbors than the men: four in ten of the men and half of the women have met at least half of their neighbors, while one-third of the men and one-quarter of the women have met fewer than one-quarter of the neighbors in their court.

Asked specifically whether they have had any problems with neighbors, four-fifths of families report at least some difficulties. Although most of these problems are seen as minor, about one in ten men and one in six women report many incidents or severe problems with neighbors. Generally, one or two neighbors are seen as causing trouble. The most common kinds of problems described (in order of frequency of mention) are: problems with children in which the parents get involved, parents not controlling their children, parents encouraging inappropriate behavior in children, parking problems (including such things as parking in other than assigned places or parking disabled cars), noise (including loud stereos or loud parties), neighbor children calling others bad names, disturbing use of alcohol or drugs, and problems with neighbors' pets. When asked specifically if they have problems with neighbors' pets, fully three-fifths of families in unrenovated quarters said they did, compared to one-third of those in renovated units. At least part of this difference is due to the fences provided with the remodeled houses.

Asked if their children have any problems with neighbors' children, three in ten families (one in six husbands and one-quarter of wives) reported one or two severe problems. The most common specific incidents described by respondents were children fighting, younger children being bullied by older children, and name calling. This kind of problem is partly produced by the age distribution of the children and it would be less likely to occur if there were older children around to break up such fights before they came to the attention of parents.

A common situation described is one in which a fight between two young children from different families turns into an argument between their parents. Sometimes such an argument becomes a shouting match between the neighbors, and occasionally it escalates into a physical fight and/or a protracted quarrel. If it gets loud and/or physical, the military police may be called. Other neighbors in the court may eventually have to take sides because it becomes impossible to maintain friendly or even cordial relations with both feuding neighbors. Interestingly, the children often go back to playing with each other while the parents have become enemies.

Some of the negative interpersonal attitudes and behavior on the part of the women can be attributed to gossip. For example, one woman may confide in another and find out from someone else that her trust was violated. The betrayed woman then turns against the gossiper and tries to elicit support from other neighbors. Such situations create a hostile atmosphere in the court and sometimes polarize it.

When neighbors in conflict are of different races, the problem may become a racial one or take on racial overtones. Respondents were asked about race relations and racial problems in the neighborhood. In almost half of the households, at least one respondent (usually the wife) said there were racial problems. Although a few reported severe racial problems, most conflicts were seen as minor or as conflicts with racial overtones. The majority were specific incidents between neighbors involving race (including children using racial epithets). Of all families interviewed, one-third noted at least one such incident. Some of these incidents began as conflicts between neighbors and evolved into racial problems when they reached the name-calling stage, a phenomenon described by the provost marshall in charge of the area. In about one in ten families, one or both of the respondents said the whites are racially prejudiced; and in one in ten, one or both said the blacks are racially prejudiced. In about one in seven families, at least one respondent clearly displayed racial prejudice during the interview.

Respondents were asked to choose one of four statements to best describe race relations in the neighborhood. The distribution of responses, as shown in Table 10.2, was similar for men and women. The majority chose the statement "People in the neighborhood tend to stick to friends of their own race, but there are no real racial problems."

When respondents were asked about their friends, they were asked to identify the race of each friend. Analysis of these choices reveals that most of the residents do indeed tend to stick to friends of their own race, although there are exceptions.[13] About two-thirds of both white men and white women have only white friends. For most white residents who have any black friends, these friends are only a small minority, especially for the men. Furthermore, friends (especially the men's) are not necessarily neighbors, so that some of the cross-racial friendships are not formed in the neighborhood but result from contact at, for example, work or church.

Like the white residents, two-thirds of the black men have only black friends (and no white friends). In contrast, only one-fifth of the black women have only black friends. For the one-third of black men with at least some white friends, the percentage of their friends who are white varies between 25% and 100%. For the four-fifths of black women who have at least some white friends, the percentage of their friends who are white varies between 10% and 67%. For about one-fifth of all black men and black women, at least half of their friends are white.

Table 10.2. Respondents' Views of Race Relations in the Neighborhood

Statement	Number of Men	Number of Women
"People of different races in the neighborhood socialize with each other and get along very well	6	8
"People in the neighborhood tend to stick to friends of their own race, but there are no real racial problems"	17	17
"There is some racial tension in the neighborhood, but it's not severe"	5	7
"There are severe racial problems in the neighborhood"	1	1
Total	29	33

When respondents were asked if anyone welcomed them when they moved in, they were asked the race of welcomers. While most welcoming neighbors were the same race as the respondent, there were many who were not. The effect of race on the pattern of greetings was greater for women than for men, and no white wives reported being greeted by a black neighbor.

Analysis of the race of neighbors cited as problems reveals no strong racial effect. While a majority of such citations by the men are cross-racial, the women are slightly more likely to name white neighbors as problems regardless of their own race.

A major source of interpersonal conflict, racial or otherwise, appears to be the way some of the residents raise a minor issue with a neighbor who, for example, has parked in the wrong space or whose child is fighting with theirs. The initial complaint is sometimes made in such a negative way that it produces a hostile response. A conversation started with an aggressive threat laden with curses is unlikely to end in congenial resolution of the problem.

Conflicts that are brought to the attention of the authorities (calling the MPs repeatedly) are dealt with in various ways, none of which is aimed at real mediation and resolution of the causes of the problem. Sometimes the officer from the sponsoring unit calls in the service members of the families involved and orders them to ensure that the conflict does not recur. Sometimes the problem is referred to the soldiers' unit commanders, who respond similarly. As a last resort, a family seen as the source of difficulties is officially forced to move off post.

In a few instances, I observed when a problem family or two left post (voluntarily or not), it took some time for the conflicts in the court to decrease and/or for the perception of problems (by both residents and authorities) to dissipate. In some cases it seemed as if the family blamed for the problems was a scapegoat for more widespread difficulties in the court. In other cases, even when the actual problems were resolved, others (such as the provost marshall or residents of other courts) thought aberrant behavior and hostile interpersonal relations still prevailed in the court. Some courts had a reputation as trouble spots, though official statistics (e.g., MP calls for domestic disturbances) did not bear this out.

It is not possible, with the present information, to trace the exact causes and consequences of these reputations, but it is likely that the social atmosphere in these courts is negatively affected. One response seems to be for residents to curtail their social interactions and to limit their contacts to one or two neighbors. This response is fostered by the knowledge that residence in the neighborhood is temporary. Such social withdrawal by others is likely to be experienced as unfriendliness and social isolation by newcomers to the court. Sensing hostility from neighbors, or at least not feeling close to them, breeds the kind of negative interpersonal behavior that may have spawned the earlier problems, leading to a circular pattern. This analysis is proposed as one reason why different courts seem to have different social atmospheres and why these climates seem to persist. However, verification would require a longitudinal study and a more saturated sampling design.

Quality of Life: Satisfaction with Life, Marriage, Children, and the Army

The respondents were asked, "How well do you feel things are going for you in general? How satisfied are you with your life?" Most were either "very satisfied" or "mostly satisfied" (three-quarters of the men and over half of the women). However, about one-fifth of the wives (seven women) indicated they were "mostly" or "very" dissatisfied with their lives, compared with only one man. About one-fifth of each group gave answers classified as "about half satisfied and half dissatisfied."

Financial problems and marital adjustment strains explain some of the pressures in their lives. In three-quarters of the families, at least one respondent answered "yes" to the question, "Do you have problems making it okay on your present income?" Asked, "Are there tensions in your marriage which bother you?," most people said "no"; but in more than one-third of the couples, at least one of the partners said "yes" (about one in ten husbands and more than one-third of the wives); an additional one-quarter of the husbands and one in ten wives said "sometimes." Fully 85% of the women reported feeling lonely at least sometimes (about one-fifth reported being lonely frequently).

While raising small children is a potential source of stress and does create some marital tension, most of the respondents are generally satisfied with their relationships with their children. There is some disagreement over discipline between husbands and wives, with a frequent cause being that the husband is considered too strict by his wife. Furthermore, almost all of the men said they wished they had more time to spend with their children. When asked to compare their relationship with their children to the relationship they had with their own parents as children, the majority (two-thirds of the men and three-quarters of the women) said it is better, mostly because they are closer to their own children and spend more time with them and/or are not as strict. This is not surprising, given the relatively large families in which most of the residents were raised.

The respondents were asked, "Now that you're away from home, what's your relationship with your parents like?" Most men and about half of the women said "same" or "about the same," while two-fifths of the men and about half of the women said "better" or "closer." Asked how often they see their parents, about half of the respondents said once a year or less and only one-quarter see their parents four times a year or more. Communication with parents by telephone is much more frequent, with a mode for men of once a month and for women of once a week or more often. However, about one-fifth of both groups talk to their parents on the phone less than once a month.

The feelings the residents of Eden Gardens have about their lives, their life-styles, and their community are bound to be related to their feelings about the Army. Like others who live on a military installation, their lives are more circumscribed and controlled by the organization than is the case for those who do not. Most of the respondents' overall feelings about Army life are positive, as would be expected among those who have already reenlisted at least once. However, there are also some very emotional negative responses. Asked about their current jobs, most of the service members are either "very satisfied" (36%) or "mostly satisfied" (27%), while some are "mostly dissatisfied" (15%) or "very dissatisfied" (12%) and a few are "about half satisfied and half dissatisfied" (9%). When asked what they like about their jobs, the service members most often mention the work itself, the responsibility, super-vising others, and the opportunity to learn. The wives vary in what they like about their husbands' jobs; most often mentioned are the hours (25%) or the lack of field duty (19%). The job aspect mentioned most often as being disliked concerns long duty hours (about one-fifth of both husbands and wives). Those wives who like their husband's hours may well be comparing them with his previous duty assignments or with those of other people they know.

When asked about reenlistment plans, most (about six in ten) of the service members say they will definitely reenlist or have already done so within the past year. The wives' feelings about reenlistment are very positive (four in ten) or mostly positive (about one-quarter). Only one in ten is negative. The wife's feelings have a strong influence on the soldier's reenlistment decision: more than half of the men say their wife's attitude is as important or more impor-tant than their own; only one in ten says the decision is his alone. Asked the reasons for a positive reenlistment decision, the respondents most often say the soldier likes the Army (mentioned in three-fifths of the households) or likes the job (about one-third), or they cite other reasons which point to the aspects of army life perceived as the most beneficial in general, to which we turn now.

Respondents were asked four open-ended questions about positive and negative aspects of army life. Their responses, shown in Table 10.3, indicate a fairly high degree of consensus and general agreement among men and women (though with some different emphases). In general, the positive fea-tures are job security, other economic benefits, and the opportunity to travel, while the negative factors involve family separations and geographic mobility. The latter two are also cited by a smaller number of families as positive aspects of Army life perceived as the most beneficial in general, to which we turn now.

Respondents were asked four open-ended questions about positive and negative aspects of Army life. Their responses, shown in Table 10.3, indicate a and security-related. The respondents view civilian job opportunities and benefits as limited and insecure compared to the guaranteed Army paycheck

Table 10.3. Responses to Questions About Army Life

Question	Response	Number of Families ($N=33$)*	Number of Husbands ($N=30$)*	Number of Wives ($N=32$)*
"What are the best things about Army life?"	Benefits	23	11	13
	Job security	22	17	12
	Medical care	20	15	12
	Travel	16	11	9
	PX (Post Exchange) and Commissary	10	4	7
	Housing	9	6	3
	Dental care	6	4	2
	Recreational facilities	2	1	1
	Physical training	1	1	0
	Field duty	1	1	0
	Other	21	14	15
"What are the worst things about Army life?"	Family separations	15	7	9
	Moving	12	5	7
	Long duty hours	11	2	9
	Unaccompanied tours	7	3	4
	Excessive field duty	7	1	6
	Behavior of some people	7	4	3
	Behavior of some people at work	6	5	1
	Inadequate pay	6	0	6
	Problems with medical care	4	2	4
	Lack of dental care	3	1	2
	Behavior of some people in community	3	2	1
	Physical training	2	2	0
	Other	22	15	14
"What aspects of Army life do you believe are good for family life?"	Benefits	18	15	7
	Meeting different people/ learning about different cultures	13	7	7
	Security	12	7	5
	Travel	11	6	7
	Separations	4	3	2
	Other	18	10	11
	Nothing	5	2	3
"What aspects of Army life do you believe are disruptive or harmful for family life?"	Separations	22	13	13
	Frequent temporary duty or field duty	22	12	14
	Unaccompanied tours	14	8	8
	Long duty hours	12	6	6
	Moving	9	6	4
	Nothing	1	0	1
	Other	12	7	6

*N indicates the number of respondents.

and benefits. Despite the desire on the part of most of the residents to stay in the Army, they view many aspects of the life-style as hardships and as placing severe strains on family relationships.

Informal Social Support and Use of Army Services

Recognizing that social support helps to alleviate the potential negative consequences of stress, respondents were asked to whom they talk when they have "personal problems or family problems or concerns."[14] As shown in Table 10.4, the three most common sources of support identified for both men and women were spouse, friends, and one or both parents. Additional sources of support for at least one-quarter of the men were work supervisor or chain of command personnel, work associates, chaplain or minister, and wife's parent(s). At least one-quarter of the women talked to a chaplain or minister, or to husband's parent(s).

Asked if they had ever been to see a chaplain for help with a problem, about one-third of the men and the women reported at least one visit (mostly just one). The most common problems were marital problems or problems with the children. Most respondents who had sought help from a chaplain felt that the visit had helped.

Respondents were asked about their use of and satisfaction with various services provided by the Army. The provision of free medical care, seen in a majority of households as one of the best things about Army life (as reported

Table 10.4.   Sources of Social Support

Source	Number of Husbands ($N = 27$)*	Number of Wives ($N = 33$)*
Spouse	24	26
Friends	18	21
Parent(s)	16	14
Work supervisor/chain of command personnel	16	3
Work associates	10	0
Chaplain or minister	7	11
Spouse's parent(s)	6	7
Neighbors	4	6
Doctor	3	2
Social worker	1	3
Psychiatrist	3	1
Psychologist	3	1

*N indicates the number of respondents.

above), is not without its problems. Though a majority of the soldiers are satisfied with the care they get for themselves at the hospital on post, they and their wives are less satisfied with the care provided to wives and children (see Table 10.5). The most common complaints (mentioned in at least one out of five households) are: difficulty in getting an appointment for a regular check-up, waiting for hours for treatment in the emergency room, hospital personnel being rude or uncaring, difficulty (or perceived impossibility) of getting dental care for which they are eligible on a space-available basis or for emergencies, and difficulty getting an appointment with a gynecologist. Some of these problems resulted in family members' not getting needed medical care; for example, some wives and children did not go to a dentist at all and some wives failed to get the prescription contraceptives they needed.

In marked contrast to the complaints about medical care, most respondents who have children attending school on post are well satisfied with the schools (see Table 10.6) and there are few complaints.

Respondents were asked if they had ever been to the Army Community Services (ACS), an Army-wide program set up to provide for family support. In slightly more than half of the households, at least one member of the couple had been to ACS. The most commonly used service (used by three in ten families) was the lending closet, which provides temporary loans of house-hold goods. Other ACS services used by at least one in ten families were: Army Emergency Relief (AER), which provides financial loans, information and/or referral, and financial/budget counseling. Satisfaction with the lend-ing closet was high; other services received assorted complaints, including that respondents had been denied the service.

ACS is intended to have a central position in providing services and service referral to army families. Though we asked residents about their use of ACS, we did not ascertain the full extent of each respondent's knowledge. We do know that there are some respondents who have never even heard of ACS (at least two husbands and six wives). Furthermore, there are others who know

Table 10.5.   Satisfaction with Medical Care at Post Hospital

Level of Satisfaction	Husbands		Wives	
	Care for self	Care for wife and children	Care for self	Care for children
Very satisfied	9	5	4	6
Mostly satisfied	3	4	7	9
Half satisfied and half satisfied	3	5	6	3
Mostly dissatisfied	4	3	0	0
Very dissatisfied	1	3	8	7
Total	20	20	25	25

Table 10.6.   Satisfaction with the Schools Their Children Attend

Level of Satisfaction	Husbands	Wives
Very satisfied	11	16
Mostly satisfied	10	6
Mostly dissatisfied	0	1
Very dissatisfied	0	2
Total	21	25

about one service ACS provides but are unaware of its other functions. This sometimes results in families' being in need of a service that ACS provides but not knowing that the service exists. For example, a few of the respondents who reported occasionally having had no food and no money did not know about the ACS food locker, which provides food in such emergencies.

In almost half of the families, at least one respondent reported using the services of the Red Cross, mostly for emergency leave and/or notification of a family emergency or a loan. Most of those who used the Red Cross were satisfied with the service they received.

Of special interest from a community perspective are the perceptions Eden Garden residents have about sources of help with a problem relevant to the community or within the purview of the community representative. We also wanted to ascertain how informed residents are about the community representational system. Respondents were asked: "There are various kinds of questions or concerns or problems you might have, such as a complaint about your quarters, a problem in the neighborhood, or questions about activities or services available. When you have such a question or problem, who would you go to for information or help?" Though multiple sources could be cited, about two-thirds of both husbands and wives identified only one source. As shown in Table 10.7, the answer given in more households than any other was the community representative, more commonly cited by wives than by husbands. The next most common answer was the housing office, which was the source most frequently cited by the men and which ranked second among the women.

Various answers were given to the question, "Who do you feel represents you on post with your concerns?", though most respondents gave only one answer, if any. The most common was the community representative (two-fifths of households; one-quarter of husbands and wives). One in six men cited his own unit or specific personnel in his unit, and one in eight women named her husband. Interestingly, about one-fifth of both the men and the women said they did not know who represented them on post.

Asked, "If you wanted to get something done in the community, who would you go to?", most respondents again cited one source, the most common being the community representative (about three-quarters of households;

Table 10.7.   Sources of Information or Help with Housing Complaints,
Neighborhood Problems, or Questions About Activities or Services

Source	Number of Families (N = 33)*	Number of Husbands (N = 30)*	Number of Wives (n = 32)*
Community representative	20	8	16
Housing office	12	9	6
MPs	6	2	4
Civilian maintenance agency	6	3	3
ACS	5	0	5
Spouse	5	1	4
Post complaint hot-line	4	2	2
Chain of command	3	3	0
Neighbors or friends	3	1	2
Chaplain	1	1	0
Other	14	12	4

half of both husbands and wives). Only one man said he did not know,
compared to six women.

Residents were then asked, "Who do you think has the power to make
decisions that affect the quality of life in family housing?" A very different
pattern of responses resulted. The most common answer was "the post commander" or "the commanding general" (about half of the households; three
in ten husbands and one-third of the wives), followed by "the residents themselves" (three in ten households; one in five husbands; one in six wives). None
of the husbands but almost one-third of the wives said they did not know.

Despite the community representative's being frequently given as a source
of information or help with problems or to get something done in the community, a series of direct questions about the community representational system
revealed a great deal of ignorance or misinformation. As shown in Table 10.8,
more than one-quarter of the men and women had never heard of the program. Even more had heard of the system but did not know any details. Only

Table 10.8.   Knowledge of Community Representational System

Extent of Knowledge	Number of Husbands	Number of Wives
Has not heard of the program	8	9
Is confusing it with another program	1	1
Has heard of it but knows no details	15	10
Knows something about it but some information is incorrect	1	0
Knows something about it but information is incomplete	3	7
Knows a lot about it	2	6
Total	30	33

a few respondents knew a lot about the community representational system. The majority of respondents (70% of men, 55% of women) did not indicate any knowledge of the monthly town meetings, and only a small minority (two men and four women) had ever been to one.

Asked about their community representative, the modal group knew there was one but did not know who she was (see Table 10.9). Others did not know there was one, gave the wrong name, knew who she was but did not know her name, or knew only the previous representative's name. Only four men and eleven women knew the current representative's name. (In all cases where the man knew her name, his wife did also.) In about one-quarter of the households, at least one of the residents had talked to the community representative at least once about a problem or concern (about one in seven men, one-quarter of the women). Among those who knew about the community representational system, attitudes varied and were more likely to be positive than negative (56% of men and 53% of women were very or mostly positive; 33% of men and 29% of women were very or mostly negative).

There is a variety of reasons for the lack of knowledge of the community representational system. Tenure is one, i.e., the longer a resident has been living in Eden Gardens, the more likely he/she is to be informed about the program. The welcoming function of the system does not appear to be operational. Information on meetings and other events is posted as well as distributed to residents in fliers. In addition, certain circulars with post announcements (e.g., temporary regulations governing lawn-watering or car-washing during water shortages) bear the name and telephone number of the community representative. Residents do not always pay close attention to such notices, however, nor do they fully understand their sources. This is partly due to the sheer number and variety of programs that operate on post. Residents are sometimes overwhelmed with information and seem to understand it best when it is given to them in person by the community representative upon their

Table 10.9. Knowledge of Community Representative

Extent of Knowledge	Number of Husbands	Number of Wives
Does not know there is one	4	2
Knows there is one but does not know who she is	15	13
Says he/she knows representative but gives wrong name or says it's a man or senior occupant	3	1
Knows who representative is but does not know her name	3	3
Says he/she does not know current representative but gives current representative's name	0	1
Knows previous representative's name but not current representative's name	1	1
Knows correct current representative's name	4	11
Total	30	32

arrival or by a court representative. Indeed, some of the misinformation residents have about the community representational system comes from neighbors.

MILITARY FAMILY LIFE

Eden Gardens is a relatively homogeneous community on some social background characteristics, such as the education and life-cycle stage of residents. However, on other important variables, it is culturally heterogeneous. The courts are certainly more racially integrated than civilian neighborhoods, probably including those in which the residents grew up. Eden Gardens is also a transient community, and long-term friendships with neighbors based on face-to-face contact are virtually impossible.

Most residents do not appear to have a strong identification with the community as a whole or to be involved in activities involving the whole community. Any social solidarity that exists does not encompass the community as a unified whole. However, most respondents are involved with at least some neighbors in social relationships involving mutual affection, activities, and aid. This is especially true for the women, whose closest friends tend to be neighbors. Further, though most families report some problems with neighbors, most problems are minor and involve very few neighbors.

The military life-style places special pressures on family life. While most families in Eden Gardens appear to have some day-to-day informal social support, it is not clear whether this support is enough to sustain these families in the event of a major military or family emergency. Most of their friendships are transitory, and it is not clear how intimate and psychologically rewarding they are. Moreover, these families could not count on some of the formal programs, including the community representational system, during a major military emergency; for the personnel who partly staff those programs would be returned to operational units and no longer available.

It is very hard to say how Eden Gardens and other family housing neighborhoods on military installations compare with similar communities of earlier periods. They are certainly larger than the family housing areas on post before World War II, when the standing Army was small. While observers are often nostalgic for the good old days of strongly supportive communities, it is not at all clear that those earlier communities had any more solidarity. Of course, it could have been the case that the residents were more similar on cultural characteristics, such as race, which foster cohesion. It is likely that social solidarity among officers' families today is stronger than it is among enlisted families, but the military unit rather than the neighborhood is more often the locus of such support. Relationships of officers with neighbors are probably no different from those in Eden Gardens.

Army enlisted families who live off post are likely to have different social support networks and life-styles from those found in Eden Gardens. This is certainly true for junior enlisted families (who are not eligible for housing on post), since their financial circumstances tend to be shakier, their housing is poorer, they generally do not have the same degree of social support, and they are younger and less experienced in coping with stress on their own. Their communities are also transient and their knowledge of Army services is very limited. Almost all young enlisted wives seem to have ties to the army community only through their husbands. This is evident, for example, in the fact that when their husbands go overseas on unaccompanied tours, they go "home"— which means they go to where their extended families and friends are.

For soldiers' families with the same rank classification as Eden Gardens residents who choose to live off post, we would expect that, on the average, they are less positively oriented to the Army, less likely to be aware of and to use the formal services provided by the Army, and less likely to be friends with other military family members.[15] Empirical tests of these expectations and of off-post family integration in civilian communities are subjects for further research.

NOTES

1. Charles C. Moskos and John H. Faris, "Beyond the Marketplace: National Service and the AVF," in *Toward a Consensus on Military Service: Report of the Atlantic Council's Working Group on Military Service*, Andrew J. Goodpaster, Lloyd H. Elliott, and J. Allan Hovey, Jr., eds. (New York: Pergamon, 1982), p. 136.
2. Charles H. Coates and Roland J. Pellegrin, *Military Sociology: A Study of American Military Institutions and Military Life* (University Park, MD: Social Science Press, 1965), p. 384. Before World War II, families on military posts were almost exclusively officers' families. For a description of the lifestyles of officers' families both before and after World War II, see Morris Janowitz, *The Professional Soldier: A Social and Political Portrait* (New York: Free Press, 1960), Chapters 9 and 10. For descriptions of trends in military families, including their numbers and compositions, see Roger W. Little, "The Military Family," in *Handbook of Military Installations*, Roger W. Little, ed. (Beverly Hills: Sage, 1971), pp. 247–270; Willard M. Bennett et al., *Army Families* (Carlisle Barracks, PA: U.S. Army War College, 1974); Nancy L. Goldman, "Trends in Family Patterns of U.S. Military Personnel during the 20th Century," in *The Social Psychology of Military Service*, Nancy L. Goldman and David R. Segal, eds. (Beverly Hills: Sage, 1976), pp. 119–133; M. Duncan Stanton, "The Military Family: Its Future in the All-Volunteer Context," in Goldman and Segal, *Social Psychology of Military Service*, pp. 135–149; David R. Segal et al., "Trends in the Structure of Army Families," *Journal of Political and Military Sociology 4* (Spring 1976): 135–139; Zahava D. Doering and William P. Hutzler, *Description of Officers and Enlisted Personnel in the U.S. Armed Forces: A Reference for Military Manpower Analysis* (Santa Monica, CA: Rand Corporation, 1982).
3. Coates and Pellegrin, *Military Sociology*, p. 384.

4. Ibid., pp. 388–389.
5. See, for example, Reuben Hill, *Families under Stress: Adjustment to the Crisis of War Separation and Reunion* (New York: Harper, 1949); Hamilton I. McCubbin et al., eds., *Family Separation and Reunion: Families of Prisoners of War and Servicemen Missing in Action* (San Diego: Naval Health Research Center, Center for Prisoner of War Studies, NHRC Report No. 74-70, 1974). For abstracts of both published and unpublished studies, see Edna J. Hunter, Donald Den Dulk, and John W. Williams, *The Literature on Military Families, 1980: An Annotated Bibliography* (Colorado Springs, U.S. Air Force Academy, TR No. 80-11, 1980).
6. Major summaries, reviews, and reports of military family research include: Bennett et al., *Army Families*; Stanton, "The Military Family"; Hamilton I. McCubbin, Barbara B. Dahl, and Edna J. Hunter, eds., *Families in the Military System* (Beverly Hills: Sage, 1976); Edna J. Hunter, ed., *Changing Families in a Changing Military System* (San Diego: Naval Health Research Center, 1977); Edna J. Hunter and D. Stephen Nice, eds., *Military Families: Adaptation to Change* (New York: Praeger, 1978); Hunter, Den Dulk, and Williams, *Literature on Military Families*; Gerald M. Croan et al., *Roadmap for Navy Family Research* (Columbia, MD: Westinghouse Public Applied Systems Division, 1980); Edna J. Hunter, *Families under the Flag: A Review of Military Family Literature* (New York: Praeger, 1982).
7. Sabra Woolley, "Ethnography of a Navy Community," in *Changing U.S. Military Manpower Realities*, Frank D. Margiotta, James Brown, and Michael J. Collins, eds. (Boulder, CO: Westview Press, 1983) is a study of a housing tract near Washington, DC whose residents are Navy and Marine Corps enlisted families (primarily pay grades E-4 and E-5). Charlotte Wolf, *Garrison Community: A Study of an Overseas American Military Colony* (Westport, CT: Greenwood, 1969) is a study of a community in Ankara, Turkey.
8. Some of the details of the description of the community, including the name, are fictitious. This has been done intentionally to protect the identity of the community.
9. One husband was away on emergency leave and the other was drunk when the interviewers arrived for their appointment.
10. The distribution for the men is: 18% rural, 21% small city (less than 50,000), 18% medium city (50,000 to 250,000), 11% suburb near a large city, 32% large city (more than 250,000). The women are somewhat more likely to come from smaller places: 19% rural, 38% small city, 16% medium city, 6% suburb near a large city, 22% large city.
11. James A. Martin of the Department of Military Psychiatry, Walter Reed Army Institute of Research, has found this in research in progress on two Army samples. Estimates of family size in the respondents' generation can be obtained from U.S. Bureau of the Census, Current Population Reports, Series P-20, No. 385, *Childspacing among Birth Cohorts of American Women: 1905 to 1959* (Washington, DC: U.S. Government Printing Office, 1984), Table 4. For women born between 1930 and 1939 (the likely cohort of respondents' mothers), about 38% of all mothers (and 55% of black mothers) gave birth to four or more children, compared to more than 60% of Eden Gardens residents who have at least three siblings.
12. For a review of some of the research supporting these and other statements about women's friendships, see Robert R. Bell, *Worlds of Friendship* (Beverly Hills: Sage, 1981), especially pp. 55–74.
13. This analysis is reported only for whites and blacks because the numbers of respondents or friends of other groups are too small for meaningful analysis.

14. The question was open-ended first and then we asked about specific others. The figures reported include both those who identified the source in response to the open-ended question and those who said yes to a specific probe. The rank order of answers to just the open-ended question was not identical but was similar.
15. John D. Blair, "Internal and External Integration among Soldiers," *Journal of Political and Military Sociology 8* (Fall 1980): 227–242, shows, for example, that career-oriented army junior NCOs are more likely to live on post with their families than are those who are not career-oriented.

11

Anzacs, Chockos, and Diggers: A Portrait of the Australian Enlisted Man

Malcolm van Gelder and Michael J. Eley

FORCE STRUCTURE AND TRADITIONS

In June 1983 Australia had 72,800 permanent service personnel, of whom 17,200 were in the Royal Australian Navy (RAN), 33,100 in the Australian Regular Army (ARA), and 22,500 in the Royal Australian Air Force (RAAF). Some 61,000 were enlisted men and women, known as "other ranks," and this number included 1,799 apprentice tradesmen and 139 junior recruits in the RAN.[1] The regular forces are supported by defence force reserves numbering almost 35,609, most of whom are in the Army, and civilian support, including those in the Department of Defence Support, numbering about 38,800. The majority of the latter are in defense industrial enterprises, scientific work, and logistic support.

The end of the Vietnam War marked the beginning of a major change in thinking and policy in relation to the Australian Defence Forces. There was a change from a partially conscript regular Army of the 1960s and early 1970s to an all volunteer Army, and there was an increasing equipment orientation in all three services. Apart from numbers, mode of enlistment, and technological orientation, however, other changes have emerged or been confirmed as well.

1. There has been a recognition of the defense industry as an industry in its own right, and a reinforcement of the concept of the profession of arms.
2. The range of employment opportunities for military women has been expanded. Women in the Navy are employed in all areas except as aircrew or at sea, and in the Army women are now able to be employed in most noncombat occupations. In the RAAF, women are now employed in a majority of musterings, including the aircraft technical trades.
3. The pattern of engagement of other ranks has changed with a distinct movement towards shorter engagements and mid-term attrition.

Given that these changes have occurred, one could speculate as to whether the services will be able to recruit and train the people necessary to man the equipment required in a sophisticated conflict environment, and less tangibly whether the services will be able to place reliance on the next generation of Australian youth to fight in the national interest. This is not meant to discount the possibility of low-level and intermediate engagements which might require little more than traditional military skills and national will.

A common assertion, in Australia at least, is that the Australian fighting man, in whatever medium of sea, land or sky, and by whatever standards, exhibits an aggressive fighting spirit on the field of battle. Notwithstanding historical differences and changes in the mode of warfare, it is readily believed that the Australian soldier will always perform with a motivation akin to that exhibited by the Australian Imperial Force in the First World War—the force which spawned the "Anzac" fighting spirit which has become something of a popular legend in Australia.[2]

The traditional image of the Australian enlisted man has been that of the fighting soldier because most of Australia's past military engagements have been on land. In the future, of course, the sociological and psychological characteristics of the Navy or Air Force enlisted man might be much more relevant to the task of successfully prosecuting a war or major engagement. But for sheer convenience the emphasis in this chapter is on describing the Australian soldier and then where possible, drawing inter-service comparisons.

HISTORICAL PERSPECTIVE

The Volunteer Spirit

From 1870 onward, volunteers rather than permanent soldiers became part of the life of Australia; and, in a frontier society which when compared with European society was relatively classless, they were bred on the philosophies of individuality, mateship, service, and equal opportunity ("give him a go").[3] When the alarm bell sounded during the Crimean War, there were sufficient volunteers in the Sudan and South Africa for whatever defense requirements were considered necessary by the British government or the colonial administrations. Geographical isolation, rural preoccupation, and a small, basically British population, all led to Australia's playing a very small military part on the world scene, and any anti militant or anti-war attitudes of average Australians were not really put to the test. In fact, the enthusiasm with which the citizens of Sydney farewelled the Sudan contingent in 1885 indicated that the people were quite prepared to support popular causes, particularly in support of the Empire.

Before this, in 1863, 1,500 volunteers had embarked for the Maori War in New Zealand. The first pitched battle in which Australians took part was probably Te Ranga in 1864, and the volunteers were praised for their dash and enthusiasm.

The separate colonies in Australia had small military forces which they agreed to combine at the time of federation. They were predominantly militia, with a small corps of permanent forces, numbering in total about 29,000 men. In 1901 the British Colonial Defence Committee advised the newly established commonwealth government that it need have the resources only to repel a squadron of three or four cruisers which might make a raid of a hasty and fugitive character. The colonial military establishment were accordingly reduced.

The federation of the Australian colonies took place in 1901, fourteen months after the outbreak of the Boer War. The first fighting forces representing the new commonwealth government sailed for South Africa in February 1902. A large percentage of the Australian contingent in the Boer War was made up of bushmen, ranging from wealthy graziers to the roughest of stockmen, who were as equally at home in the veldts of South Africa as in the plains of Australia. They could match the bushcraft of the Boer enemy. They exhibited, according to the British commander-in-chief Lord Roberts, an intelligence in fighting which he wished all British troops to have. According to Firkins, Lord Roberts recognised for the first time a characteristic of the Australian soldier which clearly differentiated him from at least the British.[4] Referring to the general question of character of the Australian soldier, Firkins asserts that "his individuality and initiative have revealed themselves so often in so many campaigns that they are recognised as fundamental to his military make up." While this is a bold claim, it can be given historical weight if one recognizes less rigidity in the Australian class structure than in that of the British: the result is that the Australian soldier, although willing to be led by his officers, is less dependent on them than his British counterpart. This relative independence might, in the confusion of war, contribute to "initiative" and more effective performance.

At Eland's river, Australians attracted a reputation as the only troops who could scout into Boer lines at night and kill sentries, and kill or capture the Boer scouts. A comment on the same battle said that the Australians had brought an "intellectual appreciation to warfare," in contrast to the bulk of the British Army, which was still adhering slavishly to orthodox means of waging war and wasting the bravery of the individual British soldier.

The rise of German imperialism saw the Australian Defence Act of 1903 providing for compulsory training in time of war. In 1910, a report by Lord Kitchener recommended a force of at least 80,000 trained men recruited from cadets at the age of eighteen. This citizen force would be directed by a professional staff corps in which, according to Lord Kitchener, no social considerations, influence, or anything but efficiency would be allowed to affect the selection and promotion of its leaders.

The scheme of training was not actually implemented until 1911, and the training was less than universal, since it could be applied effectively only to able-bodied men in the urban districts or more closely settled regions. At the outbreak of war in 1914, the army establishment comprised 3,000 permanent and 42,000 citizen soldiers, but it was swamped by the enlistment of voluntary recruits in the Australian expeditionary force. The Australian Imperial Force (or AIF) was completely volunteer, as provided by the Defence Act, though many of the first AIF had been young trainees or members of the militia. Recruiting continued to meet the needs of Australia's overseas commitments through 1914 and 1915.

By late 1915 deterioration of the military situation in Europe began to call into question the adequacy or appropriateness of the volunteer system. In August 1916 news came of heavy losses on the Somme, where the Australians suffered 28,000 casualties. The question of compulsory military service or conscription was put to a referendum on 28 October 1916 and rejected. It was again rejected on 20 December 1917 after Australia suffered a further 38,000 casualties in the third Battle of Ypres in October 1917.[5]

The inflow of recruits was meagre but adequate, and Australia remained the only participant not to compel men to serve in the war. Of a population of almost 2.5 million males in December 1911, 332,000 were sent overseas or were undergoing training at 1 November 1918; 59,000 were killed and 152,000 were wounded. There were, of course, high casualty levels in other Empire forces.

Defense cut-backs after the First World War reduced the number of citizen trainees from 128,000 in 1921 to 48,000 in 1929, and in 1929 the government suspended compulsory military training. It was only after Munich that efforts were made to increase military manpower strength; the number of citizen soldiers returned to 70,000 by March 1939.

The Second World War and Conscription

Australia followed Britain in declaring war on Germany in September 1939. Volunteers were called for the Second AIF (for overseas service), and compulsory military training for single males was introduced in October 1939. Service for conscripts was restricted to Australia and its territories, which included Papua New Guinea.

This policy of not permitting Australian conscripts to serve further afield meant that the arrival of United States conscripts in Australia from early 1942 onwards provided an awkward contrast,[6] particularly given the Japanese advances in the South-West Pacific, and the direct threat to Australia. Eventually, in early 1943, legislation was enacted to permit Australian conscripted troops to serve anywhere in the South-West Pacific area (New Guinea, New Britain, Solomons, Borneo, Dutch East Indies, Philippines and of course Australia). The remainder of the war was prosecuted with separate volunteer and conscript armies; but, as it happened, the "militia" was not required to serve beyond territory for which it had been liable from the beginning of the war in 1939.

The political and military leaders had long been worried by the existence within their army of these two armies—the volunteer and veteran AIF on the one hand and the part-volunteer part-conscript, and less experienced militia on the other. To erase the differences between the two they had taken such measures as reinforcing from a common pool of similarly trained soldiers (except all nonvolunteers went to militia units) and transferring newly promoted young AIF veterans into the militia units. The practical distinction that remained was that the Australian conscript was not sent north of the equator—a frontier that possessed no military significance.[7] He might die in Dutch New Guinea but not Luzon, in Portuguese Timor but not in British Borneo.

On the one hand, regardless of the reasons soldiers may have had initially for not volunteering, by the end of July 1945, 205,000 had transferred from the Citizen Military Forces to the AIF. On the other hand, a proportion of the men of the militia were then taking a perverse pride in not volunteering. They called each other "chocko," a term which had gone from being one of opprobrium to a title to be proud of, using it as they might "mate" or "digger."[8] They were determined to remain chockos just to show that here was one matter on which the army could not order them about. Less charitably, some might have believed (erroneously as it turned out) that chockos would be sent home as soon as the war finished whilst "volunteers" would be retained for garrison duties.

In the 1939–45 war more Australians served in full-time service (727,000) and served beyond the mainland of Australia (558,000) than in World War I. The service totals of those who served outside Australia were: Army, 397,000; Navy, 37,000; and Air force, 124,000. While a study of enlisted men in major conflicts necessarily focuses on the men on the ground, it is of significance that the proportions of those killed in the Second World War to those who served overseas were approximately the same across the three services.

Post World War II and "National Service"

After World War II the British Commonwealth Occupation Force in Japan was raised. Australia's contribution was of brigade strength with a number of ancillary units and headquarters elements. In 1950 Australia entered the Korean conflict, in which its maximum deployment was two battalions and a brigade headquarters. The commitment was beyond the resources of the regular Army (six year engagements) and reinforcements were especially recruited for Korea on short engagements (K Force). This was the commitment in which one battalion so distinguished itself that an officer of one of the original British battalions described the Australian unit as "the finest fighting infantry battalion I have ever seen."[9]

Universal conscription for all eighteen year olds was introduced in 1951 across the three services but it was simply a training scheme of sixteen weeks' duration rather than a buildup of forces to meet an actual threat. It carried a five-year part-time obligation to serve in the Citizen Military Forces. Small numbers were able to discharge their obligation in the Navy and the Air Force. Universal conscription was subsequently modified and then discontinued in 1959.

A battalion and a field battery were committed to the Malayan Emergency in 1955, and Australia participated in the "confrontation" between Indonesia and Malaysia in 1964 and 1965. The main fighting occurred in Borneo. In 1965 a battalion group was sent to Vietnam and this force was built up to a task force of 7,000 men by 1969. In addition the Navy maintained a destroyer and other support elements in Vietnam waters and the RAAF deployed three squadrons of fixed and rotary wing aircraft. All these forces were withdrawn by late 1972.

A selective national service scheme had been in operation from 1964 to 1972, its most outstanding feature being the induction by ballot of a restricted number of twenty year old men to man the Regular Army. Exempted from the ballot were those who were serving or chose to serve in the Citizen Military Force (now the Army Reserve). As it turned out, exemption from national service also meant exemption from the possibility of service in Vietnam. It was during this period that the Regular Army reached its "peace-time" peak of 44,500 men.

The use of national service conscripts in Vietnam was not the result of a lack of volunteers or lack of willingness on the part of the citizen forces to participate had they been called out. (For the citizen forces to be called out it is necessary under existing legislation for the Governor-General to declare a state of defense emergency or a state of war.) The use of national servicemen was considered by the government to be the most effective way of manning a "peacetime" regular and standing Army and discharging Australia's military obligations in Vietnam.

One nonmilitary study indicates that neither national service conscripts nor Army regulars became socialized into militaristic or reactionary views.[10] At the same time, morale among conscripts as well as regulars serving in Vietnam remained high despite some considerable anti-Vietnam (as opposed to anti-conscription) feeling in Australia. In addition, and confirmed by recent research, was the exceptional absence of alcoholism and drug usage among those who served in Vietnam and on their return to civilian life.[11]

Whilst the RAN and RAAF deployed servicemen in all the post World War II engagements, no national servicemen were inducted in those two services during the period of the 1964–1972 National Service Scheme.

THE AUSTRALIAN FIGHTING CHARACTER: LEGEND AND FACT

The Legend

While most military historians commend Australian efforts at war and there are significant differences between Australian and other forces, these differences have not been uniform. Australian troops did not always live up to the legend, and it is not correct to assert that Australians were the only claimants of a fine fighting spirit. Much the same claims have been made for New Zealand troops, and yet their cultural/historical background was in many respects quite different from that of Australia.

The Australian soldier (and by implication the Australian serviceman) has been presented as brave, industrious, and often more capable than the troops alongside whom he fought.[12] Again by reputation, the characteristic qualities of the Australian fighting man—as a volunteer, a disdainer of pomp and formality, and a practitioner of mateship—have often been ascribed to the community from which he originated.

An only too rare person, a private soldier chronicler of military events, Private William Noonan, said that "however tough the hardships and conditions, it is the facility for blending with his environment while retaining his individuality that places the Australian soldier among the world's best."[13] A British general said that to his mind the Australians were the most aggressive and managed "to keep their form in spite of their questionable discipline." He said they were "a curious mixture of toughness and sentimentality."[14]

Writers who invoke national character as an explanation of fighting prowess must necessarily be challenged to separate fact from legend, to be more precise about just how the national character was formed and how it can be discerned in action. Australia's historian of the First World War, C.E.W. Bean, undoubtedly promoted the Australian legend and exaggerated its impact, but it must be more than coincidence that similar stories of mateship and "give it a go" recur in Australia's later military engagements and life generally. "Larrikinism" is still rampant in our civilian community,[15] sometimes annoyingly so; but apparently it is the sort of larrikinism and dash which through the Second World War, Korea, Malaya, Borneo and Vietnam enabled the Australian soldier, by patterns of aggressive patrolling developed in France in World War I, to close with the enemy and dominate no-man's land.

C.J. Dennis, perhaps Australia's most popular versifier, and Anzac laureate as he was called, in writing the "Songs of a Sentimental Bloke" in 1915 promoted the romantic attraction of the larrikin type. He further captured the apparent mood of the people when we wrote "Digger Smith" in 1918, less than a year after the word "Digger" was first applied to the Anzac troops.[16]

Russell Ward has amply demonstrated how Australian patriotic attitude and "Australian" characteristics emerged first and most clearly among the convicts, Irish and bushmen as well as the Australian born, and were largely confined to the working class.[17] (It was not until the last decade, however, that some pride, albeit a little self-conscious, has been developed in tracing ancestral origins to the early convicts).

It is recognized that after the end of the First World War, but not necessarily after federation in 1901, few Australians would think of themselves as anything but Australian. War apparently produced a marked development in Australianism among the middle class, based on the achievements of the First Australian Imperial Force (AIF) and pride in the immense voluntary contribution which had been made to the war effort. This Australianism retained strong links with Britain and the British Empire. It was empire loyalty which was behind much of the enthusiasm of Australians to commit themselves to overseas wars. There are of course some more basic reasons related to travel, the search for adventure, and the willingness to partake in a good "stoush."[18] Australia was virtually the only combatant which did not adopt conscription, despite her casualty rate of 64.8% of troops in the field (the highest of the empire armies).

After the war, the digger joined the bushman as a second national stereotype or idealized Australian, but in most essential respects the "digger" was only a new version of the "bushman."[19] The bush was the model and inspirer of later forms of mateship.[20] It began with self-interest as a practical form of mutual defense for two men against the hazards of bush life. It developed in the loneliness of the bush, and in the relative absence of women and institutional religion in the bush in the early days. Its highest and best manifestations were loyalty, self-sacrifice, and hospitality. The theme of the bush has been used to describe vividly the essential characteristics of the finest infantry soldiers—"men as self-reliant and adaptable as their pioneering forebears, as tough as stringy-bark,[21] as irresistible as a bushfire."[22]

The mateship of the men on the goldfield, the diggers, was akin to that of the bushmen in many respects, except that it seemed to have laid a special stress on equality owing to the levelling influence of the diggings in a community made up of men from different nations and classes. The theme of mateship on the diggings is frequently recounted in early Australian literature.

Military life tended to reproduce the values of the mining and pastoral frontiers since the life-styles had so much in common, and two most illuminating features of the First AIF were its principles of officer recruitment and its theory of discipline. Few Australian commanders in 1918 (writes C.E.W. Bean) paid any regard to the social status of the men whom they selected to be officers; rather they considered the quality that fitted a person for leadership. The officers were expected to lead by dint of those qualities, a kind of democratic sanction, and none could expect to succeed if he relied on mere traditional forms of rigid discipline. A pre-service occupational classification of the first AIF in World War I to embark for overseas was based more on social status than the 1911 national census of the population, but it reveals the main categories to be tradesmen (34%), laborers (30%) and country callings (17%) with less than one-fifth being clerical, professional or other.[23]

It was the First AIF which forged the so-called Anzac tradition on the shores of Gallipoli and in the trenches of France, and in that tradition, Firkins distinguishes "raw courage in adversity, endurance of the worst that fate could offer, a jovial gallantry and a concern for one's mates."[24] Whether it was the influence of the bush, the activity on the goldfields, or the life-style of Australians in both country and city, it is popularly believed that the characteristic qualities of the Australian servicemen are independence, self-reliance, ability to improvise, scorn of pretension, and an outlook of egalitarianism. The Second World War AIF revived and reinforced the legend with respect to both volunteer and militiaman, as did Australian performance in Korea, Borneo and Vietnam but to a lesser degree because of the scale and nature of those actions and the absence of mobilization.

Reassessment of the Legend

The Australian mystique was formally articulated in the late 1930s when Russell Ward commenced work on his "Australian legend" thesis. Professor Manning Clark reassesses the legend in his *A Short History of Australia*, especially in terms of post-Second World War realities. Foremost is his recognition that it can no longer be said that 90% of Australians descend from the British Isles.[25] Almost 30% of Australia's population is a product of post-war immigration,[26] and 22% has no connection by birth or descent with the British Isles. Manning Clark promotes a pessimistic and gloomy impression of the years 1969 through 1980, of asphalt suburbia at its worst. He despairs that Australia as a nation has become short-sighted and that nothing, not even economic crises or world war possibilities, seems to shake it out of its materialism. Ward's "noble bushman" has given way to Clark's suburban gadget-addict, but even Clark does not ignore the continuing ideological value of the former.[27]

It is important to know that Clark, a visionary attempting to build a new society, feels that the "mateship myth" was all but laid to rest on the Vietnam battlefield, the conflict ushering in another phase of Australia's identity crisis. He does not elaborate on the point, possibly presuming its lack of contention. It may be, however, a narrow interpretation—of the events in Vietnam and the concurrent post-materialist attitudes in Australia—which fits Manning Clark's search for his new society.

Others of more conservative mind would believe that the bushman's mateship ethic was very much alive in Vietnam, a fact readily testified to by Vietnam veterans both regular and conscript. Clark seems to have assumed that political discord and student dissent were automatically transferred to the services and the battlefield, which speaks little for the basic resilience of Australian societal values and the assimilative power of the services. If Manning Clark's assertion that the mateship myth was diminished by Vietnam is meant to mean that the serviceman's will and capacity to fight is impaired, this is not necessarily in accord with other writings and findings.[28]

How much mateship and Anzac fighting qualities will re-emerge in the Australian fighting soldier of tomorrow and how much those qualities will transcend the universal tendencies towards self-gratification and materialism is uncertain. The bush or frontier spirit proved stronger than the accepted anti-militaristic attitude of the working class early in the century; but will its present counterpart, forged in the modern mining operations and increasingly mechanised agricultural and pastoral scene, fortify or reduce fighting spirit? Can the urban mateship be transferred to the battle scene as readily and as rewardingly as the earlier bush mateship?

Australia has been exposed to changes common to western society generally, but the climate, geographical boundaries, and essential institutional framework have not changed; and social and religious composition and social divisions do not seem, arguably, to have changed dramatically. Sport is still a strong influence, and traditional forms of recreation involving sun, water, surf and bush hold continued attraction.

Australia is, however, a richer, more urbanized, more technologically advanced society than it ever was. Where it was once a country typified by the bushman, the rugged pioneer and the larrikin, it is now a relatively prosperous, more cosmopolitan and urbanized country. To gauge the possible effect these changes may have had on the Australian serviceman and servicewoman, the next sections will look at some aspects of the demographic and social structure of the Australian forces.

SOCIAL AND STRUCTURAL COMPOSITION

Social Parameters

Data about nationality or ethnic origin are available only for army personnel and are limited in scope, but it appears that the Army contains fewer migrants and soldiers from migrant families than does the general population. The only ethnic groups which appear to be over-represented in the Army are those from Britain, the Netherlands and Germany. Of the other significant ethnic groups in the Australian population, Greece and Yugoslavia in particular, and Italy to a lesser extent, are scarcely represented in the Army at all by comparison. Asian born persons make up approximately 2% of the Australian population, but less than 0.3% of soldiers are from Asian backgrounds. While there is no ready explanation for this ethnic distribution, one might speculate that the military enjoys higher status within the British, German and Dutch national groups than it does with those groups of Southern European or Asian origin.

Aboriginal Australians also appear to be significantly under-represented in the Army, though this is difficult to tell with any certainty because statistics about the number of serving aborigines are not collected. Informal evidence indicates that fewer than ten recruits of aboriginal descent are enlisted each year; this would place the proportion of aboriginal soldiers at no more than 0.3% in comparison with a national population proportion of about 1%.

It would seem, then, that the Army is not a true reflection of Australia's ethnic structure, for while most ethnic groups are represented, the Army consists mainly of soldiers who are either white and Australian-born or of Anglo-Saxon origin. By comparison, aborigines, central and southern European, and Asian national groups appear to be significantly under-represented. While national origin and race are not supposed to be considered in the recruiting and induction process, neither is there any policy which aims to balance the racial and ethnic composition with that of the community. It should be noted that prospective recruits must be Australian citizens and this requirement has been strictly enforced only since 1980. The result is an interesting, though perhaps not significant, narrowness in the ethnic structure of at least the Army.

Distributions of major Christian denominations are consistent across the three services, which appear to be predominantly Anglican (approximately 40% in all services). Roman Catholic and non-Anglican protestant denominations combined have an equal share each of about 26% to 30%. While the proportions for these last two groups approximate their distribution in the general population, those claiming Anglican affiliation make up a much larger proportion in the services than they do in the general population, where only 26% claimed to be Anglican in the 1981 census. This is partly explained by the absence of a "not stated" category in military statistics, although there is a "no religion" category. For historical interest, figures extracted by Gammage about the men of the First AIF show the Protestant denominations to have been over-represented in comparison with the general population distribution of the day.[29]

The figures do not, of course, distinguish nominal from practising members of religions. It might be expected that the relative under-representation of soldiers with central and southern European national backgrounds could have decreased the representation of Roman Catholics, but no such tendency is obvious. Although the proportion of persons in the nonmilitary population who claim adherence to non-Christian religions is small (about 1%), the number in the three services is consistently almost negligible (Navy 0.1%, Air Force 0.2%, Army 0.5%).

There are significant differences between the services in the proportions of married servicemen and servicewomen. In 1983 the Air Force was the "most married" service, with 58% of its strength married, followed by the Army with 48% and the Navy, the "least married" service, with 37%. Rates of marriage for males follow this pattern, but the pattern is reversed for females: the RAAF has only 14% of its females married, compared with 15% for Army and 23% for Navy. Much of this pattern for females could be due to different patterns of age distribution and length of service among the services, where latest available statistics on turnover rate for example show Air Force women leaving the service at a rate 50% higher than Navy females.

The difference in marriage rates between the military services is no doubt related to the age distribution of those services. Navy for example, the service with the 37% marriage rate, has 60% of its strength aged 21 or less. Army, on the other hand, has approximately 30% and Air Force has only 20% in this age group. This age difference is reflected in the difference in the average ages of the enlisted personnel in the three services. Air Force is the oldest force, with an average age of 27 years. The average age of serving male soldiers is 25 years, and male sailors' average age is 23. The same trend is likely for females, (though RAAF data were not available at time of writing) with mean age for Army women being 23 and for Navy women, 21.6. Again as a matter of historical interest, the average age of the First AIF diary and letter writers researched by Gammage was 25 years.

While statistics describing the education standard of enlisted recruits do not appear to be compiled routinely in the three services, the latest Army figures which could be used as a guide indicate that about 80% of male Army recruits in recent years have completed year 10 of schooling (year 10 students are typically 16 years old). This compares with the national average of 90% of male students completing year 10. Air Force statistics show that at least a third of male RAAF recruits completed year 12 (the final year of high school). This compares very well with the current male national population average of 32%. On the other hand, available Army data indicate that only 12% of recruits had completed year 12 of schooling.

Although the absence of national norms makes accurate comparisons difficult, current army recruits are known to be at least as intelligent as those of twenty and more years ago, and mean measured intelligence of volunteer Army recruits matches closely the mean for national service conscripts between 1966 and 1970. While the mean intelligence of soldiers appears to match the population mean, the distribution of scores does differ slightly in that the distribution of volunteers' test scores is restricted at both ends of the intellectual scale in comparison with National Service recruits, with fewer voluntary enlistments occurring at both extremes of measured intelligence. The selection process, which imposes a minimum intellectual standard, is one obvious reason for this.

For male servicemen the Navy seems to attract recruits from each state, with a proportional shortfall in New South Wales (NSW) and increase in Tasmania. The Army is over-represented in South Australia/Northern Territory enlistments, and low on NSW representation. The Air Force attracts disproportionately low numbers from the two most populous states, NSW and Victoria, and high numbers from the other states. In general the distribution of female recruits follows the pattern above except in the case of Air Force, which attracts a proportionately high number of female recruits from Victoria but a disproportionately low number from NSW. The smaller, less populous states appear to be relatively over-represented, while NSW in particular, the largest in terms of population and perhaps the most significant in terms of location of serving military personnel, is under-represented.

On the basis of the limited number of social indicators discussed above, therefore, there are signs of slight differences between those who enlist in the armed forces and the general population. Perhaps most significantly, servicemen and servicewomen tend to be drawn predominantly from those areas of the population with an Anglo-Saxon background. Soldiers, though perhaps not airmen, tend to have had less secondary school education than the population as a whole. The major population centers (e.g., Sydney in New South Wales) appear to be less well represented in all services, and this may be an indication of a relative predominance of servicemen and women from rural and regional areas. Whilst not discussed earlier, there is some indication that servicemen are politically conservative. The most recent evidence of this came in the 1983 general election. Press reports noted that the only polling booth in Canberra, the national capital, to resist the otherwise consistent trend to the Labor Party was one which housed the largest army population in Canberra.

Manning Parameters

All three Australian services offer an initial fixed term of engagement: six years in the Navy (with the option of four years for female recruits), and three or six years in the other two. All servicemen are expected as a rule to serve until completion of each engagement. Some exceptions to this rule do exist;

for example RAAF allows for early release in the first ninety days, and RAN offers limited formal provisions for early voluntary discharge at some stages of service, including recruit training. The additional grounds of pregnancy or marriage exist for the voluntary discharge of females in all services. Otherwise, in all services voluntary discharge can only be achieved for strong compassionate reasons.

There is recurrent pressure to remove the short engagement option in the interest of cost effectiveness in the training and use of manpower. Army recruiting operations attempt to achieve the highest possible percentages of six-year enlistments, but despite these efforts the six-year enlistment percentage has decreased from about 60% to 40% in the last ten years. A national survey designed to assess community attitudes to the defense force indicated that young men preferred a short enlistment period to assess their career prospects before committing themselves to a lengthy engagement of six years (one-third of the lifetime of an eighteen year old).[30] A survey conducted in 1980 for the Regular Soldier Career Development Review (RSCDR) found that almost one-third of serving soldiers said that they would have preferred an open-ended engagement on enlistment.[31]

Fifty-eight percent of Army recruits are aged seventeen to eighteen years and it is this age group which displays a high level of job mobility in the community. Australian Bureau of Statistics (ABS) figures show that the average youth in this age group changes jobs at least once each year. It is for these reasons that the Army and Air Force prefer not to dispense with the three-year option. Expansion potential, manning flexibility, short-term expedient manpower, and a number of other familiar considerations are relevant to the question of term of engagement.

One major difference in selection and allocation policies of the three services is that Navy and Air Force recruits are enlisted directly into employment categories which are identified for them before enlistment. The Army on the other hand does not allocate soldiers to employments (occupational specialties) until recruit training is almost complete.

Annual male turnover is smallest in the Air Force (between 8 and 10% between 1977 and 1982), and highest in the Army (between 12 and 13% in the same period). Male Navy turnover has ranged between 9 and 12% in that time. The lower RAAF turnover may be in part related to the typically longer training time required for Air Force employments, and the consequential longer return-of-service requirement. Army has fewer of its employments attracting civil recognition than do Air Force and Navy, and this could be one factor which induces more soldiers to leave early and start a civilian career rather than serving longer with a view merely to changing employers some time in the future.

While turnover rates of noncommissioned servicewomen have been reasonably stable for both Air Force and Army in the last five years, female turnover in the Navy has almost halved in that time, dropping steadily from approximately 29% in 1977 to just over 15% in 1982. This compares with fluctuation in the Army of between 18 and 22%, and 22 and 25% in the Air Force.

In 1976 policy regarding the employment of women changed in all Australian services. Married women were allowed to continue serving, pay rates were equated with male rates, and provisions for maternity leave were introduced. Since then the proportion of females in all services has increased. In July 1982 the proportions of females in the services were: Navy, 6.7%; Army, 5.7%; Air Force, 7.2%. Navy policy seems to have changed most, in that retention of married women is more actively encouraged; and although the statistical base used makes the figure impossible to assess accurately, the incidence of serving couples is probably greatest in that service. This factor could be significant in explaining the dramatic fall in female turnover in the Navy. Separate posting locations for married partners is understood to be more accepted generally in the Navy, as separation has always been a fact of Navy life, through sea postings. Not unexpectedly, a policy which has allowed married servicewomen to remain in service has also reduced the turnover of married servicemen.

In the Army, perhaps predictably, rates of re-engagement improve as rank increases. The overall rate of re-engagement during 1981/82 was 65%. Private soldiers re-engaged at just over 40%, junior noncommissioned officers (NCOs) at 60-70% and Senior NCOs and warrant officers at 85% to 95%. While warrant officers are noncommissioned, they are usually referred to as a separate category in the noncommissioned rank structure. In the mid-1980s, unemployment in Australia had taken a marked upturn and apparently crossed that threshold beyond which uncertainty as to future employment lifts re-engagement rates significantly.

Rates of re-engagements are by contrast generally lower in the Navy where senior sailors in 1981/82 reenlisted at the rate of only 56%, with junior sailors at 45%. A slight increase in re-engagement rates occurred in technical compared with nontechnical categories.

Air Force re-engagement rates are highest of all. Senior NCOs reenlist at a rate of almost 90%, junior NCOs at between 70 and 75%, and aircraftsmen (AC) at approximately 50%.

These differential rates appear to be directly related to age, training time and the degree of civil/military alignment of trades. The figures tend to be misleading, however, in that they do not reflect different mid-term loss rates, which in turn are affected by different policies affecting such loss. For example, the Army's rate of reenlistment must be seen against the fact that around 30% of soldiers are discharged before they reach their first re-engagement point; and the Navy's against the facts that recruits may discharge during training and sailors may elect discharge after four and a half years without waiting for their re-engagement point.

The contrasting rates of re-engagement do illustrate differences in the manpower flows within the three services. RAAF has highest retention overall, retaining more young people, brighter and better educated, in a career service. Navy loses more senior ranks, due partly to family commitments. Army retains senior NCOs at an acceptable level but has a high turnover in the lower ranks.

Average length of service in the Navy is running currently at about 8.6 years for males and 4.2 years for females. The male length of service contrasts with that in the Air Force, which currently runs at about 10.4 years for males and 3.7 years for females. The average length of service for Army males is approximately 7.5 years and the female length of service 4.3 years.

Overall, manning differences between the three Australian services are relatively small. Differences that do exist in these areas can in part be traced to factors such as age, organizational structure, and some differences in service policy. Most noticeably, it seems that Air Force members are older, more are married and more are technically qualified in civil-recognized trades than members of the other two services. Sailors are younger and fewer are married, but both they and airmen seem to stay longer in their services than do soldiers.

Females in all services are younger and fewer of them are married than their civilian counterparts. This is probably best explained by the shorter general length of service of females. Furthermore, servicewomen have been more restricted in their employment and promotion opportunities. This tendency may disappear as the effects of the mid-1970s policy to enlist more women and employ them more widely begin to show during the 1980s.

The Army is different from the other services in that its enlistment policy ensures that its recruits accept a "soldier first, trade second" priority. For this reason Army recruits could conceivably be more identified with their service, at least initially, than recruits to the other services. The latter, who are mustered directly into their occupations, are more likely to have been drawn to their services for calculative-remunerative reasons—i.e., attracted by the prospect of a specific occupational category or trade training—rather than being more broadly oriented toward a service career per se. Commitment to one's service undoubtedly occurs in all three services, but perhaps at different stages and in different ways. Certainly the available statistics show that despite the possibility of earlier commitment to service, soldiers tend to leave the Army earlier.

Despite its policy of not assigning new entrants to trades until the end of recruit training, the Army has generally had no trouble attracting sufficient and suitable manpower, and in fact the defence force as a whole has never had to struggle to man its volunteer force at the level authorized by government. The evidence, inconclusive as it may be, suggests that service recruits may comprise something of a "special breed," even though in many respects they are representative of the wider community. The services appear to attract slightly different types of recruits, with the Air Force perhaps standing out as attracting recruits who most match the population norm. This could be explained by reference to the role of the RAAF, which tends to employ non-commissioned personnel in a more static and stable environment and in careers which are less different in many respects from careers in civilian areas. Despite the obvious differences between service careers (especially those in the Army and Navy) and the larger civilian society, there continues to be a willingness to enlist which implies a generally favorable community attitude toward military service.

FUTURE PROSPECTS

When Australia disengaged from the war in Vietnam, for the first time since the Second World War Australian troops were not engaged in conflict or occupation. For more than ten years the Australian services have experienced peace. As with all armed services, peace requires a re-channelling of energies; it involves re-organization, and frustration; and since the mid-1970s in Australia it has also involved relatively low levels of defense expenditure.

All these factors create pressures, on the organization as well as on the individual. To add to these pressures, Western society in the 1970s and 1980s has changed in ways which threaten to alienate it from the military. Some of these changes are of universal character and have been identified as:

1. An increasing emphasis on individual rights and individuality;
2. Development of educational systems which encourage initiative, questioning, and investigation rather than acceptance of or adherence to externally imposed rules;
3. A decline in deference and a demand for equal treatment and equal opportunity;
4. A tendency for employment to be viewed as a means to the end of higher remuneration rather than as an end in itself;
5. The "demystification" of modern life, with traditional rituals and symbols being questioned; and
6. A decrease in the importance of religion and patriotism.[32]

So while on the surface the type of recruit who enters the Australian services may not have changed, today's recruit must be able to adjust to working in an occupation that must seem "out of touch" with many of the changes that have occurred in society. At the same time, a large proportion of recruits for all services may be opting for the security, and probably the institutionalization and identification, of service life.

Institutionalization and commitment, easily fostered in time of war, are not as easily developed in an era which combines a peacetime service with conflicting social values. The task of developing commitment is not made any easier by the fact that the services are no longer "closed" communities. Changes in the services' policies in the 1970s regarding accommodation, for example, mean that an increasing number of single servicemen and women live off-base within the local communities and therefore live more than half their lives in the "other" society. The problem faced by the serviceperson in these circumstances, of coping with two value systems, cannot be discounted.

The Australian services have been conscious of social changes in the community. While still conservative and traditional by community standards, all services have changed in many ways in order to reduce the gap between their mores and social norms and those of society. The changes mentioned earlier in policies affecting the employment of women have been dramatic examples of this. It has only been since the mid-seventies that servicewomen have received pay and conditions of service equal to males. Less dramatic, perhaps, but more obvious changes have occurred in uniforms in the Army and Air Force, in an effort among other things to improve those services' public image. When long hair for males was the vogue in the late 1960s, servicemen were easily identified out of uniform because of their short hair, despite some concessions on hair length that were significant in military terms but of no consequence to the servicemen in civilian clothes trying to appear anonymous. Changing socio-sexual values in the community have resulted in less strict minor regulations in many military establishments regarding such things as sexes mingling in barrack blocks, and combined male/female single accommodation is being progressively, though not exclusively, introduced in most military areas.

Similar liberalization is gradually occurring in small ways throughout the services. For example, local leave for trainees is much more freely available now than ten years ago. Officer cadets, who were once cloistered in almost monastic isolation, are now almost as unrestricted in their off-duty time as enlisted men and women who live in barracks. Service personnel are now rarely subjected to formal room inspections and kit inspections, and they are able to add personal decoration and furniture to their rooms with a degree of freedom that was unheard of years ago.

Contrasting with these movements in social climate is a continuation of a strict code of discipline, dress and behavior while on duty. The services allow relaxation of these things after duty hours as a transition of sorts between the necessarily disciplined, regimented life of the serviceman on duty and the life "outside." By such mechanisms the role conflict is reduced and the potential for assimilation and service identification is maximized.

If the serviceman is to any extent a reflection of the community, and if that community has changed since the one which spawned the Anzacs, chockos, and diggers of earlier wars, it is reasonable to assume that the Australian serviceman of today is different from his counterpart of fifty or seventy years ago. And perhaps so it should be, or we would find a serviceman too far out of touch to earn the confidence of society. Furthermore, he now fights on a different battlefield, with different equipment. Even within the three services, differences in the type, if not the quality, of servicemen are apparent. But there are similarities between the Australian soldier, sailor and airman more compelling than the differences, and these similarities are due in no small part to the fact that they are all Australians, who at least hitherto have shared a largely common heritage and common loyalty.

NOTES

1. While the minimum age for adult entry to the Australian services is 17 years, a special category of junior recruit is enlisted in the Navy from the age of 15. Apprentice tradesmen may enlist from the age of 15½ years in all services.
2. "Anzac" is the code address adopted by General Birdwood in Egypt for the Australian and New Zealand Army Corps in 1915, and used by him in naming the landing-place at Gallipoli "Anzac Cove." The expression is now applied to Australian servicemen in later wars and to an Australian tradition sometimes heroically and sometimes ironically regarded. Although somewhat tarnished over the years, the image of the healthy, bronzed "Anzac" still lingers as part of Australia's and New Zealand's folklore.
3. K.R. Murray, "The Citizen Soldier in Australian Society. Some Thoughts." Paper presented to the Australian Study Group on Armed Forces and Society Conference 11-12 May 1979.
4. Peter Firkins, *The Australians in Nine Wars* (Sydney: Pan Books, 1982).
5. C.E.W. Bean, *Official History of Australia in the War of 1914-18*, Vol VI *The AIF in France 1918* (Sydney: Angus and Robertson, 1942).
6. Glenn A. Withers, *Conscription, Necessity and Justice: The Case for an All-Volunteer Army* (Sydney: Angus and Robertson, 1972).
7. Gavin Long, *Australia in the War of 1939-45. The Final Campaigns* Series One Army Vol VII (Canberra: Australian War Memorial, 1963), p. 77.
8. "Chocko" is World War I slang, originally an abusive name but now an honorable appellation. It came from the 8th Brigade (Tivey's Chocolate Soldiers). In World War II it was used to describe a member of the militia who did not serve outside Australia and its territories. They were called chocolate soldiers or chockos because they did not go to the Middle East. (They might conceivably "melt in the sun.")
9. Firkins, *Nine Wars*, p. 457.
10. Jane Ross, "The Conscript Experience in Vietnam," *Australian Outlook 29* (December 1975).
11. Henry S. Albinski, "The Armed Forces and the Community in Post-Vietnam Australia," *Politics 14* (November 1979): 200.
12. Bill Gammage, *The Broken Years—Australian Soldiers in the Great War* (Melbourne: Penguin Books, 1975) p. 119.
13. William Noonan, *The Surprising Battalion. Australian Commandos in China* (Sydney: NSW Bookstall Co Pty Ltd, 1945).
14. Lt. Gen Sir Adrian Carton de Wiart, *Happy Odyssey* (Sydney: Pan Books Ltd [undated]).
15. "Larrikinism," in its most favorable sense, and as romanticized by Henry Lawson and C.J. Dennis, refers to "Australian" pronounced characteristics of non-conformism, irreverence and impudence. It had its origins, according to one source, in the expression "larking about" and referred to rowdy and mischievous behavior.

16. A "digger" was originally an Australian goldminer of the 1850s and later. The term was then applied to an Australian soldier of World War I. It took the place of the time honored "cobber" in the parlance of the Australian soldier. It later became a familiar term of address such as "friend" or "comrade," and its use is now universal, not just applied to soldiers.

17. Russell Ward, *The Australian Legend*, 2nd Edition (Oxford: Oxford Univ. Press, 1966).

18. "Stoush" is slang for commotion or disturbance, ranging from a two-man fisti-cuffs to a Western Desert tank battle.

19. Geoffrey Serle, "The Digger Tradition and Australian Nationalism", *Meanjin Quarterly*, No 101, *Vol XXIV*, No. 2, University of Melbourne, 1965.

20. K.S. Inglis, "The Anzac Tradition" in *Meanjin Quarterly* No 100 *Vol XXIV* Number 1 University of Melbourne 1965 p. 50.

21. "Stringbark"—an example of the use of the name of Australian native flora to describe some person from the bush or outback. It embodies uncouth indigenous qualities, but at the same time can indicate toughness and resilience. The stringy bark is a eucalypt hardwood which can grow in poor land.

22. S. Encel, *Equality and Authority* (Melbourne: Cheshire, 1970) p. 416.

23. Gammage, *Broken Years*, p. 280.

24. Firkins, *Nine Wars*, p. 36.

25. Reduced from 98%. In the 1930s a figure of 98% was used because the Common-wealth Statistician counted everybody born in Australia, regardless of origin of parent, as British.

26. As estimated by Australian National University.

27. Manning Clark, *A Short History of Australia* (Melbourne: Macmillan Co., Pty Ltd., 1981).

28. Withers, *Conscription, Necessity and Justice*.

29. Gammage, *Broken Years*.

30. ANOP Market Research *"Community Attitudes Towards Australia's Defence Force"*, A National Communications Study for the Australian Director General of Recruiting and the Australian Government Advertising Service. October 1980.

31. Department of Defence. *Regular Soldier Career Development Review*, Canberra, November 1980.

32. F.K.N. Crook, *The Armed Forces in the Context of Rapid Social Change* ORAE Report RSS. Ottawa, April 1975, p. 91.

12

The Winds of Change: Manning the Canadian Enlisted Force*

Charles A. Cotton and Franklin C. Pinch

Canada's military, like the majority of armed forces organizations through history, depends on its host society for human resources. In the Canadian case this dependency is especially problematic, since there are no conscription laws or forms of national service which provide a stable flow of recruits. The military must compete in the national labor market, and it has done so for more than three decades since its expansion at the onset of the Cold War. A major concern in Canada during this period has been the military's capacity to maintain adequate levels of manpower, of sufficient quality and at a reasonable cost, to perform assigned national roles effectively. Institutionally, the military is particularly vulnerable to societal shifts in age distributions, labor market and educational trends, broad value trends, and shifting career expectations; and there is a need to adapt personnel policies to the changing social constituency from which recruits are drawn—always, of course, against the backdrop of the unique operational demands of military service. A substantial amount of research has been addressed to the dynamics of military participation in Canada, particularly at the enlisted level.[1]

This chapter provides an overview of the Canadian experience in attracting, training, and maintaining its integrated enlisted members during the past decade. The institutional tensions associated with these broad processes will be highlighted, as will some of the strategies which have been considered necessary to adapt to a changing society. In this regard, the material in this chapter may be of some use to planners in other nations who face similar problems in stabilizing the supply of enlisted personnel through the remainder

*Author's Note: The views and opinions expressed in this paper are those of the authors and do not represent the official views and policies of the Canadian Department of National Defence, the Royal Military College of Canada or the Directorate of Personnel Selection, Research and Second Careers.

of this century. In many respects, there is a common litany of military man-power problems in the all-volunteer forces (AVFs) of Western, liberal democ-racies, and although potential solutions must take into account national dif-ferences, the structure of the problem remains the same. This is especially true of Canada and the United States: both are concerned with issues related to recruitment, stability of skilled enlisted personnel, the expansion of employ-ment for military women, and other broad shifts in career orientations—all of which are likely to alter traditional notions of the military's institutional character.

THE STRUCTURE OF ENLISTED SERVICE

The social organization of enlisted service in the Canadian Forces (CF) reflects the influence of Canada's close historical association with Britain, and, more recently, the cultural influence of the United States. As in most militaries, officers and enlisted ranks constitute two distinct segments of the force, socially distinguishable in such manifestations as separate messing ar-rangements, accoutrements, career paths, and terms of service. Enlisted per-sonnel constitute slightly more than 80% of the regular force of around 82,000. In the main, recruitment patterns reflect this bifurcation in the func-tional and status hierarchy of military service: the egalitarian recruitment patterns of Israel, where all officers serve first as enlisted personnel, for exam-ple, are not found in Canada. There is, however, a trend toward upward mobility into the officer corps by enlisted personnel, both through the direct commissioning of senior noncommissioned officers and warrant officers and by the sponsorship of junior enlisted personnel in officer-oriented university programs. For senior ranks, commissioning provides a method of removing bottlenecks in the enlisted career hierarchy while also taking advantage of special experience-based skills needed in officer classifications. But there are examples of senior warrant officers declining the opportunity for direct pro-motion to the rank of captain, largely on the basis of their perception that it would involve a relative loss in status and influence.

Career paths for enlisted personnel are, in the main, aimed at procuring long-service members for employment in a single career field. Career paths are supported by an in-house training program and promotion system for each field. This is the typical pattern, but as we shall see later in the chapter, there are significant variations. Among other things, Canada is experimenting with concepts related to lateral entry at higher rank levels, basic trades training by outside civilian agencies, and increased flexibility in career fields; this is espe-cially the case for those areas, such as the ground combat arms, which have proven difficult to man in the 1970s.[2] The vast majority of enlisted personnel are recruited explicitly on the assumption that they will serve for an extended period in a specific military occupation. That this planning assumption has generally not held—in large part, owing to the high attrition rates during the first three years of entrants' service—has been a continuing vexation for military manpower planners. During the 1980s, this situation has abated with worsening economic conditions and a tightening of early release policies.

There are seven basic ranks, or rungs, in the enlisted career ladder in the Canadian Forces: private (Pte) to chief warrant officer (CWO). (The latter is patterned on the British Army rank of regimental sergeant major or RSM.) The modal time for progression through this system has been close to twenty-five years in the past, but there is a trend toward the promotion of personnel at a younger age, particularly in the operational segments. Only a very small percentage of entrants ever make it to the top of the enlisted hierarchy, with most leaving the military prematurely or retiring after twenty years at a lower rank. The "journeyman" or "trained soldier" rank for enlisted personnel is that of corporal (Cpl), typically attained after four years of service and the completion of advanced training in a trade; and the first supervisory level is master corporal (MCpl).

The data in Table 12.1 show the effect on the enlisted ranks of the restructuring that accompanied unification of the Canadian Army, the Royal Canadian Navy and the Royal Canadian Air Force into the Canadian Forces (CF) in 1968. The fact that pay level was tied to rank meant that, in order to equate military benchmarks with those of the Public Service of Canada (one of the Canadian government's objectives), a large number of personnel at the lowest rank level (private) had to be elevated to the rank of corporal. The unintended consequence of this "mass promotion" was that the rank of corporal ceased to be a supervisory level. Thus, a new rank—master corporal—was introduced, first as an "appointment" and later as a full-fledged rank.

To a great extent, however, the new rank structure reflects the technological requirements of a modern military force, and since, according to present logic, an advance in rank is the *prime* legitimate reason for an increase in pay, 43% of the enlisted personnel in the Canadian Forces are found at either the

Table 12.1.   Enlisted Rank Distributions in the Canadian Forces as of October, 1983

Rank	Percentage	Number
Chief Warrant Officer (CWO)	1.3	856
Master Warrant Officer (MWO)	3.5	2,293
Warrant Officer (WO)	7.0	4,574
Sergeant (Sgt)	15.7	10,244
Master Corporal (MCpl)	17.7	11,572
Corporal (Cpl)	25.3	16,516
Private (Pte)	29.5	19,339
Total	100.0	65,399

Source: CF Manpower Statistics, January 1984.

corporal or master corporal levels. Traditionalists still argue that there are "too many chiefs and not enough Indians," but at least to some extent this is based on the mistaken assumption that the corporal is still a supervisor. For all intents and purposes, corporals and privates constitute the nonsupervisory segment of the Canadian Forces: thus, formally speaking, roughly 55% of the enlisted strength perform nonsupervisory roles. Theoretically, each master corporal supervises three nonsupervisory personnel, which is about right for technical supervisory purposes but may be "top-heavy" for the operational arms of the Canadian Forces. It should be obvious from the foregoing that the present enlisted rank structure has less to do with the needs of the operational organization than it does with military rank/pay considerations and, in turn, their relationship to salary scales in the Public Service of Canada.

Comparatively, Canadian enlisted personnel are among the best paid in the world; but salary level, under favorable economic conditions, has had little effect in reducing high attrition rates in the first term of service.[3] Members are paid a direct salary regardless of their marital status, and extra allowances are generally limited to isolation, foreign, and hazardous duty categories. As suggested above, salaries are based on civil service benchmarks established on the basis of comparison between the corporal rank and comparable public service jobs. In 1982, the monthly rate for a recruit was $788; for a corporal it was $1,773 (Canadian dollars), or slightly more than $20,000 per year. In addition, beginning at the corporal rank, enlisted personnel are divided into three broad pay groupings according to specialty, with those in specialist categories 1 and 2 receiving higher monthly rates. This practice represents one of the ways in which enlisted rank compensation has had to be adjusted to the dynamics of the civilian labor force. Volunteer military labor is expensive, and the inflationary thrust is chronic, especially when there are civilian market opportunities for skilled specialists. In Canada's case, the recession in 1982 and 1983 has weakened the civilian market "pull" and thereby reduced attrition rates (by almost half).

The high rates of pay for enlisted personnel reflect the realities of volunteer recruitment in an advanced democracy. It also produces the paradox that, in some cases, the officers who lead sub-units are paid less than many of the men and women they command. Increasingly, too, there is very little difference in the fringe benefits between the officer and other rank groups. All members of the military are entitled to a full range of benefits, including fully subsidized removal expenses and one month's pay when moving from one location to another. But compensation is only one aspect of the social and motivational matrix of enlisted careers in Canada, and one cannot understand the dynamics of enlisted participation solely in monetary terms. Attitudes and orientations regarding the nature of military service conditions and obligations must also be examined. Even with high compensation levels, motivational complexities persist within both the enlisted and officer segments. Thus, a large part of this chapter is devoted to examining the social and motivational context of the Canadian enlisted experience, under three broad headings: *Entry into the military; Key issues in the career experience* (with a separate section on *enlisted women personnel*); and *Re-entry into civilian life.*

ENTRY INTO THE MILITARY

Non-officer recruitment into Canada's military is based upon enlistment into a specific trade for a three- or five-year initial term. Individuals apply to recruiting centers, where they compete against quotas and vacancies in specific occupational fields, with the quotas having been developed on the basis of computer projections of anticipated demand in a given year. Individuals who desire a specific trade often have to wait for up to a year before a vacancy becomes available. As a general rule, trades which involve training and skills of direct relevance to the civilian labor market are more attractive than those which can be classified as traditional operational functions, such as the ground combat arms and sea operations trades. Following induction, new recruits are sent for an eleven-week basic training course in one of two centralized schools, depending upon whether their mother tongue is English or French.[4] After successful completion of basic training, individuals are dispatched to specialized training schools for basic trade-qualifying courses.

It is important here to underline the fact that CF recruits enter within a unified and integrated force format, regardless of the operational element in which they will eventually serve. Those entering technical and administrative support roles, which constitute approximately 75% of the enlisted force,[5] are liable for service in any environment (land, sea, or air). This creates discontinuity and complexity in the initial socialization process, and this is of concern to military trainers. There have been, however, some significant changes in recent years, especially regarding the entry and initial socialization of recruits for the combat arms. Canadian combat troops are allocated to a regiment upon enlistment, and this affiliation remains with them throughout their career in the combat arms. (In fact, even if they transfer to another trade, they will retain this affiliation on an informal level.) Although much of combat arms basic training over the past fifteen years has been done in the two centralized schools, the trend is toward training in regimental depots. This marks a return to previous practices and is aimed at strengthening the regimental system and increasing cohesion. In fact, a number of indicators show a resurgence of the regimental system as a central component of the Canadian Forces. Similarly, a more direct hand in initial training and socialization is being taken by the naval arm.

Pressures for Change

Recruiting practices and career development models for enlisted ranks in the Canadian Forces are in the process of change in response to significant social and demographic trends in society as well as to shifts in military technology and organization. Policies and programs in existence stem largely from the 1950s, when the Cold War led to an expansion of Canada's military. In the absence of a civilian educational and training infrastructure aimed at producing the skills and expertise required, military authorities developed extensive in-house training schools and recruited primarily those who had not completed high school. Although annual recruitment quotas fluctuated from year to year as losses varied and as the economy ebbed and flowed, the basic system remained intact through the mid-seventies. Very few skilled recruits were accepted each year into military occupations which matched their civilian skills, for the military preferred to develop its own resources. Females were, almost without exception, confined to administrative support and paraprofessional medical roles.

This broad strategy for producing enlisted personnel worked well in the 1950s and 1960s when the majority of Canadian youth entered the labor force with neither a high school diploma nor a specialized skill certificate. By the middle of the 1970s, however, a number of indicators suggested a need to re-evaluate basic assumptions. The articulation between civilian and military patterns was beginning to break down. Recruiting goals were difficult to attain, and losses in training and in the early career stages rose dramatically. Less than 50% of recruits were finishing their first enlistment tour in the 1970s, despite the fact that they were all volunteers and had been carefully screened through a well-developed selection and classification system. As the 1980s began, the situation persisted; it remained relatively immune to short-run policy interventions, such as pay raises, altered eligibility standards, and changes in the training system. By this time, military authorities had become aware of the influence of external, societal trends on human resource acquisition and retention.

Research into manpower trends affecting supply began in 1974; it was aimed at a general understanding of the changing social context of military recruitment for other ranks and the development of new concepts in recruiting and career management that would serve for the remainder of the century. The research revealed that significant quantitative and qualitative changes had occurred in that segment of the age-eligible youth population which had historically provided the bulk of enlisted recruits. Results of the research are discussed in detail in published works,[6] and can be summarized as follows:

1. Revolutionary changes in the patterns of educational participation within Canada were influencing the supply of enlisted recruits.

2. Much of the attrition in training and early careers was linked to the fundamental nature of the youth segment from which the military draws most of
its recruits. The marked tendency toward job experimentation and inter-
organizational mobility in this group was at odds with the assumptions
underlying traditional recruiting and career concepts.
3. The retention of traditional policies was leading to recruitment from an
ever-narrowing segment of the potential pool. The military had failed to
develop approaches which would make it an attractive first employment
option for technically trained and occupationally experienced youth with
eleven or more years of schooling, a group which made up more than half
of the potential market by the end of the 1970s.

Implied in the above was that inroads would have to be made into the majority, better-educated segment of the potential recruit pool. This programmatic
imperative was not unique to Canada's AVF, as other nations faced the same
problems. In short, the middle class had to be brought into the mainstream of
military participation.[7] The requirement for this becomes clear when we consider the data in Table 12.2.

Table 12.2 categorizes the wastage rates among a sample of male enlistees
recruited during the summer of 1975 who answered a survey dealing with their
school, social, and employment backgrounds. They were tracked over the next
two years, and loss rates were examined in terms of those factors. This table
provides an elementary cross-tabulation of attrition by education and labor
force status upon entry into the military. The educational categories are "less
than Grade 11" and "Grade 11 or more," and the labor force categories from
which individuals entered the military are "school," "work," "unemployed."

Table 12.2. Attrition Percentages through April 1977 among Non-Officer Males Recruited
during the Summer of 1975 by Level of Education at Entry, Labor Force Status, and Attrition
Category—Canadian Forces

Attrition category	Less Schooling than Grade 11			More Schooling than Grade 11		
	School (240)	Work (311)	Unemployment (598)	School (56)	Work (71)	Unemployment (115)
Voluntary	11.0	14.0	14.0	7.0	8.0	13.0
Compulsory	21.0	22.0	33.0	7.0	10.0	13.0
Medical	1.0	3.0	2.0	2.0	0.0	4.0
Still serving	67.0	61.0	51.0	84.0	82.0	70.0
Total	100.0	100.0	100.0	100.0	100.0	100.0

Source: Claude Hamel, *The Social Correlates of Survival in Other Rank*, CFPARU Report 78-3, Toronto,
1978, p. 14.

The attrition status categories differentiate between voluntary releases, involuntary releases, other releases, and the group still serving after two years, and are expressed in percentages. The "still in service" group is most relevant for our purposes. The numbers in each category are broadly representative of their distribution over the recruited population.

Examination of Table 12.2 reveals that marginality in the labor force (unemployed) is associated with higher wastage rates in the military. This relationship holds across educational levels as the unemployed group consistently has higher loss rates. However, educational levels are also important, as the more educated group has better retention levels even among those who had been unemployed. The best retention prospects were those with higher education who entered the military directly from the school system (84%) or from a civilian job (82%). We note, too, that the differences in retention rates are largely due to higher involuntary (i.e., compulsory) losses, in that marginal recruits are less likely to meet the military's aptitude and adjustment standards.

Strategies for Change

When we look at the actual numbers involved, however, the paradox which faces military personnel authorities in Canada, given the small numbers of high quality recruits, comes into sharper focus. Nonofficer entrants who are most easily recruited are relatively incapable of career stability, whereas those who are difficult to recruit are better prospects. While the majority of potential recruits are in the better educated category, the majority of *actual* recruits come from the less educated segment. The largest group in this particular sample is that with the weakest retention prospects (retention = 51%, $n = 598$). The programmatic implication of these findings is that the military must develop new recruiting and career concepts. In the last five years, Canadian planners have begun approaches toward increasing the recruitment rate of skilled and older workers through lateral entry recruitment, and toward expanding the roles of females in the military. The goal is to establish a better fit between military and civilian patterns. This theme, with numerous Canadian examples, has been explored in a 1982 article by Pinch.[8]

Perhaps the most innovative Canadian program for enlisted recruitment is the Land Operations Trade Reassignment Plan (LOTRP), which was instituted in 1976 in the face of several years of chronic manning problems in the ground combat arms. Under this program, young persons are recruited into land combat trades with a guarantee that they will be subsequently considered for training and employment in one of the more attractive—in terms of the prevailing values of the civilian labor market—technical trades. This program, which is essentially a mode of adapting to societal trends, serves two complimentary functions in the military community. First, it helps to meet combat-arms recruiting goals, and, second, it provides other support trades with older, more experienced recruits who have been exposed to operational military life and who have proved that they can cope with the demands and values of the military community.

This policy is, from one perspective, a tacit admission by the Canadian military that the core operational trades at the enlisted level are not attractive adult career options for most of the better quality youth in society. Those which *are* attractive are the quasi-civilian support fields, especially those which offer stability of work in office or workshop environments, and the air technical/air operational support occupations. As in other AVF nations, a supply of enlisted personnel for land and sea operational service is the central manning problem. Though LOTRP is not without its own unique problems, innovative programs of this kind are necessary if the Canadian Forces are to effectively draw upon the human resource base in the future.

At the same time, however, such developments create internal tensions within the military, as programs such as LOTRP raise the issue about the place of the warrior/soldier versus that of tradesman/technician in the career and status system of the modern military. Given a choice, youth will gravitate towards areas of military employment that most closely resemble those in the civilian sector: that is, to the support component.

A great deal of research has been done in Canada to learn who participates in the military at the enlisted level. Generally, the research shows that recruitment is much more likely from the economic, social, and cultural margins of society.[9] Anticipatory socialization and self-recruitment also play important roles in attracting recruits to enter the Canadian military. High schools with cadet military programs produce a disproportionate number of recruits, and the likelihood of a family member entering military service increases dramatically in military families.[10]

In 1983 there were long waiting lists for enlisted entry, as youth unemployment levels had been driven up by a national recession. Yet the demographic projections for Canada[11] (and the low retention rates of individuals who enter the military as a last resort when they are no longer eligible for unemployment benefits) suggest that this is a short-term phenomenon. The long-term goal must be to forge closer linkages with institutions of the host society, so as to achieve a better representation of Canadian society and its labor force in the military. Recruitment is, however, only the first stage in the complex process of filling the enlisted ranks; an equally compelling task for military planners will be to improve the motivational climate for those who have already entered the military. To a degree, this can be accomplished by influencing and altering recruitment variables, but issues more directly related to the career service of enlisted personnel must also be confronted.

ISSUES IN THE ENLISTED EXPERIENCE

Early Career Attrition

Although sufficient numbers of recruits of reasonable quality can be attracted into the Canadian military, they must also be trained and retained. Despite careful screening and training, as well as comparatively good compensation, the majority of personnel enrolled do not serve beyond their first engagement (three or five years). This is especially the case in the land and sea operational forces, in which, during the 1970s, less than one in four enrollees served beyond five years.[12] Cross-national comparisons have shown that the situation is similar in other AVF militaries, although the Canadian Forces turnover rates have been the highest.[13]

Early attrition occurs for a number of reasons, few of which are amenable to full institutional control. This has led some Canadian researchers to argue that the Canadian Forces should adapt to prevailing social patterns rather than continually suffer the consequences of a poor articulation between CF career paths and prevailing civilian criteria. Similar arguments have been put forward in the United States.[14] As we have seen earlier, recruitment of high quality labor force participants and secondary school graduates into the enlisted ranks in Canada is difficult (under other than poor economic conditions), and the predominant pattern has been one of marginal recruitment. This has implications for the survival rates of recruits through basic military and trades training: Lower quality, less well-educated recruits have significantly higher attrition rates in the first two years of service.

Excessive reliance on a marginal recruitment base, however, does not fully explain prevailing patterns of early career attrition among enlisted personnel in Canada. Attitudes toward the requirements of military service and career expectations internalized from childhood onward must also be considered. In advanced democracies, including Canada, the volatility of youth attitudes regarding appropriate employment and careers is reflected within the military population. A study which examined trade satisfaction and organizational commitment in relation to career retention among Canadian Forces training school graduates in the 1970s found a 25% loss rate two years after graduation in the group (a minority) which had reported a very high level of both trade satisfaction and CF career commitment.[15]

The major conclusion to be drawn from these and other studies on Canadian enlisted personnel is that there are no simple solutions to the problem of turnover in the first few years of service. Tolerance for service irritants wanes over time, especially as marriages occur and families are formed. At a certain point, increases in compensation have little effect. Although some structural strategies, such as Canada's LOTRP (mentioned earlier), can be pursued, there are definite limits to the adaptation of such special career programs. A balance must be struck between excessive flexibility and carefully contrived rational career management systems. In addition, the requirement for operational effectiveness places limits on civilianizing reforms aimed at making the military more palatable as a career field.

Attitudinal Patterns of Enlisted Personnel

Most of the research on enlisted personnel in the Canadian Forces has been concerned with army personnel, both operational and support. We have a very unclear notion of enlisted attitudes in the navy and air force; thus, the descriptions offered below lack the strong comparative focus necessary for a more encompassing morphology of the unified force.

The majority of enlisted personnel in Canada's unified force are engaged in technical and administrative roles rather than in purely military endeavors. At the end of the 1970s, 42% of enlisted ranks were in technical support roles and 35% in administrative support.[16] They form part of the complex defense bureaucracy, which only resembles the traditional pyramid model of a combat organization. In many respects, their collective attitudes reflect that fact, and concern has been expressed in Canada over the civilianization of attitudes and the decline of the military ethos, particularly among enlisted personnel.[17] Yet these attitudinal developments are not limited to the large support segment of the military, for research has revealed problems of commitment and self-image among ground combat soldiers as well.

These issues relate directly to long-term shifts in the nature of military organization and military service—shifts reflected in the concepts of institutional and occupational models of military service as elaborated by Charles Moskos. Moskos' conceptual orientation formed the basis of a study of attitudinal patterns among male army personnel in Canada. The study used a scale measure, the Military Ethos Scales (MES),[18] based on Moskos' concepts. It showed that junior enlisted personnel in both combat and support segments tended to have an occupational orientation toward military service, defining their involvement in a contractually limited way, whereas officers and senior enlisted ranks displayed an institutional, or vocational, orientation characterized by norms of unlimited commitment.

The idea that junior troops have a calculative, somewhat extrinsic outlook on military service is, of course, not a particularly remarkable finding. However, the study also examined the systematic tensions which contrasting attitudes created within army settings: between officers and enlisted junior personnel, and between combat and support personnel. It also developed a three-way typology of latent role types based on the scalar data, dividing serving personnel into "soldiers" (who expressed a strong institutional orientation), "employees" (who expressed a strong occupational orientation), and a third, middle group called "ambivalents" (who fell between the two extremes). Overall, there were consistent and marked differences in the three groups along a number of attitudinal dimensions related to military organiza-tion and service. "Soldiers" tended to be much more supportive of the image of the combat soldier and combat institutions such as the regiment, more reluctant to accept women in combat roles, and more generally committed to the military. Among enlisted ranks, the great majority of junior troops (cor-poral and below) were classified as "employees," whereas the senior non-commissioned ranks were more likely to reflect "soldier" orientations.[19]

One of the key findings of the study on army attitudes was the marked preference of support personnel for service outside of land and sea opera-tions. Although they were currently serving in army positions, only 28.8% of senior noncommissioned ranks and 27.4% of the junior support ranks indi-cated a preference for operational land service. The majorities in both in-stances indicated a preference for service in an "air" or "static unified" milieu. Many of these saw themselves as specialists who should not have to get involved in land operations in the field.[20] This finding points up one of the unintended consequences of adopting a unified force format, since support personnel are free to consider more attractive employment situations within the total force. In the traditional three-force model, on the other hand, sup-port personnel are much more likely to be culturally adapted to their particu-lar environment. However, for Canada to attempt to return to a separate service format now or at any time in the future would create massive prob-lems, since a large proportion of support personnel have no specific element (i.e., land, sea, air) affiliation. Also, to some extent, strong branches based on occupational career fields (i.e., logistics), have developed within the Canadian Forces to give unaffiliated personnel some sense of identity and place in the scheme of things.

The Status of the Combat Soldier

In a peacetime AVF, with its high percentage of support troops, the status and self-image of the ground combat soldier is problematic. Societal norms and cultural preferences do not provide supports for committed participation to long service as a combat soldier. There is nothing especially new or star-tling in this, as ground combat forces in peacetime have long had difficulty in attracting quality recruits. However, current institutional developments make the situation more difficult because the central status of the combat soldier in the military hierarchy comes into question and is likely to remain so in a period of prolonged détente. Highly committed combat soldiers can come to believe that they are surrounded by paper pushers and bureaucrats-in-uniform who do not share their sense that the central function of the military is to fight, or at least to prepare for war.[21]

The evidence seems to suggest that the motivational flow in AVFs is away from the ground combat roles of infantry, armor, and artillery.[22] Recruits do not flock, in Canada at least, to the regimental colors, and reassignment away from the combat arms is viewed by the majority as a positive career step. This dynamic presents a problem of enormous complexity and significance to planners in Canada: for they must grapple with pragmatic policy incentives to man the combat elements in the short run, at the same time confronting the specter that some of these policies may well be eroding the essential institutional character of the military force in the longer run. Developments such as the LOTRP program referred to earlier must be seen in this light.

We must be careful, however, not to overstate the problem of attracting, training, motivating, and retraining enlisted personnel in the Canadian Forces; the situation is far from entirely negative. In comparison with members of any civilian organization that we may think of, Canadian enlisted personnel remain highly trained and organizationally committed. A cadre of "soldier" types remains for a long service career and provides the traditional backbone of the force. Perhaps this is the norm for an AVF: most enlisted personnel will serve a period of three to five years as volunteer citizen soldiers, and it may be unrealistic to expect the great majority of new entrants to remain for a full career. The difficulty comes, however, when career policies do not reflect that social reality.[23] During the past few years, CF planners have begun to confront the evidence that, for the majority of the age-eligible population, military service is not an attractive employment option, especially when other options are available. In the absence of the establishment of better social linkages with civilian institutions and better articulation of civilian and military career paths, manning instability is likely to be a recurrent theme in the Canadian Forces.

This situation calls for creative responses in institution building and policy development, and nowhere is this more apparent than in issues relating to the increased participation of women. These issues are taken up in ensuing sections.

ENLISTED WOMEN PERSONNEL

In 1982, approximately 8.7% (5,850) of the Canadian Forces enlisted force consisted of women personnel, an increase from less than 2% at the beginning of the 1960s.[24] Women are found in approximately 65% of the enlisted trades, and their distribution by rank—both as a percentage of all enlisted women and as a percentage of total enlisted strength—is shown in Table 12.3.

Women are very much under-represented in all supervisory ranks (master corporal to chief warrant officer). This means that many of the decisions regarding women's employment and careers are made by men who, as will be seen later, are not entirely positive in their attitudes toward women's participation.

The impetus for the expansion of women's roles in the military has resulted primarily from two sources: first, the Canadian Human Rights Act (CHRA),

Table 12.3.   Distribution of Canadian Forces Women by Rank as a Percentage of All Enlisted
Servicewomen and as a Percentage of the Total Enlisted Strength, 1982

Rank	Percent of Women Personnel	Number	Percent of All Enlisted Personnel
CWO	.02	1	.00
MWO	.09	5	.00
WO	.65	38	.06
SGT	4.13	243	.36
MCPL	9.40	553	.82
CPL	28.62	1,683	2.49
PTE	57.09	3,357	4.97
TOTAL	100.00	5,880	8.70

Source: CF Statistics, March, 1983

which forbade the exclusion of women from any area of employment unless such exclusion was based on bona fide occupational reasons; and, second, from the need to maintain adequate force levels in the face of inadequate male enrollment. The women's movement in Canada, and the drive for equal opportunity of employment for women in society in general has also played a part. It was on the basis of the above considerations that most of the expansion of women's roles has taken place.

As to the requirements of the CHRA, the Canadian Forces have undertaken a series of trials in order to determine the effect of women's participation in so-called near combat roles and traditionally all-male environments. Specifically, since 1979, evaluation has been undertaken of the impact of the introduction of women as members of aircrews, a noncombatant ship, two combat service support units, and in an isolated northern setting.

The training of women in aircrews is new and the evaluation will not be complete until 1985. On board ship, women have performed in traditional housekeeping and administrative roles and have also been required to perform seamanship duties alongside men. The isolation trial has been assessed as showing successful gender integration; in fact, women will henceforth assume the full range of both support and operational roles in isolated settings.[25]

In general, the trials have shown that the most serious problem has proved to be traditional male attitudes.[26] Military men still tend to view women in stereotypical ways, and women have to continually prove themselves. This, along with excessive physical demands and the absence among a significant proportion of women of a traditional soldierly approach to field tasks, poses particularly serious problems in army field units. In general, the presence of women has not been detrimental to overall operational effectiveness; however, if women are to be successfully integrated in the land operational environment, a great deal more prior preparation of the women themselves, and significant changes in attitudes among males, will be necessary. Whether or not these problems can be overcome remains an open question. It would appear that women will continue to fill noncombatant roles in the navy and air force; but the expansion of women into combatant roles has only recently been seriously broached.

As to quality of women recruits in comparison with their male enlisted counterparts, those who enrolled during the 1970s were older (94% of women as compared to 81% of men were over 18 years of age), better educated (46% of women compared to 30% of men had completed high school) and obtained higher mental ability scores (75% of women compared to 43% of men were in the top three mental ability categories).[27] By 1981, the gap between men and women had narrowed somewhat in that men showed an increase on all these dimensions; nonetheless, women enrollees continued to be of decidedly higher quality on entry. To some extent, these differences are attributable to the restricted quotas placed on positions open to women, permitting a more selective placement of female applicants. To view it another way, as long as restrictions exist on the roles for which women are considered suitable, a certain degree of discrimination against females is inevitable.

In this regard, determining the optimum number of women in each trade has been a continuing vexation to Canadian Forces policy makers. Current policy dictates that there be a minimum male content within the total manning strength of each trade. This male minimum percentage is fixed and determines the number of positions to be filled by either men *or* women within a trade. (For example, the combat arms trades accept only males, while the dental trades have 100% gender-free positions). The ratio of male to gender-free positions is based on what is somewhat arbitrarily considered a satisfactory sea/shore, operations/nonoperations, and/or field/garrison ratio. An attempt is made to ensure that men are not forced to serve a disproportionate amount of time in positions that are not open to women. That is, while some trade groupings employ both men and women, the latter are not, as a matter of policy, sent to sea or to certain other operational postings. The current proportions of male to gender-free positions are reviewed periodically, and presumably the outcome of the evaluations discussed earlier will help determine the formula to be used in the future.

With respect to retention patterns, analyses conducted on cohorts of males and females over a three-year period indicated that women had higher retention rates than males, both in general and in all specific occupational grouping comparisons. Another study, completed in 1981, showed that after the initial three-year period women's loss rates increase up to about the seven to eight year service point, when male and female attrition rates become similar. In addition, male attrition rates are higher than female rates during the last five years of service.[28] This may result from the fact that most males approaching retirement are married heads of households and thus experience greater pressure to establish themselves in remunerative second careers as mandatory retirement dates approach. In other words, situational contingencies stimulate male job search behavior at an earlier point. Since up to this time few females with full-duration careers have been married, the majority of females should experience less pressure than their male counterparts to obtain second career employment. This is, of course, a historical pattern which will presumably change as gender career lines merge in the future.

Although the data in this area are sketchy, it appears that women's voluntary loss rates are heavily influenced by marriage and child-rearing, especially in intra-service marriages. This leads us to consider another area of complexity—dual career families within the Canadian Forces.

Dual Service Marriages

With the rise in female participation in the Canadian military, the increase in marriages between male and female members who both remain in uniform has become a managerial problem.[29] At present, approximately 4% of the serving force in Canada is made up of members of dual service marriages. This is likely to rise slightly in the future as more females enter.

Although every effort is made to co-locate those involved in dual service marriages, this is not always possible; and officially, the military policy is that for the purposes of deployment, married members are considered to be single. One trend that seems to be emerging is that, should one of the marriage partners decide to leave the Canadian Forces, it is the male who tends to have higher rank and better credentials and to be likely to receive a higher civilian salary than his spouse; financially, then, the female is better off to stay in the military. It will be interesting to see if this trend continues and to observe its effects on overall retention rates of women and on the experience base of enlisted servicemen.

From the traditional perspective, complications arise when officers and enlisted ranks intermarry. Given that the pattern in Canada is for separate, i.e., segregated, messing and other social arrangements, married service couples can live rather complex social lives. Again, however, the primary problem lies in the career and social management of the force, and it is here that creative solutions will have to be sought through systematic study and policy development.

Overall, a peacetime AVF is subject to a number of external and internal pressures to modify its traditional practices for enlisted ranks. This is especially the case where the employment of women is concerned. There can be no doubt that the increase in military participation of women adds a large measure of complexity to the Canadian Forces organization and, in particular, to the career management and deployment of personnel. With respect to these issues, the balancing of human rights on the one hand and operational demands on the other is likely to occupy the CF for some years to come.

RE–ENTRY INTO CIVILIAN LIFE

Military service represents a delimited career.[30] Except for those who die while in service or those for whom special age exceptions are made, everyone must sooner or later return to civilian life, usually to a second career. This return may represent an easy transition to some, but for others there are some serious obstacles to be overcome.

For enlisted personnel, the Canadian Forces have a three-tier system that determines when a service member will retire: a three- or five-year initial engagement; a 20-years-of-service/40-years-of-age (whichever comes later) intermediate engagement; and an indefinite engagement, whereby selected service members are permitted to stay until age fifty-five. It is not unlike the "up-or-out" system of the United States forces; and, as in the United States, CF members tend to retire, on average, fifteen to twenty years before their civilian counterparts.[31] Of the 8,000 to 14,000 who leave the CF annually, few will have served to age fifty.

The senior leadership of the Canadian Forces is concerned about the ability of the service member to obtain suitable post-service employment and to adapt to civilian life in general. It is felt that post-service difficulties will reflect unfavorably on the CF as a concerned employer, thereby negatively affecting recruitment and retention of personnel. Furthermore, at some point the anxiety over making a career shift can be a demotivator, especially for personnel in nontransferable occupations (e.g., combat arms, certain sea operational occupations, etc.). Finally, there is the moral obligation that is argued to be owing to the individual who has given up a number of freedoms to serve his/her country.

From the social perspective, there is the possibility that the skills and competencies developed will be lost if service members are unsuccessful in connecting with the labor market at the appropriate level. For the individual, regardless of when he or she leaves the Canadian Forces, the annuity (pension) entitlement is unlikely to be sufficient to decently sustain self or family, and securing a civilian job will be a necessity.

While studies in the United States have addressed the long-term effect of military service upon earnings,[32] data do not exist in Canada for such an assessment. Research conducted in the Canadian Forces has been most concerned with identifying the types of problems encountered in military to civilian transition, and the variables associated with them.[33] The following describes, in summary form, what has been learned to date regarding the reentry of enlisted personnel.

Over 90% of those enlisted annuitants who leave the Canadian Forces plan to undertake employment, and their preference is to obtain a *suitable* (as opposed to *any*) job. When the composite indicator of success is taken as *not* having encountered one or more serious problems (see below), the majority (about 65%) have been found to be successful. However, the economic recession of 1981-83 caused greater difficulty for enlisted personnel who were then attempting to enter the civilian workforce. Among problems actually encountered and reported were: lacking civilian qualifications; needing to adopt civilian lifestyle and adjust to different routines, communities and work settings; coping with a lowered standard of living; finding suitable housing at an affordable price; and lacking sufficient information about job opportunities. Overall, the most serious problems have been lifestyle, job attainment, civilian certification, and simple lack of information.

In the short-term, enlisted personnel tend to move into occupational areas that have a relatively high demand and flexible qualifications for entry: for example, clerical/sales, service, and manufacturing sectors of the economy. In the beginning, representation in the managerial and supervisory levels is well below that expected on the basis of military rank, but this situation is improved in the long-term (about five years). Similarly, enlisted personnel report status and salary loss at the beginning of a second career. In the longer term, however, the majority show status and salary continuity or slight increments. About 20% continue to suffer status and salary decrements five years after leaving the Canadian Forces. These results are similar to those reported in the United States.

Correlates of success include rank, military occupation, education, and age. The first three show a positive relationship to second-career success, while the latter is negatively related. The higher the rank, the greater the success in finding a job, the higher the status of that job, and the greater the salary level achieved. Those with civilian-related backgrounds in the Canadian Forces, and who have specific civilian equivalencies when they leave, tend to have a more successful experience overall. Educational level also plays a significant role in that it is a qualification that can be most readily expressed in civilian terms. Since most enlisted personnel enter the military with less than a high school diploma, many enlisted retirees can be at a pronounced disadvantage when they leave the Canadian Forces. Among the worst off are ex-combat and sea-going personnel with a low level of formal education. Also, those who wait too long before leaving (over 45 years of age) find it difficult to obtain employment in a job market that increasingly favors younger persons.

The Canadian Forces have recognized the need to ensure that enlisted personnel have the opportunity to prepare for re-entry into civilian life, to upgrade their education, and to obtain civilian equivalencies. A massive CF program called the Second Career Assistance Network (SCAN) has been designed to meet these needs. It includes extensive transition counselling, well-developed educational programs, and the establishment of military-civilian equivalencies in training accreditation and of civilian occupational certification through professional/technical bodies.

The SCAN program's effectiveness remains to be evaluated, however. Planned research will attempt to determine, in a more precise way, the relative importance of a number of structural and motivational variables in transition success, as well as the degree to which the most disadvantaged (e.g., operational) groups of enlisted personnel can be better assisted.

STRATEGIES FOR THE FUTURE

In many respects, enlisted service in the Canadian Forces over the past decade has been influenced by demographic, social, and political/legal changes similar to those found in other nations, most notably the United States and the United Kingdom. There is the added factor of the unification of the Canadian Forces, where some structural problems remain. The difficulties in attracting and retaining well-qualified personnel have required an examination of the assumptions on which voluntary recruitment has been based; these assumptions have been found wanting, especially as regards the size of the male eligible population, educational levels, and the requirements imposed by human rights legislation respecting women's participation. Long-term stability of the force depends upon innovations which will bring personnel into the combat arms and the sea operations occupational fields; and ways have to be found to accommodate women personnel, if not in ground combat, then certainly in most other areas of military employment. Second-career programs, which take account of the uniqueness of military service, will need to be better integrated with CF career structures and with the demands of the civilian labor force. Overall, the long-term requirement is for better articulation between the military and civilian sectors.

The Canadian Forces have already begun to tackle some of these issues. The Land Operations Trade Reassignment Program (LOTRP) mentioned previously, permits initial entry into the combat arms and subsequent occupational change into a technical or administrative support employment field. This serves two purposes: first, it attracts the recruit into a hard-to-fill occupation; second, it provides a source of well-integrated support troops who can more easily identify with the norms of combat and better operate alongside their combatant counterparts. LOTRP is reinforced by a greater emphasis on the regimental system, which more readily incorporates all the functions connected with the ground combat role. Structural and interpersonal conflict is thereby reduced.

The expansion of women's roles and of the environments in which women can operate helps overcome the demographic down-curve of recruiting-age males and permits the Canadian Forces to maintain or expand its force size. It also fulfills the spirit of legislation reflecting national goals for expanding the opportunities for women. At the same time, it makes the CF more difficult to manage, especially with respect to the problem of deploying married service couples. However, so long as operational requirements come first, as they do at present, this is a manageable problem—albeit it may create disruption at the interpersonal level. Policies are needed to address many of the issues related to increased employment of women, and they will have to be under-pinned by careful research if they are to be effective.

The navy has begun to solve its enlisted recruitment problems by sponsor-ship of civilian technologists through a training program specifically geared to its needs for technicians with advanced training. The Marine Engineering Technician Training Plan (METTP) promises to be a relatively inexpensive way to ensure that key enlisted sea-going positions do not remain unfilled. As METTP is expanded to include both official language groups (English and French) and a greater number of sea-going occupations, articulation between the military and civilian training instructions will be increased. The social linkages thus formed should prove valuable, both in peacetime recruiting and in times of national emergency requiring rapid mobilization.

Finally, an emphasis on developing civilian–military equivalencies to ac-commodate retiring personnel is logically related to direct skilled recruitment. In fact, this effort is receiving much more attention, with a greater focus on operational readiness and expansion under a mobilization scenario, where it becomes important to identify those in the Canadian labor force who can be quickly trained to a military standard. Another internal thrust, which is aimed at separating skill levels from rank, will make it much easier to identify civilian–military skill equivalencies in the future. All of these initiatives point to better military–civilian articulation and the potential for the establishment of the necessary social linkages that should help the Canadian Forces stabilize its human resource base over the next decade.

As is true of most militaries, the Canadian Forces neither welcome nor easily accommodate change, regardless of its origin. But there is considerable evidence that if ways of managing and controlling necessary change can be identified, then the organization will respond favorably. The challenge for the social/behavioral research community, both in Canada and elsewhere, is to be able to provide systematic information to senior leadership, along with a clear statement of the management options that are open to them; in this regard, a modicum of success can be claimed in Canada.

NOTES

1. Almost all the research has been done by sociologists in uniform at the Canadian Forces Personnel Applied Research Unit (CFPARU) in Toronto. For a summary of the various studies and an assessment of the major implications of findings, see: E. Charles Tierney, *An Overview of Socio-Demographic Changes and Recruiting Trends in the Forces: 1968 to 1978,* CFPARU Report 79-1, Toronto, 1979. The societal context of this research is examined in the comprehensive article by Frank-lin C. Pinch, "Military Manpower and Social Change: Assessing the Institutional Fit," *Armed Forces and Society 8* (Summer 1982): 575–600. For a general assess-ment of sociological research on Canada's military, see Charles A. Cotton, "Soci-

ological Research on Canada's Military: An Assessment," (Paper presented to Conference on Future Directions of Research on the Canadian Military, York University, Toronto, November 1982).

2. Charles A. Cotton, Franklin C. Pinch, and Rodney K. Crook, "Canada's Professional Military: The Limits of Civilianization," *Armed Forces and Society 4* (Spring 1977): 365–390. Also, see Pinch, "Military Manpower and Social Change."

3. Cotton et al., "Canada's Professional Military," p. 381.

4. The organization of recruitment, training, and career management in the Canadian military reflects the bilingual and bicultural nature of Canadian society. Francophones and Anglophones are offered full careers in their mother tongues, and recruiting and promotion quotas are developed with this social imperative in mind. For an examination of some Canadian data dealing with the institutional consequences of this phenomenon, see Charles A. Cotton, *Francophone Military Participation in Canada*, CFPARU Report 76-3, Toronto, 1976.

5. Cotton et al., "Canada's Professional Military," p. 377.

6. Tierney, *An Assessment of Socio-Demographic Changes*, and Charles A. Cotton, "Educational Change and the Military Labour Market in Canada," *Interchange 11* (1981): 42–54.

7. On this point, see, for instance, Charles C. Moskos, "How to Save the All-Volunteer Force," *The Public Interest*, Number 61 (Fall 1980); Morris Janowitz and Charles C. Moskos, "Five Years of the All-Volunteer Force," *Armed Forces and Society 5* (Winter 1979): 171–217; and Gywnn Harries-Jenkins and Charles C. Moskos, "Armed Forces and Society," *Current Sociology 29* (Winter 1981). The case for similarities cannot be examined in detail here, but a comparison of Morris Janowitz and Charles C. Moskos, "Five Years of the All-Volunteer Force" with Cotton et al., "Canada's Professional Military" will underscore the similar concerns and indicators.

8. Pinch, "Military Manpower and Social Change."

9. Franklin C. Pinch, *Social, Economic and Cultural Influences on Military Participation in Two Canadian Provinces*, CFPARU Report 76-5, Toronto, 1975; Claude Hamel, *The Social Correlates of Survival in Other Rank Recruit Training*, CFPARU Report 78-1, Toronto 1978; and Charles A. Cotton, "Institutional and Occupational Values in Canada's Army," *Armed Forces and Society 8* (Fall 1981): 99–110.

10. Jacqueline A. James, *Sources of Information Affecting Application and Enrollment in the Canadian Forces*, CFPARU Report 82-5, Toronto, 1982.

11. These are discussed in Tierney, *An Assessment of Socio-Demographic Changes*.

12. Cotton et al., "Canada's Professional Military," pp. 380-381.

13. See, for instance, H. Wallace Sinaiko and Kenneth C. Scheflen, *Attrition in the Armed Services of Canada, the United Kingdom, and the United States: A Collaborative Study*, The Technical Cooperation Program, NAMRAD, Washington, DC, 1980.

14. Notably, by Moskos, "How to Save the All-Volunteer Force."

15. Peter Donnelly, E. Charles Tierney, and Charles A. Cotton, *Factors Affecting the Stay/Leave Decision of Post Pay Level 3 Graduates*, CFPARU Report 80-1, Toronto, 1980. Interestingly, this study showed the positive impact of anticipatory socialization in cadets and reserves on the retention of trainees during the first career stage.

16. Cotton et al., "Canada's Professional Military," p. 377. The situation in Canada's unified military is significant in that the support personnel, at both officer and

enlisted levels, are in a sense a "fourth element", and provide a segment which is separate from the three operational environments. The critical mass of support troops, given their relative numbers, provides the structural element which plays a critical role in civilianizing trends.

17. See, for instance, the analysis of this issue by Peter C. Kasurak, "Civilianization and the Military Ethos: Civil–Military Relations in Canada," *Canadian Public Administration 25* (Spring, 1982): 108–129.

18. Charles A. Cotton, *Military Attitudes and Values of the Army in Canada*, CFPARU Report 79-5, Toronto, 1979, and "Institutional and Occupational Values." Both references are based on Cotton's "The Divided Army: Role Orientations Among Canada's Peacetime Soldiers" (Ph.D. Dissertation, Carleton Univ., Ottawa, 1980).

19. Cotton, "Institutional and Occupational Values," pp. 105–108.

20. Cotton, *Military Attitudes*, pp. 40–52.

21. Cotton, "Institutional and Occupational Values," p. 108.

22. See the data presented in Cotton, *Military Attitudes*. More generally, this proposition finds support in a great many studies of AVF motivation at both the enlisted and officer levels.

23. Pinch, "Military Manpower and Social Change"; Moskos, "How to Save the All-Volunteer Force"; and Charles A. Cotton, *Labour Mobility Patterns and Military Manpower Supply in Canada*, CFPARU Report 75-2, Toronto, 1975. Kurt Lang has noted the military's unwillingness to try new career policies in "Military Career Structure: Emerging Trends and Alternatives," *Administrative Science Quarterly* (December 1972).

24. Personnel Selection Directive 2/83, National Defence Headquarters, Ottawa, 30 November, 1983, is the source of much of the information for this section.

25. Published Canadian Forces Policy, June 1983.

26. Franklin C. Pinch and Rosemary Park, *An Appraisal of the Social Behavioural Science Evaluation of the SWINTER Trials*, CFPARU Technical Note 5/83, Toronto, 1983.

27. Rosemary Park and Diane Forrestell, *Issues Related to the Employment of Women in the Canadian Forces*, CFPARU Technical Note 1/82, Toronto, 1982, pp. 2–4.

28. Ibid.

29. These issues with references are discussed by Pinch, "Military Manpower and Social Change."

30. The theme of military service as a delimited occupational activity and the associated problems for individuals is pursued by Marion J. Levy in "Armed Forces Organizations," in Henry Bienen, ed., *The Military and Modernization* (New York: Aldine-Atherton, 1971).

31. Robert L. Fuller, and David L. Redfering, "Effects of Retirement Planning on Retirement Adjustment of Military Personnel," *Sociology of Work and Occupations 3*, No. 4 (November 1976): 479–487; and Martin Binkin and Irene Kyriakopoulos, *Youth or Experience: Manning the Modern Military* (Washington: Brookings Institution, 1979).

32. See, for example, Melanie Martindale and Dudley L. Poston, "Variations in Veteran/Non-Veteran Earning Patterns Among World War II, Korea, and Vietnam War Cohorts," *Armed Forces and Society 5*, No. 2 (1979).

33. The remainder of this section is based on Franklin C. Pinch and Claude Hamel, *The Transition to Civilian Life Among CF Members*, CFPARU Report 78-3, Toronto, 1978.

13

Role Images, Military Attitudes, and the Enlisted Culture in Great Britain

Gwyn Harries-Jenkins

Traditionally, sociological studies of the British military have concentrated on the examination of the role and function of officers in terms of their sense of professionalism, their occupational self-image, and their status as members of a highly bureaucratic organization. In contrast, the sociological investigation of the part played within British armed forces by "other ranks"—"enlisted personnel" in American terminology—has been almost totally discounted. With the possible exception of historical studies such as Skelley's definitive work on the Victorian soldier, *The Victorian Army at Home*, no literature exists for the United Kingdom which is comparable with Moskos' seminal work, *The American Enlisted Man*.[1]

In many respects this failure to examine critically the lifestyle of these other ranks and, in particular, the "enlisted culture," can be readily rationalized. With the cessation of conscription in the United Kingdom in the early 1960s and the return to the all-volunteer force (AVF), military life in general has been foreign to a large part of the British population. Consequently the enlisted culture has attracted little attention and as an area of scholarly research it apparently has little to commend it. At the same time, media presentations have done little to suggest that this example of military subculture merits further analysis. Consequently this area continues to be neglected. This chapter sets out to examine the theme of the life and culture of other ranks in the British armed forces. The methodology is one which relies heavily on observation and the analysis of selected secondary data. While such an approach will not provide an exhaustive appraisal of contemporary military phenomena, it is intended to stimulate further research while adding to our understanding of the sociological issues which arise.

A CONCEPTUAL FRAMEWORK

An initial problem in looking at these issues is that although one talks generally of "the military," analysis leads quickly to the conclusion that the British armed forces, as those of other countries, are a far from homogeneous group. There are a number of interservice and intraservice differences in the characteristics of the enlisted culture. This is noticeable, for example, in the specific case of the lifestyle of soldiers. Here, the axiom that the British Army is nothing more than a collection of regiments which are structured and re-structured to meet specific tasks, is reflected in major differences of regimental traditions and mores. In other instances these differences suggest that a "cen-ter-periphery" model in which the center is associated with combat arms, while periphery is identified with support or technical activities, reflects accu-rately the heterogeneous nature of the enlisted culture. Alternatively, these combat/noncombat functional differences reflect the contrasting values to be found in what Moskos has termed the "segmented military."[2] This segmented or plural military will simultaneously display organizational trends which are both civilianized *and* traditional. It can be seen as a reflection of a more general phenomenon in which disadvantaged groups (the unemployed, the poor, racial minorities) are reluctant to seek employment within a structured authoritarian organization. Perhaps all that can be said with certainty is that the military in Great Britain continues to be drawn from traditional sources. When the concept of the segmented military is applied to the British armed forces, it can be concluded that some other ranks are essentially technicians in uniform with an enlisted culture, and that many of the features of their culture have a close affinity with the values of workers in the parent society. For other enlisted men, however, the culture continues to stress the ideals of soldierly honor and to uphold the mystique of the traditional military. When the effect of major interservice differences of culture and lifestyle is added to these distinctions, it can be readily concluded that this is a complex area for which the effective analysis depends upon the provision of a relevant concep-tual framework.

One such framework can be constructed on the basis of two sets of variables. These not only extend the basic idea of a segmented or plural military but also escape from a too-simplistic classification which is derived from interservice differences alone. The first set of variables consists essen-tially of those "pull" factors which attract other ranks into the British armed forces. They represent different military role images—*warrior, worker,* and *technician*—and they are a comment upon both individual motivation and group subculture. The importance of the first set of variables as pull factors is matched by a second set of variables which are essentially the "push" factors. These are variables which represent not so much an idealized military role as an attitude of mind which recognizes the potential advantages of service in the armed forces. Again, a three-fold classification can be constructed. This distinguishes *traditionalist, opportunist* and *careerist attitudes*. It suggests that the behavioral distinctions which are implicit in the role images of the first set of variables are balanced by the attitudinal differences which are to be found in the second set.

ROLE IMAGES

The Warrior

The warrior image is one in which some of the original components of military honor and duty are still operative among British other ranks—an informal code of conduct, personal dependency, group solidarity, and the pursuit of glory. The three services vary in the degree to which they have amended these historical components to fit in with the realities of life in a modern bureaucratic military, but there are persistent self-images which transcend service boundaries. Consequently, there is considerable affinity between the warrior self-image in operational units (such as the fighting regiments of the army and the seaman branches of the navy) where they are associated with combat roles. On the other hand there is a sharper contrast between these images and those held in the Royal Air Force, where few airmen are directly involved in personal combat.

Any differences between the services, however, can easily be overstated, for one of the fundamental characteristics of the warrior self-image is its universality. What this means is that features of each component are to be found in all parts of the British military. The informal code of conduct, for example, with its stress on a sense of comradeship and intense group loyalty, is a projection of a general sense of military brotherhood. This, in turn, develops a trait of personal dependency which recognizes that the survival of the group as a whole is highly dependent upon the loyalty of men to each other. Equally, the engendered sense of group solidarity with its implicit rejection of civilian values and norms reflects a sense of fraternity which is usually associated with an attachment to a specific unit. Taken further, the sense of fraternity in the military is more than instrumental. It becomes an end in and of itself, and for this reason it becomes highly suspect to the outsider.

At the same time, the outsider's reaction to the warrior self-image encourages a highly critical evaluation of the preoccupation of these other ranks with military glory. In one sense the reaction reflects a basic civilian suspicion of the ritual and trappings of a military lifestyle. Alternatively, it is indicative of the persistent concern within civilian society for the psychological implications of the seeming alacrity with which an enlisted culture embraces the pursuit of glory as an end in itself. Even though the proponents of this warrior self-image may repudiate the glory of war, their preoccupation with conflict and a sense of contest appears to distinguish them very markedly from those who prefer to stress the importance of the less martial values in a welfare society.

The Worker

The *worker* role image, in contrast, is primarily a reflection of the more instrumental values of civilian society. The main theme of the worker concept is based on the belief that there has to be a movement away from the basis of traditional authority and discipline within the military establishment. Considerable stress is placed on the functions and efficiency of a superior/subordinate relationship which depends upon persuasion and negotiation rather than upon authoritarian domination. To those other ranks who favor the image, the importance of this organizational change as a determinant of human behavior is reinforced by their perception of the need for changes in the living and working conditions of British service personnel. Cohesive social relations, it would seem, are now very dependent on a shift away from the use of negative sanctions towards a greater reliance upon positive incentives. One aspect of the latter is the shift in organizational authority; a second is the very considerable improvement in conditions of service. Consequently, as regulations which traditionally governed the way of life of other ranks have been abolished, relaxed or reformulated, so should working conditions in the military approximate more closely those enjoyed by workers within civilian society.

An important feature of the worker role image is the manner in which the identification of officers as "military managers" and of other ranks as "workers" encourages a critical evaluation of the officer–other rank relationship. There is some evidence that those who favor the worker role image equate this relationship with the less desirable features of the manager–worker conflict which is often found in civilian industry. This suggests that a traditional relationship which has been based on the concept of shared occupational interests rather than upon that of class conflict, is susceptible to change. One feature of this, which has been noted elsewhere in European armed forces (e.g., the Netherlands, the Federal Republic of Germany, and Norway), is the emergence of some form of group representation within the military organization. Taken to its extreme, this becomes a comprehensive attempt at unionization within the armed forces. So far there is little evidence of any major demand among British other ranks for such a development. Nevertheless, a feature of this worker role image continues to be the demand for the introduction into the military of the industrial practices to be found elsewhere within British society.

The worker role image is not without its critics. One issue is the point at which the military way of life can be so closely identified with civilian work that people ask "What is military?" In turn, this question raises the problem of whether the armed forces should have continuing access to scarce resources if the unique features of military life can no longer be identified. A second issue, one which is more directly related to the characteristics of the worker role image, suggests that if these characteristics are too closely based on contemporary civilian practice, they become dysfunctional within the military organization. This issue arises particularly if the image is equated with the notion of the *affluent soldier*—a notion which suggests that other ranks in the British military are relatively well-to-do, that they are more concerned with extrinsic rather than intrinsic rewards, that they have rejected the relevance of the military as a total institution, and that they see military service as essentially a "job." To put it briefly, this facet of the worker self-image is seen as playing down the importance of consensus, loyalty, morale and *esprit de corps* as features of a military culture, and as, instead, placing stress on the importance of competition, self-advancement, individual advantage, and the satisfaction of lower-order personal needs.

The Technician

The third role image, that of the *technician*, is materially different. It is firmly rooted in the technological revolution which has affected the British military as much as any industrial enterprise. It recognizes that innovation in this field has produced the complex machinery of modern warfare, the maintenance of which, whether in combat or peacetime conditions, depends upon the expertise of the military technician. This maintenance involves not only the use of developed technological skills but also the employment of highly skilled other ranks in sophisticated logistical tasks. Moreover, since the British armed forces do not rely on drafted personnel to man these technical specialties, the complex training organization which has evolved to promote the acquisition of skills inculcates and reinforces the characteristics of this image.

It is apparent that for many other ranks who identify with this technician role, the distinction between military and civilian skills has become blurred. The narrowing ability differential between military and civilian roles means that service personnel who work as military technicians have direct civilian equivalents. One danger here is that the use of civilian specialists as a reference group produces feelings of relative deprivation if conditions of military service differ from those of civilian society. This can be very marked where, within the military, technological changes are linked to organizational changes in such a way as to weaken social cohesion within the armed forces. The increasing trend in certain British army and air force units towards the civilian pattern of separation of work and residence, a trend encouraged by the economic advantages of early house purchase, has, for example, greatly encouraged the use of civilian reference groups as other ranks identify with a civilian rather than a military community. What this also suggests is that the traditional emphasis placed on such features of the enlisted culture as a strong group dynamic and a local identification now tend to be replaced in this role image by an emphasis on a mutual dependence derived from the technical proficiency of team members. In other words, the coordination of a group of specialists cannot be guaranteed by traditional means, for the technical self-image has, as one of its defining characteristics, a complex ethos which is a compound of a search for autonomy, a willingness to accept responsibility, a commitment to the task, technical ability, and a sense of belonging to a group of specialists.

MILITARY ATTITUDES

These three images—warrior, worker, and technician—represent a set of idealized roles which attract individuals to a military life-style. It is clear that where the push factors as they affect officers have been identified repeatedly with aspects of professionalism, role images for other ranks are more diverse. Soldiers are less concerned than their seniors with a single set of occupational values and there is far less homogenization than among officers. More specifically, in the absence of a singular professional ethos which has been developed as a product of selection and indoctrination processes, these other ranks demonstrate a much more diverse interpretation of the postulated attractions of military service.

This diversity is to be seen, however, not only among the *pull* factors which make a military way of life attractive to British other ranks, but also among *push* factors which emphasize the greater advantages of that life in comparison with what is happening in civilian society. Once again, three sets of attitudes can be identified, each of which merits further analysis and discussion.

The Traditionalist

In the past, the traditionalist attitude to military service has been quantitatively dominant within the British military. It is an attitude which is identified with the recruitment and retention of a group of other ranks who are concerned with the maintenance of an established way of life. These are servicemen who have not thought much about the advantages and disadvantages of service in the armed forces because they have assumed that such service is to be part of their life experience. By and large, they are individuals who are attracted to a military career because of their rejection of any postulated convergence of the armed forces and contemporary society. Indeed, persuasive evidence can be presented to suggest that the traditional military to which these other ranks wish to belong diverges along a variety of dimensions from the mainstream of developments in the general society.

One effect of this is that we can identify significant indicators of a growing divergence between societal norms and the beliefs of these traditionalists.

First, the latter continue to stress the inherent advantages of bureaucratic structures with their emphasis on the hierarchy of authority. Where civilian society may be highly critical of the mechanistic nature of the public service bureaucracy and be very concerned about the dysfunctional consequences of such an organization, the military traditionalist welcomes bureaucracy. For him it represents one persistent basis of stability in a desert of societal change. It successfully accommodates the needs of skilled technicians and technology within the military system. It provides a command structure based on age and seniority which is known and certain. Above all, bureaucracy is to the military traditionalist the most efficient means of organizing a large scale complex organization.

In addition, the traditionalist is highly suspicious of criticism of the organization. Whereas society increasingly accepts and encourages a critical evaluation of authority and power on the grounds that it is the right and duty of the individual to examine laws and their operations, the military traditionalist shies away from such evaluation. Frequently, he equates such evaluation with a less than objective approach to established structures. Alternatively, what would be seen elsewhere as a valid phenomenological approach to the study of the military organization is identified by traditionalists as a failure to understand that armed forces are not only real structures but that they have to be distinct from the actions, feelings and purposes of civilian society.

The thesis which traditionalists constantly stress is that military organizations, because their actions center on violence in situations of crisis, must develop an authority structure which is based on the existence of a sophisticated and differentially elitist model of command. Irrespective of what happens in civilian society, the sense of urgency in the military, the reality of immediate combat, and the need to impose sanctions against personnel are all stimuli which make military authority effective, in the traditionalist's view. The consequent emphasis which he places on established power structures thus serves to distinguish very markedly the norms and values of the traditionalist military man from the beliefs of civilian society. Taken to the extreme, it implies that these other ranks are deeply concerned with the upholding of the "true" values of society in the face of very considerable external pressure. To them, the military is the last repository of rules and regulated order.

The Opportunist

The opportunist, in contrast, sees service in the ranks of the British military as a chance to gain some personal advantage. The presented opportunities cover a wide range of possibilities that embrace not only financial advantage, second chance education, new skill acquisition and a change of environment but also the opportunity to obtain a measure of job security in a period of economic recession.

The complexity of individual motivation in this field has encouraged a number of studies of this particular attitude of mind. Bellany, for example, has presented a detailed statistical analysis of factors affecting voluntary enlistment into the British military.[3] He argues that in general terms there is wide agreement among interested observers that male, non-officer enlistment into the armed forces of the United Kingdom probably depends on four factors: forces' pay, average civilian pay, civilian unemployment, and the level of hostilities the armed forces are engaged in at the time. There is, however, disagreement and doubt as to whether any or all of these factors are always influential. This uncertainty persists, and, as the official conclusion put forward in 1972 decrees, there is "no evidence of any direct relationship between pay and the levels of recruitment."[4] The conclusion reached by Bellany is that, no matter what personal reasons individuals may give for joining the military, there is no doubt that as far as the army is concerned the total number of applications to enlist is a highly predictable figure—and that its size depends mainly upon the apparent financial rewards of an army job as compared to those in civilian life. What this means in practice is that the soldier tends to be recruited from the poorer regions of the United Kingdom, where average pay is low and unemployment high. Concomitantly, there is a definite tendency for rural areas and regions with relatively large service industry work forces to provide fewer would-be soldiers than the more highly industrialized parts of the country. It can also be noted that the opportunities inherent in service in the military are not readily seized upon by members of racial minority groups.

The stress which is placed upon the opportunity for financial reward and job security in the army, however, is not entirely confirmed by Bellany in his study of navy and air force recruitment. He suggests that where pay and unemployment account for about 70% of decisions to join the army, in the other two services they account on average for between 40% (RAF) and 45% (RN) of decisions to enlist. What this suggests is that opportunists in these other sectors of the armed forces are "pushed" into the military by factors other than issues of pay and unemployment alone. This conclusion is confirmed in studies of the attitudes of women toward the service opportunities in the ranks. The opportunity to overcome the effects of a poor educational record and the wish to escape from the social and occupational restrictions of their home environment are seen to be reasons why women initially favor service in the British armed forces. Thereafter, opportunities for an expanded work role, skill acquisition and general self-development, participation in unusual or expensive recreational activities, and "second chance training" are all seen to be important parts of this opportunist attitude.

Since it can be argued that male opportunists are similarly motivated, we can conclude that we are concerned here with a group of other ranks whose attitudes toward military service differ materially from the attitudes of the traditionalists. Opportunists use service to promote personal advantage, and it is very noticeable that this is the group to whom the military may be a "job" rather than a "profession." As such, the job is evaluated in comparison with other employment opportunities. Military work tasks, in particular, are identified in terms of their equivalency with civilian occupations, and the evaluation of such roles focuses on the personal advantages to be gained from acquiring occupational skills and qualifications. The most outstanding feature of this "job orientation," however, is the attention paid to the economic advantages of military service. This has become increasingly evident following the shift to the "military salary." The lessening emphasis placed on the importance of fringe benefits as part of the compensation package, the stress put on economic cash incentives to recruit and retain other ranks, and the constant comparisons made between military pay and the wage packet of civilian industry have all served to encourage the opportunist in the perception that military service is a good job from which the individual should derive as much personal benefit as possible.

The Careerist

In many ways, the motivation of the careerist closely resembles that of the opportunist, for both are concerned with the personal benefits that are to be gained from military service. The critical distinction between them, however, is that the opportunist has a very low level of commitment to the British military. The concept of "career" is entirely absent: opportunists see service in the all-volunteer force as a transitory phenomenon in the pattern of their work experience—not as a long-term commitment. The careerist, in contrast, has made a conscious choice, usually after weighing all the advantages and disadvantages, in favor of a long-term military career.

The distinction between careerist and traditionalist is also a subtle one. Both concepts are associated with a deep sense of commitment to military service which contrasts very forcefully with the instrumentality of the opportunist. Even so, the two images do differ. Briefly, the attitudes of the traditionalist can be identified with a preference for an unchanging and conventional military way of life. In the United Kingdom in particular, this is closely associated with the ethos, collegiality, and conservatism of the small group. The careerist, in contrast, is more likely to be concerned with the fulfillment of personal ambition.

Consequently, the traditionalist in his search for the maintenance of standards and the true military values tends to approach issues of personal advancement with diffidence. What is more important is the maintenance of the whole, an attitude which, carried to an extreme, encourages an uncritical acceptance of the military way of life even where this is out of step with changes in the parent society. Careerists, on the other hand, are more prone to be achievement oriented.

Irrespective of the service to which they belong or their own specialty, careerists are motivated to excel, not least because job satisfaction is closely identified with such visible signs of excellence as promotion and elitist appointments. They can be criticised—and indeed are criticised—for their rejection of commercial values and business success. Carried to its extreme, such criticism implies that the selection of a military career is the expression of a weak choice. One effect is that the military occupation is often thought to be "a berth for mediocrity." In reality, however, the selection of a military career on the part of other ranks, in common with the selection of any other long-term occupation, represents the interplay of a complex mix of social and personality factors. It may be concluded, on the basis of what Korpi and Abrahamsson respectively suggest in their discussions of recruitment to the Swedish military,[5] that careerists tend to be a group with outlooks more authoritarian than on the average. What is certain is that these other rank careerists cannot be held to be potential failures in other fields, even if they identify "career opportunity" with a noncompetitive avenue of achievement within the limited area of the military organization.

An extended analysis of motivation among these other ranks also suggests that, for the majority, the concept of career has overtones of a "calling" and a sense of military mission. In this context, the concept does represent a deliberate rejection of what is seen as the prosaic and limited horizons of a civilian occupation. But it must not be forgotten that a major feature of the military career is the manner in which it ensures the personal advancement of other ranks. For many British servicemen, the concept of career is concerned not only with the general ideal of service to the community; it also means that the adoption of a military career is one means of promoting social status, encouraging social mobility, and fulfilling the desire to excel. In short, the military is to these careerists more than an occupation. It is a means of satisfying strong personal motivations and legitimizing individual aspirations.

The concept of military careerism is one which has attracted substantial attention, although much of the writing is concerned first with officers' careers and secondly with the critical evaluation of the concept. Camacho, for example, in a controversial review of the imperatives of careerism among American officers, suggests that these imperatives evolved to such a point that they became uncontrollable. He draws particular attention to what he calls "trained incapacity" and "professional deformation" and the manner in which these affect the decision-making process to the extent that personal career goals begin to obscure the true purposes of the military organization.[6]

Irrespective of the validity of this analysis, it can be concluded that careerists among the other ranks within the British army exhibit reactions which are comparable with those noted by Camacho. Personal career goals assume an ever-growing importance as motivating factors. One effect is that individual behavior is largely a result of either explicit or implicit career considerations.

It can also be argued that individual other ranks become so committed to the military way of life that they become "locked into" the system. What is less certain is whether, in the absence of adequate research data, it can be reasonably concluded that careerists, as Camacho claims, suffer from means–goals confusion and a concomitant narrow "tunnel vision." Similarly, we have to question the extent to which these careerists are content to project an "acceptable track image," that is, to promote an image which is pleasing to supervisors within the British military. What is of particular interest in this context is the extent to which this visibility must be complementary to and supportive of the status quo. Should the extent be considerable, then it would seem that the attitudes of the careerist and the traditionalist exhibit a common concern with the maintenance of an established organizational format. Even so we may see a major difference between the concern of the traditionalist in the British military for the advancement of skills appropriate to the functional needs of the *organization* and the concern of the careerist for the development of abilities which are more appropriate to the general occupational needs of the *individual*.

ENLISTED CULTURE

The conceptual framework can be extended further by combining these two sets of variables. When the *military self-image* and *attitudes to military service* are set against each other, we can construct (see Figure 13.1), a matrix in

	Warrior	Worker	Technician
Traditionalist	X		
Opportunist		X	
Careerist			X

Attitudes to Military Service

Figure 13.1. The Military Self-Image

which some combinations of variables seem to be more likely and more related than others.

In Figure 13.1, those diagonal pairings which represent warrior/traditionalist, worker/opportunist and technician/careerist positions are most representative of the contemporary culture of other ranks in the British military. It should be noted, however, that other combinations, although less likely, may occur.

Within the enlisted culture, there are some substantial differences between the characteristics of the outlined pairs. In the traditionalist/warrior combination, for example, a major part of the base is the presence within the British army of a well defined and long established regimental system. Even where such a system does not exist in a pure form, as in the Royal Navy and the Royal Air Force, there is nevertheless still to be found among servicemen a considerable concern with such identifiable features of a regimental culture as group values, traditional norms, and idealized patterns of corporate behavior. In all services, in addition, a significant characteristic of this style of military culture is the manner in which other ranks believe that their way of life diverges sharply from more conventional civilian life-styles. Moreover, the perception of the military as a total institution, isolated from the effects of contemporary change in the parent society, reinforces the belief that enlisted culture is different from the general culture of that society.

The worker/opportunist subculture, in contrast, is more properly a reflection of what happens in that parent society or, at least, in the working class of that society. While it would be incorrect to identify these subcultures wholly with one aspect of class, status or power rather than another, it is nevertheless to be noted that the similarity between the worker/opportunist military culture and the civilian working class subculture in the United Kingdom is most marked. Consequently, much of the literature on the latter is directly relevant to this aspect of the total enlisted culture. While this draws attention to the significance of such features of the latter as language, sexual mores, attitudes toward authority, consumption patterns and so on, a most important point nevertheless is the difference between this enlisted culture and the culture of the officers' mess. The former, as a derivative of a working class culture, can be sharply distinguished from the middle class and often seemingly anachronistic culture of the latter. The enlisted culture is characterized by a sense of the personal, the concrete, the local.

It is embodied in the familiar reaction to "them" and a preference for group solidarity values which, with its own language and sense of values, rejects the outsider. Seemingly disadvantaged and preoccupied with a sense of relative deprivation, this group is epitomized by a mistrust of authority and by a rejection of the claimed legitimacy of the middle class culture of the officers' mess.

A comparable distinction can also be noted in any evaluation of the subculture of the technician/careerist. There is, however, one important difference.

The distinction between the subcultures of the worker/opportunist and the officers' mess is primarily based on a belief that these subcultures reflect substantial socioeconomic contrasts. The distinction between the subcultures of the technician/careerist and the officers' mess, on the other hand, is essentially derived from fundamental functional differences. Consequently, members of the technician/careerist group are highly critical of the way in which the culture of the officers' mess seems to be geared toward the glorification of heroic objectives rather than technical or managerial efficiency. The persistence of the "fighter spirit" among officers is considered to delay the transformation of the military establishment through a continuous technological innovation into an engineering enterprise. Indeed, it would seem that in the world inhabited by these "warrior" officers, the image of traditional military leadership is consistently perpetuated to the extent that an outdated lifestyle, an emphasis on selected normative qualities of officership, and a collegial relationship become defining characteristics of the subculture. For other ranks, therefore, the seeming unimportance of these characteristics, in combination with the persistent emphasis placed on the importance of traditionalism, serves to reinforce their preference for a way of life which recognizes the importance of technical efficiency and organizational innovation.

At the same time, the differences which are drawn between these two subcultures are paralleled by the distinctions which are believed to exist between the subcultures of the technician/careerist and other enlisted personnel in the British military. In particular, the former criticizes those facets of the general culture of other ranks which are linked with a traditional or static environment. What this means is that considerable stress is placed on the alternative benefits of technological innovation, since this encourages the development of a military subculture which is highly critical of organizational conservatism and dogmatic doctrine. Those subtle and persuasive aspects of military behavior which continue to reinforce traditionalism are especially prone to critical analysis, for to the two nontraditionalist groups of other ranks they are at best anachronistic and at worst a means of reducing the technical efficiency of the fighting force.

In complete contrast, the links which have been established between military and industrial technology serve to ensure that the subculture of the technician/careerist in the armed forces reflects very clearly many of the attitudes of the civilian specialist. Consequently, we find considerable suspicion of staff officers and a preference for the attitudes of line managers who are directly concerned with production. There is a close link established between other ranks and their officers—particularly in technical corps or branches—of a kind which is also to be found among technical staff in industry. Indeed, there may be a sense of unity in opposition to the traditionalist or the worker role image because both are seen to interfere with the maximizing of efficiency. In this respect, the technician/careerist is highly critical of organizational patterns devoted to maintaining the status quo and is vigorously opposed to the growth of the military bureaucracy.

In short, the subculture associated with the enlisted man who is a technician/careerist encourages evaluation of the postulated ability of other servicemen, irrespective of their formal rank within the military organization. Consequently, the serviceman in this situation is often at odds with the system, for his preference for technical efficiency and the development of management expertise may conflict with older, well established military traditions. The consequent sense of stress is most marked—particularly where the objectives of the technician/careerist dictate a pattern of personal advancement rather than organizational advancement or create a sense of purpose not in consonance with the wider aims of a military organization.

SOCIAL DISTANCE

Although there are differences between the defining characteristics of these pairings, their common feature is the totality of the subculture of other ranks within the British military. The differences are, in consequence, largely a gloss upon a well-established enlisted culture. It is evident that this culture, irrespective of minor variations in form, is very different from the culture of a professionalized yet highly traditional officer corps. Apart from the distinctions which have already been noted, a further fundamental and differentiating characteristic is the *social distance* which continues to divide the two groups in question. This division is in many ways the continuance of a well-established tradition which suggests that in the British armed forces, working class soldiers are commanded by officers drawn from an upper middle class. It is a social distance which has encouraged persistent media reaction, but it should not be overlooked that position in the military basically mirrors what is more generally found within British society. It is a part of the cultural system within which military organizations operate, where the highly stratified nature of British society in general rationalizes the traditional definition of the role and status of officers in particular.

The persistence of this social division is marked. About 60% of army applicants tend to be "pre-adults" who have completed their education at the earliest lawful opportunity (after twelve years of compulsory schooling) and are under the age of 17.5. That age group provided 54% of all army enlistments in 1975-80. (Looking at it another way, 40% of adult applicants vs. 32% pre-adult applicants did actually enlist.) The data from which these rates were derived are shown in Table 13.1.

For a variety of reasons the Army sets out to recruit "adults" rather than "pre-adults," irrespective of the differing number of applicants. In the Womens' Royal Army Corps, the age structure of servicewomen also shows that about half are below the age of twenty. In other words, the typical serviceman

Table 13.1.   British Army Applications and Enlistments
by Age Group (1975-1980)

Year	Applications				Enlistments			
	Adults (%)		Pre-Adults (%)		Adults (%)		Pre-Adults (%)	
1975	25,717	(40)	39,187	(60)	12,272	(47)	13,870	(53)
1976	23,622	(38)	38,284	(62)	9,208	(43)	12,133	(57)
1977	24,270	(39)	38,243	(61)	9,299	(47)	10,549	(53)
1978	22,148	(36)	39,263	(64)	9,496	(42)	13,011	(58)
1979	28,002	(42)	38,335	(58)	12,254	(47)	13,783	(53)
1980	38,195	(46)	45,098	(54)	12,317	(47)	13,639	(53)
TOTAL	161,954	(40)	238,410	(60)	64,846	(46)	79,985	(54)

Source: Ministry of Defence

at the lower rank levels, whether male or female, is a teenager or is in the early twenties. The RAF and the Royal Navy equally recruit heavily from a young age group, although in a period of economic stress they are able to expect recruits to have received more than a basic education. But for all services, this educational experience, irrespective of the standard achieved, continues to differ materially from the experience of officers. This was noted by Garnier in his studies of the British armed forces in the early 1970s. His conclusion that for the army there was a considerable reliance on the commissioning of officers who had attended fee paying schools continues to be relevant today.[7]

What this means is that other ranks in the British Army continue to have a different educational background from that of their officers. Linked to this are differences in socialization experiences. Even where both other ranks and officers are products of the state educational system, it is unusual to find that they have truly common educational experience: officers, having attended the Sixth Form in school to the age of 16 to 18, will often go on to enjoy tertiary level education; other ranks, however, will have received little beyond compulsory school education, often in a "streamed school," up to the age of 16. The sociological consequences of these different experiences, however, can be overstated, and the situation in the British military differs very little from that to be found in major British industries and the public service. Nor should too much attention be paid, as is too often done, to the peripheral yet obvious manifestations of this social distance in differences of accent, speech patterns, manners, use of language, and so on. The critical question is whether the sum of these differences produces totally different attitudes towards the vicissitudes of military life. Here, it is too easy to conclude that a highly professionalized officer corps continues to be associated with a role image which stresses the "need for service" whereas other ranks are more job-oriented. The problem is that any evaluation tends to focus on the evaluator's perceived defining characteristic of the enlisted culture, without analyzing the validity of what may at best be media images. Indeed, all that may be ultimately concluded is that the British military has been able to accommodate successfully within its organizational structure all social facets of the distance which exists between officers and other ranks in the military organization.

THE SENSE OF TRADITION

This accommodation has been achieved—and is still achieved—through the emphasis placed on the importance of tradition within the British military. The subtleties of this have long served as a fundamental characteristic of military life in the United Kingdom. An initial feature of this sense of tradition is the manner in which a regimental ethos is maintained as a central feature of the military way of life. This can be most clearly seen in the army, where other ranks normally enlist in and remain with a specific regiment or corps. It is less evident in the Royal Navy or the Royal Air Force, where service in a ship or squadron may be of a transitory nature or where service is primarily identified with a function or a geographical location. Even so, there is strong evidence here of attempts made to foster a sense of the corporate nature of military life through emphasizing the permanent traditions of a defined group.

The constituent parts of this sense of tradition can be clearly identified. Broadly speaking, a major factor is the manner in which "tradition" is identified with the definition of the military system as something more than a mere occupation. Whereas the latter can be equated with the market place and the considerable emphasis which it places on the importance of monetary rewards, the traditional military way of life is thought to be different. The sense of tradition in the portrayal of this enlisted culture consequently approximates very closely what Moskos and Faris see as "vertical identification" within a military system. They write:

> The military institution is organized "vertically," whereas an occupation is organized "horizontally." To put it in as unpretentious a manner as possible, people in an occupation tend to feel a sense of identity with others who do the same sort of work, and who receive about the same pay. In an institution, it is the organization in which people live and work that creates the sense of identity that binds them together. Vertical identification means that one acquires a sense of responsibility for the performance of the organization as a whole. In the armed forces the very fact of being part of the service has traditionally been more important than the fact that military members do different jobs. The organization one belongs to creates the feeling of shared interest, not the other way around.[8]

This sums up very succinctly the basic features of the sense of tradition which is seen to be characteristic of an enlisted culture within the British military. Other ranks can be judged, according to this interpretation, to have that "sense of identity" which is a fundamental characteristic of the regimental system and a reflection of a traditional military way of life.

What is argued in this paper, however, is that the attitudes of other ranks towards this traditional identity will vary in relation to differences between the warrior/traditionalist, worker/opportunist, and technician/careerist subcultures. It is argued that it is only in the first of these three models that there is a marked preference among other ranks in the British military for the maintenance of a regimental ethos with its attendant sense of tradition. This suggests that other ranks whose culture is more directly linked with the remaining models are less disposed to acknowledge the importance of a sense of tradition as a determinant of the contemporary life style of the British military. Indeed, it can be concluded that these servicemen may be positively opposed to the emphasis which is placed on this facet of military traditionalism.

CONCLUSION

Attention has been given to the status of other ranks within the British military. This is a complex subject, and the present discussion can only focus on a limited area of interest. Particular attention has been paid to the basic problem of identifying an enlisted culture which can be sharply differentiated from the culture of the officers' mess. Clearly, both of these form part of a more widely based military culture that can be distinguished from the general civilian culture of the United Kingdom. Even so, the military and civilian cultures are interdependent, and in the absence of a well-developed sense of militarism within British society, it would be incorrect to suggest that they are totally different. Consequently, the enlisted culture is also linked to what happens in the parent society, and any analysis has to begin from the premise that the way of life of other ranks in the British military reflects what is happening in the parent society.

It is apparent, however, that other ranks in this military are not a representative cross-section of British society. Middle-class, college-educated personnel are rarely to be found among these other ranks. Instead, both male and female personnel tend to be recruited from those who have undergone the minimum statutory period of compulsory education. It is this group who are most attracted to the military by the monetary incentives which are offered by the armed forces.

Two important reservations have to be noted, however. First, the picture which is presented of other ranks in terms of their social composition and previous educational experience differs little from that of any working-class population. Broadly speaking, other ranks in the military are no less and no more socially representative than other working class occupational groups. At the same time, the distinguishing features of the enlisted culture show that these other ranks are a far from homogeneous group. This not only serves to distinguish them from civilian groups but also makes it difficult to identify a single reference group in the parent society to which other ranks can be compared.

It is with the differences among other ranks that this paper has been concerned, and it has been suggested that three sets of "push" factors and three of "pull" factors facilitate the identification of differences of attitude towards a military way of life. What is most important, however, is the manner in which such differences are accommodated within the single military organization. It is noticeable that there is very little concern in the United Kingdom with issues of the social equity or the social justice of voluntary recruitment. As a result, "accommodation" is not identified with the problem of trying to reconcile conflicting objectives of equal opportunity and proportional representation within the contemporary military organization. Rather, "accommodation" is seen as the manner in which a sense of tradition, ideally exemplified in the continuance of the regimental ethos, is used to promote a sense of unity among other ranks within the British military system. It is this sense which is the hallmark of the enlisted culture, and it is this regimental ethos which, irrespective of differences between the characteristics of the warrior/traditionalist, worker/opportunist, and technician/careerist models, serves to summarize most effectively the ethos of other ranks in the armed forces of the United Kingdom.

NOTES

1. Alan R. Skelley, *The Victorian Army at Home* (London, Croom Helm 1977); Charles Moskos, *The American Enlisted Man: the Rank and File in Today's Military* (New York: Russell Sage Foundation, 1970).
2. Charles C. Moskos, "The Emergent Military," *Pacific Sociological Review 16*, (1973).
3. Ian Bellany, *Why Men Enlist*, Bailrigg Paper on International Security, Number 4, (Lancaster: Lancaster Univ., 1982).
4. *First Report of the Official Review Body on Armed Forces Pay*, London, HMSO (Cmnd 4954), 1972.
5. Walter Korpi, *Social Pressures and Attitudes in Military Training* (Stockholm: Almqvist and Wiksell, 1964); Bengt Abrahamsson, *Military Professionalization and Political Power* (Beverly Hills: Sage Publications, 1972).
6. Paul R. Camacho, "Dimensions of Careerism in Military Organizations" in Richard A. Gabriel and Paul L. Savage, *Managers and Gladiators: Direction of Change in the Army*, np, The Hawkes Press, nd.
7. Maurice A. Garnier, "Technology, Organizational Culture and Recruitment in the British Military Academy," *Journal of Political and Military Sociology, 3*, (1975).
8. Charles C. Moskos and John H. Faris, "Beyond the Market Place. National Service and the AVF," in Andrew J. Goodpaster et al., *Toward a Consensus on Military Service* (New York: Pergamon Press, 1983).

INDEX

About the Editors and Contributors

SUE E. BERRYMAN is a resident consultant with the Washington, D.C. office of The Rand Corporation. She has worked on military and civilian labor force policy problems at Rand for the last decade, concentrating on the transition of youth into the labor force, the human capital implications of complex technology, and women's educational and career choices. She is currently directing a project on the retention of women in the military for the Office of the Secretary of Defense.

CHARLES A. COTTON is an adjunct associate professor with the School of Business of Queen's University, Kingston, Canada, and Director of Continuing Education for the school. He holds a PhD in Sociology from Carleton University, and served in operational, research, and teaching positions in the Canadian military for 21 years. His last military position was as Head of the Military Leadership and Management Department at the Royal Military College of Canada, holding the rank of lieutenant colonel. His primary research interest is with the evolution of western military organizations.

JAMES F. DOWNS is an anthropologist who after naval service in World War II and Korea received his doctorate from the University of California, Berkeley in 1961. After conducting research on American Indians, Tibetan refugees in India, and Hawaiian school children, he turned his attention to a study of the navy as a culture and re-enlisted in the Naval Reserve as a chief petty officer. His tours of extended active duty have included service in San Diego, Washington, and USNA. He holds the rank of chief warrant officer and is currently senior social scientist at the University Research Corporation/Center for Human Services and a member of the adjunct staff, Center for Urban Ethnography, University of Pennsylvania.

MICHAEL ELEY is a psychologist and a lieutenant-colonel in the Australian Army Psychology Corps. He is on the staff of the Royal Military College, Duntroon. At the time of writing he was commanding officer of 1st Psychological Research Unit, Canberra, his background before then being in the army personnel and manpower areas.

GWYN HARRIES-JENKINS is director of adult education at the University of Hull, Hull, England. A former regular officer in the Royal Air Force, his main professional interests are the history and philosophy of the relationship between armed forces and the parent society.

JAMES C. HASDORFF is a senior historian at the USAF Historical Research Center, Maxwell AFB, Alabama. Specializing in oral history, he has interviewed numerous top-ranking air force and defense department officials.

MARTHA A. MARSDEN teaches in the School of Social Work at San Diego State University. Previously she was a research social worker at the Naval Health Research Center in San Diego. Ms. Marsden received her doctorate from the School of Social Work and Community Planning at the University of Maryland, Baltimore. Her dissertation research, sponsored by the Walter Reed Army Institute of Research, Washington, D.C., concerns the relationship of psychological androgyny to the mental health and job satisfaction of enlisted army women.

CHARLES C. MOSKOS, a former draftee, is professor of sociology at Northwestern University. He has been a Fellow at the Woodrow Wilson International Center for Scholars (1980-1981) and a Rockefeller Foundation Humanities Fellow (1983-1984). He serves as president of the Research Committee on Armed Forces and Conflict Resolution of the International Sociological Association.

JACOB NEUFELD is chief of special histories in the Office of Air Force History, Washington, D.C. He has written on a variety of military topics, including missiles, space, the F-15 fighter, jet engines, and the Vietnam War.

CONSTANCE S. OJILE is an international training consultant to the U.S. government, private industry, and major universities. She is an applied anthropologist specializing in inter-cultural training programs and cross-cultural communication. She spent three years living and working with the U.S. armed forces in Europe.

MICHAEL L. PATROW is a lieutenant colonel in the U.S. Marine Corps. He is commanding officer of Marine Amphibious Unit (MAU) Service Support Group Eleven, 11th MAU, Camp Pendleton, California. He was previously assigned as an operations research analyst in the Manpower Plans and Policy Division, Headquarters, U.S. Marine Corps.

RENEE PATROW is a lieutenant colonel in the U.S. Marine Corps. She is the deputy comptroller for the 1st Marine Division and the I Marine Amphibious Force, Camp Pendleton, California. She was previously assigned as a plans officer in the Manpower Plans and Policy Division, Headquarters, U.S. Marine Corps.

FRANKLIN C. PINCH, CD, is a lieutenant-colonel, senior behavioural scientist and director of personnel selection research and second careers in the

Canadian Forces. Educated in both psychology and sociology, he has researched and written on military manpower issues in Canada over the past decade.

DAVID R. SEGAL is professor of sociology and of government and politics at the University of Maryland, and a guest scientist in the Department of Military Psychiatry, Walter Reed Army Institute of Research. He is also an associate chairman of the Inter-University Seminar on Armed Forces and Society, and editor of its journal.

MADY WECHSLER SEGAL is an associate professor of sociology at the University of Maryland and a guest scientist in the Department of Military Psychiatry at the Walter Reed Army Institute of Research. She is the author of numerous journal articles and book chapters, with an emphasis on military organization, women in the military, and interpersonal relationships in small groups. Dr. Segal has been conducting research on military families since 1973 and she teaches a course on military families. In addition to addressing issues of community relationships, her current research on military families focuses on such work/family influences as the effects of deployment separation and reunion on marital role relationships and the effects of personnel stability in Army units on the lives of junior enlisted families.

H. WALLACE SINAIKO, a psychologist, has been program manager of Manpower Research and Advisory Services, Smithsonian Institution, since 1972. Before that he served with the Institute for Defense Analyses, and with the London branch, Office of Naval Research. He has held research appointments at the University of Illinois and the Naval Research Laboratory. He is currently chairman of the panel of military manpower trends, The Technical Cooperation Program, a consortium of the five principal English-speaking nations.

PATRICIA J. THOMAS is a branch head in the Manpower and Personnel Laboratory of the Navy Personnel Research and Development Center, San Diego. For the past decade, the focus of her research has been the assimilation of women and minorities into the navy.

MALCOLM VAN GELDER, a civil engineer and economist, was formerly in the Australian Regular Army with service in Malaya, Thailand, and Vietnam. In 1972 he transferred to the Commonwealth Public Service, but retained his interest in military personnel theory and practice. He convened the first Australian Armed Forces and Society conference in 1976.